The Physiology of Psychological Disorders

Schizophrenia, Depression, Anxiety, and Substance Abuse

THE PLENUM SERIES IN BEHAVIORAL PSYCHOPHYSIOLOGY AND MEDICINE

Series Editor:
William J. Ray, *Pennsylvania State University, University Park, Pennsylvania*

BIOLOGICAL BARRIERS IN BEHAVIORAL MEDICINE
Edited by Wolfgang Linden

HANDBOOK OF RESEARCH METHODS IN CARDIOVASCULAR
BEHAVIORAL MEDICINE
Edited by Neil Schneiderman, Stephen M. Weiss, and Peter G. Kaufmann

PHYSIOLOGY AND BEHAVIOR THERAPY
Conceptual Guidelines for the Clinician
James G. Hollandsworth, Jr.

THE PHYSIOLOGY OF PSYCHOLOGICAL DISORDERS
Schizophrenia, Depression, Anxiety, and Substance Abuse
James G. Hollandsworth, Jr.

The Physiology of Psychological Disorders

Schizophrenia, Depression, Anxiety, and Substance Abuse

James G. Hollandsworth, Jr.
University of Southern Mississippi
Hattiesburg, Mississippi

Plenum Press • *New York and London*

Library of Congress Cataloging-in-Publication Data

Hollandsworth, James G.
  The physiology of psychological disorders : schizophrenia,
depression, anxiety, and substance abuse / James G. Hollandsworth,
Jr.
     p. cm. -- (Plenum series in behavioral psychophysiology and
medicine)
  Includes bibliographical references.
  ISBN 0-306-43353-2
  1. Schizophrenia--Physiological aspects. 2. Depression, Mental-
-Physiological aspects. 3. Anxiety--Physiological aspects.
4. Substance abuse--Physiological aspects. I. Title. II. Series.
  [DNLM: 1. Anxiety Disorders--etiology. 2. Depressive Disorders-
-etiology. 3. Mental Disorders--etiology. 4. Psychophysiology.
5. Schizophrenia--etiology. 6. Substance Abuse--etiology. WM 100
H7375p]
RC514.H59 1990
616.89'07--dc20
DNLM/DLC
for Library of Congress   89-26559
                                                         CIP

© 1990 Plenum Press, New York
A Division of Plenum Publishing Corporation
233 Spring Street, New York, N.Y. 10013

All rights reserved

Printed in the United States of America

For my wife,
Brenda Dawson

Foreword

Explanations of abnormal behavior that emphasize the importance of physiological determinants of disorder are relatively unpopular among psychologists, especially among those who work as clinicians in an applied setting. The reasons for this are theoretical and historical, as well as practical. Physiology and its associated biological disciplines of biochemistry, pharmacology, and genetics are traditionally more associated with medicine; their use to underpin explanations and treatments of behavioral abnormality has consequently demanded knowledge to which most psychologists are not exposed and skills that are unavailable to them. The dichotomy thus created between medical and psychological approaches has caused many psychologists to disregard physiological factors. Even when the latter are recognized as important, many psychologists have been unwilling to admit to the fact, in the belief that by doing so they will commit themselves to an overly medical model of psychological disorder, undermining what they see as preferred views of abnormality. As I have become increasingly aware in following the progress of this book, in the United States the theoretical issues in this debate have been further sharpened by professional rivalries (present but less explicit on the European scene from which I write) between medical and nonmedical health care workers, regarding facilities for and approaches to the treatment of the mentally disturbed.

Faced with these divisions of interest, psychologists have available two courses of action. One is to distance themselves even further from a consideration of physiological factors in disorder, presumably in the hope that progress in the development of alternative perspectives will result in fully valid, self-contained models for understanding and treating psychological deviance. The other choice is to learn something about such factors and, in the course of doing so, help to strengthen the position of psychologists as professionals who, perhaps uniquely, have the opportunity to acquire a fully rounded appreciation of the *psycho-biological* nature of all behavior, not least abnormal behavior.

The philosophy that lies behind Hollandsworth's book is very much the latter. He argues cogently—with succinct reviews of the appropriate evidence—that none of the major forms of psychological disorder of concern in contemporary society can be fully understood without taking into account the contribution of physiological mechanisms. Importantly, however, he does so without falling into the trap which, ironically, has ensnared much organic psychiatry: that because psychological disorders are associated with aberrant physiology, this necessarily validates a narrow etiological model of such disorders as discrete disease entities, enshrined at a descriptive level in such classificatory schemes as DSM-III-R. While using current psychiatric nosology as a framework for organizing his material, and as a vehicle for communication, Hollandsworth does not merely attempt to seek a compromise with the medical position over disorder. Instead he interprets the physiological evidence in a different way, drawing for part of his theoretical analysis on constructions of the physiology of abnormality which, as it happens, have actually been rather critical of conventional disease notions of psychological disorder. I am referring here to contemporary biological theories of personality and temperament. These theories, developed by psychologists themselves, argue for the existence of intrinsic nervous system differences between individuals, differences that act as predispositions to various forms of disorder and which, when pushed into dysfunctional states, represent the physiological component in psychological abnormality. According to such theories, the understanding of the contribution of biology to the etiology of disorder then becomes, not the search for discrete cause, but an appreciation of how and why normal physiology takes an abnormal functioning. Looked at in this way, the physiological analysis of disorder is not an alternative to the psychological or the social. Instead it supplements these approaches, providing a bridge between brain and behavior that many clinicians have been unwilling to cross—currently fruitless discussions about the relative importance of psychological (i.e., cognitive) versus physiological "causes" of panic disorder are a good example.

The discoveries that are now being made in the neurosciences and related disciplines already attest to the importance of psychologists acquiring a knowledge of the physiology of the disorders they study and treat. Equally important is the opportunity such knowledge imparts to them in being able to shape future interpretations—and hence applications—of it. Hollandsworth's book enables the practicing clinician to do both of these things and, although the message it conveys is one which I suspect may require of some readers that they set aside their preconceptions, I urge them to try.

GORDON CLARIDGE

Department of Experimental Psychology
Magdalen College
University of Oxford
Oxford, England

Preface

This book is written for students and practitioners of professional psychology who would like to know more about the physiological aspects of the major disorders they encounter with their clients. It is written in the opinion that most courses in physiological psychology taught in graduate training programs generally fail to make that discipline relevant to the clinical interests of students. Part of this failure appears to be the reliance on literature that is based primarily on data drawn from infrahuman subjects. In addition, there is a tendency in these courses to emphasize physiological rather than psychological dysfunction. The present work attempts to remedy this shortcoming by approaching the subject from a clinical perspective and relating information on physiological function to each of four problem areas. As such, this book can be used as a supplemental text in courses in either physiological psychology or advanced psychopathology. Practitioners who have completed their formal training may also find the work useful when consulting with their medical colleagues. With that in mind, special attention has been paid to issues involving an interdisciplinary approach to the treatment of these disorders.

The book is divided into three parts. Part I, Chapters 1–3, focuses on the interrelationship of biological and psychological functions, introducing basic principles and concepts to provide a framework around which the subsequent chapters are developed. Part II, Chapters 4–7, looks at specific disorders in terms of how certain physiological factors affect their development and expression. The diagnostic areas covered include schizophrenia, depression, anxiety, and substance use disorders. Part III consists of a single chapter that discusses some of the implications of what has been developed in the previous chapters.

Doubtless, some readers will be disappointed to find that I have failed to include some clinical areas that are of particular interest to them. This will most likely be the case in regard to personality disorders and disorders of childhood. It was necessary, however, to limit the scope of the book in some manner. To attempt to cover all of the major diagnostic categories listed in the DSM-III-R is simply too great an undertaking if I am to provide students and practitioners with a useful guide of modest proportions at a reasonable cost. Perhaps in the future, if requests for the present work suggest that the need is there, a second volume covering the remaining diagnostic categories in the DSM-III-R will be attempted.

Fortunately, I have been able to draw on the comments and suggestions of many students and colleagues in writing this book. Among those who read the manuscript and provided constructive feedback are John Alcorn, Bill Daigle, Desiree Kilcrease, Jeff Matranga, David McGalliard, Pat Leverett, Rosamond Myers, Ramona Netto, Ralph Ott, Jana Sealey, Gary Simmons, and Jayne Williams. I am especially indebted to Milt Becknell, Lynwood Wheeler, Evan Bradford, Lisa Moon, and Theresa Wozencraft for their contribution as research assistants during the preparation of the work. Martha Cain deserves special commendation for the patient and painstaking care with which she reviewed the manuscript. Her comments and suggestions were invariably on target and helpful. In addition, I would like to thank Martha for preparation of the subject index, which is her work alone.

In particular, I wish to acknowledge the insightful and scholarly suggestions of my colleague, Gordon Claridge, as well as the hospitality he and his wife, Rosemary, showed me during my stays in Oxford. I also would like to add a special word of thanks to Eliot Werner, my editor at Plenum. Finally, I would be remiss not to mention the support and good cheer of Phil, Carole, and the regulars at the Gardener's Arms.

JAMES G. HOLLANDSWORTH, JR.

Hattiesburg, Mississippi

Contents

Prologue

A man kneels, arms outstretched, eyes wide. A lantern on the ground throws its light on his white shirt so that he stands in stark contrast to the black forms huddled around him. Soldiers with heavy coats and tall hats lean forward, their rifles pointing at his heart. Other prisoners cower beside him, some shielding their faces with their hands. Others lie already dead on the ground. This is Goya's *The Third of May, 1808, in Madrid: The Execution on Prince Pio's Hill*, or simply, *The Third of May*. Goya painted it in 1814, six years after the event took place during the occupation of Spain by Napoleon's troops.

Although *The Third of May* is one of Goya's most powerful paintings, it is not his most remarkable. Another depicts a ghoulish figure holding a body in its hands. In the picture the ghoul has already eaten the head and is tearing off the left arm with its mouth, eyes large with excitement. Another scene is that of a young couple with silent smirks mocking the village idiot, who is masturbating. Yet another painting depicts two men standing in mud up to their knees with raised cudgels and bloodied faces, unable to flee but also unable to end the contest with a final blow.

These works are referred to as Goya's "black paintings." Unlike his other efforts, these were not intended for public display. Goya painted them on the walls of a country house near Madrid in which he lived as an old man. It appears that he never spoke about them to anyone, even after he left for France in 1824 to live in exile until his death four years later (Gudiol, 1971).

* * *

Much of the impact of Goya's later paintings is attributed to an illness he suffered in 1792. Prior to that he was a painter of pleasant

1

times—colorful scenes of picnics and games, elegant tapestries, and cartoons (outline sketches) in the delicate, ornamental style of the period. After the illness, which left him permanently deaf, his paintings reflected a harsh, cynical view of the world, depicted so powerfully in his black paintings. John Canaday writes,

> Goya's life was split in two near its midpoint by an illness that very nearly killed him. . . . But he lived, and the traumatic experience released powers never before expressed. . . . A new Goya emerged—Goya the humane and bitter social observer, the scourging and despairing delineator of vice and cruelty, the fantasist whose pictured nightmares explored the most desperate realities. (1968, pp. 91 & 93)

Art critics agree that his later works represent the climax of his imaginative and creative genius (Licht, 1979).

Goya actually had several bouts with an unexplained illness throughout his life. The first occurred in 1778 at the age of 32. Fortunately, on that occasion he recovered unscathed. However, as his success mounted and the pace of work accelerated, he was suddenly stricken again in 1792. His numerous symptoms included paralysis of the right side, vertigo, impairment of balance, hearing, and speech, tremors, noises in the head, convulsions, mental confusion probably accompanied by hallucinatory experiences, as well as comatose or semi-comatose states. Recovery was slow but steady so that within a year he regained all his faculties, save his hearing, which never returned. Unexpectedly, many of the symptoms recurred in 1809 and again in 1819 (Harris, 1971).

The popular explanation of Goya's illness is that he was suffering from syphilis. At the time little was known about the effects of this disease. Consequently, it was something of a wastebasket explanation for illnesses people could not explain in other ways. We now know that in its final stage syphilis does attack the central nervous system, inducing many of the symptoms that Goya experienced. However, when syphilis reaches this point total incapacitation and death soon follow. Thus, it is highly unlikely that Goya could have displayed these symptoms at the age of 46 in 1792 and live another 36 productive years before dying of a stroke at 82 (Karlen, 1984).

Other maladies have been offered as possible explanations of Goya's illness. These include disorders of the inner ear, schizophrenia, or manic-depressive psychosis. In 1972 Dr. William Niederland, a psychiatrist, proposed yet another explanation of Goya's illness. In the early 1930's, while making some extra money as a public-health physician during his residency in Düsseldorf, Dr. Niederland treated workers who were scraping and repainting the city's bridges. In their occupation these workers were constantly exposed to lead-based paints and, as a result, suffered from plumbism or lead poisoning. Many showed signs of central nervous system dysfunction (encephalopathy) and neuromuscular problems (neuropathy) similar to Goya's.

Although lead can enter the body through the lungs, the principle route of absorption is through the digestive tract. In the years before public health legislation, lead poisoning was common among children who ate paint chips or mouthed objects covered with lead-based paint. It was also common among adults who drank water from lead pipes and from containers fabricated with lead solder.

Lead is a chemical element (Pb) that exerts its toxic action by combining with enzymes involved in the synthesis of products essential to normal cell function. It is stored in the liver, kidneys, and bones. Over time most of the lead in the body makes its way to the bones. On occasion, when the acid-base balance of the body is disturbed, lead stored in the bones is released into the blood, an event that precipitates a sudden rush of neurological problems, including convulsions, delirium, and coma. In chronic cases, mental changes and the impairment of vision due to optic nerve atrophy may occur. Neuromuscular effects include paralysis (usually bilateral, although the right side may suffer alone, especially if the individual is right-handed). Overall, lead poisoning may present a picture of general muscular weakness and wasting. Patients can experience a good, if slow, recovery, provided that they abstain from contact with lead. Reexposure, given the persistence of lead in the bones, can result in relapses requiring further treatment (Walton, 1977).

During his bouts with illness, Goya suffered from paralysis of the right side (Goya was right-handed), tremors, coma, delirium, transient blindness, mental confusion, depression, paranoid thinking, and vertigo—symptoms that Dr. Niederland recognized as similar to those of the Düsseldorf painters with whom he worked many years before. What, however, would have been the source of Goya's exposure to lead? It is known that lead poisoning was common among painters during his time. A classic treatise by Ramazzini published in 1703 on occupational hazards devoted an entire chapter to the dangers of the materials used by artists. He noted: "I have observed that nearly all the painters whom I know, both in this or other cities, are sickly . . . for their liability to disease [because of] the materials of the colors that they handle and smell constantly" (quoted in Niederland, 1972, p. 416). Paints of the 18th and early 19th centuries were often metal-based, such as red lead, cinnabar of mercury, white lead, and many other pigments containing a number of toxic, heavy metals. Furthermore, factory paints were unknown so that the artist of Goya's day had to mix his own pigments, a process which involved grinding these poisonous compounds by hand.

Still, this does not explain why Goya's reaction to these paints was so severe in comparison to other artists of the period. Nevertheless, there may be several answers to this question. First, it is known that there are individual differences in susceptibility to lead poisoning. Dr. Niederland, for example, found that only some of the bridge painters in Düsseldorf came down with symptoms of the disease. In addition, an answer may lie in Goya's painting technique. Goya made massive use of lead white in his paintings, both as a primer and as a primary color. Furthermore, Goya was amazingly prolific, painting portraits in as few as one or two sessions and some pieces in less than an hour. It is estimated that he completed over 1800 works of art over his lifetime, many of them large commissions. Dr. Niederland calculates that Goya worked at such a frenetic pace that he was able to complete several large canvases in the same time it would take other painters to finish only one. As a result, it is possible that Goya absorbed two to three times as much lead as most painters. Importantly, his illnesses kept him away from his paints, possibly allowing the accumulation of lead to drop slowly until his health was restored. However, after each illness Goya eventually returned to work, thus reexposing himself and perpetuating his illness.

*   *   *

This unusual tale of biohistory illustrates the proposal that human thoughts, feelings, and actions are the complex product of many factors, the relative importance of each depending on the nature of the response, the context in which it occurs, the presence of biological predispositions, and the sum total of past experience that we bring with us to the situation.

With Goya as an example, it can be seen that although his illness profoundly affected his work, it did not *cause* him to paint as he did. We must consider a number of other factors, such as his obvious gift for artistic expression. Although he studied under some of the best teachers in Europe, Goya must have inherited much of his talent, for if art were simply a matter of training and practice, we would expect masterpieces from the brushes of commercial artists.

In addition, there is the influence of the times in which Goya lived. During the latter part of his life, Europe was in political and social turmoil. In 1808 Napoleon invaded and occupied Spain. During this period the French troops treated the Spanish people with contempt and subjected them to cruel and barbarous acts. Goya witnessed many of these atrocities and depicted them in a series of 82 etchings entitled *The Disasters of War*. This graphic portrayal of savage acts portended the black paintings that were to come. Thus, it is to a foundation of natural talent honed by study and practice and immersed in a sea of human cruelty that we add his illness, which, in turn, may have served as an important catalyst for his best work. As such, Goya's life serves to illustrate the complex interaction of many factors that come together in the ultimate expression of the human experience.

Part I

Introduction

This book begins with a chapter on diagnosis, the process by which psychological disorders are organized according to systematic rules of classification. In a very real sense, a diagnostic system provides the language that allows practitioners and researchers interested in psychological disorders to communicate. However, the diagnostic categories one uses also affect the way one looks at these problems. For example, calling the fear of being around people a "social phobia" places it in the same category as the fear of dogs, snakes, insects, and mice (i.e., "simple phobias"). In this way, making a diagnosis does more than simply describe the disorder; it makes a statement about the origin and nature of that particular problem.

An example of how diagnostic decisions affect one's conceptualization of psychological disorders can be found in the application of the "disease model" to psychosocial problems. The issues surrounding this application are discussed in Chapter 1, particularly as they relate to social-learning or psychodynamic alternatives. Unfortunately, it appears that proponents of the different approaches tend to line up on opposite sides of this debate and thus treat psychological disorders as if they were either discrete disease states (e.g., caused by some specific biochemical anomaly) or the result of bad experiences entirely. However, it is concluded in Chapter 1 that many psychological problems share characteristics of both biologically-based *and* psychologically-based models. Consequently, rather than adhering to one or the other, this chapter offers an alternative—the systemic model of dysfunction—that incorporates aspects of both.

The application of the systemic model to psychological disorders is developed in Chapter 2. This approach, which attempts to explain how differences in biological make-up predispose individuals to different dis-

orders, bridges the gap between physiological and psychosocial explanations of psychological dysfunction. It is argued in Chapter 2 that
individuals are different in terms of the kinds of nervous systems they
possess, just as they differ in terms of their physical characteristics.
Furthermore, it is thought that these differences, which are probably
genetic in origin, are expressed as variations in thought, feeling, and
activity. This perspective emphasizes the belief that the development of
a specific psychological disorder is thus the product of biological predispositions and personal experience.

In spite of a long history of interest in individual differences, there
is still a tendency to divide psychological disorders into two categories—
those that are "organic" or "natural" (i.e., biologically-based) and those
that are not. While this dichotomy works fairly well for some problems,
such as organic mental syndromes, it breaks down rapidly as we move
to disorders for which learning, biological predisposition, environmental influences, and subjective factors all seem to play a role. In this
regard, recent developments in the areas of behavioral medicine, life
stress research, and developmental psychology are reviewed in Chapter
2 to illustrate the need for a broad perspective that cuts across traditional
disciplines by taking biological as well as psychosocial factors into
account.

Chapter 3 explores in greater detail how genetically-based predispositions interact with environmental experience to affect a person's
growth and development. In this chapter it is suggested that our genotype has three different kinds of effects—passive, reactive, and active.
A passive genotype effect occurs when parents provide both our genotype and the environment in which we grow up. A reactive effect, on
the other hand, occurs in response to the different ways people around
us react to those genetic characteristics that make us unique. And finally, the third type of effect occurs when our genotype leads us to play
an active role in seeking out those environments that allow us to explore
and cultivate our genetic potential.

Determining the degree to which genetic and environmental variables interact and the relative contribution of each is difficult and depends on, among other things, the nature of the psychological disorder
we want to predict. Genetic factors may play an important role in some
instances and essentially no role in others. However, it is clear that
satisfactory answers to these complex questions will not come solely
from either the biological or environmental side. Until both dimensions
are taken into account, it is likely that our understanding of why we do
what we do will be incomplete.

Chapter 1

Diagnosis

The disorders covered in this text are defined according to the diagnostic criteria presented in the revised, 3rd edition of the *Diagnostic and Statistical Manual of Mental Disorders* (DSM-III-R) (American Psychiatric Association, 1987). The DSM-III-R and its predecessor, the DSM-III, are widely accepted in North America as the standard classification system for mental disorders. The DSM system is referred to routinely in most books on abnormal psychology as well as in works dealing with the treatment of these areas from a variety of different perspectives.[1] As the author of one textbook puts it, "The reason for using the DSM-III criteria for disorders is simple: The vast majority of clinicians—regardless of their professional identity as psychologists, social workers, or psychiatrists—use DSM-III as their classification system" (Mehr, 1983, p. 97). Although the system is American rather than international in scope, several issues concerning its use warrant discussion, particularly since the questions they raise provide a basis for understanding why a book on the physiological factors in these disorders was written in the first place. (See Panel 1.1, "A Note on Terminology.")

The Psychiatric Diagnostic System

Definition of Diagnosis

The term "diagnosis" has several meanings. One definition relates to its use medically; another is concerned with its meaning in a more generic sense. Failing to realize that diagnosis can be used in two differ-

[1]Some of the many examples of works that use the DSM include Altrocchi (1980); Davison and Neale (1982); Hersen (1983, 1985); Maxmen (1986); I. G. Sarason and Sarason (1984); F. J. Turner (1984); and S. M. Turner and Hersen (1984).

PANEL 1.1

A Note on Terminology

The terms one uses say a lot about the assumptions one makes regarding the nature of the phenomena being studied. For example, the term *mental disorder* implies something different than the terms *mental illness* or *mental disease*. The latter two are deemed unsuitable for the purposes of this book for several reasons. For one, both "illness" and "disease" may imply an exclusively medical perspective. For another, the term illness is generally used in relation to more serious, often incapacitating disorders like schizophrenia. On the other hand, disease may imply the narrow (i.e., discrete state) meaning of the term. The present volume emphasizes a wide range of problem areas that may respond to any number of different treatment modalities. Consequently, the more generic term *disorder* is used rather than illness or disease.

There are problems with the term *mental* as well. "Mental" suggests "a priori assumptions regarding the locus of problems as within the skin" (Schacht & Nathan, 1977, p. 1023). The intention of this work is to recognize the potential contribution of a number of factors, only some of which are under the skin. As an alternative, the term *psychological*, which would seem as more general in its meaning than mental, has been used. Thus, the current volume will refer to *psychological disorders* rather than *mental illness* or *mental disease*.

A similar question can be raised by the use of the word *physiology* rather than *biology* in the title. "Biology" is more inclusive and covers a wide range of topics related to living matter. Some of these areas include reproduction, growth, structure, and origin. "Physiology," on the other hand, applies more specifically to the functions of living organisms or their parts. Thus, genetics (the study of heredity) is a subfield of biology while cardiology (the study of the heart and its functions) is a specialty area in physiology.

It can be argued that because of its broad scope, "biology" is more appropriate for that aspect of psychology that explores the relationship between brain and behavior (Rosenzweig, 1982; Davis, Rosenzweig, Becker, & Sather, 1988). Others have argued, on the other hand, that biological psychology, with its focus on molecular, synaptic, or neural systems, encourages a reductionistic view that tends to ignore the behavioral or psychological aspects of human functioning (Shuttlesworth, Neill, & Ellen, 1984).

The issues are complex, and it is unlikely that any decision concerning the use of either term will be completely satisfactory. Nevertheless, the discipline of physiology has enjoyed a long and honored relationship with psychology, and, as the study of function, seems the natural complement to psychology by dealing with some of those gaps between stimulus and response that psychology does not take into account (cf., Skinner, 1987). In addition, the decision to use *physiology* in the title is based, in part, on the expectation that this book will be particularly useful for students interested in "physiological psychology," which is still the most common designation for courses in the area.

ent ways has lead to misunderstandings regarding its application to problems that are seen as primarily psychological, rather than medical, in nature.

Medically, diagnosis is "the act or process of identifying or determining the nature of a disease through examination" (American Heritage Dictionary, 1978, p. 363). Clearly, a key word in this definition is "disease." It has been questioned whether the use of diagnosis in this sense is appropriate for many of the so-called "problems in living" that are not considered to involve a disease process (McReynolds, 1979).

The second, broader definition is "a precise and detailed description of the characteristics of an organism for taxonomic classification" (p. 363). Diagnosis used in this manner provides a basis for communication between persons interested in the same phenomenon.

> The first and fundamental step in the study of behavior, including abnormal behavior, is the grouping of observations into an organized scheme so as to make sense of the bewildering array of response patterns. Classification is the basis of any science because it is the process of identification of a phenomenon so that events can be measured and communication can occur between scientists and professionals. (H. E. Adams, Doster, & Calhoun, 1977, p. 47)

The present work intends to use diagnosis as it applies to the description and classification of disorders. Consequently, it will not imply medical causation, although a medical (i.e., psychiatric) classification system is employed and although in most instances medical (i.e., physiological) factors may play a significant role in the process.

Development of the DSM-III and -III-R

The American Psychiatric Association's initial effort to classify "mental" disorders was the DSM-I, which appeared in 1952. It contained a glossary of terms that provided descriptions of diagnostic categories and reflected the influence of Adolf Meyer's psychobiological model of psychopathology. Consequently, mental disorders in the DSM-I are described primarily as "reactions" to psychological, social, and biological factors.

Approximately 10 years later it was decided to bring the DSM more in line with the World Health Organization's classification of diseases and morbid conditions. The latter system, which grew out of a conference in Paris at the turn of the century, is revised approximately every 10 years and is known as the ICD *(The International Statistical Classification of Diseases, Injuries, and Causes of Death)*. As a result, the DSM-II appeared in 1968 in conjunction with the eighth revision of the ICD (ICD-8).

By 1974, as work began on the ICD-9, it was clear that the DSM-II also needed revision. Its diagnostic criteria were too sketchy to allow for reliable classification. Consequently, the American Psychiatric Association, through its Council on Research and Development, appointed a task force to develop a DSM-III to appear with the ICD-9 when it was published in January 1980.

From the start, the DSM-III represented a radical departure from its predecessors. Just as the DSM-I reflected a particular etiological viewpoint, so did the DSM-II, which was influenced during its development by psychoanalytic theory that dominated the Association. The Task Force for the preparation of the DSM-III, however, was headed by Robert Spitzer and consisted of a group of psychiatrists and consultant psychologists primarily involved with diagnostic research rather than clinical practice. The goal of the Task Force was to develop an empirically-based manual that would "raise the low level of reliability of psychiatric diagnosis through the use of explicit and carefully defined criteria" (Bayer & Spitzer, 1985, p. 188). With their common interest in research, the committee adopted an approach based on the "rigorous application of the principles of testability and scientific verification" (p. 188). Not surprisingly, the group was viewed almost immediately as unsympathetic to those whose theory and practice derived from the psychoanalytic tradition.

The process of developing the DSM-III was both arduous and controversial. The Task Force was attacked by many of its colleagues who saw it as abandoning psychiatry's psychoanalytic heritage. For example, an editorial in the *Journal of the American Academy of Psychoanalysis* accused the new manual of being a threat to those who were attempting to "maintain American psychiatry as a humane, open, and socially progressive force" by reducing clinical disorders to sets of symptoms that were "scientific, behaviorist and measurable" (Schimel, 1976, pp. 133–134). More specifically, Schimel observed, "I do not find within the definitions of DSM-III the kinds of neurotic patients I have worked with for thirty years; only disembodied fragments. I do not find the hysterics, the obsessionals, the anxiety ridden, the socially or situationally afflicted. I believe the direction of DSM-III to be profoundly regressive, even antisocial. It is not true; it does not fit the troubled human beings we see in our offices or hospital clinics. Our patients are people, not target symptoms" (p. 134).

Schimel, as well as others, defended the psychoanalytic perspective on the grounds that its tenets were just as plausible as those of the Task Force. It was asserted that "a century of experience with the psychodynamic point of view had given inferences about the unconscious, intrapsychic conflicts and defense mechanisms, a status close to those derived from direct observation" (cited in Bayer & Spitzer, 1985, p. 195).

The debate came to a head over one issue—deletion of the term "neurosis" from the manual. To the Task Force, neurosis was an etiological construct rather than a descriptive term and thus should not be included. Originally, it referred to Freud's notion of a process involving unconscious conflict, a subsequent instigation of anxiety, and eventually the maladaptive use of defensive mechanisms that resulted in symptom formation. Freud, however, also used it descriptively (i.e., to indicate painful symptoms in individuals whose reality testing was intact). Over the years, the term has been extended to include almost any unpleasant subjective state in which anxiety is a principle component.

Predictably, practitioners who favored the psychoanalytic perspective saw deletion of the term as a threat to their orientation and, more specifically, as jeopardizing their ability to obtain third-party reimbursement (e.g., from insurance companies) for long-term therapy. Consequently, the struggle over neurosis became an important political issue in the years 1975 to 1979. At the heart of the struggle were the votes of the representatives of the Assembly of District Branches and the Board of Directors (the American Psychiatric Association governance structure). The Task Force faced the possibility of not having their report accepted by the organization that had commissioned them to write it in the first place.

In the end, after a series of negotiations and political maneuvers, the DSM-III was adopted. As a concession to the psychoanalysts, the term neurosis was reinstated as an optional diagnosis for several categories. Thus, dysthymic disorder, which was called "chronic depressive disorder" in earlier drafts of the DSM-III, could be diagnosed as "depressive neurosis." Other diagnostic categories allowing for this option were the anxiety, somatoform, dissociative, and psychosexual disorders.

Work on a revision of the DSM-III began in May of 1983, little more than three years after the DSM-III appeared, and the revised manual became available for general use in May 1987. The revision represented an effort to improve the reliability and clinical usefulness of the DSM-III. The group who worked on the DSM-III-R consisted of 25 advisory committees involving over 230 consultants and was again headed by Spitzer. Feedback was encouraged from clinicians who actually used the DSM system by making a draft of the DSM-III-R available at a reasonable price ($7.50) with specific instructions for participation in the revision process. After much debate and study, most of the changes in the DSM-III-R resulted in only a refinement of diagnostic criteria and the reorganization of some diagnostic categories under new headings, particularly among childhood disorders. Despite doubts surrounding the revision (cf. Fisher, 1986a, 1986b; Landers, 1986), the DSM-III-R involved only a minor adjustment to the classification process and did not represent anything approaching the dramatic theoretical shift that occurred when the DSM-III was initially adopted.

Criticisms

If the reception of the DSM-III *within* the psychiatric community in North America was hostile, it was met with an even more disgruntled and skeptical reaction from without. Just as deletion of the term neurosis served as a rallying point for psychoanalysts, a statement that "mental disorders are a subset of medical disorders" (Spitzer, Sheehy, & Endicott, 1977, p.4) ignited opposition among psychologists. Although the Task Force voted against including this statement in the final draft, psycyhologists reacted swiftly. Their major concern was the fear that they would not be able to obtain third-party payment if these disorders were designated as medical conditions.

The situation was aggravated by the Task Force's decision to expand the scope of disorders covered in both the DSM-III and, subsequently, the DSM-III-R. The DSM-III identifies 230 separate categories of disturbance representing a 60% increase of those listed in the DSM-II and a 280% increase over the DSM-I (McReynolds, 1979). Some of the newly-included disorders are drug abuse, psychosexual dysfunction, and specific developmental disorders (i.e., problems with reading, arithmetic, and language). McReynolds (1979) argues that the DSM-III took social and behavioral problems and recast them as psychiatric disturbances.

The possibility that many psychological problems might come under the exclusive purview of the medical community evoked considerable alarm. As one practicing psychologist put it: "DSM-III scares the hell out of me. It is going to concretize everything as a medical disorder; for example, 'disorder of shyness.' Physicians have their areas of competence, but they are hardly competent in everything" (Miller, Bergstrom,

Cross, & Grube, 1981, p. 389). Nevertheless, Spitzer defended the increased scope of the DSM-III, stating: "If there is general agreement among clinicians, who would be expected to encounter the condition, that there are a significant number of patients who have it and that its identification is important to their clinical work, it is included in the classification" (Spitzer et al., 1977, p. 3).

In response, the American Psychological Association established a task force of its own, which offered six major criticisms of the DSM system—(1) use of a disease-based model to describe problems in living; (2) unreliable diagnostic categories; (3) a mixed classification system that categorizes problems on the basis of symptom clusters in some instances, sometimes on the basis of theoretical considerations, and at times on the basis of developmental influences; (4) the establishment of categories on the basis of committee vote rather than empirical evidence; (5) use of diagnostic labels that have the potential for political and/or social misuse; and (6) the limited ability of the document to indicate which treatment modality is appropriate for which disorder and what to expect in terms of clinical outcome. Other criticisms of the DSM during this period echoed these sentiments (Begelman, 1976; Schacht & Nathan, 1977).

Some of this reaction, however, may have been premature (Millon, 1983). For example, the criticism of poor reliability appears to have been based more on the weak record of the DSM-II than that of the DSM-III, which was designed specifically to deal with this problem (American Psychiatric Association, 1980, p. 8). In fact, reliabilities of the diagnostic categories derived from extensive field testing as well as data generated through the use of the DSM-III in clinical practice suggest that considerable progress has been made in this area (e.g., DiNardo, O'Brien, Barlow, Waddell, & Blanchard, 1983).

In retrospect, other criticisms by the American Psychological Association Task Force appear unnecessarily severe. The criticism that diagnostic categories were established on the basis of consensus "rather than empirical evidence" would seem to ignore the reality that science always progresses through consensus (Mahoney, 1976). In a like manner, the expectation that a diagnostic system be able to identify preferred treatment modalities may be asking a bit much, given what we know. It is still debated whether certain treatments are more effective for specific disorders or whether most interventions affect essentially the same result (Kazdin, 1986; Rachman & Wilson, 1980; VandenBos, 1986). Until this issue is resolved, it will be difficult to match the most effective treatment modality with a specific diagnostic category. In fact, a reliable classification system such as the DSM-III or III-R may be seen as a prerequisite for gaining the knowledge that will allow us eventually to make these determinations (Stiles, Shapiro, & Elliott, 1986).

The same reasoning applies to the criticism that the DSM uses an inconsistent classification system (i.e., symptomatic versus developmental versus theoretical). This objection suggests that an integrated model for classifying disorders be in place before diagnostic criteria are used. If we assume that a classification system is closed to further revision once it is established (cf., Zubin 1977), the problem is real. However, development of diagnostic categories is an open-ended process that "evolves and develops through guesswork, hunches, and assumptions as research progresses" (H. E. Adams et al., 1977, pp. 47–48; see also Feighner et al., 1972). As such, "systems of classification must be treated as tools for further discovery, not as bases for polemic disputation" (Zigler & Phillips, 1961, p. 616).

Persistent Issues

At least two of the six questions raised by the American Psychological Association Task Force do represent ongoing concerns for anyone using the DSM-III-R. The first deals with the potential for the system's misuse while the second concerns the endorsement of a disease-based model for disorders that are primarily psychological in nature.

To Diagnose or Not to Diagnose

Many psychologists do not see the need for a diagnostic system at all (e.g., Rogers, 1951). It is argued that diagnostic labels can be used as a powerful tool to disenfranchise or otherwise injure such groups as women, minorities, or gays. For example, the proposal to introduce three new diagnostic categories in the DSM-III-R (masochistic personality disorder, paraphilic rapism, and premenstrual dysphoric disorder) met with strong opposition from feminists. Although these diagnoses were either dropped or moved to an appendix entitled "Proposed Diagnostic Categories Needing Further Study" (p. 365), the DSM continues to be met with skepticism by many who see it as a threat to individual rights.[2]

It is not surprising, therefore, to find that there are many psycholo-

---

[2]See Delworth (1986); Fisher (1986); Fleming and Nichols (1986); M. Kaplan (1983a, 1983b); Kass, Spitzer, and J. B. Williams (1983); Schacht (1985); Schoenewolf (1986); Spitzer (1985); and J. B. Williams and Spitzer (1983) for examples of this debate.

gists who prefer not to use the DSM at all. A survey of 601 Clinical and Counseling Psychologists drawn from the National Register of Health Service Providers in Psychology revealed that while the vast majority (90.6%) of them used the DSM-III, they did so primarily because it was required for third-party payment (Miller et al., 1981). In 1983 Smith and Kraft surveyed 546 members of Division 29 (Psychotherapy) of the American Psychological Association. The majority of respondents (73%) were employed full-time in the practice of therapy and primarily identified with an eclectic (32%) or psychoanalytic (24%) orientation. More than half (52%) did not see a need for a classification system at all, while almost two-thirds (58%) objected specifically to the DSM-III. Furthermore, most respondents (79%) expressed the opinion that not enough had been done to develop an alternative to the psychiatric system.

In spite of the interest in an alternative to the DSM system (McLemore & Benjamin, 1979) and several thoughtful moves in that direction (e.g., Kanfer & Saslow, 1965; H. E. Adams et al. 1977), the competition has not gotten very far. Part of the reason is that psychologists can not agree among themselves on what kind of system should be used. While almost 4 out of 5 respondents to the Smith and Kraft (1983) survey said that not enough had been done in the development of another system, 75% also opposed the behavioral analysis alternative, despite the fact that more work had been done in this area than any other (Foltz, 1980). Furthermore, the magnitude of the task itself has presented apparently insurmountable obstacles. The American Psychological Association Task Force met for two years (1977–1978) before disbanding because "the job proved to be scientifically and financially overwhelming, and politically unpopular" (Fisher, 1986a, p. 24).

Nevertheless, there can be no question that, in spite of the controversy, the DSM-III has gained widespread acceptance in North America. (As of its 13th printing in 1986, more than half a million copies of the DSM-III had been distributed, while sales of the DSM-III-R exceeded 280,000 within two years of its appearance.)[3] A possible reason for the success of the DSM-III is that, given what it is intended to do, it is reasonably effective. Generally, its diagnostic criteria are seen as being both clinically meaningful (Achenbach, 1980) and reliable (Millon, 1983). Furthermore, the multiaxial format used in the DSM-III and -III-R endorses a view that psychological disorders result from the interaction of multiple factors.

The issue of whether one should diagnose at all may be more a question of how the DSM system is used. It is possible that practitioners

---

[3]D. Bardes, American Psychiatric Press (personal communication, March 2, 1989).

see less need for a diagnostic system since they are interested in the individual client for whom the specific details of his or her life are more important than being placed in a general diagnostic category. On the other hand, researchers studying a certain disorder in different locations or at different times can benefit from the use of standard criteria that allow them to determine whether they are dealing with the same thing (Stiles et al., 1986). Using Millon's example, it is important to know whether researchers studying "borderline personality" at Massachusetts General are dealing with the same disorder as investigators at the Menninger Clinic, the Michael Reese Hospital, or the Langley Porter Institute.

> It has been suggested that the classification or diagnosis of people and their behavior is unnecessary, harmful, or degrading. . . . A similar argument against classification is the assumption that each individual or response pattern is unique—consequently, classification is a meaningless activity. Although both of these assumptions may be valid, any science, including psychology, searches for common elements in events in order to integrate these events into a conceptual scheme. A classification system is a conceptual model of the real world that ignores many unique features of responses or individuals. Whether a particular model is justified is determined by how accurately the model facilitates the prediction, control, and understanding of behavior. (H. E. Adams et al., 1977, p. 48)

Along these lines, it has been argued that categorizations are inevitable and that making them at various levels involves distinctive gains and losses (Mischel, 1979, p. 744). Categorizations can range from wide-band, low-fidelity assessment of people in general to narrow-band, high-fidelity decisions concerning the treatment of the individual (Wiggins, 1973). Thinking in terms of stereotypes is an example of a broad-band process. It allows us to make broad discriminations but obscures the interaction of certain behaviors in particular contexts. Applied to psychological disorders, this level encompasses global constructs such as personality traits (e.g., Eysenck, 1967) or personality archetypes (e.g., Jung, 1924). On the other end of the continuum is a narrow-band analysis that involves the prediction of certain behaviors in specific situations. Assessment at this level makes fine-grained discriminations regarding individual clients.

Mischel (1979) has argued for a middle level of analysis that is broad yet rich in distinctiveness. This level maximizes parsimony (i.e., a few broad categories are formed) and richness (i.e., there are many features common to members of each particular category). As such, it is most useful for describing not only what we are like in general but also how we differ from others. Making this sort of distinction allows for an access to information about particular types of persons in order to flesh out the specifics of a particular case. Accurate diagnosis using a system like the DSM-III-R represents this level of analysis and can provide clinical guidelines based on knowledge gleaned from many similar cases.

Recognizing the appropriate reasons for providing diagnostic labels may serve to guard against their misuse. If diagnosis serves to stereotype an individual, it presents a clear threat to that individual's rights. On the other hand, use of a diagnosis to relate an individual's problem(s) to a relevant body of knowledge may be a potentially beneficial application of the diagnostic process. Hopefully, this text will stand as a positive example of how the latter can occur.

The Disease-Based Model

Some critics of the DSM system recognize the value of an accurate diagnosis but are concerned with the DSM's endorsement of a disease-based model. In this regard, there are two important issues associated with viewing psychological disorders as manifestations of a disease process. One issue deals with the way in which the term disease is *defined*; the other concerns the manner in which diseases are *treated*. Both issues have important implications for the assumptions upon which this book is based.

Issues of Definition. Like the term diagnosis, "disease" has more than one meaning. Also, as in the case of diagnosis, confusion about how it is used can lead to misunderstandings.

In one sense, disease refers to a specific disorder of an organ or body part, often caused by the presence of some pathogen. Although there are a few conditions listed in the DSM-III-R (e.g., dementia associated with alcoholism) that are caused by a single, identifiable pathogenic agent, in general, psychological disorders display few characteristics that allow us to treat them as distinct diseases.

For one thing, psychological disorders usually involve more than one etiological factor. Psychological disorders also usually lack the clear-cut signs and symptoms characteristic of physical disease. Furthermore, the symptoms of a psychological disorder normally can not be supplemented by more reliable diagnostic information from other sources, such as the laboratory (cf., Cowdry & Goodwin, 1978; Garfield, 1986; Quay, 1986). Finally, a psychological disorder is not conveniently localized in a particular organ system. Instead, its diagnosis depends on a disruption of function involving a broader range of personal, social, and legal factors.

It is not surprising, therefore, that many health-care professionals prefer some form of social-interpersonal model rather than one promoting a disease-based etiology (e.g., Carson, 1969; H. B. Adams, 1964). Almost half (47%) of the respondents to the Smith and Kraft (1983) survey endorsed this position. Accordingly, there has been widespread objection to the use of a disease-based model with "problems in living." Albee (1977), for example, argues that "the unvarnished fact is that most of the emotional problems of living do not belong in the category of disease. To attribute marital conflict or delinquency . . . to a biological defect, to biochemical, nutritional, neurological, or other organic conditions, in the absence of compelling evidence, is to sell our psychological birthright for short term gain" (p. 10).

Nevertheless, we have to be careful not to throw the baby out with the bath water. Although psychological disorders share little in common with infectious diseases (Buss, 1966), this does not mean that the notion of a disease-based etiology has no relevance or value when attempting to understand these problems. There is, as noted above, more than one use of the term *disease*.

> Physical diseases can be broadly divided into two types. There are, on the one hand, some diseases characterized by a clearly discontinuous change in bodily functioning and traceable to some discrete cause, often external in origin; the infectious illnesses are examples. But other diseases have a different quality. These are the *systemic* diseases, which have their origins in the internal state of the organism and arise as a transformation and ultimate breakdown of otherwise normal functions. A good example is essential hypertension. (Claridge, 1985, p. 9, italics in original)

More specifically, systemic diseases can be distinguished by three characteristics (Claridge, 1985). First, a systemic disease is defined in reference to normal functioning and is therefore understood best in terms of its relationship to a normal state. Second, it is assumed that a continuity between health and disease exists. And finally, systemic disease is thought to result from multiple, rather than single, causes. In many ways, it might be more appropriate to think of this type of disorder as a systemic *dysfunction* rather than a disease.

As noted earlier, essential hypertension is a good example of a systemic disorder. It is defined in terms of a deviation from normal rather than by the presence of some pathogen. Also, there is a continuity between normal and high blood pressure so that the decision regarding diagnosis and treatment is often a matter of judgment rather than some absolute standard. And finally, the development of essential hypertension appears to result from a number of factors, some inherited by the person and some found in his or her interaction with the environment. The "disease" aspect of hypertension comes into play when, as a

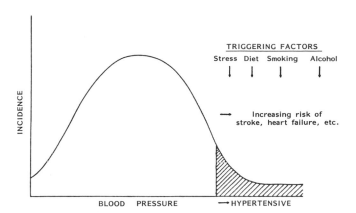

Figure 1.1. The continuum of blood pressure as disposition to hypertension-related disease. (From G. Claridge [1987], 'The schizophrenias as nervous types' revisited, *British Journal of Psychiatry, 151,* p. 736. Copyright © 1987 by The Royal College of Psychiatrists. Reprinted by permission.)

result of this dysfunctional state, a cardiovascular crisis (e.g., stroke, heart failure) eventually occurs. (The continuum between high blood pressure and hypertension-related diseases is illustrated in Figure 1.1.)

The model of systemic dysfunction can be applied to psychological disorders as well. One example is found in the observation that certain anxiety states appear to result, at least in part, from a biological predisposition toward physiological hyper-reactivity. Gray's (1982) work in this area has done much to define the mechanisms by which this occurs and will be discussed at length in Chapter 6. Another example involves a tendency, which appears to be inherited, for persons who exhibit antisocial behavior to display characteristics of chronic "sensation seeking" (Zuckerman, 1983, 1984). Sensation seeking is "the need for varied, novel, and complex sensations and experiences and the willingness to take physical and social risks for the sake of such experience" (Zuckerman, 1979, p. 10). Most if not all of us enjoy a certain amount of novelty or variation in our daily routine. However, when this natural predisposition is taken to an extreme, all sorts of disruptions in normal personal and social functioning can occur.

Another example is schizophrenia (Claridge, 1987). Schizophrenia is defined in terms of a deviation from normal functioning. Furthermore, there is a continuity of functioning between the premorbid condition and a schizophrenic episode, which often makes it difficult to determine when the disorder is in "remission" and when it is not. In addition, no single factor can be claimed to "cause" schizophrenia.[4] Like hypertension, the "disease" aspect of the disorder results from a breakdown in normal functioning.

> The schizophrenic 'break' can indeed be seen as a discontinuity in behaviour—and therefore of brain function, thus preserving intact the notion of schizophrenia as a disease. However, this is perfectly compatible with the underlying disposition being dimensional, and describable as biological and psychological traits which, in the absence of triggering factors and when occurring in moderate degree, merely represent ways in which healthy human nervous systems vary. (Claridge, 1987, p. 736)

(The continuum between a predisposition toward schizophrenia and an actual schizophrenic "break" is illustrated in Figure 1.2.) In this manner, schizophrenia provides another example of how an inherited biological predisposition, through an interaction with life experiences, can contribute to the development of problems that are psychological in nature.

Thus, psychological disorders, as systemic dysfunctions, may reflect "genetically influenced variations in brain organisation which underlie temperamental and personality differences" (Claridge, 1985, p. 10). These differences, in turn, interact with environmental factors to transform these biological predispositions into signs of the disorder. In a like manner, Depue & Monroe (1986) have suggested that these types of disorders may result from "poorly modulated regulatory activity or, more simply, dysregulation." This dysfunction is the result of a "sys-

---

[4]The basis for viewing schizophrenia as a systemic disorder will be discussed at length in Chapter 4. Let it suffice at this point to assert that schizophrenia is the result of many factors (Zubin, 1986), some of which probably reflect a genetic predisposition to the disorder (Gottesman & Shields, 1982). Other etiological factors include the individual's premorbid level of functioning, which provides evidence for his or her coping skills, and environmental factors in the form of stressful events. Moderating variables, such as the person's physical and economic situation or social support system, are also important. In terms of diagnosis, there is still considerable controversy surrounding what the classic symptoms of the disorder mean in terms of prognosis and whether they constitute a single disorder or several (Mackay & Crow, 1980; Taylor, 1972). Furthermore, there are no diagnostic tests that allow for schizophrenia to be defined as a discrete disease state. For example, while schizophrenic patients may evidence more dopamine binding sites at postmortem than normals, the dopamine hypothesis of schizophrenia is still too elementary and nonspecific to warrant the use of dopamine or its metabolites as a reliable biological marker for the disorder (Karson, Kleinman, & Wyatt, 1986; Murphy & Buchsbaum, 1978). It should be added that the systemic perspective of schizophrenia presented here is compatible with several other explanations of the disorder. For example, the vulnerability model of schizophrenia (Zubin & Spring, 1977) is based on the assumption that some persons exhibit a genetically-based susceptibility to the disorder and that a schizophrenic episode develops when a "vulnerable" individual is subjected to a series of stressful environmental events that combine to surpass the threshold of vulnerability.

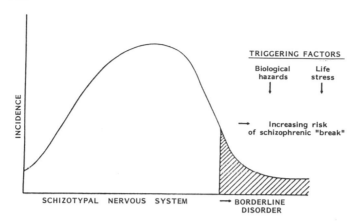

Figure 1.2. The hypothetical continuum of "schizotypy" as predisposition to schizophrenic disorder. (From G. Claridge [1987], 'The schizophrenias as nervous types' revisited, *British Journal of Psychiatry, 151*, p. 736. Copyright © 1987 by The Royal College of Psychiatrists. Reprinted by permission.

temic biologic vulnerability that increases the probability of dysregulation . . . when the vulnerable system is challenged by endogenous or exogenous stressors" (p. 41).

A model of individual differences in terms of one's susceptibility to a particular disorder provides a conceptual foundation for the present work and strengthen the rationale for viewing psychological disorders from a physiological perspective. This perspective assumes that a more accurate picture of how these disorders operate may be found in an understanding of the interaction of environmental and physiological factors, rather than either one or the other alone. Furthermore, a focus on individual variation allows one to evaluate the role of physiological factors over the entire range of psychological problems, rather than being limited to those disorders, such as schizophrenia, that traditionally have been thought to involve some sort of biological dysregulation as a basis.

Issues of Treatment. The different uses of the term "disease" have created problems in terms of treatment as well. At first glance, we might assume that all diseases should be treated medically. In fact, medicine is defined as "the art or science of treating disease" (American College Dictionary, 1958, p. 756). While this may be appropriate when we are talking about a discrete disease, the picture changes considerably when we take into account the complexity and interactive nature of a systemic dysfunction.

An example of problems that can occur by treating all diseases as if they were discrete can be found in the debate over prospective payment for medical care in the United States (Uyeda & Moldawsky, 1986). To curb escalating costs, in 1983 Medicare instituted a cost-containment program that tied payment for treatment to predetermined rates depending on the diagnosis assigned to the patient at discharge. This system, which is based on the average cost of treating diagnostically-related groups or DRGs, was phased in over a five-year period and applies to all general medical facilities.

The use of DRGs as a basis for payment has disclosed some interesting information about the treatment of different types of disorders. More specifically, it has been found that the DRG system works best for surgical procedures, less well for acute medicine, and hardly at all for inpatient psychiatric care (Nightingale, 1986, p. 71). The reason seems clear. The cost of surgery is easier to predict because these procedures usually deal with discrete disorders, such as a diseased appendix or a cancerous tumor. Psychiatric disorders, on the other hand, take a more unpredictable path and thus may not lend themselves as well to plans involving prospective payment.

At present the DRG system is being extended to include such health-care facilities as psychiatric, rehabilitation, children's, and alcohol/drug hospitals, which were initially exempt from this cost-containment system (Binner, 1986). The arguments against applying DRGs to psychiatric diagnoses reflect the problems related to treating all diseases as if they were discrete. As discussed earlier, systemic diseases differ from discrete ones in a number of ways. They have multiple causes, lack clear-cut signs or symptoms, cannot be verified by more precise information, and are not localized in a particular organ system. Although there may be a number of good reasons for expanding the scope of DRGs to include psychiatric facilities (Kiesler & Morton, 1988a), a number of problems in terms of prospective payment for these disorders remain, particularly when we take into account the interpersonal, legal, and social considerations involved.

As a result, many health-care providers are concerned with the effects of "medicalizing" problems in living so that "mental disorders are loosely defined as those human problems psychiatrists treat" (McReynolds, 1979, p. 126). Although part of the concern is financial, there is realistic apprehension as to what happens if psychiatrists, as medical doctors, were to attempt to treat psychological disorders with medication alone. Consequently, McReynolds (1979) argues that "the medical model is no longer heuristic in social science. What good it brought to our discipline was exhausted long ago. It now entraps our thinking and limits our research and practice" (p. 125). In this case, he is referring to a medical model that treats diseases as discrete states.

On the other hand, it may be short-sighted to insist that medical treatment is suited for discrete diseases only. To do so fails to appreciate the contributions medical treatments do have for disorders that share characteristics of systemic illness. Thus, while certain psychosocial interventions may be of value for treating hypertension (McCaffery & Blanchard, 1985), it would be unreasonable to insist that they can take the place of antihypertensive medications for all patients suffering from the disorder (Blanchard et al., 1985).

Unfortunately, the traditional distinction between mind and body appears to have led many psychologists and psychiatrists (e.g., Ludwig, 1975) to think of problems in terms of one of two broad categories— those that are "organic" or "natural" and those that are not. Clearly, this dichotomy works in some areas, such as organic mental syndromes (e.g., senile dementia). However, it breaks down rapidly as we move into areas for which learning, biological predisposition, environmental influences, and personal factors all play a role (Zubin, 1972).

The present volume will argue that anyone dealing with psychological problems can benefit from an appreciation of the subtle interaction of multiple factors that *together* result in a clinically meaningful syndrome. Problems that used to be thought of as either physical or psychological are now approached by interdisciplinary treatments that attend to aspects of both.[5] This is not to say that there is a medical basis for every problem. It is to say, however, that an understanding of physiology can make the practitioner more aware of the many elements that make up a psychological disorder and lead to an appreciation of the complex interaction of factors that contribute to its expression.

Summary

In this chapter it has been argued that assigning a diagnosis involves more than identifying the specific cause of a particular problem. It is a process of classification by which the complexity of clinical reality

[5]Examples of the appropriate use of an interdisciplinary approach can be found in Alford and Williams (1980); Becker and Schuckit (1978); Bellack (1986); Emmelkamp (1982); Foa, Steketee, and Ozarow (1985); Hersen (1979, 1986); Lieberman and Davis (1975); Mavissakalian and Michelson (1983); Mavissakalian, Turner, and Michelson (1985); Miller, Norman, Keitner, Bishop, and Dow (1989); Rush, Hollon, Beck, and Kovacs (1978); Stern (1978); Telch, Agras, Taylor, Roth, and Gallen (1985); Turner, Hersen, Bellack, Andrasik, and Capparell (1980); and P. H. Wilson (1982).

is organized. This allows researchers and practitioners to benefit from the shared learning that results from being able to talk about problems with similar characteristics.

The present work is based on the diagnostic system contained in the DSM-III-R. This system provides a framework for organizing the vast array of information that exists for four diagnostic categories—schizophrenia, depression, anxiety, and substance abuse. One reason for using the DSM-III-R is that the diagnostic categories it entails are generally reliable and widely used, at least in North America. Therefore, a majority of the readers of this book should be familiar with the DSM-III-R.

This is not to say that using the DSM-III-R is not without cost. Diagnostic reliability is achieved, in part, through narrowness and closure. Consequently, using the DSM-III-R may imply a degree of consensus among health-care professionals that, in actuality, does not exist. This is particularly true when one takes into account that the same disorder may be diagnosed differently in different cultures. Thus, there are some important unanswered questions that are not as easily dealt with within the framework of the DSM-III-R. For example, the question of whether schizophrenia and manic-depressive illness exist on a continuum that encompasses the entire range of psychosis (cf. Claridge, 1985; Crow, 1986; Zigler & Glick, 1988) is more difficult to address when these separate diagnostic categories are dealt with in two different chapters. Nevertheless, some sort of organizational structure must be used. Therefore, the possibility that overlap between the different diagnostic categories occurs and that the lines of distinction between them have been somewhat arbitrarily drawn is acknowledged but left to other, more capable authorities to explore.

There are other problems with the DSM-III-R. Of particular concern is the possibility that use of a diagnostic system will lead to "labeling" one's clients and to seeing them not as persons but as disorders. However, this is an ever-present danger for any health-care provider, regardless of the system he or she uses to comprehend the client's problems. A second persistent concern involves the application of a disease-based model to disorders that are primarily psychological in nature (i.e., problems of living). In this chapter it has been argued that the broad rather than narrow meaning of the term "disease" be used. In this regard, these disorders may be viewed as the result of systemic dysfunctions rather than diseases per se.

The advantages of using a systemic model should be evident in the chapters that follow and will be reviewed again in the final chapter of the book. For now, it will be sufficient to say (1) that the disorders covered in this volume will be viewed as deviations from normal function rather than discrete disease states. In addition, it will be assumed (2) that there is a continuity between health and illness and (3) that, unlike discrete diseases, systemic dysfunctions result from multiple rather than single causes. As a result, treatment of these disorders would seem to call for the cooperative effort of several professions rather than the limited efforts of a single discipline. This preference for an interdisciplinary approach to treatment is a theme that will be developed throughout the book and that provides an underlying rationale for its being written.

Chapter 2

Temperaments

Pavlov's assistant led "Brains" out of her kennel to the laboratory. She had been given her nickname because of the rapidity with which she could be conditioned. This, however, had come as something of a surprise, since Brains was a withdrawn, frightened animal. Although she had been raised in the laboratory with "utmost gentleness," she was always nervous around people, often slinking along behind the experimenter with her tail between her legs or cringing to the floor at the slightest movement or sound. Nevertheless, she had proven to be a valuable subject in many experiments. (Pavlov, 1960/1927, pp. 287–319).

Pavlov had not expected a dog like Brains to be easily conditioned. He believed that such animals would be too distracted or withdrawn to attend sufficiently when the experimental stimuli were presented. Initially he chose friendly, active dogs who seemed at ease around people and in the laboratory. Unexpectedly, these animals proved to be much less satisfactory as subjects. They became drowsy and even fell asleep when placed in the experimental apparatus that limited their movement. After awhile, Pavlov despaired at achieving anything with these animals; that is, until he altered his experimental conditions to suit them. He found that

> In dogs of this type many conditioned reflexes must be developed concurrently, and with a great variety of stimuli; no stimulus must be repeated more than once in a single experiment, and long pauses between the applications of the various stimuli must be avoided; not only excitatory but also inhibitory reflexes must be developed. In short, when we make rapid and considerable variations in the experimental environment such dogs become quite satisfactory subjects for the experiments. (p. 286)

However, there was little Pavlov could do about Brains, who became so sensitive that she reacted defensively to even the slightest sound. Finally, in 1924 there was a terrible storm in Petrograd (now Leningrad) where Pavlov conducted his experiments. The kennels were flooded, and the animals were made to swim a quarter mile to the main building, where they huddled together on the floor. Brains never seemed to recover from this ordeal and developed a hypersensitivity that precluded her being used further in experiments.

There are two points to be made about Pavlov's experience with Brains and her canine comrades. First, although they were raised in a controlled laboratory environment, there were conspicuous individual differences between animals that could not be explained satisfactorily in terms of past experience alone. Second, these individual differences proved to be so durable that Pavlov had to modify his experimental methodology to take them into account.

Nervous Types

I. P. Pavlov, the Nobel laureate in physiology, is best remembered for his work on classical conditioning. Every undergraduate knows that he taught dogs to salivate at the ringing of a bell. It is less well known that he also made a major contribution by developing a theory of individual differences.

Pavlov's interest in individual differences resulted from his observations of laboratory animals like Brains. He noticed that the dogs demonstrated a wide variation in temperamental characteristics, such as aggressiveness, timidity, and friendliness. Furthermore, since he studied the same animals for long periods of time, even years, he became very familiar with their individual mannerisms or "personalities." Soon he was able to predict how different animals would behave during his experiments.

From these observations Pavlov developed a theory of "nervous types" (Gray, 1964). He postulated that individual nervous systems differ in several important ways. One of these is a tendency toward *excitation* or *inhibition*. Pavlov believed that inhibition varies among individuals just as excitation does, but independently so that it is possible to exhibit different combinations of the two factors. For example, one person might display a strong excitatory tendency with little inhibition; another may demonstrate both strong excitation as well as inhibition. The key is the *balance* or equilibrium of the two opposing forces.

Pavlov defined the *strength* of a nervous system in terms of its ability to maintain a balance between inhibition and excitation. "Strong" nervous systems are well-balanced and thus are able to respond over long periods, even in the presence of powerful stimulation. "Weak" ones, on the other hand, over-respond to mild or even weak stimuli and thus become exhausted quickly. Furthermore, at very high levels of stimulation weak systems respond with a paradoxical reduction in strength due to excessive inhibition that is designed to defend the nervous system from further stimulation.

Pavlov considered animals that were either "sanguine" *or* "phlegmatic" to have strong nervous systems in that they responded in a relatively stable manner (i.e., did not veer dramatically toward increased excitation or inhibition). The "choleric" animal, on the other hand, evidenced a tendency toward excitability, just as the "melancholic" animal displayed a preponderance of inhibition.

Pavlov noted that these attributes reminded him of people, prompting him to generalize his observations to human beings. (See Panel 2.1, "An Example of the Melancholic Temperament.")

> The melancholic temperament is evidently an inhibitory type of nervous system. To the melancholic, every event of life becomes an inhibitory agent; he believes in nothing, hopes for nothing, in everything he sees only the dark side, and from everything he expects only grievances. The choleric is the pugnacious type, passionate, easily and quickly irritated. But in the golden middle group stand the phlegmatic and sanguine temperaments, well equilibrated [sic] and therefore healthy, stable, and real living nervous types no matter how different or contrasted the representatives of these types may seem outwardly. The *phlegmatic* is self-contained and quiet,—a persistent and steadfast toiler in life. The sanguine is energetic and very productive, but only when his work is interesting, *i.e.*, if there is a constant stimulus. When he has not such a task he becomes bored and slothful, exactly as seen in our sanguine dogs, as we are accustomed to call them. (Pavlov, 1928, p. 377, italics in original)

Pavlov's death in 1936 brought an end to a remarkable career that spanned more than half a century and coincided almost completely with that of another famous theorist of the period, Sigmund Freud. However, unlike Freud's ideas, Pavlov's theory of "nervous types" had little influence in the West, particularly the United States. There were two reasons for this.

The first was the popularity of psychoanalysis, which specifically rejects the notion that mental events can be reduced to physiological concepts (Parisi, 1987). After struggling for a number of years to develop a theory of the mind that was based on natural science, Freud (1954) abandoned his *Project for a Scientific Psychology* in 1902 and concluded that mental events involve a different class of phenomena all together. Seven years later Freud visited the United States and gave a famous series of lectures at Clark University. During the next 30 years his influ-

PANEL 2.1

An Example of the Melancholic Temperament

The genius of Charles Dickens allowed him to capture the essence of a character in just a few words. An excellent example of the melancholic temperament is thus provided by his description of Pip's adversary in *Great Expectations*.

> Bentley Drummle, who was so sulky a fellow that he even took up a book as if its writer had done him injury, did not take up an acquaintance in a more agreeable spirit. Heavy in figure, movement, and comprehension—in the sluggish complexion of his face, and in the large awkward tongue that seemed to loll about in his mouth as he himself lolled about in a room—he was idle, proud, niggardly, reserved, and suspicious. He came of rich people down in Somersetshire, who had nursed this combination of qualities until they made the discovery that [he] . . . was just . . . a blockhead. (Dickens, 1953, p. 192)

ence continued to grow, with many of his adherents fleeing Nazi Germany for the United States and England in the 1930's. As a result, psychiatry in the West (particularly in the United States) became dominated by psychoanalytic thought. Later this influence spread to clinical psychology in the United States (but not in England) through psychiatry's control of internship training sites in Veterans Administration medical centers following the Second World War (S. B. Sarason, 1981).

A second development that worked against the influence of Pavlov's theory of individual differences was the strong environmentalist bent of experimental psychology in the United States during the same period (Cravens, 1978). J. B. Watson, the father of behaviorism, took an extreme environmentalist position in the 1920's by proposing that a child at birth is equipped with little more than the "structure" of his or her body and a few rudimentary, unlearned responses (Bergmann, 1956). Although the environmentalist argument does not necessarily preclude a role for biological differences in individual make-up (Eysenck, 1982), the strongly environmentalist position served to blunt the impact of Pavlov's theory of nervous types on American psychology.

> A notable feature of the behaviourist movement, which originated and especially flourished in the United States, has been its studied disregard of individual variations between people, except in so far as these can be explained as due to differences in each person's set of learned habits. Thus, although

embracing the general principles of conditioning discovered by Pavlov, be-
haviourist psychologists ignored that part of his writings which referred to
the possibility of there being intrinsic biological constraints on individual
action. (Claridge, 1985, pp. 41–42)

In spite of the failure of Pavlov's nervous types to gain much head-
way in the United States, an interest in his theory did survive elsewhere.
In the Soviet Union, after a brief period of disfavor following his death,
Pavlov's writings regained their earlier prominence in directing Soviet
research. Although Pavlov's theory has undergone considerable revision, his influence remains today due to the continuation of research in
the decades since his death by experimental psychologists in Eastern
Europe, such as Teplov and Nebylitsyn in Russia and Strelau in Poland
(e.g., Nebylitsyn & Gray, 1972).

In a like manner, Pavlov's ideas were kept alive in England by
psychologists such as H. J. Eysenck. Eysenck began with Pavlov's proposal that the nervous system is under the control of the two opposing
forces—excitation and inhibition. Like Pavlov, Eysenck argued that individuals differ in terms of the relative balance of the two, some showing a greater tendency toward excitability while others toward more
inhibition. This distinction became the basis for his concept of
introversion-extraversion, which interacts with two other personality
dimensions—neuroticism and psychoticism. Variations within each of
the latter can thus be accounted for by differences in introversion-
extraversion. For example, it is said that an introverted "neurotic" tends
toward chronic anxiety, which includes disturbances such as phobias
and obsessive-compulsive disorders. The extraverted neurotic, on the
other hand, is more likely to develop disorders like hysterical neurosis.

There is a direct relationship between Pavlov's nervous types and
Eysenck's concept of introverted and extraverted personalties (Eysenck
& Levey, 1972). A "weak" nervous system creates an introvert, while the
"strong" system results in an extravert. The introvert is more easily
aroused, more sensitive to stimuli, and more inclined to withdraw from
strong stimulation. The extravert, on the other hand, with a more bal-
anced nervous system, can tolerate a more stimulating environment,
and, in fact, requires a certain level of stimulation for normal functioning. Brains, a canine introvert, was therefore more easily conditioned,
while her more sociable companions had a tendency to become bored
during experiments and fall asleep.

Pavlov's concept of nervous types survives today as a form of *temperaments*, a developmental model of individual differences based on
constitutional factors (Diamond, 1957). Temperaments are defined as

"that individual peculiarity of physical organization by which the manner of thinking, feeling, and acting of every person is permanently affected" (American College Dictionary, 1958, p. 1246). In a sense, temperaments are neurophysiological templates that "determine the broad direction in which personality, in its fuller sense, develops" (Claridge, 1985, p. 30).

> Individuals differ according to certain fundamental nervous properties, probably genetically determined, which underlie temperamental qualities like reactivity, sensitivity, attentiveness, and ability to regulate the demands of the environment. An important common feature of these properties seems to be the role they play in maintaining, or failing to maintain, an excitatory-inhibitory balance in the nervous system. (Claridge, 1985, p. 178).

This approach is illustrated nicely by Kagan's work on the temperamental contributions to social behavior (Kagan, 1989). Working with 20- to 30-month-old infants, Kagan and his colleagues have identified two subgroups of children who respond in dramatically different ways when placed in an unfamiliar situation.[1] One group, which represents approximately 10% to 15% of the children tested, become quiet, vigilant, and restrained. The other group responds in a spontaneous and apparently fearless manner. Kagan refers to the first group of children as *inhibited* and the second group as *uninhibited*. Not only do these individual differences in behavioral style appear to be biologically based, they appear to persist as the child grows older.

Other examples of different types of temperaments can be found in the work of Thomas and Chess, who initially identified nine dimensions in their study of children (Thomas & Chess, 1977; Thomas, Chess, & Birch, 1968). Their categories included activity level, rhythmicity, approach or withdrawal, adaptability, intensity of reaction, threshold of responsiveness, quality of mood, distractibility, and attention span/persistence (Thomas, Chess, Birch, Hertzig, & Korn, 1963). More recent investigators, notably Buss and Plomin (1975, 1984), have refined these dimensions, at first reducing them to four and later to three basic traits—emotionality, activity, and sociability. Although the number and meaning of these personality dimensions is still much in debate (cf., McCrae & Costa, 1986; Waller & Ben-Porath, 1987), it is generally held that there are regularities in behavior that endure across time, that pre-

---

[1]Studies that describe this work include Garcia-Coll, Kagan, & Reznick, 1984; Kagan, Reznick, Clarke, Snidman, & Garcia-Coll, 1984; Kagan, Reznick, & Snidman, 1987, 1988; Kagan, Reznick, Snidman, Gibbons, & Johnson, 1988; Reznick et al., 1986.

dict behavior, and that can be assessed with a reasonable degree of reliability (Block, 1981; S. Epstein, 1979; Costa & McCrae, 1988; Small, Zeldin, & Savin-Williams, 1983).

In many ways, the study of temperaments is a "bottom-up" approach in that these dispositions are thought to reflect the activity of low-level structures in the brain. As such, models of temperament can be said to deal with the biological structure of personality rather than its function per se. Thus, dimensions of temperament are broad rather than specific, descriptive rather than functional. More recently, however, the interest in individual differences has broadened beyond the study of temperaments to include *neuropsychology*, which is concerned with functional capabilities rather than general predispositions (Hartlage & Telzrow, 1985). In the past neuropsychology has not been concerned with psychopathology to a great degree and has focused instead on higher mental functions, such as intellectual and cognitive processes. However, the notion that psychological disorders result from a functional dysregulation that interacts with biological predispositions has provided a new way to approach psychopathology (Golden & Sawicki, 1985).

Whereas the traditional approach to temperaments relied heavily on psychophysiological studies to elucidate individual differences along such dimensions as arousability and inhibitory control, the more recent application of neuropsychological research methods has resulted in a focus on hemispheric function. Some of this work has attempted to explain various pathological conditions in terms of a cerebral dysfunction in one of the two hemispheres (e.g., Flor-Henry, Koles, Howarth, & Burton, 1979). Other research has focused instead on the communication between hemispheres (e.g., Wexler, 1980). Whichever approach is taken, however, it is likely that our understanding of individual differences in terms of physiological factors will encompass aspects of both traditional psychophysiological and more recent neuropsychological models.

The study of temperaments can thus be summarized as follows. It is assumed that individuals are different in terms of the kinds of nervous systems they possess, just as they differ in terms of their physical characteristics. These differences, probably genetic in origin, involve both broad dispositions and variations in neuropsychological function. This causes certain individuals to be more susceptible than others to different types of psychological dysfunction (i.e., to different forms of psychopathology) resulting from an interaction with their psychosocial environment (Claridge, 1985, pp. 4–5). (See Panel 2.2, "The Ancient Theory of Temperaments.")

PANEL 2.2

PANEL 2.2

The Ancient Theory of Temperaments

The proposal that personalities vary because of constitutional differences between people has been around for a long time. The Greek physician Galen (c. 130–200 B.C.) asserted that each person has four "cardinal humors" (blood, phlegm, bile [choler], and black bile [melancholy]). It was believed that a proper balance of these four humors was responsible for health, with disease resulting from an excess or an insufficiency of one or another of them. Each person's "temperament" was thought to reflect a unique balance of the four cardinal humors, so that some people were sanguine (i.e., having blood as the predominant humor), others phlegmatic, and so on. This theory was attacked vigorously by Paracelsus (1493–1541) toward the end of the Middle Ages, during which time it was the basis for all manner of medical treatments, such as blood-letting. Ironically, however, the death knell to Galen's theory was struck by a physician hoping to verify, rather than attack, it. Santorio (1561–1636) was a Venetian physician who developed devices to measure the body's temperature (a synonym at that time for "temperament") and other functions. Among his instruments was the recently-invented clinical thermometer, a primitive heart rate recorder, a hygrometer (an instrument for determining the humidity of the atmosphere), and a specially designed "weighing chair." With these tools Santorio set out to prove Galen's theory by demonstrating that disease is an imbalance between what the body takes in and what it excretes. Although his quantitative approach provided the basis for the scientific study of metabolism, it also ended Galen's dominance of medicine by exposing his theories to the scrutiny of experimental investigation. (Readers desiring to learn more about the original theory of temperaments are referred to Boorstin [1983], Part X.)

The Integration of Biological and Psychosocial Factors

Obstacles to Integration

The study of individual differences (i.e., temperaments) provides a way in which both biological and psychosocial factors can be taken into account. Nevertheless, the integration of biologically-based models of individual differences with theories of psychological dysfunction has been slow.[2] The old reasons for this lack of integration would appear less important today. The psychoanalytic movement no longer dominates psychiatry as it did and has gone through major revisions itself (e.g., Wachtel, 1977). The strict environmentalistic position emblematic of behaviorism earlier in the century has been modified as well (e.g., Meichenbaum, 1977). Nevertheless, obstacles to a meaningful integration of biological and psychosocial models persist. Some deal with the turf-guarding (e.g., economic and political concerns) that occurs when separate disciplines are divided among different professions. Other obstacles concern legitimate theoretical issues, while yet others involve a research methodology that fosters the isolation of knowledge from different sources.

Economic and Political Obstacles. Recently when I wondered aloud why psychologists did not show more appreciation for the biological aspects of behavioral problems, a colleague noted that to do so would be giving "more ammunition to the psychiatrists." Her point was well-taken in the sense that the areas of biology and behavior traditionally have been divided into two, separate professions—medicine and psychology. This arrangement provides the basis for a natural rivalry that tends to interfere with a meaningful integration of the two perspectives.

More specifically, as competition in the United States for the health-care dollar becomes more keen (cf., Cheifetz & Salloway, 1984), the need for the various professions to emphasize differences rather than similarities in their approach also increases. Consequently, it becomes important for psychologists to demonstrate how their services are different

---

[2]This point was brought home to me a number of years ago when I attended the annual convention of the Association for Advancement of Behavior Therapy (AABT) in Chicago. At that meeting I went to a symposium entitled "Neurology, Physiology, Pharmacology and Behavior Therapy: Completing the Gestalt" (Uchalik, 1978). The room in which the symposium was held was quite large and could hold more than 500 people. For this particular program, however, there were probably no more than a dozen in attendance. Understandably, the presenters were disappointed at the low turn-out and devoted a good bit of the discussion to the question of why there was not more interest in what seemed to them an important and timely topic. Nevertheless, attendance at this symposium was probably an accurate indication of the distrust many psychologists had at that time regarding biological factors and perhaps illustrates the tendency for proponents of various approaches to emphasize their own areas at the expense of others. There have been changes since that meeting in 1978. During more recent meetings of AABT there have been numerous presentations involving the interface of biology and behavior that have attracted large audiences. Examples of these presentations include Agras (1985), J.G. Beck (1985), Goldman (1988), Holroyd (1987), Linehan (1987), and Strickland (1985).

from and perhaps superior to those of psychiatrists, while psychiatrists, of course, make the same argument. Thus, each profession attempts to capitalize on what it knows best, a practice which contributes to the continued isolation of biological from psychosocial factors. An excellent example of this rivalry can be found in the controversy discussed in the preceding chapter that surrounded the adoption of the DSM-III and its revision. It is clear that as long as the delivery of health- care services continues to be an "I win; you lose" situation, an appreciation of what both sides have to offer will be frustrated.[3]

Theoretical Obstacles. In addition to economic/political obstacles, there are barriers that arise because the two teams in the health-care arena simply think differently (Kingsbury, 1987; S. Lieberman, 1986). For example, on the psychiatric side of things the dominance of psychoanalysis has given way to a call for the "remedicalization" of the discipline (Ludwig, 1975). While this development certainly encompasses the biological viewpoint (e.g., Kety, 1974), the approach also has been criticized as too narrow by failing to take into account the social, psychological, and behavioral dimensions of these problems (Engel, 1977; Fabrega, 1975). In fact, the biomedical approach tends to divide disorders into two distinct and mutually exclusive categories. There are "natural" disorders that reflect "biological brain dysfunctions, either biochemical or neurophysiological in nature" (Ludwig, 1975, p. 603). This category, which includes disorders such as schizophrenia and manic-depressive psychosis, is said to come under the purview of psychiatry. Conversely, the "nonpsychiatric disorders" (which include "problems of living, social adjustment reactions, character disorders, dependency syndromes, existential depressions, and various social deviancy conditions" [p. 604]) are seen as the proper domain of other health-care professionals, such as psychologists and social workers.

Needless to say, there are many who object to this sharp distinction between biological and psychosocial problems and who challenge the reductionism of medical research. They object to medicine's "lemon squeezer approach" in which the causes of a complex disorders like schizophrenia are reduced to a single variable, such as a biochemical

---

[3]It must be acknowledged that many of these statements in this section over-simplify a complex state of affairs. There are many divisions and subdivisions within both medicine and psychology. For example, the alienation of psychiatry from the main stream of medicine continues to be an area of concern (Lipowski, 1988). As a result, some psychiatrists advocate the merger of biological and psychological care, but under the auspices of medicine only! Subsequently, the fragmentation of health care can be seen as one of the major challenges facing health-care professionals of all persuasions.

anomaly, with little consideration given to their psychosocial components (Claridge, 1985, p. 185).

> While reductionism is a powerful tool for understanding, it also creates profound misunderstanding when unwisely applied. It has led to narrow emphasis on the single-lesion theory of pathogenesis—the molecular biologic analogue of the germ theory—in which complex causation is neglected and a single technologic solution is sought for the single lesion. . . . Reductionism is particularly harmful when it neglects the impact of non-biologic circumstances upon biologic process. (Holman, 1976, p. 21)

Understandably, Engel (1977) and others have argued that the *biomedical* model be replaced with a *biosocial* one that encompasses both biological as well as psychosocial variables, particularly in terms of "how disease and behavior interrelate" (Fabrega, 1975, p. 1500).

Psychologists, on the other hand, have also hindered integration by eschewing an interest in the biological aspects of behavior. Skinner's (1950) criticisms in this regard are well known and reflect the belief held by behaviorists "that most of man's behavior could be understood and controlled as a function of environmental variables" (R. P. Lieberman & Davis, 1975, p. 307). More recently, however, psychologists have dared open the "black box" with their investigation of cognition. Ironically, this new interest has also hampered the acceptance of physiological factors by explaining non-environmental contributions to behavior primarily in terms of cognitive constructs.

A good example of this can be found in the emergence of cognitive reconceptualizations of personality. In 1968 Mischel attacked the traditional view that behavior is determined by underlying personality dispositions or traits. In its place, Mischel developed a cognitive model of personality that replaces psychodynamic formulations with the cognitive constructs, such as encoding and categorization, expectancies, subjective values, and self-regulatory plans (Mischel, 1973, 1979). The result is that consideration of biological variables is neglected in two ways—behavioral constancy is attributed to cognitive factors while the criticisms of personality "traits" continue to work against the notion of behavioral constancy from other than cognitive sources (e.g., biological predispositions).

Methodological Obstacles. A final reason why biological and psychosocial theories of behavior have been slow to converge rests on a research methodology that obscures the interrelatedness of different disciplines (cf. Cronbach, 1975). For example, pharmacological researchers interested in the specific action of a certain drug are not interested in psychosocial effects on individual responsivity to that drug. Consequently, they conduct double-blind experiments designed to minimize variability due to psychosocial factors. Another example can be found among psychologists who attempt to minimize the effects of differences due to biological make-up. This takes the form of the assumption, termed the "equipotentiality premise," that principles of learning cut across all individuals as well as most species (Seligman & Hager, 1972; see Hollandsworth, 1986, Chap. 4, for further discussion).

The exclusionary nature of much research is illustrated in the rivalry of genetic versus environmental explanations of behavior (Rowe, 1987). Geneticists have avoided the idea that there may be an interaction between biological and environmental factors because this interaction makes interpretation of genotypic effects difficult (Plomin, Defries & Loehlin, 1977). Environmentalists, on the other hand, "have been equally reluctant to accept the idea of organismic specificity, since the existence of specificity makes it difficult to utilize a global, main-effects model" (Wachs, 1983, p. 403). The result has been that individual differences are consigned to what Cronbach has called "that outer darkness known as error variance" (1967, p. 27). Thus, research methodology allows us to focus only on those variables of particular interest and to ignore other factors entirely (Minke, 1986). In turn, this practice may lead us to dismiss results that can not be explained in terms of our chosen theory, perpetuating the segregation of knowledge along the lines of orthodox belief (cf. Garcia, 1981).

Aids to Integration

In spite of these obstacles to integration, there has been persistent movement in that direction over the past two decades (e.g., Staats, 1983). For example, several lines of research have lead investigators to conclude that the interaction of biological and psychosocial factors simply can not be ignored. Of these, the areas of behavioral medicine, environmental stress research, and developmental psychology would seem most important.

Behavioral Medicine. It is doubtful that any health-care area has developed as rapidly as behavioral medicine. From its inception as a specialty in 1977 (Schwartz & Weiss, 1977), behavioral medicine has enjoyed consistent and widespread growth. Currently there are hundreds of workshops, courses, and training programs in behavioral medicine each year that involve the interaction of many disciplines, including nursing, medicine, psychology, social work, physical therapy, and others.

Behavioral medicine, by definition, is an interdisciplinary approach that represents "an emerging network of communication among an array of disciplines not previously well-connected" (Agras, 1982, p. 797). It is an outgrowth of the conclusion that many problems can not be dealt with satisfactorily from one perspective alone. Consequently, many of the barriers between the biomedical community and other health-care providers have been lowered, resulting in a new view of health and illness that takes into account psychosocial as well as biological factors.

Life Stress Research. Although the study of how stressful environmental events affect health may be seen as one aspect of behavioral medicine, life stress research predates behavioral medicine (Mason, 1975a, 1975b) and, in fact, can be said to have been a major factor contributing the emergence of behavioral medicine in the first place.

One result of research in this area is the finding that a large proportion (as much as 25%) of a community is *chronically* distressed (Link & Dohrenwend, 1980). Although some of these cases can be explained in terms of prolonged life difficulties, most of these individuals show evidence of a persistent disorder that can not be explained in terms of environmental factors alone (Depue & Monroe, 1986). In fact, the presence of a prior disorder is by far the most powerful predictor of a subsequent disorder, accounting for as much as 30 to 40% of the total variance, independent of environmental factors. By comparison, environmental variables account for only 1 to 9% of the variance in these studies.[4]

Depue and Monroe (1986) conclude from their review of this literature that the "stable attributes of the individual are equal to, or more powerful than, socioenvironmental factors in predicting human disorder" (p. 48). They specifically criticize focusing on socioenvironmental factors only because to do so assumes that individuals are "homogeneous entities who vary in level of disorder as a function of socioenvironmental factors alone" (p. 48). Depue and Monroe assert that "the most powerful prediction scheme is likely to be one that incorporates both socioenvironmental factors . . . and stable individual attributes" (p. 49). Among these attributes is a biologically-based vulnerability toward specific disorders.

[4]Examples of the inability of environmental variables by themselves to explain various chronic disorders can be found in Friedman and Booth-Kewley (1987); Grant, Patterson, Olshen, and Yager (1987); Rabkin and Struening (1976); and I. G. Sarason, de Monchaux, and Hunt (1975). The predictive power of a prior disorder is dealt with in McFarlane, Norma, Streiner, and Roy (1983); Monroe (1982); Monroe, Imhoff, Wise, and Harris (1983); and A. W. Williams, Ware, and Donald (1981).

Developmental Psychology. Developmental psychology is a third area in which there has been an interest in how differences in biological make-up interact with environmental experiences. Traditionally, there has been a separation between theorists who emphasize environmental forces and those who argue for the central role of inherent (i.e., naturalistic) factors in directing development. The "nurture" side recognizes the crucial role of biological influences at birth; they argue that variability thereafter is primarily the result of environmental factors (e.g., Ross, 1980).

An alternative view stresses the interaction of both environmental and genetic factors for understanding human development (e.g., Scarr & McCartney, 1983; Wachs, 1983). From this perspective, our genetic make-up is said to play a major role in determining which environments are experienced and what effects they have.

> What people experience in any given environment depends on what they attend to, how much they learn, how much reinforcement they feel they get for what behaviors. And what they experience in any given environment is a function of genetic individuality and developmental status. (Scarr, 1985, p. 510)

Detrimental environments, such as those that involve poverty, malnutrition, or child abuse, will interfere with or place upper limits on our development. Less intrusive surroundings, however, provide a foundation of experience that fosters development generally but which does not explain very much in terms of individual maturation. These personal characteristics are seen as being determined primarily by genetic factors. This approach, which has renewed an interest in how biological factors interface with learning environments to foster normal (or abnormal) growth, is so important to the current volume that it is discussed at length in the following chapter.

Summary

In summary, an interest in individual differences that transcend environmental influence goes back almost a century. One aspect of this interest has been a focus on biologically-based predispositions, particularly those that involve a balance between excitation and inhibition. More recently, these basic tendencies have been elaborated on by the application of knowledge gleaned from the study of hemispheric function. Together, these two lines of inquiry suggest that our psychological status at any given time is the product of an interaction between physiological regulation and environmental experience.

In spite of this tradition, the study of psychological disorders continues to be divided among a number of different disciplines, each of which emphasizes its own areas of expertise. Cross-disciplinary ventures, although faced with several obstacles, would seem to offer the best promise for understanding psychological problems in the future (Agras, 1987; Russo, 1988). Recent developments in the areas of behavioral medicine, life stress research, and developmental psychology illustrate the need for a broad perspective that takes physiological as well as psychosocial factors into account.

Chapter 3

Genes and Environment

On December 19, 1985, Lazaro Faraga, 27, was driving from Texas to Miami with his girlfriend, Sherry Royal. In the car with them were Sherry's 5-year-old daughter, their younger twins, and a 2-month-old infant. Just a few days earlier Faraga had been released in Dallas on a $75,000 bond for trafficking in cocaine. Near Jackson, Mississippi, the two got into an argument, apparently over the paternity of the youngest child. Stopping his car in the right lane of the interstate, Faraga first tried to push Sherry and her daughter, who was clinging to her legs, into the path of an oncoming truck. As the argument heated, truck drivers and other motorists stopped to see what was happening. Sherry got back into the car and shut the door. However, Faraga got the door open and pulled her and the infant from the car. Tearing the child from his mother's arms, Faraga slammed it on the hood of a yellow car that had pulled over. Then he picked up the baby, raised it over his head and threw it onto the pavement in front of oncoming traffic. In terror, Sherry scooped up the child and ran to a truck that also had stopped, only to find the passenger door locked. Faraga again grabbed the infant and threw it to the pavement a second time. The baby died of multiple skull fractures and injuries to the brain. Faraga was later found guilty of capital murder and sentenced to death.[1]

---

[1]The events surrounding this heinous act are summarized in an article that appeared in the Jackson, Mississippi, *Clarion-Ledger* on July 30, 1987 (p. 3B). That particular report concerned a unanimous decision by the Mississippi Supreme Court to uphold the death sentence imposed by a lower court. Faraga's appeal was based on the admission by his court-appointed lawyer during the trial that the defendant might be guilty of murder but not of capital murder. Faraga argued that his attorney should not have admitted his guilt and that he should have been tried for child abuse instead of murder. Furthermore, he contended that the pills he was taking for ulcers had made him crazy. Nevertheless,

Why did Lazaro Faraga do such a thing? Several explanations come to mind, but most likely none of them involves genes or heritability. In fact, it would seem preposterous to attribute this action to some genetic program. On the other hand, almost any explanation of this severely abnormal behavior would seem lacking. Although Faraga tried to fake insanity at his trial, he was not psychotic, nor was he under the influence of drugs at the time of his arrest. All that we can say is that he was angry. So how do we explain his actions in light of the fact that everyone gets angry, even extremely angry, without resorting to this kind of frenzied brutality?

There is probably no simple explanation for what Faraga did. His actions appear to have been the unfortunate combination of many factors, some of which were situational. After all, there had been an argument. However, there are any number of potential contributing factors, such as how he handled his anger in the past, his conflicts with those close to him, as well as the possibility of a history of drug abuse. To this profusion of factors we can add, perhaps surprisingly, genetic considerations, for this element provides yet another perspective on the reasons for Faraga's violent crime.

Behavioral Genetics

What we think, do, and feel is influenced by factors from two sources—ourselves and our environment. The environment is an omnipresent, multidimensional, and dynamic source of change. However, to a large extent we determine what we experience in terms of our environment.

There are two ways in which we can affect what we experience. One way is through the selective attention to or distortion of what goes on about us. This involves how we perceive the environment and is determined by our expectations, attitudes, or beliefs. However, our perceptions are the product of previous experience so that how we perceive

---

Justice Hawkins, writing for the court, stated, "When proof of certain facts is overwhelming, however, an attorney may find it strategically prudent to concede such facts while still denying that his client is guilty of the crime charged in the indictment." Hawkins noted further that Faraga was sane and that "the proof offered at the trial was overwhelming that he did murder the infant." A more complete accounting of the crime and the trial that followed can be found in issues of the *Clarion-Ledger* published on December 20, 1985 (p. 1A), December 21, 1985 (pp. 1B, 4B), January 17, 1986 (p. 1B), February 18, 1986 (p. 3B), and February 19, 1986 (pp. 1B–2B).

the environment is essentially self-perpetuating. What we have experienced in the past to a large extent determines what we experience in the future.

What, then, do we contribute to this process that is distinctively our own? One thing we do offer is our genetic make-up—the unique combination of attributes inherited from our biologic parents. This represents a second way in which we, through our strengths and weaknesses, can shape experience.

> Genes direct the course of human experience, but experiential opportunities are also necessary for development to occur. Individual differences can arise from restrictions in environmental opportunities to experience what the genotype would find compatible. With a rich array of opportunities, however, most differences among people arise from genetically determined differences in the experiences to which they are attracted and which they evoke from their environments. (Scarr & McCartney, 1983, p. 433)

Genes and environment both play important yet different roles in our development. The environment provides the context in which growth occurs while our genotype gives direction to that growth. The relative importance of each factor varies, depending on the person's stage of development and the manner in which these factors interact (McCall, 1981).

Genotype → Environment Relationships

There are three ways in which genes influence what we experience. First, there is a *passive* effect that occurs when our genes *and* environment come from the same source. This occurs primarily during infancy and occurs when a child's parents provide both the genes and the environment that are favorable (or unfavorable) for the development of a particular trait. This type of effect is referred to as a passive genotype → environment relationship because it occurs independently of the individual. In other words, the child has nothing to do with determining either his or her genetic make-up or his or her environment (Plomin, DeFries, & Loehlin, 1977).

The development of verbal abilities is an example of a passive effect. A child's ability to read is influenced by his or her inherited ability to read as well as the availability of books in the home. Parents who read well and who enjoy reading are likely to have children who are good readers for both genetic as well as environmental reasons. In situations such as this, however, it is impossible to sort out which is more important to the child's development, because the child's genes, the parent's genes, and the rearing environment provided by the parents are related (Bell, 1968). Only when this interrelatedness is disrupted, such as occurs when the child is adopted, can we begin to gain some sense of what role each of these factors plays.

A *reactive* genetic effect, on the other hand, occurs when our genotype elicits different types of responses from our social and physical environment. The smiley, active baby is a case in point when he or she receives more attention and social stimulation than his or her more cantankerous companion. In a like manner, cooperative and attentive preschoolers may receive more pleasant and instructional interactions from adults than children who are uncooperative or easily distracted (Scarr & McCartney, 1983). This type of effect extends beyond the environment provided by our parents and includes teachers, peers, or other adults who may recognize an emerging trait and respond by providing special opportunities for its development.

A third type of genotype → environment relationship, referred to as an *active* genotype effect, occurs when we seek out environments that are compatible with or supportive of our genetic potential. Thus, the skilled athlete may seek out opportunities in sports while the bright child may pursue the company of others who can foster his or her intellectual growth. Which sport or area of study a child chooses will be determined to a large extent by environmental opportunities and social values. However, no amount of education, training, or environmental support can make the athletically inept individual a star or the retarded child a scholar. For this reason, it can be said that the active genotype effect is the most direct expression of genotypic influence on individual experience.

Examples of Genotype → Environment Relationships

The division of genotype → environment relationships into three types is merely one of conceptual convenience. In real-life situations these effects are mixed, ambiguous, and variable. For example, when is the out-going, sociable baby evoking responses that reinforce this behavior (a reactive effect) rather than simply reflecting a natural tendency around loving and attentive parents (a passive effect)? Or when is the young scholar being a good student because his or her parents and teachers have encouraged it (again, a reactive effect), rather than being studious because he or she finds it inherently rewarding (an active effect)? Nevertheless, it is still worthwhile to look at examples of each effect separately in order better to understand how genes and environment interact.

Obesity: A Passive Effect. One of the more controversial areas of debate in the nature-nurture controversy is the inheritance of obesity. A number of studies suggest human obesity and fatness are highly heritable (Börjeson, 1976; Brook, Huntley, & Slack, 1975; Fabsitz, Feinleib, & Hrubec, 1980; Feinleib et al., 1977). The problem with doing research in this area, however, is that the inheritance of obesity represents a passive genetic effect. That is, our parents may provide both the genetic propensity toward being overweight as well as the environment for consummatory behavior. This makes the determination of whether obesity is caused by genes or environment difficult to ascertain.

Adoption studies provide one means of trying to sort out genetic from environmental factors in this regard. Children who are adopted grow up in homes in which the adoptive parents contribute only the environmental part of the obesity equation. Adoption studies of obesity, however, have resulted in contradictory results. Hartz, Giefer, and Rimm (1977) concluded that the family environment was far more important than heredity in determining the percentage of overweight in adults. Garn, Cole, and Bailey (1977) reached a similar conclusion with children using relative weight and skinfold thickness as dependent measures. On the other hand, Annest, Sing, Biron, and Mongeau (1983) found exactly the opposite in their study of overweight children. Unfortunately, all three of these adoption studies are flawed by a lack of information on the biologic parents and the failure to explore the entire range of body weight. In addition, three of the four studies deal with children only.

In 1986 Stunkard and his associates conducted an adoption study that was designed to correct the methological shortcomings of the earlier investigations. Using the Danish Adoption Register, Stunkard and his colleagues collected information on 5455 children who represented every nonfamilial adoption granted in Denmark between 1924 and 1947. Next, they mailed out a general health questionnaire to 4643 of the adoptees who were still alive and living in Denmark. Of these questionnaires, 3651 were returned for a response rate of 79%. The mean age of those who returned the questionnaire was 42.2 years and included 56% who were women.

From this data base the investigators randomly selected 540 adoptees that fell equally into one of four weight categories—thin, median weight, overweight, and obese.[2] A second questionnaire was then mail-

[2]Weight was defined in terms of a body-mass index, which is calculated by dividing the subject's weight in kilograms by the square of the subject's height in meters. There were approximately 130 to 140 subjects in each weight class.

ed to these adoptees, their parents (both biologic and adoptive), and biologic siblings who were still alive. By getting information from several sources, the investigators were able to determine reliably the weight of adoptees as well as that of their parents.

These data were analyzed by comparing the adult weight of the adoptees with the weights of both their biologic and adoptive parents. The findings were highly significant and indicated a strong relationship between the weight class of the adoptees and the body-mass index of their biologic parents. In fact, they found that 80% of the adopted offspring of two obese parents become obese as compared with no more than 14% of the offspring from two parents of normal weight. However, there was no relation between the weight class of the adoptees and the body-mass index of their adoptive parents. Furthermore, the relation between biologic parents and adoptees was not confined to the obesity weight group but was present across the whole range of body fatness.

The authors concluded that "genetic influences have an important role in determining human fatness in adults, whereas the family environment *alone* has no apparent effect" (p. 193, italics added). However, they are careful to point out that this finding did not mean that fatness, including obesity, is determined at conception like eye color or that the environment has no effect. In fact, since the genetic key to fatness may lie in activity level rather than appetite or food preference (L. H. Epstein & Cluss, 1986), it may be possible to counter the expression of a genetic tendency toward fatness through the application of weight management programs that include both exercise and proper dietary control.

Obesity illustrates a passive genotype → environment relationship in that an infant inherits from his or her biological parents both a genetic tendency toward a particular weight as well as a rearing environment that is either favorable or unfavorable toward that predisposition. If the environment is favorable (e.g., supports overeating), a positive genotype-environment correlation is said to exist. If the environment works against the natural tendency (e.g., reinforces a strict dietary regimen), the genotype-environment correlation is said to be negative.

Nurturing: A Reactive Effect. It has been known for a long time that the cries of a newborn are diagnostically important for determining its physical health (Lester & Zeskind, 1978, 1979; Ostwald & Murry, 1985; Tronick, 1989). In fact, the nature of an infant's cry sounds are often included as part of the neurological examination (Prechtl & Beintema, 1964) and mentioned in pediatric textbooks as an important component in the clinical evaluation of a neonate's medical status (e.g., Behrman &

Vaughan, 1983, p. 1554). Down's syndrome, for example, is noted for the unusually low-pitched pain cries it can produce (Freudenberg, Driscoll & Stern, 1978; Lester, 1985).

Inasmuch as an infant's cries evoke different responses from adults who hear them, this area of research serves to illustrate the nature of a *reactive* genotype → environment relationship. For example, the high-pitched cries of a premature infant are considered more aversive and elicit greater autonomic arousal in mothers and fathers than those of a full-term infant (Frodi et al., 1978; Frodi, 1985).

In 1980, Zeskind published a study in which he attempted to determine how different sorts of infant cries elicit different types of responses in adult caregivers. Thirty parents and 30 nonparents listened to tape-recorded pain cries of 16 two-day-old infants. Half of the cries were from healthy, low-risk infants, while the other half were recorded from healthy infants at high-risk due to a large number of obstetric complications.

Zeskind found that, in terms of an expressed desire to take "effective action," parents could discriminate between the cry sounds of infants at risk as opposed to those who were not. Nonparents, however, were not able to do so. He speculated that while inexperienced caregivers can distinguish the "cry sound" from other infant noises and know what it means, experience with infants may be necessary to translate certain cries into meaningful signals that call for decisive action. More specifically, experienced parents are able to discriminate between "sick" cries by indicating a desire to provide "tender and caring" responses as opposed to the tendency to render more effective responses in reaction to cries that signal urgency. Zeskind also proposed that there may be a biological synchrony between the organization of the infant's stressed central nervous system and the organization of the sensory capacities of the listener.

The evocative power of an infant's cries does not, however, always result in an effective or appropriate parental response. In another study, Zeskind and Lester (1978) found that inexperienced adults rated the cries of high-risk infants as "more aversive, grating, sick, urgent, distressing, piercing, discomforting, and arousing than low-complication infant cries" (p. 580). Consequently, it is possible that the infant at risk may not get the care he or she needs as a result of a grating or aversive cry that leads the caregiver to avoid interacting with the child (Bell, 1968, 1971). An extreme example might occur when high-pitched, grating, and excessive crying contributes to child abuse or neglect (Frodi, 1985; Gil, 1970; Parke & Collmer, 1975; Ramey, Hieger, & Klisz, 1972). It would be interesting to know what role, if any, this factor had in precipitating the death of the infant described at the beginning of the chapter.

Talent: An Active Effect. Not all genotype effects are passive or reactive. We may also act upon our environment in ways that complement or foster certain inherited potentialities. The most obvious case of this is when we seek out opportunities to develop a special talent. As Kempton observed in his review of Duberman's biography of Paul Robeson, "We get out gifts from nature but we realize our talents with their cultivation" (1989, p. 3).

Bloom (1985) and a team of research assistants at the University of Chicago conducted a five-year study of 120 superstars—Olympic swimmers, tennis players, concert pianists, sculptors, world-class mathematicians, and scientists. Most of his subjects were under 35 years of age with memories of childhood that were still fresh. Furthermore, their parents and teachers were often still living and thus available to tell their side of the story.

What these researchers found was that although these superstars had many different talents, they shared a number of similarities in terms of their childhood experiences. The influence of the home was seen as particularly important. Rather than being child prodigies, people whose talents were obvious at an early age, most of the children were not identified as gifted until after several years of hard work on their talent. What the children did have in the early years were alert and caring parents who noticed initial signs of potential and encouraged its development.

Success, even under these conditions, did not occur overnight. None reached a peak with his or her talent in less than 10 years of hard work and all went through the same three stages. First was a period of "falling in love" with their chosen pursuit. At this stage, the parents sought out teachers who were good with children and not necessarily the most skilled technically. These teachers were remarkable for their quickness to praise and their warm, friendly manner. The second stage involved the development of precision and the establishment of sound technique. This stage was also important for developing a sense of competence. The sort of teacher the child needed at this stage was more demanding, more of a perfectionist, someone who would make the child practice until he or she got it right. The final stage involved the child's making it on his or her own. This occurred when the child developed a personal style with the help of a final teacher who was both a master of the talent as well as a good role model.

These superstars illustrate how we go about shaping those environments that are necessary for the development of our special talents. The support and interest of the parents represent a positive genotype-environment correlation. But this does not diminish the importance of the role the young stars themselves played in shaping environmental experiences to develop natural abilities. For example, some parents who were interviewed recalled another son or daughter who was even more gifted but not willing to work as hard. The superstar, by contrast, made a string of choices that placed practice before pleasure, the development of a particular skill before the pursuit of other interests. In this regard, the children who later developed into superstars illustrate an *active* genotype → environment relationship.

Summary. The relationship between genes and environment occurs in three basic ways. In the case of a *passive* effect, our genetic make-up and environment are linked by a common factor, our biologic family. The term "passive" is used to indicate that the individual does not contribute to this situation; it is provided without asking and usually without our thinking about it. Nevertheless, this effect can be extremely important, especially during the very early years of development. The second or *reactive* effect extends beyond the family to include anyone with whom we come into contact. This type of effect involves the different ways people respond to us because of our physical attractiveness, temperaments, or natural abilities. Consequently, the reactive effect is most important during early childhood when basic skills and competencies are being developed and our sense of identity is being established. This developmental step paves the way for an *active* effect in which the individual seeks out those experiences that are important for the realization of our inherited abilities. This effect becomes more pronounced with age as the talents are developed and, of course, can continue throughout adulthood. Furthermore, an active effect is not limited to our interaction with other people but can entail any sort of environmental circumstance, social or physical, that enables us to realize our genetic capability.

Scarr's Model of Genotype → Environment Relationships

The interrelatedness of factors that contribute to a child's growth and maturation can be viewed within the context of Scarr's model of behavioral development, which is presented in Figure 3.1 (Scarr & McCartney, 1983, p. 425). The end-point of the process is the child's phenotype—his or her observable characteristics arising from an interaction of the genotype with the environment. The child's phenotype is

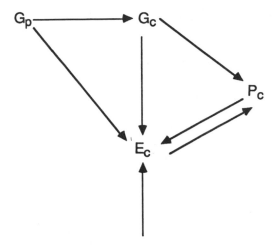

Figure 3.1. A model of behavioral development. (From S. Scarr and K. McCartney [1983], How people make their own environments: A theory of genotype → environment effects, *Child Development, 54,* p. 425. Copyright © 1983 by the Society for Research in Child Development, Inc. Used with permission.)

indicated by P_c in the figure, while G_c represents the child's genotype and E_c the rearing environment. The $G_c \rightarrow P_c$ relationship indicates maturation, which is controlled primarily by the genetic program. Notice that the parents' genotypes (G_p) contribute to both G_c and E_c. It will also be noted that P_c affects the rearing environment, representing an interaction between the child and his or her environment. A final aspect of the model is the presence of environmental factors that arise independently of either the parents or the child, as indicated by the arrow pointing to E_c from the bottom of the figure.

Many theories of human development include the person-environment interaction ($E_c \leftrightarrow P_c$). However, in most models the basis of this relationship is ambiguous. This is not the case for Scarr's model, which shows that the child's genotype affects both his or her phenotype *and* rearing environment ($G_c \rightarrow P_c$; $G_c \rightarrow E_c$). Since the genotype is determined *before* either the phenotype or the rearing environment, it can be seen that the correlation between the latter two is actually a function of the former. This demonstrates how our genes influence experience, as discussed in the first part of this chapter.

In terms of the different ways in which the genotype affects our environment, it also can be seen in Scarr's model that the passive effect involves the influence of G_p on P_c via G_c and E_c. The reactive effect is represented by the impact of G_c on P_c via E_c, while the active effect is portrayed by the interaction between P_c and E_c, given the effect of G_c on P_c.

It should be noted, however, that these genotype effects interact with other factors and thus can not be said to provide a complete picture of development by themselves. For example, there are environmental factors that arise independently from either the child or the parents and that interact with these effects since all three types involve pathways through the environment (E_c). Consequently, the correlation between P_c and E_c can be either positive, as when the rearing environment is compatible with or supports a genetic predisposition, or negative, as occurs when the environment serves to counteract or to interfere with the progression of natural development.

With this in mind, Scarr's model of behavioral development can be summarized as three propositions (Scarr & McCartney, 1983, p. 427). First, the process by which a child develops is best described by the three kinds of genotype → environment relationships discussed earlier—passive, reactive and active. Second, the relative importance of the three kinds of genotype effects changes as development progresses so that the influence of the passive type declines from infancy to adolescence while the importance of the active type increases. And finally, the importance of environmental experience also increases over time in conjunction with the shift from passive to active effects as individuals find increasing opportunities to select their own environments.

Proximal versus Distal Effects

Scarr's model shares with other developmental theories an interest in the interaction of the person with his or her environment ($P_c \leftrightarrow E_c$). This interest emphasizes *proximal* effects, those factors that occur in temporal proximity to the events they predict. This is reasonable, given that these factors are usually obvious and frequently offer the most parsimonious explanation for what has occurred. However, Scarr's model also directs attention to *distal* variables, such as the parent's genotype (G_p), that can also play an important role in determining a particular outcome.

The importance of distal variables can be seen in Scarr's (1985) research on the effect of maternal behaviors on children's intellectual and emotional development. It is well known that a mother influences the child's behavior and that the child, in turn, exerts a reciprocal effect on the mother (Baumrind, 1971; Bell, 1979). To study this, Scarr and her research colleagues chose two proximal variables—maternal control of children rated from 15-minute observations of teaching situations and scores from interviews with mothers about their methods of disciplining their children in the face of typical misbehavior. Both measures yielded acceptable reliability and were scored to indicate both positive and negative parental management techniques. On the positive end of the continuum are techniques such as reasoning, explaining, and other verbal messages. On the negative end is physical punishment. In the middle are various forms of verbal admonishment.

In one study, the researchers were interested in whether maternal disciplining skills and control techniques could predict the child's Stanford-Binet IQ scores. It turns out they could, both concurrently (rs = .42–.49) and 18 months later (R^2 of .23). The nature of these relationships indicated that positive maternal behaviors were related to higher intellectual performance. If we were satisfied with proximal variables only, we would conclude that parents who do not discipline their children in positive ways could have more intelligent children if they would use more reasoning, understanding, and verbal skills and less physical punishment.

As Scarr points out, the problem is that the influence of distal factors had not been considered. Consequently, when Scarr entered the mothers' educational level in years and vocabulary scores from the Wechsler Adult Intelligence Scale (WAIS) into the regression equation, it was found that the mothers' IQ, as determined by the WAIS, dominated all other variables and by itself predicted *both* the children's IQ and the mothers' parenting skills. In other words, brighter mothers appeared to have brighter children and also tended to use more positive methods of discipline. Furthermore, the mothers' educational level was of little importance in that it did not add significantly to the predictive power of the relationship generated by the vocabulary scale of the WAIS. In fact, the only significant independent predictor among these variables of the children's IQ at 42 to 48 months of age was the mothers' WAIS vocabulary score.

Intelligence is thought to have a strong genetic component, so this set of results may have been peculiar to IQ. Consequently, Scarr also explored the relationship of the mothers' disciplining patterns with the children's communication skills as measured by the Cain–Levine Social Competence Scale (Cain, Levine, & Elzey, 1963). Again, the mothers' positive control techniques during the discipline interview predicted the children's communication skills later. This would seem to imply that if mothers manage their children in more positive ways, the children will be able better to carry messages, remember instructions, answer the telephone, and tell stories. However, when the mothers' vocabulary score from the WAIS was considered, the mothers' parenting skills as well as educational level again failed to add to the predictive power of the mothers' IQ in foretelling the child's communication skills at 42–48 months of age. In other words, it appears that mothers who are smarter behave in more benign ways toward their children as well as have children who have better verbal skills. This would suggest that improving the mothers' discipline techniques will not dramatically improve the children's language skills, even though focusing on the proximal variables alone would seem to offer this hope.

This is not to say that the mothers' genetic make-up is the only or even primary determinant in their children's overall development. When these same variables were entered into an equation that attempted to predict social adjustment (e.g., whether a child is attentive and expressive rather than withdrawn), the proximal variable (positive maternal discipline techniques) did predict the well-adjusted children. In this case, the maternal vocabulary score did not make a statistically significant contribution to the children's social adjustment, apart from its contribution to how mothers discipline their children. Consequently, changing the mothers' discipline and control techniques might have a payoff for the children's social adjustment.

The point of all of this is that while the genetic contribution to development cannot explain everything, it often does have an effect that may be masked by more immediately obvious variables, such as interpersonal transactions and environmental contingencies. Again, this is not to say that the latter are unimportant. Rather, it is to say that the genetic factors should not be ignored, for their contribution, although subtle, may be central to a child's development. Returning to the murder of the infant discussed earlier, it would seem that proximal variables, such as the argument, were sufficient in and of themselves to explain Faraga's crime. It is interesting to consider, however, how more distal factors might have played a role in affecting the disastrous outcome.

Environmental Factors

The potential for our genetic make-up to affect behavior is no different from any other causative factor; its importance depends on a number of considerations, such as the nature of the problem and the presence or absence of other, mediating or competing factors. In other words, although genetic factors may affect events in a manner in which we are not normally aware, this does not mean that they are invariably the cause "behind" a particular disorder, and in many instances they may have a minor role or no role at all. Furthermore, it may be useful to remember that heritability is not absolute, nor it is unchangeable.

Heritability Is Not Absolute

It is generally accepted that causal factors for any disorder can be categorized in three ways: (1) necessary and sufficient,(2) necessary but not sufficient, and (3) facilitating or predisposing (Goodwin & Guze, 1984). An example of the first category is a particular genotype (an abnormal gene on chromosome 4) that causes Huntington's Chorea—a fatal, progressive dementia (Gusella et al., 1983). In this case, the presence of the single gene is both *necessary and sufficient* for the development of a complex of symptoms that include disturbances in mood, restlessness, poor self-control, and eventual deterioration of cognitive function. The strong genetic pattern is such that the disorder among persons living in the eastern United States can be traced to six individuals who emigrated in 1630 from a small village in Suffolk, England. One family has been traced for 300 years with at least one family member in each of the 12 generations expressing the disorder (Vessie, 1932).

Fortunately, the number of disorders for which a single causative factor is both necessary and sufficient is relatively rare. Many more factors fall into the second or *necessary but not sufficient* category. In fact, a majority of physical infectious diseases involve several causes, all of which are necessary but no one of which is sufficient by itself to cause a disorder (Meakins & Christou, 1979; Plaut & Friedman, 1981; Sartwell & Last, 1980; Susser, 1973). For example, only a portion of persons exposed to the tuberculosis bacterium show clinical evidence of TB. Other factors, such as the resistance of the host, malnutrition, alcohol abuse, and possibly a genetic predisposition, appear to determine who gets TB and who doesn't. AIDS and susceptibility to the HTLV-III virus is another example of a situation in which exposure is necessary but not sufficient for the disease to develop (Baum & Nesselhof, 1988; Martin & Vance, 1984).

The third category includes factors that are *facilitating or predisposing*. Here the link between the cause and its effect is much less direct. For example, the loss of parents during childhood is related to the development of a number of psychological problems, even though it is neither necessary nor sufficient to produce any one of them (Maxmen, 1986). In this case, the presence of other causative factors or moderating variables (e.g., poverty, life stress, genes) will determine the clinical outcome.

Most psychological disorders would seem to fall in either the second (necessary but not sufficient) or third (facilitating or predisposing) categories (e.g., Heston, 1966; Rosenthal et al., 1968; Rosenthal, Wender, Kety, Welner, & Schulsinger, 1971). Schizophrenia, for example, is thought to be a "psychobiological complex involving multiple etiologies, which include genetic, developmental, psychosocial, and possibly even infectious factors" (A. R. Kaplan et al., 1976, p. 343). An analysis of various twin and adoption studies suggests that 73% of the variance in predicting schizophrenia can be accounted for by genetic factors, leaving 23% to the environment (Fulker, 1979). However, not all schizophrenics have the same symptoms, which leads to the question of whether this indicates a role for different genes or different environments (Hay, 1985). Thus, the evidence for its heritability coupled with equally strong evidence for an important environmental role suggests that the genetic basis for schizophrenia, while important, is still only relative in terms of its effect.

Alcoholism is another case in point (Schuckit, Goodwin, & Winokur, 1972; Tarter & Edwards, 1986). Using the adoption methodology employed by researchers in the areas of schizophrenia and obesity, Goodwin and his associates followed the offspring of alcoholic, biological parents who were reared by nonalcoholic, adoptive parents.[3] A control group consisted of individuals who were reared by their nonalcoholic, biological parents. The incidence of alcoholism in the offspring of alcoholic parents reared in nonalcoholic, adoptive homes was 22%, while only 4.4% of the children in the control group became alcoholic.

While this research suggests that heritability is a factor for some people, it does not show that genes are either necessary or sufficient to cause alcoholism. Many people who become alcoholic appear to lack a genetic basis for the disorder (i.e., their biological parents were not alcoholic). Furthermore, even if they have a genetic make-up that predisposes them toward alcoholism, abstinence will insure that they do not become alcoholic. In fact, alcoholism appears to be linked to a number of variables, including life stress, psychological disorders, as well as social and cultural influences (cf. Roebuck & Kessler, 1972), so that our genetic make-up is seen as playing a facilitating or predisposing role only.

Heritability Does Not Mean Unchangeability

Even in a worst-case scenario in which an inherited trait is both necessary and sufficient, the environment still plays a crucial role, for there are many examples of how environmental factors can affect or

---

[3]This series of studies includes Goodwin, Schulsinger, Hermansen, Guze, and Winokur (1973); Goodwin et al. (1974); Goodwin, Schulsinger, Knop, Mednick, and Guze (1977b); as well as Schuckit, Goodwin, and Winokur (1972).

modify even the most virulent genetic disorders. The phenylketonurias (PKU) are considered as representative of the necessary and sufficient category since this group of disorders is transmitted as an autosomal recessive trait. Nevertheless, the mental retardation that invariably develops as a result of neurologic lesions produced by a reduced tolerance to phenylalanine can be lessened by the provision of a diet low in phenylalanine during infancy or early childhood. In the same vein, although a disabling genotype may be both necessary and sufficient to cause profound mental retardation, the environment in which we place the mentally retarded person is of great importance for his or her development. Thus, not only do genetic factors vary in terms of the degree of their influence, they are also malleable in terms of their ability to be influenced by environmental factors.

Another example of why heritability does not mean unchangeability can be found in Lewontin, Rose, and Kamin (1984). Using an analogy from agriculture, they note that a handful of open-pollinated corn (i.e., seeds that are not genetically identical) can be randomly planted in two plots side-by-side. One plot is left to its own without extra watering or fertilization. The other is monitored closely and provided with extra water and nutrients to enrich the soil. After several weeks, the young corn in the two plots will be quite different. The neglected plot will yield corn that is *on average* shorter than the corn in the neighboring plot. However, in both plots there will still be considerable variation in height among the individual plants, suggesting that height has a genetic component. However, it would be misleading to say that height was genetically determined, since it is clear that other factors, such as water and fertilizer, also determined how high the corn grew.

This example is used as an argument against the assertion that there are genetically-based differences in intelligence between races. Individuals who grow up in impoverished environments will not do as well on average as those who have the benefit of a good education, literate family members, and social reinforcement for learning. Consequently, it may be misleading to attribute differences in intelligence between groups of people to racial (i.e., genetic) causes unless environmental factors are also taken into account (see Angoff, 1988, for an excellent discussion of this issue).

On the other hand, it would be equally misleading to assert that genetic factors play no role whatsoever. While the *average* level of intelligence may be affected by environmental considerations, *individual variability* may be determined to a large degree by genetic factors. For example, adopted children may generate IQ scores that are above those of their biological parents. Yet the correlation of their scores with those

PANEL 3.1

Heritability

Contributed by Martha Cain

Heritability is defined as the extent to which differences in genotype and environment contribute to the development of phenotype (an observable characteristic which can be measured) (Gottesman & Shields, 1982). Heritability is a descriptive statistic, and as such does not refer to an individual but to a population (Plomin, DeFries, & McClearn, 1980). The question addressed in the study of heritability is whether individual differences in behavior are influenced by genetic differences and, if so, what is the relative influence of heredity and environmental factors.

Genes, which are actually sequences of DNA nucleotide bases, do not directly cause behavior; they work indirectly via physiological systems. Genes control the production of proteins which then go on to determine anatomical, biochemical, and physiological characteristics in association with the internal and external environments. The outcome of all these processes may include some effect on behavior.

Initial queries may look at how many genes and which chromosomes are involved in expressing a particular behavior, after which the focus shifts to the developmental course of these particular genes, the type of gene action (additive-dominance), their interaction with the environment, pathways between the primary effect of the genes on protein production and regulation, and their ultimate effect on behavior (Elston, 1986; Hay, 1985). Complicating this type of investigation is the general rule that a single gene affects more that just a single phenotype (Plomin, DeFries, & McClearn, 1980).

Genetic variation results from either a single gene or the combined effect of several genes (polygenes). In the field of medical genetics, a large number of single genes have been identified which regularly produce easily recognized phenotypes that fall into classes that do not overlap with the normal phenotype and are thus qualitatively different (Gottesman & Shields, 1982). Principles of Mendelian genetics, with dominant and recessive segregating genes, are applicable to these genes, which are not easily deflected from their course and have few links in the causal chain connecting them to their specific traits.

Linkage of a particular phenotype (or disorder) to a single locus marker demonstrates that transmission occurs at the single locus and allows persons with that marker to be identified. Linkage studies to known markers seek to determine whether there are genes contributing to a particular disease located on these known chromosome markers (Hay, 1985). Even when the precise gene product cannot be specified or its mode of genetic transmission identified, a biological finding can serve as a marker of genetic vulnerability if it is heritable and segregates with the illness in pedigrees where it is found (Reider & Gershon, 1978). One problem associated with vulnerability markers in the study of mental disorders is the episodic nature of their clinical manifestations. Even in persons who have a particular disorder, there may be long periods of their lives in which there are no detectable signs of illness.

Nevertheless, the single-locus Mendelian type of heritability rarely occurs in complex phenotypes. Inherited traits most often depend on multifactorial variables with many indistinguishable loci contributing additively to genetic vulnerability and numerous environmental factors acting similarly (Gershon, 1983; Cloninger & Reich, 1983). The more complex the phenotype, the more steps in the chain of events and the greater number of environmental and genetic factors that are important to phenotypic variation.

Most of the variability determined by polygenetic effects is the result of simultaneous occurrences of many small discontinuities which are not individually detectable when put together and smoothed by environmental factors (Plomin et al., 1980). Over a population, however, they result in a bell-shaped continuous variation in a trait (Gottesman & Shields, 1982). Each multiple gene, or polygene, has a small, multiply-mediated effect on variation of a trait when compared to the total variation for that trait. As Gottesman and Shields (1982) note, "The expression of the trait, e.g., height, blood pressure, or disease resistance, depends much less on which unspecific genes in the specific trait system an individual possesses than on the total number pulling him toward the tail of the distribution of values" (p.7).

An example of polygenetic effects can be found in relation to the question of cell number. Recent research suggests that the number of cells governs the amount of neurotransmitter synthesizing enzymes in the brain (Reis, Fink, & Baker, 1983). Consequently, it is possible that genetic determinants of cell number play a role with respect to the expression of diseases, including those associated with aging (Kety, Rowland, Sidman, & Matthysse, 1983). For example, it is now established that there is a progressive decrease in the nigrostriatal system in aging humans. This appears to be associated with a reduction of the number of dopaminergic neurons in the substantia nigra. Individuals with more dopaminergic neurons would be expected not to express symptoms of such degeneration (Parkinsonism) until a more advanced age than those born with a fewer number of cells, if the rate of decline of cells is comparable. In neurological or psychiatric disease a large reservoir of cells may be protective against the expression of symptoms when brain cells are progressively lost. A question yet to be answered is whether variations in cell number could be one genetic element of diseases such as schizophrenia, manic-depressive illnesses, and Parkinson's, in which neurons of a particular neurochemical class and their receptors are involved.

Adoption studies, in which psychiatric conditions occur more often in adoptees who have biological relatives with the same illness than in those who do not, offer powerful evidence for genetic transmission of many of these disorders (Tsuang & Vandermey, 1980; Slater & Cowie, 1971). A second type of evidence occurs in twin and family studies in which individuals more closely related to the one with the disorder are more likely to show evidence of the illness (Gershon, 1983; Plomin, 1989). This increased susceptibility is often found in monozygotic twins, who are expected to show greater concordance than dizygotic twins. Crossover between the major diagnostic groupings of mental disorder (schizophrenia and affective disorders) is small and thus implies genetic specificity of each disorder.

from their biological parents is higher than the correlation of scores from their adoptive parents (Scarr & Weinberg, 1977, 1978, 1983).

In short, there are many good reasons why we should not credit genetic factors with more power than they deserve. It can be seen that far from providing a basis for some form of genetic determinism, our genotype exerts an influence that is relative in its effect and somewhat malleable in terms of its outcome. Furthermore, rather than being impersonal and dehumanizing, a person's genotype may provide the ultimate expression of his or her individuality.

> If there is a central message from behavioral genetics, it involves individual differences. With the trivial exception of members of identical multiple births, each one of us is a unique genetic experiment, never to be repeated again. Here is the conceptualization on which to build a philosophy of the dignity of the individual! (Plomin, DeFries, & McClearn, 1980, p.11)

Summary

It has been argued in this chapter that genetic factors play an important and often unrecognized role in determining how we think, act, and feel. Sometimes the effect is passive in that it is provided without our knowledge or desire. On other occasions, it is implemented through the different ways people around us respond to those characteristics that make us unique. Yet, in other situations we play a more active role in seeking out those environments that allow us to explore our genetic potential.

This interaction of our genotype with our environment is a fluid, dynamic process that changes with time so that the older we get the more important our environmental experiences become (Plomin, 1989). At an earlier age it may be that certain experiences are necessary for development. As we grow older, however, we assume more control over what we do and thus the passive effect of our genetic make-up becomes less important. The role of our genotype at this point is in terms of the strengths and weaknesses it has provided that lead us to seek out those environments we find most rewarding.

The nature of the interaction of genetic and environmental variables is complex and depends on, among other things, the nature of the disorder or behavior we want to predict. In some instances, genetic factors will play a more important role than others. Whatever the case, it is clear that satisfactory answers to the complex questions will *not* come solely from either the genetic or environmental side. Behavior and development are a function of the transaction of genes and environment. Until both dimensions are taken into account, it is likely that our understanding of why we do what we do will be, at best, incomplete and, at worst, misleading.

The Case of Lazaro Faraga

And so we return to Lazaro Faraga. Purely psychological explanations of his crime, which might include both environmental as well as psychodynamic models, suggest that any one of us is capable of committing this act, given similar past experiences and being placed in the same situation. However, an alternative view would argue that genetic differences must be taken into account and that the interaction of these differences with a particular set of circumstances resulted in the infant's death. It can be argued that other people would have reacted differently, even if they were faced with exactly the same set of experiences, for no one else shares Lazaro Faraga's genotype.

In other words, Faraga's unique genetic make-up insures that it is impossible for anyone else to become the environmental clone of this man. No one else would have interacted with his environment in exactly the same way. For example, what was it about Faraga that contributed to his anger and his ability to handle it? How did people react to him? Why did he become involved with drugs like cocaine and how did they affect his judgment, mood, and rationality? What sorts of environments did he seek out, and how did these environments contribute to an inability to control his emotions?

Clearly, there are no final answers to these complex questions at this time. And, of course, no attempt is being made to explain this bizarre event in terms of genetic factors only. On the other hand, Faraga's crime does serve to illustrate that while the environment provided a context, genetic factors could have set in motion a number of events that came together tragically one day on a highway in Mississippi.

Part II

Clinical Disorders

To this point we have talked in terms of principles that apply generally to the development of psychological disorders. In this regard, it has been argued that these disorders are not like a discrete disease but rather an indication of a systemic dysfunction that represents a deviation from normal functioning. Individual differences in terms of a susceptibility to certain dysfunctions may provide the basis for understanding how different persons develop different disorders. This approach highlights the interaction of one's biological self and one's life experiences. The complexity of this interaction, particularly as it relates to personal growth and development, suggests that the relative contribution of the two areas depends not only on the disorder being studied but on the point in its development at which the interaction occurs.

The next part of the book attempts to apply these principles to four diagnostic categories—schizophrenia, depression, anxiety, and substance use disorders. These disorders were chosen for three reasons. First, together they represent the vast majority of adult cases that present themselves for treatment in either inpatient or outpatient settings. Second, the research base for the physiological basis of these disorders is both extensive and sound. Third, many characteristics of these "core" disorders are shared by other forms of psychopathology found in children and adults. An understanding of the physiological aspects of these problem areas may therefore generalize to other areas of clinical concern.

In spite of the literally thousands of research studies that have been conducted in each of these areas, there is no overriding set of findings that can be applied generally across diagnostic categories. Consequently, each of the four clinical chapters takes a slightly different approach, depending on the literature that is available and considerations that set one disorder apart from another. Each chapter offers a brief diagnostic summary based on the DSM-III-R and a discussion of the evidence for the heritability of that group of disorders. In addition, the physiological basis for the symptoms characteristic of these disorders as well as the CNS mechanisms that are thought to underlie the expression of each disorder are highlighted.

Chapter 4

Schizophrenia

Perhaps no psychological disorder is more crippling than schizophrenia. Its characteristic psychotic symptoms involve disturbances in thought processes, perception, and affect that invariably result in a severe deterioration of social and occupational functioning. Furthermore, the course of schizophrenia is lengthy and almost always involves a number of debilitating residual symptoms.

There is no single model or concept of schizophrenia. This point was underscored in 1972 when a joint American-British project compared the frequency with which a group of New York psychiatrists and a group of psychiatrists in London made the diagnosis (Cooper et al., 1972). It was found that the American physicians applied the diagnosis of schizophrenia about twice as often as their British colleagues. This discrepancy occurred because in the United States the symptoms said to be indicative of schizophrenia were broader and more numerous than those used for the same diagnosis in Great Britain. Although the more recent diagnostic criteria of schizophrenia contained in the DSM-III-R (See Panel 4.1, "Schizophrenia: Diagnostic Summary.") represent a shift toward the narrower conception preferred in Western Europe, disagreements over how schizophrenia is diagnosed in different countries remain (Kuriansky, Deming, & Gurland, 1974).

At least part of the reason for differences in opinion over the diagnosis of schizophrenia can be traced to the history of the disorder. Just before the turn of the century, in the sixth edition of his textbook, Kraepelin combined three syndromes (catatonia, paranoia, and hebephrenia) into a single category called "dementia praecox." To justify his decision, he pointed out that all three disorders affect patients early in life, are invariably chronic and deteriorating, and are probably organic in their etiology (Kraepelin, 1902/1899, 1971/1919).

PANEL 4.1

Schizophrenia: Diagnostic Summary*

The DSM-III-R favors "positive" (i.e., psychotic) symptomatology in making the diagnosis of schizophrenia. Of these symptoms, the presence of delusions is among the most important. Some delusions may involve persecutory ideation, while more bizarre forms include "thought broadcasting" (e.g., the patient believes that others can hear what he or she is thinking), "thought insertion" (e.g., the patient's thoughts are not his or her own but have been inserted by someone else), or "thought withdrawal" (e.g., thoughts have been removed from the patient's head). Although popularized in cartoons, delusions of grandiosity (e.g., believing that one is Napoleon) are less common.

Another complex of positive symptoms characteristic of schizophrenia involves thought disturbances evidenced by loose associations and/or poverty of content of speech. Other symptoms, such as neologisms (new words, distortions of words, or words given a highly idiosyncratic meaning), perseveration (persistent repetition of words, ideas, or topics), clanging (speech in which the sounds of words rather than their meaning determine word choice), and blocking (interruption of a train of speech before the thought has been completed) may occur, but less frequently. In addition, schizophrenics often experience hallucinations. Auditory hallucinations (usually voices) are the most common, although tactile (e.g., tingling) and somatic (e.g., snakes crawling inside the abdomen) hallucinations are occasionally evident. Visual, gustatory, and olfactory hallucinations also occur, but less frequently.

"Negative" symptoms listed in the DSM-III-R include flat or inappropriate affect, impaired sense of self, and inability to initiate goal-directed activity. Another negative symptom is decreased psychomotor behavior reflected by a diminished reactivity to the environment or a reduction in spontaneous movement. The diagnosis of schizophrenia requires that continuous signs of the disorder, including an active phase with psychotic (i.e., positive) symptoms, have been present for at least six months.

The onset of schizophrenia is usually during adolescence or early adulthood, although the disorder may begin in middle to late adulthood. Its development is usually characterized by a *prodromal phase*, in which there is a clear deterioration from the person's previous level of functioning. This deterioration may be evidenced by social withdrawal, difficulty at work or school,

---

*Material for this section is taken directly from the DSM-III-R (*Diagnostic and Statistical Manual of Mental Disorders* [Third Revision, Revised], American Psychiatric Association, 1987).

neglect of personal hygiene and grooming, and disturbances in affect, communication, and ideation.

The prodromal phase is followed by the *active phase*, in which psychotic symptoms necessary for the diagnosis appear. Onset of the active phase may be precipitated by a psychosocial stressor. The final or *residual phase* is similar to the prodromal phase except that affective blunting and impairment of role functioning are more common. A return to full premorbid functioning is rare. Furthermore, persons with schizophrenia are at increased risk for a shortened life span due to a higher than normal suicide rate and increased incidence of premature death from other causes.

The DSM-III-R recognizes five types of schizophrenia, four involving the active phase and one dealing with the residual. Each is different in terms of prognosis and response to treatment. The *catatonic type* is characterized by marked psychomotor disturbance that may involve stupor, rigidity, excitement, or posturing. Stereotypic or repetitious behavior and mutism may occur as well. This type of schizophrenia is much less common today than it was a number of years ago.

The *disorganized type* of schizophrenia is characterized by incoherence, marked loosening of associations, or grossly disorganized behavior. In addition, affect is flat or grossly inappropriate. Delusions or hallucinations are common but lack a coherent theme, as in the *paranoid type* of schizophrenia. The latter involves a preoccupation with one or more systematized delusions or auditory hallucinations related to a single theme. Associated with this type are such features as generalized anxiety, anger, argumentativeness, and possibly violence. Unlike the other forms of schizophrenia, functional impairment for the paranoid type may be minimal if the delusions are not acted upon.

Perhaps the most common type of schizophrenia is the *undifferentiated type*, a frequent diagnosis for long-term residents in mental hospitals. The primary feature of this type is the presence of prominent psychotic symptoms (e.g., delusions, hallucinations, incoherence, or grossly disorganized behavior) that cannot be classified as one of the other three types already mentioned.

The final form of schizophrenia is the *residual type*, a diagnosis used when there has been at least one episode of schizophrenic symptoms but no prominent psychotic features even though signs of the disorder persist. For example, eccentric behavior, illogical thinking, and mild loosening of associations may occur. If delusions or hallucinations are present, they are not prominent or accompanied by strong affect.

The DSM-III-R includes a broad category (psychotic disorders not elsewhere classified) of five disorders that involve psychotic symptoms which cannot be classified as one of the other disorders already mentioned. The relationship of these disorders to schizophrenia is unclear.

Brief reactive psychosis involves the sudden onset of psychotic symptoms of short duration (i.e., more than a few hours but less that one month) with an eventual return to full level of premorbid functioning. A precipitating event is always involved and would be seen as very stressful to almost anyone in similar circumstances. *Schizophreniform disorder*, on the other hand, presents in a manner identical to schizophrenia with the exception that its duration, including the three phases, is less than six months.

Schizoaffective disorder is a controversial diagnostic category that was originally thought to be a subtype of schizophrenia. This disorder involves symptoms that may mimic both schizophrenia and mood disorders at one point or present with psychotic symptoms only at another. However, it does not appear that this disorder is part of a continuum between the two major disorders based on its differential response to chemical interventions, most notably to lithium (Hay, 1985). An *induced psychotic disorder* occurs when a delusional system develops in a second person as a result of a close relationship with another person who already has a psychotic disorder in which delusions are a significant feature. The same delusions are shared, at least in part, by both parties, and the content of these delusions is often in the realm of possibility and may be based on the common experience of both persons. If the relationship between the two is interrupted, the delusional beliefs of the second will usually diminish or disappear. Although most commonly seen in relationships involving two persons ("folie à deux"), the disorder also has been known to involve up to 12 people in a family.

The final diagnosis in this category is *psychotic disorders not otherwise specified*, which was termed atypical psychosis in the DSM-III. This diagnosis is used when there are psychotic symptoms that do not meet the criteria for any other nonorganic psychotic disorder. It is also used in those cases in which there is insufficient information to make a specific diagnosis; with further information, a more appropriate diagnosis can be made.

In 1911 Eugen Bleuler (1950/1911) coined the term schizophrenia and added a fourth subtype—simple. In addition, Bleuler attempted to simplify Kraepelin's 36 symptom categories by distinguishing between *fundamental* symptoms (the "4 A's" of autism, loose associations, inappropriate affect, and ambivalence) and secondary symptoms (e.g., neologisms, poverty of ideas, catatonic posturing, hallucinations, delusion, etc.). Of these, Bleuler came to believe that disordered associations was "the distinctive and unifying construct that defined schizophrenia" (Magaro, 1984, p. 142).

It has been suggested that both views of schizophrenia encouraged its being thought of as a single construct; Kraepelin proposed one syndrome consisting of three previously unconnected disorders while Bleuler reduced many symptoms to a few (Magaro, 1984). As a result, research on the disorder from 1900 to 1950 rarely distinguished between different types of schizophrenia. If heterogeneity was recognized at all, it was in terms of the grouping of the three basic clinical subtypes proposed by Kraepelin with the possible addition of Bleuler's fourth category.

Schizophrenia, however, does not lend itself to being thought of as a single construct. Reliability coefficients for its diagnosis are generally low (Kappas range from .27 to .77 for an average of .56; Neale & Oltmanns, 1980). Magaro suggests that there are three possible explanations for this. For one, approaches to diagnosing schizophrenia vary considerably, as discussed earlier. Second, the diagnostic system prior to the introduction of the DSM-III was basically unreliable (see Chapter 1). And third, the variable course of the disorder itself makes a reliable diagnosis difficult (cf. Carlson & Goodwin, 1973).

Positive and Negative Symptoms

One of the first steps toward developing a more reliable diagnosis for schizophrenia was K. Schneider's (1959) attempt to identify the "first-rank symptoms" (FRS) of the disorder. His symptom-specific approach is still widely used and emphasizes the so-called *positive* symptoms of schizophrenia, such as hallucinations and delusions. These are contrasted to its more *negative* aspects, such as poor social relationships and poverty of speech, which Schneider does not consider to be as important. Although developments like Schneider's FRS have added greatly to the reliability with which the diagnosis can be made, positive symptoms are not unique to schizophrenia per se and may be evident in a number of other disorders as well (DeVaul & Hall, 1980; Freeman, 1980; Newman, 1980). Furthermore, schizophrenia's negative symptoms would also appear to be essential for the diagnosis as Kraepelin and Eugen Bleuler saw it (Venables, 1983).

Another attempt to establish symptom-specific criteria for schizophrenia was the World Health Organization's International Pilot Study of Schizophrenia (IPSS) (Carpenter, Strauss, & Bartko, 1973; Carpenter & Strauss, 1974). A total of 1202 patients from Columbia, Czechoslovakia, Denmark, India, Nigeria, China, the United Kingdom, the Soviet Union and the United States were administered the Present State Examination (PSE) (Wing, Cooper, & Sartorius, 1974). The PSE is a structured mental status interview consisting of 360 items rated by the examiner for their presence or absence. An additional 55 items thought to define clinically relevant symptoms were added for the study. Since the instrument is of British origin, it is heavily weighted toward the FRS criteria.

A comparison between schizophrenic and nonschizophrenic

groups revealed 69 statistically significant symptoms, of which 12 appeared to be most discriminating. These were restricted affect, poor insight, thoughts aloud, waking early, poor rapport, depressed facial expression, elation, widespread delusions, incoherent speech, unreliable information, bizarre delusions, and nihilistic delusions. It can be seen that the discriminating items reflect a mixture of positive and negative symptoms. In addition, it should be noted that, contrary to Schneider, no one symptom was found to be pathognomonic to schizophrenia. In other words, all 12 symptoms distinguished between the two groups but no symptom was common to all schizophrenics. As the authors noted, "The criteria used in this system do not constitute a definition of schizophrenia, but rather provide an operational method for identifying patients who would be commonly considered schizophrenic in many centers, and thus permit more accurate communication and testing of clinical and research findings" (Carpenter et al., 1973, p. 1277).

The authors of the PSE had also hoped to identify a cluster of diagnostic items that would hold up reliably across cultures. They did find that there was good agreement between a computer-generated model and the local diagnosis of clinicians in various parts of the world for many patients, namely those with positive and therefore clearly recognizable symptoms. This suggested that there is what might be termed a "nuclear" form of the disorder. However, the computer program also found that almost 50% of patients diagnosed as schizophrenic in the various countries failed to meet the criteria for this nuclear condition. Thus, the study has a double-edged significance (Claridge, 1985). On one hand, it supports the notion that it is possible to define a diagnosis of schizophrenia reliably, if the criteria are drawn tightly. On the other hand, it does not settle the question of what sorts of behaviors and symptoms should be called schizophrenic.

Crow (1980) has proposed that there are two types of schizophrenia. Type I schizophrenia is characterized by hallucinations, delusions, and thought disorders (i.e., positive symptoms). This is the "acute" form of the disorder that exhibits a good response to neuroleptics and has a potentially favorable prognosis. Its pathology appears to be implicated with alterations in dopaminergic transmission. Type II schizophrenia, on the other hand, is characterized by negative symptomatology (e.g., flattened affect, poverty of speech, etc.) and is more chronic in its course. This type is often accompanied by intellectual deterioration and may involve cell loss or structural changes in the brain (Golden & Sawicki, 1985). (Also see Seidman, 1983, for an extended discussion of brain dysfunction and its relationship to the negative and positive signs of schizophrenia.)

Whatever the case, the problem of diagnosis is complicated further by the uncertainty of the disorder's prognosis. Just as there is no single symptom or set of symptoms pathognomonic for the disorder, *"there is no such thing as a specific course of schizophrenia"* (Ciompi, 1980, p. 420, italics in original). Ciompi followed 289 schizophrenics for an average of 37 years and found that approximately half had a favorable outcome. For 10% of these cases, there was a single acute episode followed by complete remission; another 25% remitted after a series of episodes. On the other hand, 18% followed a course of chronic deterioration after either single or multiple episodes (6% and 12% of the patients, respectively).

The presence of negative symptomatology is related to poor prognosis (Mackay, 1980). These symptoms focus on the patient's social skills and ability to work with people. In fact, social factors appear to be important both prior to and following a schizophrenic episode. The patient's premorbid adjustment, which refers to the ability to function in one's social role prior to hospitalization, has been found to be predictive of length of hospitalization (Phillips, 1953). Something as simple as knowing whether the patient has ever been married (for older males) is of significant predictive value (Garmezy, 1978). Other significant predictors (phrased in terms of a favorable prognosis) include acute onset, clear precipitating factors, married, good premorbid adjustment, presence of depressive features, lack of schizoid features, feelings of guilt, presence of disorientation or confusion on admission, above average IQ, absence of marked emotional blunting during hospitalization, and no schizophrenia in blood relatives (Stephens, Astrup, & Mangrum, 1967). The predictive value of premorbid social function and employment status was verified by Strauss and Carpenter (1977) in their 2- to 5-year follow-up study which involved the nine countries participating in the IPSS. In fact, social contacts and work function were two of the three "key predictors," with duration of hospitalization prior to initial evaluation the third.

These findings suggest that the interpersonal or social aspects of the person's adjustment (i.e., negative symptoms) are the best predictors of a poor prognosis in schizophrenia and are supported by Manfred Bleuler's (1978) classic follow-up of 208 schizophrenic patients over a 23-year period. He concluded that a poor prognosis was almost always associated with a difficult or hopeless home environment. Others, such as Stephens (1978), also have observed that the major factors that relate to hospitalization and relapse are social in nature.

Investigators who are attracted to the more positive or psychotic symptoms of the disorder often lose sight of the importance of the social or interpersonal aspects of schizophrenia. Claridge (1985) and others have argued that both aspects of schizophrenia are important. In this regard, schizophrenia may be somewhat different from other important clinical disorders. In schizophrenia, disordered thinking is seen as contributing to the secondary symptoms of social isolation. In the case of depression, the disruption of social relationships is thought to contribute the decrease of attentional capacity and other cognitive impairments characteristic of that disorder (Gale & Edwards, 1983). Nevertheless, antipsychotic medications seem to be primarily effective for acute (i.e., positive) symptoms only and may even exacerbate negative symptomatology (Angrist, Rotrosen, & Gershon, 1980; Klein & Rosen, 1973; Owen et al., 1978; Seeman, Lee, Chou-Wong, & Wong, 1976).

The relevance of this distinction to the present chapter is that if schizophrenia is a unitary and reliably-defined construct, some sort of homogeneous set of findings in regard to its physiological basis should emerge. To the degree, however, that the diagnostic term *schizophrenia* encompasses a wide range of dysfunctional systems, then research on its physiological basis should result in a heterogeneous set of findings that will be more difficult to interpret. As we shall see, the latter situation seems to be very much the case.

Models of Schizophrenia

Perhaps the dominant theory of schizophrenia in recent years has been the disease model (Henn & Nasrallah, 1982). This perspective asserts that schizophrenia results from "abnormalities in brain structure, arising in part from genetic factors leading to biochemical and physiological differences in the central nervous system of affected individuals" (Henn & Kety, 1982, p. 3). Other factors, such as an injury to the brain or a viral infection affecting the central nervous system (CNS), may serve to precipitate the disorder in persons with a genetic predisposition. In this manner, schizophrenia is seen as a discrete disease state that is etiologically and symptomatically distinct from normal or healthy states. If a continuum exists, it is between schizophrenia and manic-depressive psychosis and not between schizophrenia and some variation of normal functioning (Crow, 1986; Zigler & Glick, 1988). Efforts to identify the pathogenic factors have subsequently relied most heavily on morphological, neurohistological, or biochemical techniques.

Opposed to the disease model is a group who strongly criticize this

view (e.g., Laing, 1969). Probably the best known advocate of this position is Thomas Szasz (1974). He has argued that mental illness is a myth
concocted by social institutions and agencies in order to manage those
members of society who are non-normal (i.e., irrational, irresponsible,
deviant, or criminal) (Szasz, 1987). According to Szasz, physicians who
treat the "mentally ill" are practicing a "deception" and are acting moral-
ly and politically as agents of the state. In this respect, treatment is either
a form of social coercion (as with psychopharmacological medications)
or a sham (in the case of psychotherapy) (Szasz, 1979). In this regard,
the "antipsychiatrists," as they are called, believe that pursuing a disease model of schizophrenia is, in reality, a witch hunt.

> The concept of mental illness is analogous to that of witchcraft. In the fif-
> teenth century, men believed that some persons were witches, and that some
> acts were due to witchcraft. In the twentieth century, men believe that some
> people are insane and that some acts are due to mental illness. (Szasz, 1971,
> p. xix)

They argue that abnormal behavior must be considered in terms of its
social context. (Some of these issues were discussed in Chapter 1.) Consequently, Szasz and others view such disorders as schizophrenia as
psychological reactions of extreme proportion provoked by abuses of
social authority, which, in turn, is used to control the disorder once it
has occurred.

There is a third approach to schizophrenia that falls between the
disease model and the antipsychiatric alternative (cf. Claridge, 1985).
This approach agrees with many of the antipsychiatrists' criticisms of
viewing schizophrenia as a discrete disease but disagrees with the exclu-
sion of all biological or physiological considerations. Claridge argues
that "in recognizing this important difference between physical and
mental disease we should not, like Szasz and other antipsychiatrists,
overreact into excluding from consideration one of the strongest points
of similarity, namely the grounding of psychological abnormality in the
biology of the organism" (p. 174).

The alternative model proposes that schizophrenic symptoms represent an aberration in CNS processes that underlie cognitive and personality characteristics shared by healthy and unhealthy persons alike
(Claridge, 1987). Consequently, it is assumed that there is a continuum
between normality and abnormality with certain disorders (e.g., borderline personality) symptomatic of both states. In fact, it has been
suggested that the difference between a highly creative, "normal" individual and a schizophrenic is only a matter of degree (Venables et al.,
1978).

More specifically, Claridge (1972, 1987) and others (e.g., Siever, 1985) have argued that individual differences in terms of disposition to schizophrenia are determined by the presence of a "schizotypal" nervous system.[1] Some of the characteristics of the schizotypal personality are magical thinking, social isolation, recurrent illusions, constricted or inappropriate affect, and undue social anxiety. Claridge has argued that the mechanism for these characteristics is a deviation in the set-point for homeostatic regulation of the CNS, possibly as a result of a weakening of inhibitory control or alterations in the functional and structural properties of hemispheric organization (Claridge & Broks, 1984).

Attempts to determine how hemispheric dysfunction is related to schizophrenia per se have been influenced by Broadbent's work on attention (1958, 1971, 1977). Broadbent proposed that attention involves two separate, hierarchical steps. The first is referred to as "filtering" and involves a global, low-frequency process designed to detect single features from the multitude of stimuli encountered at any point in time. The next stage involves organizing related features along some relevant dimension. This is referred to as "pigeon-holing" and allows for stimuli to be packaged into more manageable units for further processing.

Attentional deficiencies in schizophrenia may involve errors at both stages. The "faulty-filter" hypothesis argues that the acute schizophrenic "is characterized by an inability to restrict the range of his attention so that he is flooded by sensory impressions from all quarters" (Venables, 1964, p. 41). In this manner, the schizophrenic becomes aware of stimuli of which normal individuals are not conscious (Frith, 1979). (See Panel 4.2, "The Personal Experience of Schizophrenia.")

It has been hypothesized that this deficiency involves those parts of the limbic system that act in a reciprocal fashion to "gate-in" and "gate-out" stimuli. (This corresponds on a psychological level to a person's "openness" or "closedness" to the environment [Venables, 1973].) For schizophrenics, this gate seems to be permanently switched to the open mode. This can be demonstrated in the laboratory by having schizophrenics attempt to screen out distracting stimuli or divide their attention between two conflicting tasks (McGhie & Chapman, 1961). For example, if the schizophrenic subject is required to process information delivered to one ear while ignoring contemporaneous stimuli presented to the other ear, he or she will exhibit a tendency toward "overinclusive-

---

[1]The term *schizotypy* was initially used by Meehl (1962) and others (e.g., Rado, 1956; Rado & Daniels, 1956) to denote individuals with schizoid types of personalities as identified by a subset of items from the MMPI.

PANEL 4.2

The Personal Experience of Schizophrenia

The "faulty filter" hypothesis is illustrated dramatically by the following description by a young woman of what it was like in the early stages of a schizophrenic break.

> At first it was as if parts of my brain "awoke" which had been dormant, and I became interested in a wide assortment of people, events, places, and ideas which normally would make no impression on me. Not knowing that I was ill, I made no attempt to understand what was happening, but felt that there was some overwhelming significance in all this, produced either by God or Satan, and I felt that I was duty-bound to ponder on each of these new interests, and the more I pondered the worse it became. The walk of a stranger on the street could be a "sign" to me which I must interpret. Every face in the windows of a passing streetcar would be engraved on my mind, all of them concentrating on me and trying to pass me some sort of message. Now, many years later, I can appreciate what had happened. Each of us is capable of coping with a large number of stimuli, invading our being through any one of the senses. We could hear every sound within earshot and see every object, line, and colour within the field of vision, and so on. It's obvious that we would be incapable of carrying on any of our daily activities if even one-hundredth of all of these available stimuli invaded us at once. So the mind must have a filter which functions without our conscious thought, sorting stimuli and allowing only those which are relevant to the situation at hand to disturb consciousness. And this filter must be working at maximum efficiency at all times, particularly when we require a high degree of concentration. What happened to me in Toronto was a breakdown in the filter, and a hodge-podge of unrelated stimuli were distracting me from things which should have had my undivided attention. (MacDonald, 1960, p. 218)

ness," that is, the inability to focus attention on specific tasks (Payne, Mattussek, & George, 1959).

Others have argued that the problem is not so much a problem of filtering as it is with what schizophrenics do with information once it has been perceived. Hemsley (1975), for example, has proposed that schizophrenics display an inability to organize stimuli at the second or pigeon-holing stage. This may lead to the misinterpretations or faulty attributions characteristic of the more delusional aspects of the disorder.

Whatever the case, these models of schizophrenia that emphasize the information-processing aspects of the disorder also recognize the possibility that there is most likely a biological basis for these deficits. This would explain why schizophrenia appears to be, at least in part, inherited. (See Panel 4.3, "The Heritability of Schizophrenia.") In fact, the observation that the risk for any individual's developing schizophrenia varies depending on the degree of relatedness to someone diagnosed as schizophrenic (e.g., monozygotic twins are more often concordant for schizophrenia than dizygotic twins) provides an empirical basis for assuming a continuity between schizophrenia and normal states. In this regard, schizophrenia may be conceptualized in terms of a "multifactorial-polygenetic-threshold" model[2] (Gottesman & Shields, 1982), which postulates that the disorder occurs "once an individual has passed beyond a certain threshold, determined by a combination of genetic loading and accumulated life experience" (Claridge, 1985, p. 131). How these various factors come together to result in the expression of schizophrenia will be considered in the next section.

Physiological Factors

Physical Factors

There are a number of specific physical factors of possible etiological significance that have been identified in the medical literature, although the specific mechanisms by which they induce schizophrenia are unclear. For that reason they will be discussed only briefly here. Some of the more important of these factors include neurological disease, birth injury, neuroanatomical abnormalities, cerebral atrophy, and viral infection. Essentially none is seen as being sufficient to cause schizophrenia, although it has been suggested that there may be essentially two subgroups of schizophrenics—those whose disorder arises from a genetic predisposition and others whose problems are associated with clear-cut cerebral disease, abnormality, or insult (Murray, Lewis, & Reveley,

---

[2]More recently, investigators (e.g., Sherrington et al., 1988) have argued for a single-gene theory of schizophrenia. Support for this proposal, however, is uncertain given other evidence that points to a heterogeneous group of genetic factors that may contribute to the disorder (Kennedy et al., 1988). The issue is complicated further by the possibility that a single gene can have multiple effects (McKusick, 1969). This principle, which is known as "pleiotropism," could account for the heterogeneity of the schizophrenic phenotype without assuming a polygenetic basis for the disorder (McGuffin, Farmer, & Gottesman, 1987). Whatever the case, the hypothesis that persons inherit a genetic predisposition to schizophrenia is generally accepted.

PANEL 4.3

Heritability of Schizophrenia

There are three major approaches to the study of the heritability of schizophrenia. The first of these, the *concordance approach*, compares the rate of schizophrenia across groups that differ in terms of their biological relatedness. Compared to an incidence rate of 0.9% for schizophrenia among the general population, the risk of schizophrenia increases 4-fold (to 4.2%) for the parents of schizophrenic children, 7-fold (to 7.5%) for children with schizophrenic siblings, and almost 10-fold (to 9.7%) for the children of schizophrenic parents (Rosenthal, 1970). If a person has the misfortune of being the child of parents who are both schizophrenic, then the risk for developing the disorder increases to 46.3% (Gottesman & Shields, 1982). The morbidity rate drops dramatically, however, as the distance between an individual and a biological relative with schizophrenia increases (2.1% and 1.7% for second- and third-degree relatives, respectively).

A second strategy for studying the genetics of schizophrenia is the *adoption approach*. One form of this approach focuses on children of a schizophrenic parent (or parents) who are adopted at an early age. In this manner, the relative contribution of the child's genetic make-up to his or her development can be compared with that of the rearing environment (see Chapter 3 for a discussion of this point). The evidence generated by this approach is fairly consistent and indicates that biological relatives are as much as 10 times more likely to be diagnosed as schizophrenic than the child's adoptive relatives (Kety, Rosenthal, Wender, & Schulsinger, 1968). Conversely, it also has been demonstrated that children whose biological parents are normal but who are adopted by a schizophrenic parent do not develop schizophrenia at an increased rate (Rosenthal, 1970).

The third approach to the study of the heritability of schizophrenia is the *high-risk approach*. This strategy involves identifying high-risk individuals (such as children of schizophrenics) and following them for a number of years (e.g., Venables et al., 1983; see Garmezy, 1978, for a critique). For example, Mednick and Schulsinger (1968) studied over 200 children around the age of 15 whose mothers had been diagnosed as chronic schizophrenics. Many of these children exhibited patterns of psychophysiological responsivity that differed from age-matched controls but that were similar to adult schizophrenics. In particular, children in the high-risk group showed a tendency for marked autonomic instability, particularly as measured by electrodermal responses. A few years later Mednick and his co-workers (Mednick & Schulsinger, 1973) followed up 90% of the original high- and low-risk subjects and found that a large proportion of those subjects exhibiting excessive autonomic lability at the earlier assessment had developed full-blown symptoms of schizophrenia. Using a similar approach, Venables and his associates (Venables et al., 1978) found that genetically high-risk children exhibit a greater "openness" to environmental stimuli.

Even though evidence for the genetic contribution to schizophrenia from these approaches argues for the presence of a significant genetic predisposition for the disorder, it should be noted that the proportion of the variance this factor(s) explains is relatively small. As Rosenthal (1970) has noted, the rate of schizophrenia in relatives of a schizophrenic patient is always less than would be predicted by a straightforward genetic model of the disorder. It was suggested, therefore, that environmental factors must be playing a significant role as well. More specifically, Fulker (1979) performed a biometric analysis on the various twin and adoption studies on schizophrenia and estimated the additive genetic variance at 73%, leaving 27% for environmental variance. An analysis by Henderson (1982) using twin and family data rather than adoption data estimated genetic variance at 71%, cultural effect at 20%, with the remaining 9% arising from the twin environment itself.

Among the various environmental influences linked to schizophrenia, the rearing environment has been the beneficiary of the greatest amount of research. Nevertheless, a high prevalence of schizophrenia among biological siblings of schizophrenic adoptees and its absence in their adoptive siblings provides evidence against an exclusive role for family-associated environmental factors (Plomin, DeFries, & McClearn, 1980). This does not, however, rule out the possibility that rearing factors may potentiate or diminish the effects of vulnerability or predisposition (Kety, Rowland, Sidman, & Matthysse, 1983). Other environmental factors that have found to be related to schizophrenia include, among others, birth injury and season of birth (Kinney & Jacobsen, 1978). As of yet, however, no single environmental factor has been identified as pathognomonic for the disorder (Gottesman & Shields, 1982).

In summary, it can be said with some degree of confidence that genetic factors are important in the transmission of schizophrenia. At present, whether the mode of transmission is polygenic or monogenic is unclear (Kennedy et al., 1988; Sherrington et al., 1988). Whatever the case, the risk of developing schizophrenia is known to increase in proportion with the degree of relatedness to a schizophrenic relative (Gottesman, 1978). These conclusions are compatible with a diathesis-stress model of the disorder in which a genetic predisposition interacts with stressful life events so as to result in the expression of the disorder. There is no evidence, however, that one particular environmental influence is predominant for the development of schizophrenia. In addition, "no environmental causes have been found that will invariably or even with moderate probability produce genuine schizophrenia in persons who are unrelated to a schizophrenic index case" (Gottesman, 1978, p. 67). Nevertheless, Cromwell (1978) has pointed out that even if the prevalence of schizophrenia were determined to have a definite genetic basis, this would indicate nothing more than evidence for the genetic transmission of some trait found in schizophrenics but not necessarily unique to schizophrenia.

1985). Generally, however, it is assumed that cerebral disease or injury interact with a person's genetic vulnerability to precipitate the disorder.

Neurological Disease. Neurological disease or insult has been linked to schizophrenia because a number of syndromes, such as temporal lobe epilepsy, Huntington's chorea, brain tumors (particularly in the temporal lobe and diencephalon), and encephalitis, present with symptoms that are typical of schizophrenia (Ashton, 1987). In addition, schizophrenic patients may exhibit other signs of neurological dysfunction. For example, 18 of the 21 schizophrenic patients (86%) studied by Cox and Ludwig (1979) exhibited neurological "soft signs," although there was no evidence of neurological disease.

Brain Injury. Injury to the brain, particularly during birth, also is thought to precipitate schizophrenia in individuals who are genetically predisposed. For example, Mednick and Schulsinger (1968, 1973) found that children of schizophrenic mothers who experienced complications during pregnancy or birth were five times more likely to develop symptoms of the disorder than children of schizophrenic mothers who had unremarkable deliveries. The pathogenic cause is thought to be neonatal hypoxia, which in some cases might be sufficient to produce schizophrenic symptoms even in the absence of a genetic predisposition.

Neuroanatomical Abnormalities. Several studies have investigated the differences between schizophrenic patients and controls in terms of the relative weight, thickness, or size of various structures in the brain (Weinberger & Wyatt, 1982). One finding that has attracted particular interest involves the corpus callosum. Several postmortem studies have suggested that the corpus callosum of schizophrenics is thicker than that of normals and that increased thickness is related to early rather than late onset of the disorder (Bigelow, Nasrallah, & Rauscher, 1983).

In one study Rosenthal and Bigelow (1972) measured the brain specimens of 10 chronic schizophrenics and 10 control patients in terms of a number of anatomical characteristics (e.g., volume of the thalamus, brain weight, average cortical mantle width). Of these measures, only the average width of the corpus callosum was significantly different,

with averages of .518 and .611 cm for controls and schizophrenic patients, respectively. Furthermore, the range of widths (.454–.571 cm and
.558–.638 cm, respectively) indicated that there was little overlap between the two groups. These data have been interpreted by Randall
(1980) and others as an indication that schizophrenic symptoms are due
to the presence of an increased number of myelinated interhemispheric
nerve fibers that link functional areas of the brain that are not connected
in normal subjects. The problem with this research, however, is determining whether these differences are a cause or a consequence of the
disorder (Stevens, 1982).

Cerebral Atrophy. There is evidence that the brains of schizophrenics
are approximately 6% lighter than the brains of patients with other
psychological disorders and that schizophrenics have larger than normal
ventricles (R. Brown et al., 1986; DeLisi et al., 1986). In addition, the
brains of schizophrenics have been found to have fewer neurons in the
cerebral cortex (Benes, Davidson, & Bird, 1986) and reduced volume in
the region of the amygdala and hippocampus (Bogerts, Meertz, Schönfeldt-Bausch, 1985).

Johnstone and her associates (Johnstone, Crow, Frith, Husband, &
Kreel, 1976; Johnstone et al., 1978) compared schizophrenic patients
with non-schizophrenic institutionalized patients and found that the
former exhibited increased cross-sectional ventricular size, suggesting
atrophy of the brain. The increased size was related to the more negative
features of the disorder, such as affective flattening, retardation, and
poverty of speech, as well as impaired performance on IQ tests. Weinberger and his associates (Weinberger et al., 1980; Weinberger, DeLisi,
Neophytides & Wyatt, 1981) conducted a retrospective chart analysis of
51 chronic schizophrenic patients in terms of their premorbid adjustment. Computerized tomography (CT) scans revealed evidence of brain
atrophy that was significantly related to poorer premorbid adjustment
(e.g., negative symptoms), particularly during childhood. They concluded that the neuropathological process occurs early in the development of schizophrenia and may predispose or eventually cause the disorder in adolescence. Nevertheless, factors related to poor premorbid
adjustment may be responsible for brain atrophy rather than the other
way around.

Viral Infection. Schizophrenia has also been viewed as resulting
from a slow or latent viral infection (Crow, 1980, 1983), an idea intro-
duced more than 60 years ago by Menninger (1926). The viral hypothesis
is one way of explaining the curious observation that schizophrenics are

more likely to be born in the early winter months than other times of the year (Bradbury & Miller, 1985; Crow, 1986). It has been established that viruses are capable of producing mental disorders (e.g., Creutzfeldt-Jakob disease), may remain latent for years, and may show a particular affinity for the limbic system. Nevertheless, no virus has been definitely associated with schizophrenia. Some studies (e.g., Crow et al., 1979; Tyrrell, Parry, Crow, Johnstone, & Ferrier, 1979) have identified a virus-like agent in subgroups of schizophrenic patients, but others were unable to replicate this finding (Mered et al., 1983). However, other investigators have found antibodies for the cytomegalovirus in the cerebrospinal fluid of subgroups of schizophrenic patients (Albrecht, Torrey, Boone, Hicks, & Daniel, 1980). In addition, the presence of viral antibodies may be linked to both neurological soft signs and CT abnormalities (Kaufmann, Weinberger, Yolken, Torrey, & Potkin, 1983).

Summary of Physical Factors. Physical factors in the etiology of schizophrenia are not necessarily incompatible with other perspectives. For example, the idea that birth injury or neurological disease may be precipitating factors is compatible with the threshold model of the disorder alluded to earlier. The thickness of the corpus callosum has been tied to the schizophrenic's inability to process information effectively, just as increased ventricular size can be said to relate to schizophrenia's negative symptomatology. Furthermore, Crow (1985) has asserted that a virus responsible for schizophrenia may become incorporated into the gene that determines hemispheric dominance and thus may contribute to the lateral dysfunction of the cerebral hemispheres. Nevertheless, it is also clear that the effects of these factors alone are inadequate to explain the complex expression and course of the disorder.

Biochemical Factors

The biochemical model of schizophrenia looks at the disorder in terms of the excess, deficiency, or imbalance of various biochemicals in the brain (Barchas, Elliott, & Berger, 1977). Many biochemical theories have been advanced, but only three of the major ones will be reviewed here. In addition, the probability that schizophrenia results from a complex interaction of several biochemical factors will be addressed.

Early Hypotheses. An early model of schizophrenia suggested that the disorder results from the production of toxic compounds in the brain. In 1952 Osmond and Smythies observed that the synthesis of epinephrine requires an N-methylating enzyme (phenylethanolamine-

N-methyl transferase) and that mescaline, a powerful hallucinogen, is an O-methylated derivative of the catecholamines. (See Panel 4.4, "Neurotransmitters.") This observation was followed by the discovery that serotonin is similar in structure to other methylated indoleamine derivatives (e.g., psilocybin and LSD) that are capable of producing schizophrenic-like symptoms (cf. Claridge, 1978). Consequently, it was suggested that schizophrenia arises from the abnormal accumulation of a psychotogenic N- or O-methylated biogenic amine derivative (Kety, 1967).

Research into the "transmethylation hypothesis," as it is called, has attempted to find evidence of psychotogenic agents in bodily fluids, to induce the accumulation of these compounds in the brain, and to identify the enzymes that might be responsible for the aberrant metabolic process. Efforts in all three areas have been disappointing (Barchas, Elliott, & Berger, 1977). Although various methylated biogenic amines continue to be offered as the endogenous psychotogen, none has been shown to occur exclusively in schizophrenics. Nevertheless, as Kety (1967) noted, the transmethylation hypothesis will probably continue to attract attention since for every substance eliminated several new ones appear to take its place.

Another early theory of schizophrenia implicated monoamine oxidase (MAO), the primary catabolizing agent for of the catecholamines. In 1973 Wyatt and his associates compared the MAO activity in blood platelets in 13 monozygotic twins discordant for schizophrenia and in 23 normal volunteers. There was high positive correlation between twins (suggesting that MAO levels are genetically determined and not the consequence of the disorder itself), but there was an inverse correlation between the degree of schizophrenic symptomatology and MAO levels (Spearman rank-order correlation of $-.54$). Consequently, it was suggested that MAO levels might serve as a genetic marker for vulnerability to schizophrenia (Wyatt et al., 1973).

Other investigators have reported that reduced levels of MAO are related to auditory hallucinations and delusions in a subgroup of schizophrenic patients (Schildkraut et al., 1976; Sullivan, Cavenar, Stanfield, & Hammett, 1978), and another study found that MAO activity differentiated between chronic schizophrenics and normal controls with paranoid patients having the lowest levels of all (Potkin, Cannon, Murphy, & Wyatt, 1978). Other studies, however, have failed to detect differences between acute schizophrenics and normal controls (Carpenter, Murphy, & Wyatt, 1975; Reveley, Glover, Sandler, & Spokes, 1981).

In 1979 Wyatt, Potkin, and Murphy reviewed 26 studies and con-

PANEL 4.4

Neurotransmitters

There are more than 30 substances in the body that are thought to play a role in effecting synaptic transmission in the central nervous system (CNS). Some of these compounds are well known, such as dopamine, norepinephrine, 5-hydroxytryptamine (serotonin), acetylcholine, and gamma-aminobutyric acid (GABA). The means by which these neurotransmitters are metabolized is reasonably well understood and the nature of their action has been identified (Ciaranello & Patrick, 1977; Elliott, Edelman, Renson, & Berger, 1977). Nevertheless, knowledge of the exact mechanism by which they operate is much less certain, and there are other compounds that play a role in the transmission of signals in the CNS. Some of these may be neurotransmitters that have not yet been identified, while others may serve as "second messengers" by translating the neurotransmitter's signal into appropriate biochemical reactions within the cell. Still other substances may serve as neuromodulators by "fine-tuning" activity within the synaptic cleft itself.

In spite of the complexity of the neurotransmission process, a great deal has been learned since 1895 when Oliver and Shafer demonstrated that extracts from the adrenal gland produce physiological effects similar to those resulting from stimulation of the sympathetic nerves (Elliott, Holman, & Barchas, 1977). We know now, for example, that neurotransmitters are synthesized in the nerve terminal from precursors taken into the cell from the interstitial fluid and transported down the neuronal axon via microtubules. The synthetic process takes place in one or several steps and involves various enzymes, some of which are involved in the synthesis of more than one neurotransmitter. Mitochondria in the immediate intracellular fluid provide the metabolic energy for synthesis to take place. After the neurotransmitter has been formed, it is stored in vesicles until needed. Depolarization of the cell membrane by an action potential results in the release of the neurotransmitter from the vesicles into the synaptic cleft, where it binds to postsynaptic receptors in a "lock-and-key" type of arrangement. This allows for the propagation of the impulse to other neurons. The binding of transmitter molecules to the postsynaptic membrane is not an all-or-none proposition, for they are constantly disassociating from the receptor site, freeing it to be restimulated. This explains why the strength of postsynaptic stimulation depends on the amount of the transmitter available to be released. The transmission process ends when the neurotransmitter is catabolized by degradative enzymes in the synaptic cleft or transported back into the terminal ending, where it is either broken down or reabsorbed into the vesicles for

...ge. Pharmacological agents can alter synaptic transmission by affecting any of these steps.

Catecholamines

The catecholamines are a group of important biological agents synthesized from the amino acid tyrosine. They serve as both hormones and neurotransmitters. The adrenal medulla (situated on top of the kidneys) is the principal source of the hormonal catecholamines, mainly epinephrine. Norepinephrine, on the other hand, is synthesized primarily in the peripheral sympathetic neurons and is released directly onto the smooth musculature of blood vessels, digestive tract organs, various secretory glands, and other structures in the face and head. Neurons in the brain synthesize both norepinephrine and dopamine for activity in the CNS since peripheral catecholamines cross the blood-brain barrier only to a limited extent.

The three catecholamines (dopamine, norepinephrine, and epinephrine) represent three successive steps in a metabolic pathway. After tyrosine is converted to L-DOPA (dihydroxyphenylalanine) by tyrosine hydroxylase, a second enzyme (L-aromatic-amino acid decarboxylase) converts L-DOPA into dopamine. (The same enzyme is also responsible for the synthesis of serotonin.) Dopamine is catalyzed by dopamine-beta-hydroxylase into norepinephrine, which, in turn, is converted into epinephrine by an N-methylating enzyme (phenylethanolamine-N-methyl transferase). The catecholamines are broken down both inside and outside of the neuron. The primary catabolizing agent for intraneuronal inactivation is monoamine oxidase inhibitor (MAOI). Other enzymes break down the catecholamines in the liver and kidneys. Eventually, the byproducts of the later process are eliminated from the body in the urine.

There are numerous catecholamine pathways in the brain (as determined from studies in the rat) and the sympathetic branch of the autonomic nervous system (ANS) (Lindvall & Björklund, 1974; Ungerstedt, 1971). Centrally, norepinephrine is found primarily (70%) in the cells of the locus ceruleus, which projects numerous pathways to the spinal cord, cerebellum, hippocampus, hypothalamus, septum, and cortex. Dopaminergic pathways originate in the substantia nigra and project rostrally to the caudate-putamen, cortex, and portions of the limbic system. These pathways connect both the emotive and intellectual parts of the brain and thus provide a basis for the idea that the central catecholamines are extensively involved in psychological disorders.

Catecholaminergic activity can be affected in several ways. For example, the MAO inhibitors block the degradation of the catecholamines once they have been taken back up into the nerve terminal, increasing intraneuronal catecholamine levels and allowing for a more potent response when the nerve is stimulated again. The administration of L-DOPA bypasses the rate-limiting effects of the synthesizing enzymes entirely (except for L-aromatic-amino acid decarboxylase) and results in increased levels of dopamine. This explains its usefulness in the treatment of Parkinson's disease. Drugs can affect the catecholamines by affecting their storage (reserpine), release (amphetamine), re- uptake (imipramine or cocaine), and receptor interaction (the phenothiazines). In addition, stress is thought to cause an increase in the tissue levels of the synthesizing enzymes for the catecholamines (Thoenen, Otten, & Oesch, 1973).

5-Hydroxytryptamine (Serotonin)

In the 1950s two investigators independently discovered a substance that produced vasoconstriction and contraction of intestinal smooth muscle (Page, 1954). Its psychotropic properties were expected when it was identified in the mammalian brain and also found to be structurally related to lysergic acid diethylamide (LSD) (a potent hallucinogen and serotonergic receptor agonist that is discussed in Chapter 7). Since its discovery, serotonin has been found to be involved in a number of functions of the CNS, including sleep, sexual behavior, pain sensitivity, thermoregulation, and control of pituitary hormones (Barchas & Usdin, 1973).

Serotonin is synthesized from tryptophan, as essential amino acid (meaning that it must be supplied by the diet). As noted earlier, one of the synthetic enzymes (L-aromatic-amino acid decarboxylase) also converts L-DOPA to dopamine. There are several metabolic pathways responsible for the catabolism of serotonin, one of which involves MAO. Another pathway has been postulated as providing a means by which endogenous psychotogens causing schizophrenia might be formed (Koslow, 1977)

The anatomy of serotonergic pathways reveals that most serotonergic cells (at least in the rat brain) are found in the raphé nuclei with ascending projections to a wide variety of structures in the limbic system and cortex. Descending pathways are thought to innervate the medulla and spinal cord. Less is known about the regulatory mechanism of serotonin. It is known that after its release into the synapse it is rapidly taken back into the presynaptic terminal. It is thought that the tricyclic antidepressants affect this process (Berger, 1977).

Acetylcholine

Acetylcholine is well known for its role in the peripheral nervous system as the neurotransmitter at the site of neuromuscular junctions, postganglionic parasympathetic fibers, and preganglionic fibers of both the sympathetic and parasympathetic branches of the ANS. However, its role in the CNS is less well understood, although it is believed to be involved with arousal mechanisms, temperature regulation, and memory (DeFeudis, 1974). It has also been suggested that acetylcholine may play a role in schizophrenia (Barchas et al., 1977) and the mood disorders (Berger & Barchas, 1977) through its interaction (i.e., balance) with other neurotransmitters.

The precursor of acetylcholine, choline, is probably synthesized in the liver and transported across the blood-brain barrier as either free choline or as phosphatidyl choline (Cooper, Bloom, & Roth, 1986). The enzyme (acetyl transferase) converts choline into acetylcholine. Acetylcholinesterase in the neuronal tissues inactivates acetylcholine once its has been released into the synaptic cleft by breaking it down into choline and acetic acid. Approximately 30–50 % of the choline is then taken back up by the nerve terminal. There are no known agents that block the uptake mechanism. However, there are a number of compounds that inhibit cholinesterase, although many of these do not cross the blood-brain barrier. (Goldstein, Aronow, & Kalman, 1974).

Gamma-Aminobutyric Acid (GABA)

In the early 1950s GABA was found to be present in very high levels in the brain and spinal cord (Roberts, 1975). Like acetylcholine, GABA is synthesized from its precursor in a single enzymatic step. Its pathways connect with dopaminergic neurons of the limbic system. GABA is an inhibitory transmitter affecting both pre- and postsynaptic activity. It is thought that its mechanism of action postsynaptically involves the opening of chloride channels with a resultant influx of this negative ion into the cell. This causes the neuron to become hyperpolarized, making it less responsive to other stimuli. On the presynaptic side, GABA reduces incoming signals by afferent depolarization. The net result of both actions is to prevent neurons that are usually paroxysmally active from responding to normal or excessive stimulation (Haefley, Pieri, Pole, & Schaffer, 1981). GABA neurons innervate the locus ceruleus and raphé nuclei, a process which is thought to provide the basis for the anxiolytic action of the benzodiazepines in reducing the experience of anxiety (Gray, 1982, 1983).

cluded that low levels of MAO are not necessarily related to acute symptoms of schizophrenia but may be significant for a subgroup of chronic patients. However, there is still the possibility that MAO levels are related to medications, diet, activity, hospitalization, sex, age, or nonspecific effects of stress or psychoses rather than the disorder itself. In addition, the finding that patients suffering from both schizophrenia and affective disorder exhibit lower levels of MAO activity than controls suggests that MAO may be involved in these types of disturbances generally but not schizophrenia specifically (Meltzer & Arora, 1980). (This view is compatible with the observation that the positive signs of schizophrenia are not unique to that particular disorder.) On the other hand, the MAO theory complements both the dopamine and transmethylation hypotheses since MAO metabolizes all of those compounds. Consequently, low levels of MAO might induce high levels of dopamine or other psychotogenic amines.

Dopamine Hypothesis. A biochemical model of schizophrenia that has received a great deal of attention is the dopamine hypothesis. This theory, which postulates that schizophrenia is caused by an excess of dopamine-dependent neuronal activity in the brain (Meltzer & Stahl, 1976), was suggested by several lines of evidence. It is thought, for example, that antipsychotic medications exert their therapeutic effect by reducing dopaminergic activity. It is known that the ability of the phenothiazines to bind to dopamine receptors is highly correlated with their clinical potency (Seeman et al., 1976; Snyder, 1976). Furthermore, a side effect of these medications is a syndrome resembling Parkinson's disease, which involves a decrease in the synthesis of dopamine. Another side effect of these medications in some patients is the development of tardive dyskinesia. This condition is thought to involve dopaminergic supersensitivity resulting from the tonic blockade of postsynaptic dopamine receptors (Creese & Snyder, 1980; Hollister, 1977; Klawans, 1973; List & Seeman, 1979). In addition, AMPT (alpha-Methyl-p-tyrosine), which inhibits the synthesis of the catecholamines (which include dopamine), has been found to potentiate the antipsychotic action of the phenothiazines (Carlsson, 1974). In contrast, L-DOPA, the immediate precursor to dopamine, induces psychosis in some patients receiving the drug as a treatment of Parkinson's disease (Goodwin & Murphy, 1974). On the other hand, compounds structurally similar to the catecholamines may induce or exacerbate psychotic symptoms, as in the case of amphetamine psychosis (first reported by Young and Scoville in 1938).

Attempts have been made to find differences between schizophrenic patients and normal controls in terms of dopaminergic activity in the brain. Lee and Seeman (1980) conducted postmortem examinations of 59 normals and 50 schizophrenics and found significant elevations of dopaminergic receptor sites in the patients, even those who had no history of being treated by neuroleptics. Crow and his associates found the same thing in patients who had not received neuroleptic medication at least one year or more before their death (Crow, Johnstone, Longden, & Owen, 1978). Other researchers, while finding increased dopamine receptors among schizophrenic patients, have suggested that these differences may be entirely iatrogenic (i.e., due to the neuroleptic medications; see Mackay et al., 1982). Whatever the case, it is now accepted that all of the antipsychotic drugs do exert their effect through the common mechanism of dopamine receptor antagonism so that dopamine must be involved with schizophrenia in some way (Ashton, 1987).

There are four dopaminergic pathways or systems in the brain (see Figure 4.1). The nigrostriatal system arises from the substantia nigra and projects to the corpus striatum. It is primarily concerned with the control of muscle tone and movement, and it is the degeneration of dopaminergic cell bodies in this system that causes Parkinson's disease (Hornykiewicz, 1973). A second dopaminergic system is the tuberoinfundibular pathway, which arises from cells in the median eminence and projects to the hypothalamus. This system appears to deal with the release of prolactin and other hormones from the pituitary and does not appear to be related to schizophrenia. The chemoreceptor trigger zone in the medulla is also under dopaminergic control but does not appear to be involved with the disorder either. The final system, the mesolimbic pathway, arises from a group of cells in the ventral tegmental area and projects to many limbic structures and the frontal cortex. This system is suspected of being involved in schizophrenia for two reasons. For one, these structures contain high concentrations of dopaminergic receptors. Second, evidence from postmortem, EEG, CT, and cerebral blood flow investigations of schizophrenia all implicate the limbic system and its frontal lobe connections.

There are three types of dopamine receptors in the brain, each of

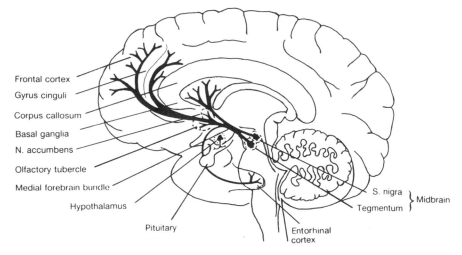

Figure 4.1. Dopaminergic pathways in the brain. (From H. Ashton [1987], *Brain Systems, Disorders, and Psychotropic Drugs,* p. 394. Oxford: Oxford University Press. Copyright © 1987 by Heather Ashton. Reprinted by permission.)

Multiple dopamine receptors

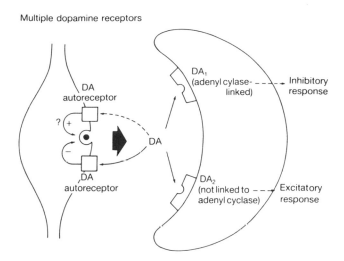

Figure 4.2. Presynaptic and postsynaptic receptors for dopamine (DA). Postsynaptic receptors mediate tissue responses and include dopamine-1 (DA₁) receptors linked to adenylate cyclase and dopamine-2 (DA₂) receptors not linked to this enzyme. Presynaptic autoreceptors may modulate dopamine release. (From H. Ashton [1987], *Brain Systems, Disorders, and Psychotropic Drugs*, p. 391. Oxford: Oxford University Press. Copyright © 1987 by Heather Ashton. Reprinted by permission.)

which is biochemically, pharmacologically, and functionally distinct (Creese, 1982). Although the nature of their interaction is unclear (Beart, 1982), it does seem that either separately or together they serve inhibitory and excitatory functions and that much of this activity is mediated by other neurotransmitters, particularly serotonin and norepinephrine (Cools, 1982). Two types of receptors are postsynaptic (see Figure 4.2). One of these, dopamine-1 (DA-1), is linked to the "second messenger" adenylate cyclase and is thought to be responsible for excitatory responses. The second, dopamine-2 (DA-2), is not linked to adenylate cyclase and appears to be inhibitory in its effect. The general consensus now is that while there are no differences in DA-1 receptor binding between schizophrenics and controls, there is a significant increase in DA-2 receptor binding in the former (Cross, Crow & Owen, 1981).

The third receptor type, dopamine-3 (DA-3), is presynaptic and is thought to modulate the synaptic release of dopamine via a negative feedback loop (Dourish & Cooper, 1985; Meltzer, 1980; Tepper, Groves, & Young, 1985). The DA-3 receptors (called "autoreceptors") are present in the nigrostriatal and mesolimbic systems of the cerebral cortex and are located on the body, axons, and dendrites of the neuronal cells themselves. The release of dopamine at the synapses is controlled by a complex feedback system involving cholinergic, GABA-ergic neurons, and the autoreceptors. When the latter are stimulated by dopamine or its agonists, there is a decrease in dopamine release and hence a reduction in dopaminergic activity. Since the autoreceptors are more sensitive than postdopaminergic receptors to dopamine agonists, low levels of the latter may produce paradoxical effects that are opposite to postsynaptic dopamine receptor stimulation (i.e., cause a reduction in dopaminergic activity).

The antipsychotic drugs appear to exert their effect through the blockade of dopamine receptors in the brain (Ashton, 1987). Since many of these drugs are capable of antagonizing all three types of dopamine receptors, it is unclear which of the three are important in schizophrenia. Initially, it was thought that their antipsychotic effect involved adenylate cyclase, the postsynaptic second messenger which is coupled to the DA-1 receptors (Kebabian, Petzold, & Greengard, 1972). This was because the ability of the phenothiazines to inhibit adenylate cyclase correlated well with their clinical potency (Iversen & Iversen, 1975). More recent evidence, however, suggests that antagonism of DA-1 receptors is not necessary for an antipsychotic effect (Ashton, 1987). The butyrophenones and benzamides, which are also clinically potent, exert only weak DA-1 receptor activity. On the other hand, the correlation between DA-2 binding potency and antipsychotic potency is good for all of the antipsychotic medications. The importance of the DA-3 receptors is not yet known, although a new approach in the pharmacological treatment of schizophrenia is directed toward the development of drugs that selectively stimulate the autoreceptors thus reducing dopamine synthesis and release.

Although the blockade of DA-2 receptors may be responsible for producing an antipsychotic effect, the mechanism by which this occurs is unclear. A problem in this regard is the phenomenon of a "therapeutic time-lag" (Ashton, 1987). (Although DA-2 receptor antagonism occurs quickly, the antipsychotic effects of the medication do not become apparent for some weeks.) It has been argued that over time the administration of antipsychotic medications causes the dopaminergic cells to become tonically depolarized (Bunney, 1984). This is called a "depolarization block" and may have the greatest effect on reducing dopaminergic transmission. For example, it has been found that there is an almost complete silencing of firing of dopaminergic neuron activity in the substantia nigra and ventral tegmentum with chronic administration of these drugs. It is thought that a depolarization block results from the failure or exhaustion of normal feedback mechanisms. More specifically, the blockade of postsynaptic receptors decreases dopamine's synaptic action which causes the homeostatic increase in the firing rate of dopaminergic cells. Initially, this reduces the effectiveness of the dopaminergic blockade and thus might explain the failure of the antipsychotic medications to exert an acute effect. Over time, however, the compensatory response fails, perhaps as a result of autoreceptor supersensitivity (i.e., the increased dopaminergic activity in the synapse stimulates inhibitory feedback). At this point, postsynaptic blockade is enhanced and a clinically beneficial response appears (Creese, 1983).

The possibility that antipsychotic medications have an effect on all three receptor types explains why these drugs produce adverse as well as therapeutic effects. For example, Parkinsonian symptoms and tardive dyskinesia are both associated with alterations of the dopaminergic system, although in different ways. If the postsynaptic receptors become supersensitive as a result of continued dopaminergic blockade, the resultant increase in dopaminergic activity may aggravate schizophrenic symptoms and induce tardive dyskinesia. On the other hand, if the DA-3 autoreceptors become supersensitive (thus inhibiting dopamine release and causing a reduction in dopaminergic activity), Parkinsonian symptoms may develop. In this situation, there is also the possibility for a potentiation of negative symptomatology. (The development of a depolarization blockade will also contribute to the same syndrome as that caused by autoreceptor supersensitivity.)

In spite of the knowledge of how the antipsychotic medications affect dopaminergic activity, there is still no direct evidence that schizophrenia is caused by a defect in the dopaminergic transmission system (Neale & Oltmanns, 1980). For example, efforts to monitor dopaminergic activity by measuring a dopamine metabolite (homovanillic acid) in cerebrospinal fluid and the examination of catecholamine-related enzymes in autopsied brains have found no reliable difference between schizophrenics and normal controls (Post, Fink, Carpenter, & Goodwin, 1975; Rimón, Roos, Räkköläinen, & Alanen, 1971).

Also it must be noted that the antipsychotic drugs have a significant effect primarily on the positive symptoms with very little effect on negative aspects of the disorder, such as poverty of speech and flatness of affect (Johnstone, Crow, Frith, Carney, & Price, 1978). Consequently, dopamine receptor activation, if present in schizophrenia, must be responsible for only some aspects of the disorder, namely those seen in the acute stage. Chronically, dopamine may not be involved at all, although it may contribute to negative symptomatology through inhibition or underactivity rather than excitation or overactivity (Alpert & Friedhof, 1980; Chouinard & Jones, 1978; Crow, 1982). However, the dopamine hypothesis has generated a great deal of research over the past few decades. Some see this to be the greatest contribution of the dopamine theory of schizophrenia, regardless of whether it eventually proves to be correct (Meltzer, 1979).

Interactional Hypotheses. Although the dopamine hypothesis continues to generate support, it is probable that no single agent is responsible for schizophrenia and that other neurotransmitters operating in conjunction with dopaminergic systems provoke the acute aspects of the disorder. Along these lines, it has been suggested that the basic defect in schizophrenia involves a lack of inhibition of the GABA-ergic system and that antipsychotics work by preventing an overload of dopaminergic impulses normally dampened by that system (Roberts, 1977). The GABA connection, however, is doubtful at this point (Ashton, 1987).

Another hypothesis involves an imbalance between dopaminergic and cholinergic activity, with there being a relative predominance of the former over the latter (J. M. Davis, Janowsky, & Casper, 1977; K. L. Davis, Hollister, Berger, & Barchas, 1975). To test this theory, J. M. Davis (1974) gave schizophrenic patients a drug (methylphenidate) that blocks the re-uptake of dopamine, thus increasing dopaminergic activity. Normal subjects experienced a mild euphoria while the schizophrenic subjects become psychotic. He proposed a two-factor theory in which one factor, an unidentified biochemical compound, "turns on" schizophrenia while the second factor, dopamine, "turns up the gain." Both factors must be in operation for a schizophrenic episode to be expressed. The phenothiazines block the dopaminergic stimulation (i.e., turn down the gain), while dopaminergic stimulants, such as amphetamine and methylphenidate, turn up the gain in persons with the first factor. In terms of this model, the antipsychotic agents work by turning down the gain (i.e., blocking dopaminergic activity).

Whatever the case, the biochemical models of schizophrenia are still highly speculative. Perhaps the best that can be said about these theories at this point is that schizophrenia appears to be the manifestation of an imbalance of the functionally interdependent dopaminergic, noradrenergic, and serotonergic pathways connected in series in the limbic system (Cools, 1975). In addition, biochemical factors must also be considered in terms of their interaction with environmental considerations. And finally, it is probably unrealistic to expect any biochemical theory to explain schizophrenia in its entirety (cf. Murphy & Buchsbaum, 1978). At best, it might be said that the dopamine and related hypotheses may help delineate a biologically homogeneous subgroup of patients for whom positive symptomatology is the defining feature and for whom psychopharmacologic interventions are optimally effective (Haracz, 1982).

Psychophysiological Factors

Research on the psychophysiology of schizophrenia has relied on a variety of responses and methods (for reviews see Spohn & Patterson, 1979, and Venables, 1981). Of these, perhaps the most closely studied areas have been the orienting response and evoked potentials. Work on the former has generally used electrodermal measures and has focused primarily on schizophrenic hyper- and hypo-responsivity to simple stimuli. Studies involving evoked potentials, on the other hand, have looked at the tendency for individuals to augment rather than reduce their perception of simple stimuli. Examples of some of the stimuli used in these studies include tones or flashes of light. This research can be conceptualized as focusing on the *vertical* organization of the brain, particularly as it relates to the interaction of the brain stem with areas of the midbrain (e.g., limbic system).

Orienting Response. One of the most widely studied psychophysiological variables in schizophrenia has been the electrodermal orienting response or orienting reflex (OR). The OR is thought to be triggered by change or movement of a stimulus in the perceptual field thereby signaling a "mis-match" between the sensory input and a "neuronal model" of that field (Sokolov, 1963). Repeated presentations of the novel stimulus alter the neuronal model causing OR activity to subside or habituate. If schizophrenia is characterized by an impairment in response to the external world, then some defect in OR function would be expected (Bernstein, 1964).

The investigation of schizophrenic OR has generated conflicting results. Zahn, Rosenthal, and Lawlor (1968) reported that schizophrenic patients gave larger electrodermal responses and showed less habituation than normals in response to audible tones. Bernstein (1964, 1970), on the other hand, suggested that schizophrenics are hypo-responsive in terms of the frequency, amplitude, and habituation of the OR response to both visual and auditory stimuli. Gruzelier and Venables (1972) attempted to reconcile these differences by reporting that a group of schizophrenic patients they studied evidenced a bimodal pattern of responses. About half of their subjects demonstrated apparent electrodermal hypo-responsivity (e.g., low baseline levels with little if any orienting activity), while the remainder exhibited a large number of high amplitude, fast-recovery skin conductance responses that failed to habituate (see also Venables, 1977).

Although the bimodal distribution of schizophrenics was independently replicated by Rubens and Lapidus in 1978, a reanalysis of the 1968 data by Zahn in 1976 failed to reveal a bimodal distribution among his original subjects. His reanalysis, as well as other data (e.g., Patterson, 1976; Straube, 1979), seem to emphasize the relative prevalence in the schizophrenic population of nonresponders characterized by a pattern of low spontaneous activity and withdrawal. This pattern is interpreted as evidence of the presence of protective inhibition of schizophrenics to help them deal with overstimulation. Also, it may be that "faster habituation suggests that perception among chronic schizophrenics is relatively diffuse and undifferentiated" (i.e., fewer and broader response dimensions) (Bernstein, 1970, p. 154). However, Frith, Stevens, Johnstone, and Crow (1979) reported that only 4 out of 45 patients they studied (none of whom had been on neuroleptics for at least four weeks prior to assessment) were nonresponders.

These findings have been explained in terms of experimental artifact, methodological shortcomings, or the presence of subgroups of schizophrenic patients (Venables, 1983). Zahn (1976) suggested that the failure to confirm was due to changes in hospital discharge policies so that the patients tested by Gruzelier and Venables in the 1970s were more heavily weighted toward subjects who were less resistant to the phenothiazines. It was also suggested that the differences were due to the medications themselves, a possibility disputed by Gruzelier and Hammond (1976) who were unable to show any clear connection between drug status and hypo- or hyper-responsivity. Perhaps the most likely explanation concerns the possibility of subgroups among the schizophrenic population, particularly in terms of positive versus negative symptoms. Straube (1979) compared nonresponders to responders and found that the former were significantly higher on ratings of emotional withdrawal, conceptual disorganization, somatic concern, depressive mood, and motor retardation, a finding similar to Gruzelier's results reported in 1976. In like manner, Gruzelier and Manchanda (1982) studied 48 undrugged hospital admissions. Of these, 29 had larger amplitude right-hand responses to tones whereas 19 had larger left-hand responses. The former (suggesting left hemisphere involvement) displayed "classical" or Bleulerian schizophrenia—blunted affect, emotional withdrawal, impaired social functioning, disorganized thought, and retarded motility. The latter manifested florid symptoms including "hypomanic affect, pressure of speech, ideas of reference, depressive hallucinations and delusions, hypochondriasis, grandiosity and situational anxiety" (p. 488).

It has been proposed that both the hypo- and hyper-responsivity shown by schizophrenic patients relate to a dysfunction in the limbic system, particularly in the amygdaloid or hippocampal areas (McGuinness & Pribram, 1980). Spohn and Paterson (1979) suggest that disturbances in the balance of cholinergic activity account for this dysfunction, providing basically a biochemical substrate for these functional "lesions." The limbic dysfunction hypothesis can also be linked to the dopamine hypothesis (e.g., Meltzer & Stahl, 1976) or a combination of the two (e.g., cholinergic and dopaminergic systems) (Mesulam & Geschwind, 1978). Other work has been directed toward explaining this responsivity in terms of the balance of the hemispheres, an area to be discussed shortly. However, electrodermal levels and responses have been found to operate independently of generalized hemispheric influences. Consequently, they probably relate more to discrete aspects of stimuli and response processing and thus may involve reticular-thalamic (i.e., vertical) pathways.

In summary, schizophrenic ORs may reflect different stages or phases of the disorder with hyper-responding associated with positive symptomatology and hypo-responding negative symptomatology. Whatever the case, it is clear that schizophrenics tend to respond *inappropriately*. Claridge (1985) suggests that this be taken as evidence for a dysfunction of the schizophrenic brain's ability to maintain a homeostatic condition so that arousal is either too high or too low.

Evoked Potentials. Evoked potentials (EPs) are averaged electroencephalographic (EEG) waveforms recorded from subjects stimulated by light flashes, tones, electric shocks, or any sensory event that has an onset fast enough to produce adequate synchrony of the brain's response (Buchsbaum, Haier, & Johnson, 1983). As such, EPs complement the use of the electrodermal orienting response in demonstrating the presence of reliable differences across individuals. Of particular interest in this regard is the concept of augmenting and reducing, which refers to the finding that individuals vary in the extent to which their nervous systems either amplify or diminish the effects of stimulation. This dimension was first suggested by Petrie's (1960) work on individual differences in the perception of painful stimuli. Work with EPs using light as a stimulus has found that *augmenters* exhibit elevated EP amplitudes with increasing flash intensity while *reducers* show either smaller increases or even reductions with increments in intensity. Work with cats has shown that the mechanism for augmenting-reducing is based on the interaction of the cortical visual system and the brain stem and ascending reticular system rather than differences in peripheral visual mechanisms or thalamic responsiveness, thus linking the construct to basic arousal structures (Lukas & Siegel, 1977). Cats who are augmenters appear to be more active and responsive, more aggressive, and generally more emotional. Furthermore, they tend to explore their surroundings more inquisitively. Reducers, on the other hand, are observed to behave in a more timid and inactive manner.

Silverman has suggested that the states of chronic withdrawal seen in schizophrenia represent an excessive narrowing of attention resulting as a defensive maneuver against threatening or otherwise intense stimulation—the reducing effect (Silverman, 1967). This hypothesis has been supported by the finding that acute schizophrenics not on medication tend to be reducers in terms of visual (Landau, Buchsbaum, Carpenter, Strauss, & Sacks, 1975) and somatosensory EPs (G. C. Davis, Buchsbaum, van Kammen, & Bunney, 1979). Connolly, Gruzelier, Manchanda, and Hirsch (1983), however, found both augmenting and reducing among a group of 22 schizophrenic subjects as compared to 22 normal controls. Since these differences depended on the site of the EEG reading (left or right temporal), they interpreted their findings as indicating a left hemisphere abnormality as well as the possibility of a generalized hemispheric imbalance. Other investigators have also demonstrated that schizophrenics show deviant types of responding when the strength of the sensory stimulus is progressively varied (e.g., Landau et al., 1975). Claridge (1972), for example, found that when physiological arousal was very low, schizophrenic sensitivity to environmental stimuli (as measured by EPs) seems to be very much increased. Shagass (1977), on the other hand, found that schizophrenics exhibited low amplitude EP responses in response to stronger stimulus intensities.

The two conclusions that may be derived from the EP studies of schizophrenia are that, first, many schizophrenics seem to be reducers, a finding that is compatible with the stimulus overload hypothesis. The second conclusion we can draw is that schizophrenics may exhibit a paradoxical profile of responses that is different from that of normals. More specifically, when physiological arousal is very low, sensitivity to environmental stimuli seems much increased. (In normals, the level of attentiveness to external stimuli is more directly related to level of arousal.) This has lead Claridge to observe:

> It seems very likely that underlying augmenting-reducing is some sort of regulatory mechanism which modifies the brain's response to external stimulation and that this, in turn, is intimately connected, through feedback

loops, to general arousal systems. Normally, these circuits would be expected to work smoothly together, making it possible for the nervous system to maintain an appropriate strength of sensory response for its prevailing level of arousal. What appears to happen in the schizophrenic brain is a kind of "uncoupling" effect; or, put another way, a weakening of its regulatory properties. If this were true then it would almost certainly cause the brain to veer to extremes of activity, not just in one system (say, general arousal), but also as reflected in the mutual disconnection of *different* systems. (Claridge, 1985, p. 117, italics in original)

Hemispheric Factors

Unlike the psychophysiological approach with its interest on the *vertical* function of the brain, hemispheric research has emphasized the brain's *horizontal* organization (e.g., across hemispheres). Like psychophysiological studies, this research is tied to information-processing models of schizophrenia (e.g., Magaro, 1980). But whereas psychophysiological research elucidates the nature of the relationship between attention and arousal, hemispheric research tells us something about the detection and integration of environmental stimuli.

The possibility that schizophrenia is caused by a temporal-limbic dysfunction of the left hemisphere is long-standing (e.g., Flor-Henry, 1983). Although some evidence comes from the observation of a higher proportion of mixed or reversed dominance in schizophrenics than in normals (Gur, 1977), the strongest data supporting a left-located cerebral dysfunction in schizophrenia come from studies employing EEG (e.g., Flor-Henry, Koles, Howarth, & Burton, 1979), neuropsychological (e.g., Abrams & Taylor, 1979), and behavioral measures (e.g., Gur, 1978). These studies have shown greater 13–20 Hz EEG power from the left temporal region in schizophrenics, more aphasia screening test errors for schizophrenics, and schizophrenic dysfunction in the processing of verbal information presented with a tachistoscopic apparatus. Other studies have demonstrated the difference between schizophrenics and normals in terms of hemispheric function. Some of these responses include higher right ear auditory thresholds, suggesting left temporal lobe pathology (Gruzelier & Flor-Henry, 1979; Bazhin, Wasserman, & Tonkonogii, 1975). Other data suggest a pattern of left hemispheric dysfunction and overreaction when verbal and visual stimuli are presented on tachistoscopic tasks (Gur, 1978). Within subjects, schizophrenics appear to have a particular problem processing information presented to the left, normally language-dominant hemisphere (Colbourn, 1982). Consequently, it has been proposed that "the florid syndrome with its pressure of speech and flight of ideas implies an overactivation of left hemisphere functions, whereas sluggish thinking and speech, impoverished sometimes to the point of muteness, which characterized the group with larger right-hand responses, implies a reduction in left hemisphere activation" (Gruzelier & Manchanda, 1982, p. 493).

The evidence for left hemispheric dysfunction, however, is inconclusive, particularly since it is extremely difficult to place dysfunction definitely in either hemisphere. Another school of thought argues that the dysfunctional hemisphere is the right one (Oepen et al., 1987). Citing the work on split-brain patients, which suggests an interhemispheric functional balance of inhibition and release (e.g., Bogen, 1985), they see schizophrenia as a consequence of an overactive right hemisphere. Noting that the right hemisphere is especially activated by emotional stimuli (Bryden & Ley, 1983), these investigators, using half-field presentation of tachistoscopic stimuli (faces and words), found that acute schizophrenics demonstrated impairment of right hemispheric function with simultaneous improvement of left hemispheric performance.

In spite of the relative degree of specialization of the two hemispheres in terms of language and spatial functioning, both sides of the brain are involved in the processing of information received from the outside world. Consequently, it is probably insufficient to attempt to explain schizophrenia in terms of a deficit in one hemisphere or the other (Wexler & Heninger, 1979). This has lead to the proposal that, rather than a dysfunction in either one of the hemispheres, the problem lies in interhemispheric regulation (Flor-Henry, 1976).

There are two possible models involving the interaction of both sides of the brain. The first, proposed initially by Beaumont & Dimond (1973), is that there is poor communication between hemispheres; "the two cerebral hemispheres are partially disconnected and . . . this reflects some change in the efficiency of the corpus callosum" (p. 662). They report that, compared to control groups of normals and nonschizophrenic psychiatric patients, schizophrenics do equally as well matching shapes and letters when they are presented to the same hemisphere but less well when presented to different hemispheres. They suggest that schizophrenics have a partial brain disconnection. Another hypothesis along the same line has suggested that in schizophrenia there is an increase in interhemispheric inhibition, making the two hemispheres functionally isolated from each other (Galin, 1974). This might explain the sense of a dual personality or a splitting of ideas from affect.

An alternative explanation is just the opposite; there is too much communication between hemispheres. This could result in the brain's inability to function effectively as a total unit due to an overload of the system. Findings consistent with this hypothesis come from the work of Green and his colleagues (Green, Glass, & O'Callaghan, 1979; Green & Kotenko, 1980). They examined the ability of schizophrenics to recall stories presented over headphones to both ears simultaneously or individually. Schizophrenics were able to perform better when the story was presented in one ear only, suggesting that engagement of both hemispheres caused interference with verbal processing. They also found a left ear disadvantage in monaural speech comprehension, which they interpreted as the relatively inefficient transmission of complex auditory information by the ipsilateral auditory pathways. Randall (1980) has thus argued that there is an abnormally high number of fibers connecting equivalent areas of the two hemispheres. A similar proposal is offered by Wexler (1980) who suggests that there may be a weakening of interhemispheric inhibition resulting in overexcitation of both hemispheres at the same time.

Venables (1981) has linked hemispheric dysfunction to deficiencies in information processing highlighted by the attentional models of schizophrenia discussed earlier in the chapter. He has proposed that the left hemisphere attends to contralateral stimuli while the right attends to both contralateral and ipsilateral stimuli (Heilman & van den Abell, 1979). In this regard, it is suggested that it may be the function of the right hemisphere to conduct the global or preattentive structuring of the perceptual field (i.e., filtering) with the left hemisphere performing the second or pigeon-holing function. In support of this view, patients who have experienced right posterior lesions "behave as though this pre-attentive structuring had not occurred. Their focal attention wanders aimlessly across a chaotic field or adheres to a salient stimulus for lack of further direction" (Kinsbourne, 1974, p. 278). A failure of right hemisphere functioning may in turn lead to left hemisphere overloading in keeping with the observation of its overactivation in schizophrenic patients (Venables, 1984).

Whatever the case, it appears from several sources that schizophrenics evidence lateral asymmetry. Data from studies of the OR discussed earlier suggest that schizophrenics, as compared to normals, evidence greater differences in electrodermal responses when recordings made from the right and left hands are compared (Gruzelier & Manchanda, 1982). The same phenomena have been found with EPs investigating the augmenting-reducing phenomenon referred to earlier (Connolly, Gruzelier, Manchanda, & Hirsch, 1983). Consequently, we have the disquieting possibility that the increased response variability observed among schizophrenics occurs not only within the same individual over time but also within the individual at the same time on different sides of the body!

Summary of Physiological Factors

Drawing a consensus from the data from the thousands of studies arising from both the medical and psychological perspectives is difficult. Part of the reason is that much of this work is focused on relatively narrow aspects of schizophrenia. Consequently, the convergence of these different lines of investigation has not been explored as systematically as the individual areas. A second reason for the lack of integration is the difficulty of interpreting the data we do have. Psychophysiological, neuroanatomical, and biochemical indices are essentially single outcomes of a complex process resulting from activity of a total operating system. Thus, as illustrated in the case of lateral dysfunction, it is extremely difficult to know what part of the system is dysfunctional, much less why. Venables (1981) has suggested that studying EEG measures of brain function is like attempting to discover what is being made in a factory by listening to its walls.

With this in mind, all that can be said by way of generalization is that the schizophrenic brain simply does not function in a coordinated manner much of the time. There appears to be a lack of ability to maintain homeostasis in terms of inhibitory control as well as a an inability to integrate information across hemispheres. This has lead to the suggestion of an "uncoupling" in schizophrenia that affects the schizophrenic's ability to relate his or her emotional state with his or her intellectual one (Claridge, 1985, pp. 124–126). The "splitting" of affect from the intellect was thought originally to be the central characteristic of schizophrenia and provided the impetus for Eugen Bleuler (1950) to coin the term.

Treatment Implications

After a lifetime of study Manfred Bleuler (1978) came to view schizophrenia as resulting from the interaction of an inherited disposition with adverse environmental experiences. Together, these factors precipitate the maladaptive development of a schizophrenic personality characterized by disharmonious human relations. One aspect of the this developmental process is the schizophrenic's attempt to reconcile his or her personal view of the world with objective reality. This is accomplished by the production of idiosyncratic mental images that shape the world according to his or her own psychophysiological or hemispheric disposition. According to Bleuler, effective therapy for schizophrenia therefore should attempt to reverse this process by using therapeutic forces that contribute to a harmonious development of a person's personality. To this end, social and environmental factors become central to the treatment of schizophrenia.

> A community, whether it be in a hospital or in a family, is of paramount importance. In this community the schizophrenic must reach a state of equilibrium between an optimal amount of activity which stimulates him, and an optimal amount of routine and order which helps to calm and control him. When ready, the patient needs to be confronted with new situations and responsibilities which encourage him to mobilize his vital forces. During certain phases of his illness he will require a calming agent such as psychotherapy or drugs. The success of a therapy is contingent upon the organization of an active community, opportunities for the patient to become involved, and possibilities for tranquilization. (M. Bleuler, 1979, pp. vii–viii)

Bleuler's clinical observations are entirely compatible with the discussion of physiological factors here. It has been argued that the schizophrenic inherits a biologic predisposition toward the disorder. Whether through the excessive activity of the dopaminergic system or other neurotransmission systems in conjunction with it, there seems to be a loosening of the normal regulatory process of the CNS (i.e., positive symptoms). This is reflected by abnormal responses to the environment, including interpersonal stimuli, due to an uncoupling of the normal integration of arousal with attention so that the intensity of stimuli is either under- or overestimated. In addition, there is evidence of attentional deficits in the ability to screen out irrelevant stimuli and appropriately categorize information that is perceived. The latter may reflect a lateral dysfunction of the cerebral hemispheres. Consequently, the schizophrenic is faced with a bewildering and threatening world with which he or she has difficulty coping. The result of these experiences, in turn, may lead to a number of secondary adaptive processes (i.e., negative symptoms) that, in many cases, are more debilitating than the symptoms characteristic of the early stages of the disorder. Consequently, it is clear that the treatment of the schizophrenic patient must proceed along two parallel lines—appropriate medication and an active psychosocial intervention (Wallace, Donahoe, & Boone, 1986).

Medications

Antipsychotic medications have assumed a major role in the treatment of schizophrenia, particularly in its acute phase (Klein & Davis,

1969). For example, Cole and his associates (Cole, Goldberg, & Davis, 1966; Cole, Klerman & Goldberg, 1964) reported that 75% of schizophrenic patients given a phenothiazine improved substantially after six weeks of treatment, with only a few patients experiencing further deterioration. This group was compared to the patients who received a placebo in a control condition. Fifty percent of this group deteriorated over the same period with only 25% showing substantial improvement. The effectiveness of the antipsychotic medications in the treatment of schizophrenia as demonstrated by this and other studies has been consistently favorable (J. M. Davis, Schaffer, Killian, Kinard, & Chan, 1980).

These medications, however, are not without limitations. As noted earlier, they are effective primarily for relieving acute or "positive" symptomatology (Wallace et al., 1986). Furthermore, their effectiveness appears to wane as the disorder progresses so that in the maintenance phase their effect is not as great as during the acute phase. For example, a majority of patients experience relapse within 3 to 5 years of discharge in spite of continued neuroleptic treatment (Kohen & Paul, 1976). And finally, there are numerous aversive side effects that may discourage the patient from continued use of these medications and possibly lead to severe complications, such as Parkinsonianism or tardive dyskinesia.

Psychosocial Interventions

Even when the antipsychotic medications do work, the schizophrenic patient is still faced upon discharge from the hospital with the daily problems in living that proved so difficult to cope with in the early stages of the disorder's onset. It has been estimated that as many as half of medicated patients still are unable to adapt to living successfully in the community (Hogarty et al., 1979). This problem was highlighted by G. W. Brown and his associates (Brown, Carstairs, & Topping, 1958; Brown, Monck, Carstairs, & Wing, 1962) in their prospective study of male schizophrenics. They found that, contrary to expectations, discharged patients who returned to live in their marital or parental home were more likely to relapse, showed more disturbed behavior, and remained unemployed longer than patients living either with siblings or by themselves. (Large hostels were also predictive of poor adjustment.) Furthermore, those patients whose relationship with their family was "highly emotionally involved" were even more likely to relapse.

To sort this out, G. W. Brown, Birley, and Wing (1972) completed a prospective study of 101 schizophrenic patients who were discharged to live with their relatives. Among several variables studied was the degree of emotional involvement of the patient's relative(s), scaled to provide an index referred to as "expressed emotion" (EE). EE has a negative connotation but should not be thought of as involving only negative feelings, such as hostility or anger. "Emotional overinvolvement" was also found to be an important component (Brown et al., 1972). G. W. Brown concluded that the degree of EE experienced in the home was directly related to relapse with 58% of patients in high-EE homes relapsing as compared to 16% in low-EE homes. In a replication of these findings by Vaughn and Leff four years later (1976), it was found that a remarkable 92% of discharged schizophrenic patients relapsed within nine months if they (1) lived in high-EE homes, (2) interacted with a high-EE relative more than 35 hours a week, and (3) were not on medication. This compared to only a 15% relapse rate for patients who also were not on medication but who were discharged to low-EE homes.

Based on the early observation that physiological arousal was related to withdrawal in schizophrenic patients, Venables and Wing (1962) proposed that the mechanism linking high-EE to relapse was physiological arousal. This hypothesis led to the investigation of the relationship between physiological arousal and EE in schizophrenic patients by Tarrier and his coworkers (Tarrier, Cooke, & Lader, 1978a, 1978b; Tarrier, Vaughn, Lader, & Leff, 1979). After several unsuccessful attempts to demonstrate the effects of EE on arousal in the laboratory, the investigators moved to the patients' home environments. They found that when the schizophrenic subject was talking to the interviewer, there were no differences in arousal as measured in terms of electrodermal activity and heart rate changes. However, when the key relative entered the room and joined in the conversation, clear and significant differences between patients with high- and low-EE relatives were obtained. This study was subsequently replicated by the finding that arousal, as measured by spontaneous electrodermal activity, differed between patients who had low- versus high-EE relatives, again only when the relative was present (Sturgeon, Kuipers, Berkowitz, Turpin, & Leff, 1981). It was concluded from these studies that the schizophrenic patient's physiological arousal in interpersonal settings is an important contributory factor in relapse. Furthermore, the data suggest that while a high-EE relative may instigate and maintain arousal, a low-EE relative appears to facilitate the patient's adaptation to the social situation and may actually help dissipate arousal.

An attempt to link arousal directly to relapse, however, has not been as successful. One study randomly assigned recently discharged patients to either a psychosocial intervention designed to lower EE or individual counseling. Although the psychosocial treatment was highly successful, arousal was not related to relapse and thus did not appear to be the mediating factor (Sturgeon, Turpin, Kuipers, Berkowitz, & Leff, 1984). Turpin (1983) has argued, however, that since the assessment of arousal for this study took place in the laboratory, the relationship between arousal and relapse was attenuated because of the stringent demand characteristics of the experimental setting which exert a "normalizing effect" on the subject's behavior that is not reflected in his or her daily life. Methods that allow for the monitoring of patients in more naturalistic settings, such as the telemetered EEG experiments of schizophrenics during psychotic episodes (Stevens et al., 1979), may help shed some light on this issue. Whatever the case, the work on EE has made it clear that the home environment of the schizophrenic plays an important role in his or her recovery and the possibility of relapse (Leff & Vaughn, 1985).

As a result of this research, a broad-spectrum, family-centered treatment approach for schizophrenia has been advocated. Vaughn and Leff (1976) have suggested that the first step is to identify high-risk EE families using a streamlined version of Brown-Rutter Family Interview (Brown & Rutter, 1966; Vaughn & Leff, 1977). Other problematic social situations, such as complicated social situations (e.g., disturbing sexual relationships), should also be monitored. In addition, the use of medication to reduce the patient's disturbed behavior at home or work may reduce the level of emotion expressed by others. Since medication-taking in an outpatient setting is often under the patient's control, self-management training would seem to be an important part of the overall treatment program as well.

A comprehensive treatment package that takes all of these factors into account has been developed by Falloon and his associates (Falloon, 1985; Falloon, Boyd, & McGill, 1984). This approach, designed to improve the family's ability to cope, begins with an assessment of the family's problem-solving effectiveness, an analysis of the family system as a unit, and at least two sessions at the outset of treatment devoted to educating the family on the diagnosis, etiology, management, and course of schizophrenia. Other components include communication training, training in structured problem-solving, and other behavioral strategies, such as self-management skills (including medication adherence training), social skills (including job-finding and job interview training), and anxiety management training.

This behavioral treatment package has been compared to individual therapy in a controlled study (Falloon et al., 1982). (Both conditions had the same pharmacological and rehabilitation components.) The efficacy of the program was demonstrated after nine months with the family-treated patients evidencing a higher rate of total remission of schizophrenic symptoms, fewer episodes of depression, and lower ratings of negative symptoms assessed by independent raters. In fact, only one family-treated patient had relapsed as compared to almost half (44%) of the individually-treated patients.

Summary

These results highlight the need to view schizophrenia from a perspective that integrates psychological, medical, and psychosocial models (Magaro, 1984; Schooler, 1986). Regardless of its biochemical or genetic basis, schizophrenia is, in its most basic sense, a problem of daily living (cf. "Where Next?", 1988). Although understanding its physiological roots may help us understand the schizophrenic's disordered thinking, this does not mean that successful treatment must proceed on that level only. Perhaps ironically, appreciating the physiological factors in schizophrenia only serves to heighten the emphasis on the nonmedical aspects of its treatment.

Chapter 5

Mood Disorders

The mood disorders[1] encompass a diverse range of syndromes reflecting a variety of states (cf. Zung, 1973). The most common of these is depression, of which there are at least four types (Akiskal, 1979). The first type, normal depression, is a relatively brief response that often results from common psychobiological processes, such as those which occur during premenstrual or postpartum periods (Dalton, 1984; Pitt, 1973). By definition, normal depression is not a diagnosis under the DSM-III-R. Situational depression, the second type, usually lasts longer than normal depression (from several weeks to several months) and often reflects good reality testing (Fenichel, 1945). If it persists, this type of depression may be assigned the diagnosis of adjustment disorder with depressed mood. The third type, secondary depression, refers to a state of demoralization following a chronic psychiatric or medical problem (Klein, 1974; Lipowski, 1975; Robins & Guze, 1972). Secondary depression is diagnosable as a mood disorder as long as the pre- or coexisting condition is also noted. Primary depression, on the other hand, is not linked to a preexisting medical or psychiatric problem (Kocsis, 1981), is grossly out of proportion to any life event, and affects cognitive, psychomotor, and vegetative processes. Primary depression is diagnosed according to its severity (e.g., dysthymia versus major depression) and in terms of the presence or absence of manic episodes (e.g., unipolar versus bipolar). (See Panel 5.1, "Mood Disorders: Diagnostic Summary.")

The history of depression has been marked with controversy and confusion. Initially, depressive episodes within and across individuals were thought to share a common set of characteristics, originate from a common cause, and therefore respond to one type of treatment (S. H.

[1]In the DSM-III the mood disorders were referred to as the affective disorders.

PANEL 5.1

Mood Disorders: Diagnostic Summary[1]

Symptoms or behaviors that distinguish unusually high or low mood swings from normal feelings are referred to as a mood syndrome. For example, a mood syndrome indicative of depression is characterized by the presence of such symptoms as weight loss, fatigue, feelings of worthlessness, or diminished ability to think or concentrate. A mood episode is a mood syndrome that cannot be attributed to a known organic factor or some other nonmood disorder like schizophrenia. A mood disorder, in turn, is determined by the pattern of mood episodes. For example, the diagnosis of major depression is made when there is a history of one or more major depressive episodes without corresponding manic or hypomanic episodes.

In the DSM-III-R mood disorders encompass two major subcategories—bipolar disorders and depressive disorders. Bipolar disorders are characterized by the presence of at least one manic or hypomanic episode along with one or more major depressive episodes. If there is a history of manic episodes, a diagnosis of bipolar disorder is made. However, if the "highs" are hypomanic only, the diagnosis is cyclothymia. An additional subclassification, bipolar disorder not otherwise specified, includes episodes with manic or hypomanic features that do not meet the criteria for one of the two specific bipolar disorders.

The depressive disorders, on the other hand, involve one or more episodes of depression without a corresponding history of manic or hypomanic episodes. The diagnosis of major depression is made if there are one or more major depressive episodes, while the diagnosis of dysthymia is used if there is a history of depressed mood over a two-year period that does not meet the criteria for a major depressive episode. As with the bipolar disorders, there is a residual diagnosis of depressive disorder not otherwise specified.[2]

---

[1]Material for this section is taken directly from the DSM-III-R (*Diagnostic and Statistical Manual of Mental Disorders* [Third Revision, Revised], American Psychiatric Association, 1987).

[2]There is a separate diagnostic category referred to as adjustment disorders. These disorders involve maladaptive reactions to identifiable psychosocial stressors provided the response does not persist longer than six months. One of the adjustment disorders is "with depressed mood." This disorder will not be dealt with separately here or elsewhere since it is assumed to share many of the physiological characteristics of the depressive disorders. Another adjustment disorder, "with work (or academic) inhibition," is also related to the disorders discussed in this chapter in that it reflects the disruption of normal functioning that often accompanies depression.

The essential feature of a *manic episode* is an elevated, expansive, or irritable mood. Some of the behaviors manifested during a manic syndrome include inflated self-esteem, decreased need for sleep, pressured speech, flight of ideas, or psychomotor agitation. By definition, a manic episode is differentiated from a hypomanic one in terms of degree of impairment. A manic episode causes severe impairment of occupational or social functioning and may be serious enough to warrant hospitalization in order to prevent harm to the client or others. A hypomanic episode, by contrast, is not severe enough to cause marked impairment in social or occupational functioning and usually does not require hospitalization. Often the person in the midst of a manic episode does not recognize that he or she is ill and thus resists efforts to be treated. However, this does not mean that the person is completely out of touch with reality, as would occur in the midst of acute psychosis.

Although a person's first manic episode is usually experienced in the early 20s, it can appear at any time during adulthood. Its onset is usually sudden, with a full set of symptoms appearing within a few days. The episode may last from a few days to several months and often terminates abruptly. Its complications may include natural consequences resulting from impaired judgment and include such problems as financial loss or psychoactive substance abuse. Often manic episodes occur following major psychosocial stressors or childbirth; they may also be precipitated by antidepressant medications or electroconvulsive therapy.

A *major depressive episode* is identified by a depressed mood (possibly an irritable mood in children or adolescents) or loss of interest or pleasure in all activities for a period of at least two weeks. Some of the behaviors that indicate a major depressive syndrome include unusual weight loss or weight gain, insomnia or hypersomnia, feelings of worthlessness or inappropriate guilt, diminished ability to think or concentrate, or recurrent thoughts of death, often with suicidal ideation, plans, and even attempts. Occasionally delusions or hallucinations may be present. When they are, their content is usually consistent with the predominant mood (i.e., mood-congruent). A common delusion involves being persecuted because of some moral transgression or personal inadequacy.

Features of a major depressive episode may vary considerably across different age categories. In children the episode may be accompanied by somatic complaints, psychomotor agitation, anxiety, and phobias. With adolescents, there may be negativistic or antisocial behavior, such as the use of alcohol or illicit drugs. In elderly adults, some of the symptoms of depression (e.g., disorientation, memory loss, and distractibility) may suggest dementia. If the necessary criteria are met, additional diagnoses on either Axis I or III should be considered.

A major depressive episode is usually thought to make its initial appearance in the early 20s but may occur at any age. Although its onset can be sudden, it usually develops over several days to weeks and may last six months or longer if untreated. There is inevitably some impairment of social or occupational functioning, which in severe cases may warrant hospitalization due to the person's inability to take care of himself or herself. The most serious problem in this regard is the possibility of suicide. A major depressive episode may be triggered by any number of other problems, such as chronic physical illness, psychoactive substance dependence (particularly to alcohol and cocaine), and psychosocial stressors, such as the death of a loved one, marital separation, or divorce.[3]

There are three types of *bipolar disorders*—mixed, manic, and depressed. Differentiation of type is based on clinical features of the current or most recent episode. The episode that occasions hospitalization is typically manic, although over time both manic and depressed episodes usually alternate. It is estimated that anywhere from 4 to 12 persons per 1000 (0.4% to 1.2%) in the adult population have experienced this disorder, with equal occurrence among males and females. Furthermore, it is known that bipolar disorder occurs at a much higher rate in first-degree biological relatives of people with the disorder than in the general population.

Cyclothymia is also a chronic mood disturbance of at least two years' duration (one year for children and adolescents) and involves numerous episodes of hypomania alternating with periods of depressed mood or loss of interest. The severity or duration of cyclothymic mood swings, however, is not sufficient for a diagnosis of major depression or bipolar disorder. Although the diagnosis of cyclothymia usually does not warrant hospitalization, some degree of impairment in social or occupational functioning is likely, especially during the hypomanic phase. (A diagnosis of bipolar disorder is made if a manic episode, as opposed to a hypomanic episode, occurs during the first two years of cyclothymia.)

Cyclothymia often begins in adolescence or early adulthood, usually without a clear onset and following chronic course. It is not unusual for a person with cyclothymia to develop a bipolar disorder; in fact, some investigators believe that cyclothymia is a mild form of bipolar disorder. The nature of predisposing factors is unclear, although it is thought that anywhere from 4 to 35 adults in a 1000 (0.4% to 3.5%) experience this disorder at some point in their lives. Like bipolar disorder, cyclothymia occurs equally in males and females. In addition, first-degree biological relatives of persons with the disorder are more likely to exhibit symptoms of major depression or bipolar disorder than people in general.

Major depression is characterized by one or more major depressive episodes without a history of either manic or hypomanic episodes. Major de-

[3]It should be noted that uncomplicated bereavement (a V code in the DSM-III-R) is not considered a mental disorder, even when associated with a full depressive syndrome. Only when symptoms such as morbid preoccupation with worthlessness, suicidal ideation, marked impairment in functioning, or prolonged duration exist is bereavement considered to be indicative of a major depressive episode.

pression is subclassified as being either "single episode" or "recurrent," depending on the past history of the disorder. Although some people experience only one episode of major depression and return to a normal level of premorbid functioning, more than half of the persons who experience their first episode will eventually have another and thus meet the criterion for major depression, recurrent type.

Major depression is one of the most common disorders in the United States and Europe. Estimates of adults experiencing the disorder at some point during their lives range from 9% to 26% for females and from 5% to 12% for males. At any one time it is estimated that 4.5% to 9.3% of female adults and 2.3% to 3.2% of male adults have the disorder. First-degree biological relatives of people with the disorder are 1.5 to 3 times more likely to experience the disorder than are persons among the general population.

For a number of years it was common practice to make a distinction between "endogenous" and "reactive" depression. The former was based on the presence of such symptoms as agitation, insomnia, anorexia, visceral problems, psychomotor retardation, and other vegetative signs. This type of depression was thought to be more responsive to somatic (e.g., pharmacological) treatments and was contrasted with reactive depression, which was thought to be indicative of more externally-oriented problems associated with a person's interpersonal or social role inadequacies. Although the endogenous-reactive terminology does not appear in the DSM-III or DSM-III-R, it is possible to subclassify major depression as being "melancholic type." This distinction is used to suggest that the disorder may be particularly responsive to certain somatic therapies, including tricyclic and MAOI antidepressants, lithium, or electroconvulsive therapy.

The essential feature of *dysthymia* is chronic, depressed mood most of the time for at least two years. Frequently, dysthymia appears to be the consequence of a preexisting, chronic nonmood disorder, such as anorexia nervosa, psychoactive substance dependence disorder, or a chronic physical illness classified on Axis III. When this is the case, the disorder is diagnosed as "secondary" to the preexisting problem. When the mood disturbance is not related to a preexisting nonmood disorder, it is classified "primary." The onset of dysthymia is usually in childhood, adolescence, or early adulthood, and for this reason the disorder is often referred to as depressive personality. Social and/or occupational impairment in persons with dysthymia is usually mild to moderate, but hospitalization is rarely required as a result. Dysthymia is a common disorder that apparently affects females more often than males. It appears to be more common among first-degree biological relatives of people with major depression than among the general population. Frequently, major depression is superimposed on dysthymia and should be recorded as an additional diagnosis. Also, in persons with dysthymia there may be a coexisting personality disorder, such as borderline, histrionic, narcissistic, avoidant, or dependent.

Rosenthal & Klerman, 1966). This *unidimensional* view was essentially Freud's position and is therefore shared by many psychoanalytically-oriented therapists (Mendelson, 1974).

The unidimensional view is contrasted with a *multidimensional* perspective which posits that depression encompasses several different syndromes (Klein, 1974). These disorders are thought to vary along several different dimensions, two of which have received particular attention. The first dimension involves the distinction between depression that presents with depressed mood only (unipolar disorder) and depression that entails manic episodes as well (bipolar disorder). A second dimension deals with depression that appears to be biologically-based (endogenous depression) as opposed to those forms that seem to result from the person's interaction with his or her environment (reactive depression).

The unipolar–bipolar distinction is based on the belief that a biochemical imbalance(s) causes some persons to become depressed and others to exhibit severe shifts in mood that swing between sadness and elation (Perris, 1982). This discrimination was originally proposed by Leonhard (Leonhard, Kroff, & Schultz, 1962) and has been favored by a number of other investigators (e.g., Perris, 1966, 1969; Winokur, Clayton, & Reich, 1969). Although not everyone agrees with the idea (e.g., Gershon, Baron, & Leckman, 1975), evidence from genetic and family studies, metabolic analyses, investigations regarding differential responses to treatment, and clinical observations of the course and prognosis of different states support the distinction (for reviews, see Andreasen, 1982; Depue & Monroe, 1978).

A second distinction has been made between those forms of depression that are thought to follow an autonomous course and those that seem more related to situational factors (Paykel, Prusoff, & Klerman, 1971). The first form, endogenous depression, usually requires hospitalization and is characterized by progressively severe symptoms that are primarily vegetative in nature. This type of depression is thought to be genetically based and to respond positively to somatic therapies, such as antidepressant medications and electroconvulsive therapy (ECT). The second form, reactive depression, is less severe and is characterized by more subjective or cognitive symptoms. Also, reactive depression is thought to be more responsive to psychosocial interventions.

There have been three lines of evidence supporting the endogenous–reactive distinction. For one, factor-analytic studies of depressive symptoms usually generate two factors corresponding to the two types (Carney, Roth, & Garside, 1965; Kiloh & Garside, 1963; Paykel, Klerman, & Prusoff, 1970). Second, studies employing ECT have claimed greater success with endogenous patients than with reactive ones (Carney et al., 1965; Carney & Sheffield, 1972, 1974; Mendels, 1965). And finally, the use of antidepressant medications has supported the distinction by identifying the modal responder—"an endogenous depressive with vegetative signs and a good premorbid personality who is ahedonic and nondelusional and has experienced few previous episodes or none" (Kocsis, 1981, p. 301) (also see Bielski & Friedel, 1976, and Kuhn, 1958).

There have been criticisms of the endogenous–reactive distinction as well. Fowles and Gersh (1979) have noted that factor-analytic studies are based on clinical ratings and therefore bias the results in favor of the dichotomy. Also, factor structures vary across studies and, at best, account for only a modest portion of the variance. In terms of a differential response to treatment, it has been pointed out that ECT is generally used with the more seriously depressed patients who have the potential to demonstrate greater gains than less severely impaired patients whose functioning is closer to normal to start with. And finally, evidence from studies involving antidepressant medication has been questioned after several double-blind investigations found no evidence to support the utility of making a differential diagnosis in terms of endogenous versus reactive depression (e.g., Burt, Gordon, Holt, & Hordern, 1962; Greenblatt, Grosser, & Wechsler, 1964; Hordern, Burt, & Holt, 1965; Paykel, 1972; Raskin & Crook, 1976).

Problems with the endogenous–reactive distinction led Kendell to conclude that "it does not really do justice to the variety and diversity of depressive illness" (1976, p. 19). Furthermore, differentiating between endogenous and reactive depression is often difficult (Akiskal, Bitar, Puzantian, Rosenthal, & Walker, 1978), since the dichotomy appears to represent "a continuum rather than a means of dividing patients into relatively clear-cut groups" (Klerman, 1975, p. 1010). For these reasons, the distinction was de-emphasized in the DSM-III (and subsequently the DSM-III-R) so that endogenous depression survives today only as an optional fifth digit ("with melancholia") in the diagnostic code for major depression. Nevertheless, the distinction retains its usefulness to the degree that it reminds us that many forms of the disorder do not appear to share a common etiology or follow a similar path.

The Reward System of the Brain

It is likely that aspects of both the unidimensional and multidimensional views are correct. There can be no doubt that "depression" is a broad term for a variety of disorders that involve different etiologies, follow a divergent course, and respond differentially to various treatment interventions. However, it is also probably accurate to say that all of these disorders are mediated to some degree by a common mechanism—the reward system of the brain (Akiskal & McKinney, 1973). According to this perspective, "depressive illness, as a final common pathway, is the culmination of various processes that conceivably converge in those areas of the diencephalon that modulate arousal, mood, motivation, and psychomotor function. The specific form that the syndrome will take in a given individual depends on the interaction of several factors" (Akiskal & McKinney, 1975, p. 290). Some of these factors include genetic vulnerability, developmental events, social support, physiological stressors, and personality characteristics.

The reward system is composed of neural structures located in the medial forebrain bundle and periventricular areas of the central nervous system (CNS). These nuclei are innervated by noradrenergic and dopaminergic fibers that provide numerous connections with the arousal system in the reticular formation of the brain stem (Akiskal & McKinney, 1975). There are also pathways to both the psychomotor system (pyramidal and extrapyramidal tracts) and the stress-neuroendocrine system (particularly the hypothalamic-pituitary-adrenal axis). Given the interconnection of these different systems, impairment or dysfunction in one can result in functional shifts of the other systems as well. This explains how a disruption of normal functioning in the reward system can result in a range of diverse effects involving arousal, endocrine function, and psychomotor activity.

There are many factors that are thought to affect the reward system of the brain (Willner, 1985). Some of these operate over long periods of time, while others consist of events that immediately precede a depressive or manic episode. The latter include stressful life events, particularly those that deal with personal loss, separation, or adversity (Fava, Munari, Pavan, & Kellner, 1981; Lloyd, 1980; Paykel et al., 1969). Immediate precipitants of depression, however, are rarely sufficient by themselves to explain why people get depressed. For example, the incidence of clinical depression following conjugal bereavement is only 5%, with less than 1% resulting in hospitalization (Clayton, 1979; Parkes, 1972). In fact, many if not most episodes of depression occur in the absence of stressful life events entirely (Lloyd, 1980).

These observations highlight the importance of long-term or predisposing factors (Akiskal & Tashjian, 1983). Significant among these factors are such conditions as prolonged unemployment, financial difficulty, and family/marital problems (Aneshensel & Stone, 1982; Jahoda,

1979). Brown and Harris (1978) found that the major predictors of depression for working class women in London were being unemployed and having three children living at home. Mildly stressful events are also important because of their ability to sensitize the brain to subsequent presentations of the stressor (Anisman & Zacharko, 1982). In this regard, it has been observed that 40% of mildly depressed patients develop a severe depressive episode within 3 to 4 years (Akiskal et al., 1978).

The presence or absence of social support in conjunction with other factors is also an important predictor of depression. Aneshensel and Stone (1982) found that in their large community sample the group that had good social support, no recent loss events, and a low level of "strain" experienced the lowest rate (less than 2%) of depression. This was compared to a second group with poor social support, two or more recent loss events, and a high level of strain, who exhibited an incidence rate of almost 50%. Brown and Harris (1978) found that only 1% of women who had good social support exhibited symptoms of depression as compared to 100% of women suffering from a high level of strain who did not have access to intimate, confiding relationships and who had suffered early maternal loss.

Although often occurring together, stress and the lack of social support are thought to exert different effects on the reward system of the brain (Willner, 1985). This hypothesis is based on the observation that rewards operate in two ways—as incentives and as satisfiers. *Incentives* induce behavior by informing a person that he or she is approaching a goal (Bindra, 1978). Consequently, engaging in a sequence of behaviors that leads to the attainment or consumption of some reward may be as rewarding as the goal itself. On the other hand, rewards also function as *satisfiers* (e.g., the pleasurable feelings that follow a good meal) and thus exert their influence at the point of attainment or consumption. Satisfiers are thought to result from activities that maximize chances of survival and include such activities as those related to feeding, reproduction, security, and affiliation (cf. Meddis, 1977).

Willner (1985) has proposed that the incentive and satisfaction functions of reward provide a basis for distinguishing between endogenous and reactive types of depression. He argues that the former results from the development of a biological insensitivity to reward, which leads to a loss of incentive and therefore a reduction of performance behaviors. Prolonged or uncontrollable stress may be particularly important in this regard since it appears to cause biochemical changes that reduce the ability of pleasurable stimuli to activate the reward centers. Reactive depression, on the other hand, is said to involve the absence or removal of the rewards themselves, particularly those associated with social or interpersonal needs. Consequently, prolonged stress may be of particular etiological significance in the development of the endogenous form of the disorder while the lack of social support may result in a more reactive type. The distinction is of some interest because it explains why, in the case of endogenous depression, the provision of tangible rewards or social support appears to have little effect. In addition, Willner's proposal suggests why somatic interventions for reactive depression may be ineffective if they fail to take into account the person's interpersonal environment.

Physiological Factors

All persons are not equally at risk for developing a mood disorder. It appears that certain individuals inherit a vulnerability to these disorders and are thus unusually susceptible to the effects of environmental stress or the lack of social support (cf. Fulker, 1981). This may be particularly true of persons who later develop symptoms of endogenous depression (Akiskal, 1983). (See Panel 5.2, "Heritability of Mood Disorders.")

According to Eysenck's model, the prototype of the endogenously depressed person is the introvert who is emotionally unstable (i.e., neurotic) (Eysenck, 1967). A critical review of the area by Akiskal, Hirschfeld, and Yerevanian (1983) concluded that of all of the personality characteristics believed to be related to depression, introversion has generated the strongest support. Anxiety-prone personality characteristics have also been linked to depression. Gray (1982) noted that many of the symptoms that define so-called "neurotic" depression (e.g., obsessional thoughts, irritability, restlessness, and difficulty falling asleep) are also those that describe the anxious temperament.

Secondary Depression

There is considerable overlap between anxiety and depression. It is estimated that anywhere from one-third to one-half of patients with symptoms of panic disorder, generalized anxiety disorder, agoraphobia, or obsessive-compulsive disorder also experience major depression (Grunhaus & Birmaher, 1985; Sheehan, 1982). On the other hand, as many as 10% to 20% of individuals with clear-cut depressive episodes also experience panic attacks (Grunhaus & Birmaher, 1985).

In most cases, separating the two diagnostic groups is difficult, and

PANEL 5.2

Heritability of the Mood Disorders

Contributed by Martha Cain

As early as 1921, Kraepelin observed that mood disorders run in families (Kraepelin, 1921). He described a circular form of insanity, classified as "manic-depressive insanity" (now referred to as bipolar disorder), and estimated that heredity factors were involved in 80% of the cases he treated. Since Kraepelin's observation, it has been established that the prevalence of bipolar disorder is much higher in first-degree biological relatives of people with the disorder than in the general population. Although less than one person in a hundred (0.7%) will experience a bipolar disorder during his or her lifetime, the prevalence of the disorder increases 10 times for first-degree biological relatives of persons with a manic-depressive disorder (7.6% for parents and 8.8% for siblings) (Rosenthal, 1970). Furthermore, it has been estimated that approximately 11% of children of manic-depressives become manic-depressive themselves.

There is also evidence that unipolar disorder has a genetic basis. The morbidity risk of developing a major depression for first-degree biological relatives of persons with unipolar disorder is 28%, compared to 9% for the population in general (Cadoret & Winokur, 1975a). Concordance rates for mood disorders among twins also suggest the importance of genetic factors. As many as 70% of monozygotic twins exhibit comparable symptoms of a mood disorder, compared to 19% for dizygotic pairs (Gershon, Denner, & Goodwin, 1975)

Heritability may play a role in determining whether a mood disorder will present with both manic and depressive episodes (bipolar disorder) or with depression only (unipolar disorder) (Dunner, Greshon, & Goodwin, 1976; Gershon, Bunney, Leckman, Van Eerdewegh, & DeBauche, 1976; Hay, 1985). However, this relationship is far from straightforward. Although family pedigrees of bipolar patients reveal a higher frequency of mood disorders among their relatives than do the pedigrees of unipolar patients, these disorders do not always "breed true" since the relatives of bipolar patients are more likely to exhibit symptoms of a unipolar rather than bipolar disorder (Helzer & Winokur, 1974; James & Chapman, 1975; Perris, 1966; Winokur, Clayton, & Reich, 1969). Mendlewicz and Rainer (1977) also found that the biological parents of a person who was adopted and later developed symptoms of a bipolar disorder were more likely to have a mood disorder as well, but not necessarily a bipolar one. Consequently, they proposed that a bipolar disorder reflects a more severe genetic and/or environmental load than major depression.

Two different modes of transmission for mood disorders have been suggested. The first of these is a form of X-linked, dominant gene inheritance (Cadoret & Winokur, 1975b), although this may occur for the bipolar but not unipolar type (Mendlewicz & Fleiss, 1974). Since it is rare for both fathers and sons to exhibit a bipolar disorder, locus on the X chromosome has been suspected. Also, the high incidence in females, especially those related to manic-depressive probands, suggests an X-linked dominant allele (Hay, 1985). An X-linked locus of the gene on the X-chromosome would allow a depressive disorder to be transmitted to female offspring by either or both parents, but to males only by the mother. Theoretically, father-to-son inheritance of the trait should not occur. Controversy on this issue exists, however, especially regarding reported discoveries of father-to-son transmission of bipolar disorders (Hays, 1976; James & Chapman, 1975; Loranger, 1975).

Other areas of research on the X-linked dominant gene theory have suggested linkage between bipolar disorders and the loci for the Xg blood system (Mendlewicz & Fleiss, 1974) as well as for color blindness (Mendlewicz, Fleiss, & Fieve, 1972; Reich, Clayton, & Winokur, 1969). However, after an extensive review of the literature, Gershon et al. (1976) concluded that chromosomal linkage does not occur between bipolar disorder and color blindness, but that what does occur is that color blind individuals simply have a higher incidence of mood disorder than the general population. The hypothesis that bipolar illness is inherited as an X-linked dominant trait, closely linked spatially with the Xg locus, is thus not supported. This failure, however, does not disprove a single-major-locus etiology for bipolar illness (Stone, 1980), and it is currently held that the X-linked mode of transmission may occur in a minority of bipolar families (Dunner, Fleiss, Addonizio, & Fieve, 1976; Gershon, Dunner, Sturt, & Goodwin, 1973).

In a more recent study of a genetically isolated population, the Old Order of Amish of Pennsylvania, a gene that may predispose a person to bipolar illness was isolated on chromosome 11. Relatives who resembled one another in terms of manic-depressive symptomatology also resembled one another with regard to certain genes known to be located on chromosome 11 (Egeland et al., 1987). However, two other studies using non-Amish pedigrees did not find bipolar linkage to chromosome 11 (Detera-Wadleigh et al., 1987; Hodgkinson et al., 1987).

Unipolar disorders, on the other hand, are thought to be manifestations of polygenic rather than major-single-locus abnormalities (Baker, Dorzab, Winokur, & Cadoret, 1972). Polygenic inheritance involves the summation of many different genes, normally distributed in the population, which contribute to the phenotypic expression of a trait. The mode of transmission, which is based on a computational model developed by Slater (1966), implies that a large contribution to the onset of a disorder may be accounted for by environmental factors and personality variables (Depue & Monroe, 1979).

Both bipolar and unipolar mood disorders are thought to be affected by environmental factors, although to a different degree. This possibility was emphasized in early work by Scandinavian researchers who associated unfavorable environments with the onset of overt manic-depressive psychosis and suggested that differences between the various mood disorders were the result of the interaction of genetic, constitutional, social, clinical, and neurophysiological factors (Perris, 1966; Stenstedt, 1952). This conclusion is consistent with the proposal of a "multiple threshold" model of transmission provided by Gershon, Baron, and Leckman (1975). This model suggests that susceptibility to a particular disorder is determined by a combination of genetic and independent factors which create a "net liability" that manifests as the disorder when it crosses a particular threshold. Greater liability is seen as being expressed as a bipolar disorder.

Differences in the relative strength of the genetic versus environmental factors in various individuals are postulated to account for proportionate differences in severity of the disorder. Thus, depending on the particular genetic-environment interactions, individuals who began life as more predisposed on the basis of inheriting more risk genes would manifest a disorder when environmental factors accumulated, while other persons would not (Stone, 1980, p. 156). In addition to heterogeneity rising from genetic differences, the degree of clinical variability among the mood disorders is influenced by heterogeneity stemming from psychosocial and environmental differences. Thus, while heredity appears to account for much of the variance in etiology of bipolar and unipolar disorders, the psychosocial factors of the disorder are believed to facilitate and significantly influence its actual development and expression (Kety, 1979; Schulsinger, Kety, Rosenthal, & Wender, 1979).

Another aspect of the mood disorders that is thought to be influenced by both genetic and environmental factors is age of onset (Cadoret & Winokur, 1975b). For example, the possibility of genetic heterogeneity in unipolar disorders has been suggested on the basis of early and late onset groups (Cadoret & Winokur, 1975b; Perris, 1966). The greater discordance for unipolar monozygotic twins suggests that environmental factors play a crucial role in the onset and phenotypic expression of this disorder. Bipolar conditions, which usually exhibit an earlier onset, are thought to involve a larger complement of genetic vulnerability and are thus considered to be the severest form of a mood disorder (for a review, see Allen, 1976).

A polygenetic mode of transmission appears to be most consistent with the unipolar data, while there is strong support for X-linked dominant transmission for the bipolar disorders. Perhaps the best summation of the studies is that in the mood disorders the frequency of expression of bipolar and unipolar disorders varies significantly between comparable populations, between generations, and between geographic regions in the same population (Gershon, 1982). However, no genetic transmission model applies to all populations studied.

all that can be said is that the two disorders occur together with some frequency. For example, one study reported that depressive episodes occurred in 44% of patients with anxiety disorders followed for 6 years in a hospital clinic (Noyes, Clancy, Hoenk, & Slymen, 1980), while another study found depression in two-thirds (66%) of patients followed over a 5- to 12-year period (Cloninger, Martin, Clayton, & Guze, 1981). Also, a quarter of the 25 obsessional patients followed by Capstick and Seldrup (1973) had a diagnosis of depression that either preceded or followed the obsessional state. In one group of patients with agoraphobia and/or panic disorder, 68% had a past or current episode of major depression, of which 85% were termed endogenous (Breier, Charney, & Heninger, 1984). In addition, since antidepressant drugs have some utility in treating panic disorder, agoraphobia, and obsessive-compulsive disorder (Grunhaus & Brimaher, 1985; Klein, Gittelman, Quitkin, & Rifkin, 1980), the distinction between depression and anxiety is blurred further. Consequently, structured interviews like the Anxiety Disorders Interview Schedule (Di Nardo, O'Brien, Barlow, Waddell, & Blanchard, 1983) and Schedule for Affective Disorders and Schizophrenia (Endicott & Spitzer, 1978) may be particularly helpful in sorting out which disorder predominates.

There are also a number of medical conditions that result in secondary depression (see Table 5.1). Most of the organic syndromes reflect actual damage to the brain. For example, dementia may present with depressive features but is distinguishable from the mood disorders because of the presence of memory and cognitive impairment (Blazer, 1983). It should be noted, however, that depression may also cause cognitive deterioration so severe that a diagnosis of dementia is inappropriately made, creating a condition known as pseudodementia (Haggerty, Golden, Evans, & Janowsky, 1988; Wells, 1979). In addition, lesions in the brain resulting from neoplasm, stroke, or infection may cause expansive or uninhibited behavior that is difficult to distinguish from mania, especially if the damage is located in the frontal lobes (Ashton, 1987). Various endocrine disorders may also affect changes in mood. Grave's disease (hyperthyroidism), Addison's disease,[2] hyper-

[2]Addison's disease results from the failure of the adrenal cortices to produce adrenocortical hormones, primarily aldosterone and cortisol. Lack of the former greatly reduces the reabsorption of sodium in the kidneys so that excessive amounts of sodium ions, chloride ions, and water are lost in the urine. This causes dehydration and acidosis, which generally depresses CNS activity. The loss of cortisol makes it impossible for the individual to maintain a normal blood glucose concentration between meals or to convert glucose stores into usable energy. This results in a generalized suppression of many other metabolic functions of the body.

Table 5.1.   Medical Conditions Associated with
Organic Mood Disorders

Endocrine causes	Collagen disorders
Acromegaly	Systemic lupus erythematosus
Hypoadrenalism	Polyarteritis nodosa
Hyperparathyroidism	
Hypoparathyroidism	Cardiovascular disease
Hypopituitarism	Cardiomyopathy
Hyperthyroidism	Congestive heart failure
Hypothyroidism	Myocardial infarction
Vitamin and mineral disorders	Infections
Beri-beri (vitamin B1 deficiency)	Encephalitis
Hypervitaminosis A	Hepatitis
Hypomagnesemia	Influenza
Pellagra	Malaria
(nicotinic acid deficiency)	Mononucleosis
Pernicious anemia	Pneumonia
(vitamin B12 deficiency)	Syphilis
Wernicke's encephalopathy	Tuberculosis
Neurological disorders	Malignancy
Dementia, Alzheimer's type	Carcinoid
Huntington's disease	Pancreatic carcinoma
Multiple sclerosis	Pheochromocytoma
Stroke	
Tuberous sclerosis	Metabolic
Wilson's disease	Porphyria
	Intoxication states

Note. From M. E. Thase (1987), Affective Disorders, in R. L. Morrison and A. S. Bellack (Eds.), *Medical Factors and Psychological Disorders: A Handbook for Psychologists*, p. 89. Copyright © 1987 by Plenum Publishing Corporation. Reprinted by permission.

parathyroidism, acromegaly, and hypopituitarism are all associated with depression. Finally, the presence of a slow-acting neurotropic virus has been suspected in some cases of depression (Amsterdam et al., 1985). In terms of making a differential diagnosis, sleep patterns, particularly the length of time asleep until the first rapid-eye-movement period (REM latency), may provide a reliable psychophysiological marker to differentiate between primary and these forms of secondary depression (Coble, Foster, & Kupfer, 1976).

Drugs, some of which are listed in Table 5.2, can also cause depression (McClelland, 1986; Tyrer, 1981). Several antihypertensive medications, for example, may induce depressive states by their interference with the release and storage of monoamines in the brain. Reserpine,

Table 5.2. Medications Associated with Organic Mood Disorders

Type names	Generic names	Selected trade
Antihypertensive	Reserpine	Serpasil, Sandril
	Methyldopa	Aldomet
	Propranolol hydrochloride	Inderal
	Guanethidine sulfate	Ismelin sulfate
	Hydralazine hydrochloride	Apresoline hydrochloride
	Clonidine hydrochloride	Catapres
Antiparkinsonian	Levodopa	Dopar, Larodopa
	Levodopa, carbidopa	Sinemet
	Amantadine hydrochloride	Symmetrel
Hormones	Estrogen	Estrace, Menrium, Premarin
	Progesterone	Progestasert
Corticosteroid	Cortisone acetate	Cortone acetate
Antituberculosis	Cyloserine	Seromycin
Anticancer	Vincristine sulfate	Oncovin
	Vinblastine sulfate	Velban
Antiulcer	Cimetidine	Tagamet

which depletes stores of monoamine at the nerve terminals, can cause depression so severe that suicide is a realistic possibility (Ashton, 1987). Also, any of the CNS depressants, including alcohol, barbiturates, narcotics, and anticonvulsants, can cause depression.

Physiological Symptoms of Depression and Mania

There are a variety of symptoms said to be indicative of either a depressive or a manic episode. For example, a depressed person may experience feelings that range from sadness, hopelessness, and despair on one end of a continuum to anxiety, fear, agitation, irritability, and even specific phobias on the other. Depressive behaviors may also exhibit a wide range of characteristics, from motor retardation and slowed speech to agitation and hand-wringing. Other symptoms of depression include decreased autonomic responsivity, a loss of appetite, fatigue, and a loss of interest in sexual activity. Mania, like depression, is characterized by a variety of symptoms. These may range from elevation of mood, hyperactivity, and self-important ideas to irritability, anger, and brief periods of depression. In short, the physiological symptoms of depression and mania vary widely and reflect physiological activity in three areas—the central nervous system, the endocrine system, and the peripheral nervous system.

Central Symptoms. In terms of the CNS functioning, one of the most common symptoms of depression is the disruption of sleep. Electroencephalographic (EEG) studies on sleep patterns have generated relatively consistent findings that differentiate depressed from normal individuals or even depressed persons from insomnia sufferers (Gillin, Duncan, Pettigrew, Frankel, & Snyder, 1979). The usual pattern of sleep for the depressed individual involves less total sleep, longer latency before sleep, more early morning awakenings, more intermittent time awake during the night, less delta sleep, less sleep efficiency, and shorter REM latency than normal subjects. In fact, REM latency is inversely correlated ($r = -.57$) with the severity of depression (Kupfer & Foster, 1972). Consequently, it is often said that sleep for the depressed person is fragmented and shallow. However, this pattern is not inevitably the case. Some depressed patients may exhibit excessive sleep, increased eating, and considerable weight gain rather than the usual disruption of sleep and the associated loss of appetite and weight (Ashton, 1987).

Studies of waking EEG in patients with mood disorders have generated less consistent results (Ashton, 1987). Alpha activity does not appear to separate manic or depressed subjects from normal ones, but beta activity has been found to be increased in both depression and mania. The lateralization of EEG activity, on the other hand, appears to differentiate between depressed patients with high and low anxiety (Perris, 1980).

The literature on somatosensory evoked potentials (EPs) suggests a decreased amplitude and prolonged latency for individuals who are depressed. Interestingly, this diminished responsivity disappears with recovery (Shagass, Ornitz, Sutton, & Tueting, 1978). However, EPs may be dependent on stimulus intensity (Buchsbaum, 1979). Buchsbaum, Goodwin, Murphy, and Borge (1971) measured EPs using four intensities of light for two groups of patients, one with a history of only depression (unipolar) and the other with a history of both manic and depressive episodes (bipolar). The bipolar patients evidenced relatively greater increase in EP amplitude with increasing stimulus intensities (augmentation) than their unipolar counterparts. Unipolar patients, on the other hand, were found to be reducers (i.e., they exhibited reductions in amplitude with increasing intensity).

Finally, cerebral blood flow has been recorded in depressed patients using the xenon-133 inhalation technique (Mathew et al., 1980). Greatly reduced values for gray-matter blood flow was found when 13 patients were compared to age-matched controls. Furthermore, there was a significant inverse correlation between depression and the reduction of blood flow to both hemispheres (rs of −.63 and −.62 for the left and right hemispheres, respectively). Despite the absence of interhemispheric differences, the decrease in blood flow was most marked in the frontal regions. These findings would suggest that there is a reduction in neuronal metabolism in depression consistent with decreased mean integrated EEG amplitude, decreased amplitude of cortical evoked responses, slowed psychomotor responses, and cognitive dysfunction (Weckowicz, Yonge, Cropley, & Muir, 1971). In addition, it has been suggested that the cerebral vasodilation that results following electroconvulsive therapy (ECT) may be responsible for some of its antidepressant effects.

Endocrine Symptoms. Several diseases affecting the endocrine glands (e.g. hyper- and hypothyroidism) are well-known causes of altered mood states. In addition, depression has been linked in women to fluctuations in sex hormones just prior to menstruation or after giving birth (Abramowitz, Baker, & Fleischer, 1982; Hopkins, Marcus, & Campbell, 1984). Consequently, it is thought that the endocrine system may be helpful in diagnosing and understanding the mood disorders (Depue, Kleinman, Davis, Hutchinson, & Krauss, 1985; Skutsch, 1985).

> The logic of this new strategy can be summarized very succinctly. Neuroendocrine function is regulated by the limbic system and hypothalamus of the brain. These same areas of the brain are thought to be the site of primary pathology in the affective disorders. Since direct, invasive studies of the limbic system in human patients are not feasible, the study of neuroendocrine function can be used to obtain indirect knowledge about it. In principle this strategy could reveal specific disturbances of limbic-neuroendocrine function in patients with endogenous depression. (Carroll, 1982, p. 292)

Two endocrine systems have been studied extensively in this regard. The first of these, the hypothalamic-pituitary-adrenal cortex (HPAC) system, responds to a variety of psychological and physical stressors. In depression, it is common to find elevated plasma concentrations of cortisol, increased urinary excretion of cortisol and its metabolites, blunted circadian rhythm, and possible elevations of adrenocorticotropin hormone (Carroll, 1982; Sachar, 1982; Thase, Frank, & Kupfer, 1985).

Another effect of depression on the functioning of the HPAC system is the inhibition of negative feedback, which has been related to hyperactivity of the central cholinergic systems (Carroll, 1982). This can be demonstrated by the dexamethasone suppression test (DST). Dexamethasone is a potent, synthetic corticosteroid. A bedtime dose of 1.0 to 2.0 mg normally shuts down HPAC activity for 24 hours. In a significant number of depressed patients plasma cortisol levels either remain high or escape the initial suppression before the 24-hour period is over.

Carroll (1982) has reported that this test identifies melancholic (i.e., endogenous) depression with 67% sensitivity (i.e., the ability to discriminate among depressed patients with abnormal results) and 95% specificity (i.e., the ability to discriminate among nondepressed patients with normal results). However, other investigators have found sensitivity rates that range from 15% to 30% (see Thase et al., 1985) and false-positives that exceed 30% (Meltzer, Fang, Tricou, Roberston, & Piyaka, 1982; Stokes et al., 1984). Some of these differences may be due to variations in diagnostic criteria, recent weight loss, drug or alcohol abuse, medications (e.g., certain antihypertensives and contraceptives), the presence of some other intercurrent medical condition (including relatively minor allergic and respiratory conditions), or even the lack of biometric reliability between centers administering the test (Carroll, 1982; Stokes et al., 1984). In addition, there is the question of whether DST abnormalities indicate HPAC hyperactivity or some other physiological abnormality, such as of the pituitary gland. Nevertheless, the DST appears to be a reasonably good marker for depression and may actually signal therapeutic improvement by normalizing several days or even weeks before other indications of recovery (Carroll, 1982). Interestingly, most patients who exhibit DST nonsuppression also have shortened REM latency (Thase et al., 1985).

Functioning of the pituitary-thyroid system is also frequently disturbed in depression (Lipton, Breese, Prange, Wilson, & Cooper, 1976). This possibility was suggested by evidence that a small number of depressed patients have an organic disorder caused by hypothyroidism and a large number of manic and depressed persons show transiently elevated thyroid hormone levels which may be related to monoaminergic stimulation of beta-adrenergic receptor sites (Whybrow & Prange, 1981). This system can be tested by injecting thyrotropin-releasing hormone (TRH), which stimulates the release of thyroid-stimulating hormone (TSH) from the pituitary. In normal individuals the administration of TRH produces an exaggerated release of TSH (Gold & Pottash, 1983). However, a significant minority of depressed individuals (e.g., 25%–40%) exhibit a blunted response (Kirkegaard, 1981; Targum, 1983).

Since there is little overlap between the results of DST and TRH tests (Rush et al., 1983), the two endocrine abnormalities do not appear to be caused by the same mechanism. However, most depressed individuals who exhibit a blunted TRH response also have shortened REM latency, although attempts to relate this finding to neurochemical studies have yielded conflicting results (see Thase et al., 1985).

Peripheral Symptoms. Psychophysiological measures of peripheral symptoms have included cardiovascular responses, salivation, sweat-gland, and electromyographic (EMG) activity (Lader, 1983). Salivation and sweat-gland activity may be reduced in severe depression and return to normal on recovery (Dawson, Schell, & Catania, 1977; Palmai, Blackwell, Maxwell, & Morganstern, 1967). However, both of these measures, as well as cardiovascular changes in particular, may reflect the degree of agitation or anxiety present in depression and thus may be increased rather than decreased (Craighead, Kennedy, Raczynski, & Dow, 1984; Dawson et al., 1977; Friedman & Bennet, 1977; Lader & Wing, 1969; Noble & Lader, 1971a, 1971b).

The situation in regard to electromyographic (EMG) activity, on the other hand, is less clear. Initially, it was thought that depressed persons exhibited increased levels of EMG activity (Rimón, Sternbäck, & Huhmar, 1966) thus producing a state of hyperponesis (i.e., exaggerated activity within the motor portion of the nervous system) that was thought to be related to the development of neuronal fatigue characteristic of the disorder (Whatmore, 1966). However, the finding of increased EMG among depressed patients is either inconsistent (Goldstein, 1965) or lacking (Shipman, Oken, Goldstein, Grinker, & Heath, 1964). It may be that an increase in generalized muscular tension is characteristic of psychiatric patients in general but not of depressed patients in particular (Pétursson, 1962).

Another aspect of EMG activity in depression has focused on the differences in facial muscle activity between nonhospitalized depressed patients and nondepressed normals during emotional imagery (Schwartz, Fair, Salt, Mandel, & Klerman, 1976a, 1976b). The idea is that EMG activity is related to smiling (as opposed to frowning) and thus provides a direct psychophysiological measure of mood (Schwartz et al., 1978). Nevertheless, at least one other investigation failed to find differences in levels of EMG activity between depressed and nondepressed patients who were hospitalized (Oliveau & Willmuth, 1979).

Summary of Physiological Symptoms. In summary, it can be said that physiological measures of the mood disorders are congruent with the array of symptoms originating from both the cognitive and behavioral assessment modes. Central measures suggest a shallow and fragmented pattern of sleep, which would be expected to contribute to feelings of fatigue and inability to think or concentrate. Depressed individuals also display a tendency to "reduce" sensory stimuli, while manic ones "augment." Furthermore, evidence of reduced cerebral metabolism in depression is in keeping with impaired cognitive ability, slowed speech, and even hopelessness and despair. The endocrine measures, on the other hand, suggest a strong relationship between the mood disorders and stress, a factor of some importance as noted earlier. And finally, an important diagnostic consideration is that peripheral indices of depression may be related to the presence of anxiety, fear, or agitation.

Physiological Mechanisms

When considering physiological aspects of the mood disorders, there are several cautions to keep in mind (Thase, 1987, p. 71). First, if one accepts the multidimensional nature of these disorders, there is no reason to expect that a single biological disturbance underlies all of the mood disorders. Second, since studies in the area normally present grouped data, it is possible that evidence for biological subtypes has been obscured (Buchsbaum & Rieder, 1979). Third, it should be expected that some individuals (particularly those who present with only a single episode of nonmelancholic major depression) may show little evidence of any biological dysfunction at all. Fourth, even if a physiological abnormality is detected, it does not indicate biologic causality. Many symptoms, such as disruptions of sleep, diminished activity level, and weight loss, may reflect the rigors of hospitalization, the effects of medication, or some other aspect of the clinical state itself. And finally, biological markers may be transient (i.e., apparent during periods of acute symptomatology only). Consequently, studies that do not track these disorders over a period of time may produce either misleading or insignificant results.

The Monoamine Hypothesis. The predominant biochemical models of depression today are referred to collectively as the *monoamine hypothesis*. This theory posits that disturbances in the catecholamines, norepinephrine and dopamine, and the indoleamine, serotonin, are responsible for both depressive as well as manic episodes (Bunney & Davis, 1965; Glassman, 1969; Schildkraut, 1965). It is known that these monoamines are important neurotransmitters in the regulation of sleep, appetite, and emotional processes and that many antidepressants produce increased levels of the monoamines in the neuronal synapses.

Therefore, it has been predicted that depression is associated with decreased monoamine activity resulting from either a reduced synthesis, increased degradation, or altered synaptic function, and that mania may involve increases in monoaminergic activity.

After 20 years of research on the monoamine hypothesis, the results are still equivocal (Zis & Goodwin, 1982). The most widely studied index of norepinephrine activity is its key metabolite, MHPG (3-methoxy-4-hydroxy-phenylglycol). Some depressed patients do demonstrate reduced levels of urinary MHPG excretion over a 24-hour period (Deleon-Jones, Maas, Dekirmenjian, & Sanchez, 1975; Schildkraut, 1982; Thase et al., 1985). It is also of interest to note that MHPG levels in the bipolar patient are low during depressive and elevated during manic episodes. However, a number of questions regarding the reliability and validity of MHPG as a marker for depression remain (Baldessarini, 1985; Kelwala, Jones, & Sitaram, 1983). For example, other lines of investigation have failed to reveal definite evidence of either a norepinephrine deficiency in major depression or an excess in mania (Zis & Goodwin, 1982).

The evidence for a disturbance of dopaminergic function in the mood disorders is also unclear (Thase et al., 1985), with the possible exception of psychotic depression, during which increased levels of a dopamine metabolite (homovanillic acid) and decreased dopaminergic enzyme (dopamine beta-hydroxylase) have been reported (Meltzer, Cho, Carroll, & Russo, 1976). The role of serotonin is not well understood either. Although an effort has been made to categorize depressed patients in terms of serotonin's principal metabolite (5-hydroxyindole-acetic acid) (see van Praag, 1980), the usefulness of this procedure has been questioned (Koslow et al., 1983).

More recently, the monoamine hypothesis has been modified by expanding it to include another neurotransmitter, acetylcholine. Since it is known that cholinergic agents do have profound effects on mood, EEG sleep, and neuroendocrine function (Sitaram, Nurnberger, Gershon, & Gillin, 1982), it has been suggested that the problem in depression and mania is an imbalance between the monoamines and acetylcholine (Janowsky, Risch, & Gillin, 1983).

An appealing aspect of this hypothesis is its ability to relate depressive symptomatology to alterations in REM sleep. REM activity is regulated by the interaction of two REM-inhibiting centers (the locus ceruleus and raphé nuclei) and the pontine reticular formation, which stimulates REM sleep (Hobson, McCarley, & Wyzinski, 1975; McCarley & Hobson, 1975) (see Figure 5.1). Acetylcholine activates the pontine reticular formation, which means that increased concentrations of this neurotransmitter will promote REM sleep and suppress activity in the

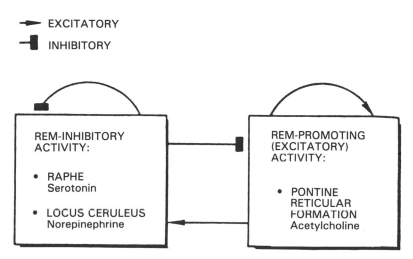

➤ EXCITATORY

⊣ INHIBITORY

Figure 5.1. Reciprocal interaction model of sleep control. In waking, locus ceruleus (using the neurotransmitter norepinephrine) and dorsal raphé neurons (using the neurotransmitter serotonin) inhibit the population of pontine reticular neurons. Over the course of the sleep cycle, these inhibitory monoamine influences diminish because of negative (inhibitory) feedback; when pontine reticular formation neurons are released from inhibition, they become active and, using acetylcholine, generate the events of REM sleep. (From R. E. McCarley [1982], REM Sleep and Depression: Common Neurobiological Control Mechanisms, *American Journal of Psychiatry, 139*, p. 566. Copyright © 1987 by American Psychiatric Association. Reprinted by permission.)

locus ceruleus and raphé nuclei. In addition, cholinergic agonists have been found to induce depressive symptoms in both normal and depressed subjects (Janowsky, El-Yousef, Davis, & Sekerke, 1972; Janowsky, Risch, Parker, Huey, & Judd, 1980; Risch, Cohen, Janowsky, Kalin, & Murphy, 1980). Consequently, an imbalance favoring acetylcholine over the monoamines norepinephrine and serotonin might result in both depressive symptoms and increased REM activity (e.g., reduced REM latency). Restoration of the balance should, in turn, lessen depression and return REM activity to normal.

This model is not without problems, however. One is the failure of agents with purely anticholinergic properties to exert an antidepressant effect. Nevertheless, the emphasis on neurotransmitter *balance* rather than excess or deficiency is consistent with explanations as to how antidepressant medications work, as will be discussed in the next section. Furthermore, a model that implicates more than one neurotransmitter allows for the possibility that there are several subtypes of depression rather than a single, uniform state. For example, one type may be related to monoaminergic dysfunction (Maas, 1975; Schildkraut & Kety, 1967), while another may involve impaired functioning of acetylcholine-related systems (Janowsky et al., 1972). Yet other forms of the disorder might involve a combination of the two.

Monoamine Receptor Changes. Receptors for the monoamines are dynamic structures that change in response to variations in agonist supply. Decreased levels of these neurotransmitters will result in a compensatory increase in activity while increased levels will result in decreased activity. In other words, these receptors adapt to variations in neurotransmitter concentration in an attempt to maintain the previous level of activity.

This is accomplished in two ways. In the short run, changes in agonist supply stimulate one of the two different types of presynaptic receptors (Langer, 1977, 1980). These "autoreceptors" are located on the axon and dendrites of the presynaptic neuron (see Figure 5.2). Presynaptic alpha receptors, alpha$_2$, exercise negative feedback, while presynaptic beta receptors exert positive feedback. Consequently, when

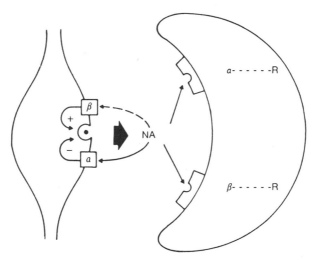

Figure 5.2. Presynaptic and postsynaptic receptors for noradrenalin (NA). Presynaptic alpha receptors mediate a negative feedback system for noradrenalin release under most physiological conditions; presynaptic beta receptors mediate a positive feedback system for noradrenalin release when the concentration of neurotransmitter in the synaptic cleft is low. Alpha and beta postsynaptic receptors mediate different responses to adrenergic stimulation (e.g., vasoconstriction and vasodilation of blood vessels, respectively). (From H. Ashton [1987], *Brain Systems Disorders and Psychotropic Drugs*, p. 309. Oxford: Oxford University Press. Copyright © 1987 by Heather Ashton. Reprinted by permission.)

levels of norepinephrine are low, presynaptic beta receptors stimulate further release of the neurotransmitter. When the concentration of norepinephrine is high, alpha$_2$ receptors dampen this activity. Binding studies have shown that the alpha$_2$ receptors for depressed persons exhibit greater than normal sensitivity (Garcia-Sevilla, Guimón, Garcia-Vallejo, & Fuster, 1986).

Over the long run, the actual number of both pre- and postsynaptic receptor sites will increase or decrease depending on the level of neurotransmitter available. An oversupply will decrease the number (i.e., density) of receptor sites while a deficiency will have the opposite effect. This process may provide a mechanism by which antidepressant medications exert their therapeutic effect. It is known, for example, that the clinical effects of the antidepressants take from 3 to 6 weeks to emerge (Baldessarini, 1985) and that although their initial effect in terms of enhancing transmitter action is almost immediate, tonic changes in both pre- and postsynaptic receptor sensitivity correspond more closely with the clinical response (Charney, Menkes, & Heninger, 1981b). Also, it should be noted that cocaine and amphetamine, which are both immediate and potent simulators of monoaminergic activity, are without antidepressant effects.

In this regard, the chronic administration of certain antidepressants has been shown to result in a decrease in the density of alpha$_2$ receptors, which lessens negative feedback and thus increases the amount of norepinephrine released (Charney et al., 1981b). Although this mode of action is compatible with the monoamine hypothesis, the ability to down-regulate alpha$_2$ receptors is not shared by all antidepressant agents, which suggests that an additional mechanism(s) may be involved (Charney et al., 1981a). There is also evidence for the down-regulation of postsynaptic beta receptors following the chronic administration of antidepressant medication (e.g., Cohen, Campbell, Dauphin, Tallman, & Murphy, 1982; Mishra, Gillespie, Youdim, & Sulser, 1983). Although both postsynaptic alpha and beta receptors exert several different effects depending on the tissues or organs in which they are located, both types of receptors essentially increase activity. Consequently, a down-regulation of these receptors would make the system *less* sensitive to monoaminergic stimulation, which is contrary to what would be predicted by the monoamine hypothesis (i.e., that an increase in monoaminergic activity is necessary for an antidepressant effect).

Since the effects of antidepressant medications on presynaptic alpha$_2$ receptors and postsynaptic beta receptors would appear to be operating in opposite directions, some researchers have suggested that the mode of action for these drugs is to increase the *stability* of monoaminergic transmission. This might occur if these diverse effects tend to cancel each other out and thereby limit the capacity for severe or maladaptive fluctuations in synaptic transmission (Maas, 1979; Svensson & Usdin, 1978; Willner & Montgomery, 1980). Such an action might explain not only the efficacy of these drugs over a wide range of symptoms in depressive disorders but also their relative lack of effect in normal subjects (Harrison-Read, 1981).

The process of receptor modification, however, is not as straightforward as it may sound. Not only does it vary depending on the amount of time involved and the amount of receptor agonist available, but it also may encompass more than one neurotransmitter. For example, it has been demonstrated that the down-regulation of beta-adrenergic receptors requires both noradrenergic and serotonergic input, with possibly other hormones being involved as well (Barbaccia et al., 1983; Racagni & Brunello, 1984; Sulser et al., 1983). It is also clear that changes in sensitivity of some receptors, such as those for serotonin, depend on the area of the brain studied, the behavioral response measured, and the type and dose of the agonist used to elicit the response (Ögren et al., 1983; Fuxe et al., 1983).

Stress and Social Support in Depression

Although antidepressant medications appear to exert their effect by regulation of pre- and postsynaptic receptor sensitivity, the concentration and balance of neurotransmitters available to act on these sites is still an important factor. In this regard, the effects of stress and the lack of social support on monoaminergic activity are relevant to an understanding of how mood disorders occur (Anisman & Zacharko, 1982; Barnett & Gotlib, 1988). Both factors are thought to affect the reward system of the brain, although they appear to do so in different ways (Willner, 1985). As noted earlier, stress, particularly if it is uncontrollable, may affect the reward system's ability to respond to pleasurable events and thus result in psychomotor retardation and despondency. The lack of social support, on the other hand, appears to be related more directly to the absence of rewards per se and is characterized by increased anxiety and hostility.

Stress can precipitate a depressive state by affecting both the amount and balance of neurotransmitters in the brain. Aversive events give rise to the individual's attempt to cope. This coping normally proceeds along behavioral lines with a concomitant increase in the utilization and synthesis of brain monoamines. When behavioral coping is successful, the neurochemical systems are not taxed. If behavioral coping is not possible or is ineffectual, such as when the experience is perceived as uncontrollable, monoamine utilization may exceed synthesis. The resultant reduction in monoamine stores is thought to promote or exacerbate a depressive state.

Another effect of stress is to disrupt the balance of neurotransmitters. More specifically, stressful life events may increase cholinergic activity relative to that of the monoamines (Gillin et al., 1979; Janowsky et al., 1972). The predominance of cholinergic activity in the hypothalamus and forebrain is thought to affect the incentive function of the reward system by reducing its sensitivity to rewards (Willner, 1985). Given the interconnectedness of these centers with other parts of the brain, this may lead to a general suppression of behavior and the inability of the individual to sustain efforts to cope with the aversive events that initiated the process in the first place. Among endogenously depressed patients this imbalance is indicated by the failure to suppress serum cortisol in the DST and by decreased REM latency. This pattern is also observed in "depressive personalities" and may give some idea of how a genetic predisposition to depression might exert its effect.

The effect of stress on depressive states may be self-limiting. It has been suggested that feedback loops mediated by presynaptic beta receptors respond to the decrease in the function of monoamines by gradually increasing the synthetic capacity of monoaminergic neurons. Consequently, the likelihood of recovery increases in inverse proportion to the degree of severity of the depression. There are two implications to this observation. First, the more severe the endogenous depression, the more likely it is to recover. Second, mild depression may continue indefinitely if left untreated. In addition, this mechanism may help explain the cyclic nature of the disorder. Interestingly, it has been suggested that antidepressant drugs and ECT work because they mimic the adaptive process to stress (Antelman & Chiodo, 1984; Stone, 1979), although the way in which this occurs is unclear (Willner, 1985).

The lack of social support, on the other hand, is thought to be linked to reactive depression, particularly among people who enjoy social relationships (Beck, 1983). Unlike endogenous depression, which involves the balance of norepinephrine and acetylcholine, reactive or "neurotic" depression is thought to be mediated by forebrain activity of serotonin. Serotonin is an inhibitory neurotransmitter and exerts a dampening effect on the amygdala. Therefore, the reduction in the level of serotonin may result in the release of aggressive behavior. The result may be expressed as irritability, anxiety, agitation, or hostility, and may include serious suicide attempts. It is interesting to note that depressives with abnormally low levels of a serotonin metabolite, 5-hydroxyindoleacetic acid (5-HIAA), in the cerebral spinal fluid are more likely to have attempted suicide and more apt to have used a violent method (e.g., hanging, drowning, or several deep cuts on the wrist) (Åsberg, Träskman, & Thorén, 1976; van Praag, 1982). One study followed up 119 suicidal patients and found that all 7 who subsequently succeeded in killing themselves had exhibited abnormally low levels of 5-HIAA when initially examined (Träskman, Åsberg, Bertilsson, & Sjôŝtrand, 1981). Furthermore, 6 of the 7 died of violent means (3 by drowning and 3 by hanging).

It should be noted, however, that "pure" syndromes resulting from either stress or the lack of social support are uncommon and that a majority of depressions show a mixed pattern involving both endogenous and reactive symptoms. Consequently, the interaction of these diverse neurochemical systems may complicate the diagnostic picture considerably. Eating, for example, is suppressed by reducing activity in the dorsal norepinephrine system. Consequently, endogenous depression is most clearly associated with the loss of appetite and weight. However, low serotonin activates feeding, so the effect of the two dysfunctions occurring together is intermediate or variable, and weight gain is not uncommon (Mathew, Largen, & Claghorn, 1979).

This interaction may confound other depressive symptoms as well. The DST, which indicates an imbalance of acetylcholine and norepinephrine, is abnormal in only some 40–50% of endogenous depressions. Serotonin, on the other hand, stimulates adrenocorticotropic hormone (ACTH) secretion and is an essential link in the ACTH response to stress. Consequently, it may be that the endogenous depressives who show normal dexamethasone suppression are those who have low central serotonin turnover. In other words, reduced serotonin activity may calibrate the DST, such that it no longer provides an accurate measure of central acetylcholine-norepinephrine balance even when the latter is abnormal. The same sort of masking of these imbalances may also occur with the interaction of serotonin and dopamine in the nigrostriatum.

More on Mania

The physiological mechanisms of mania are less well understood than are those for depressive states. It is known that manic episodes may be precipitated by antidepressants that increase levels of both dopamine and serotonin. However, there are two reasons why mania does not seem related to an increase in serotonin (Willner, 1985). First, there is evidence that levels of norepinephrine increase at the onset of a manic episode and that serotonin is low during both phases of bipolar disorder. Second, specific serotonergic antidepressants do not precipitate a manic break. In one study, a patient was medicated with desipramine (a commonly used antidepressant that blocks the neuronal uptake of norepinephrine but not serotonin) and later with zimelidine (which blocks the neuronal uptake of serotonin) (Extein, Potter, Wehr, & Goodwin, 1979). The former induced hypomania and rapid mood cycles while the latter did not.

If it is true that the synthesis of norepinephrine is increased in the face of stress (and being depressed can be a stressful condition), there may be a tendency for it, like any biological system, to overshoot. According to this theory, the switch from depression to mania reflects the overcompensation of norepinephinergic neurons. However, it is unknown what differentiates the unipolar from the bipolar patients, although the latter appear to exhibit more extreme "normal" mood swings between episodes of the disorder (Depue et al., 1981).

Treatment Implications

Therapies for the mood disorders, particularly depression, reflect a multidimensional model with their tendency to include a "smorgasbord of treatment components" (McLean, 1981, p. 205). These include procedures designed to counter biological vulnerability, reduce environmental stress, improve coping skills, and increase social support (Rehm, 1981). In light of the physiological aspects of the mood disorders just discussed, an approach such as this would seem justified. For example, it is clear that some types of depression are essentially unresponsive, at least initially, to environmental or social influence and require an intervention that targets the endogenous factors thought to be responsible. This may involve using a "somatic" intervention, of which there are two major types—pharmacological and electroconvulsive. (A third type of somatic treatment involving the adjustment of circadian rhythms will also be briefly discussed.) Second, the potential importance of stress as both a predisposing and precipitating factor must be taken into account. This can be done by altering the stressfulness of the individual's living situation and by providing him or her with more effective coping skills to deal with stress that can not be avoided. Finally, the social/interpersonal aspects of the mood disorders would seem to be important in terms of creating as well as ameliorating these disorders, even in apparently endogenous cases.

Somatic Interventions

It has been thought for some time that the physiological symptoms of depression are predictive of the patient's responsiveness to somatic treatments. In a large prospective study, Weckowicz and his colleagues (Weckowicz et al., 1971) were able to predict treatment outcome in terms of three different treatment approaches (ECT, psychotherapy, and anti-depressant medications). Patients displaying signs of low autonomic (sympathetic) reactivity and low salivation responded best to ECT. Patients low on psychomotor retardation and high on autonomic reactivity and salivation responded best to psychotherapy. The patients high on psychomotor retardation but also exhibiting "atypical" depressive symptoms (e.g., schizoid or involutional depression) responded best to medication. These results, however, were far from conclusive, particularly in terms of the effectiveness of the drug intervention. Although other studies have failed to demonstrate the value of making these sorts of distinctions, the antidepressants, lithium, and ECT continue to play a major role in the treatment of the mood disorders (Abrams, 1988).

Antidepressants. There are three main types of antidepressant medications—tricyclics (TCAs), monoamine oxidase inhibitors (MAOIs), and newer "second generation" drugs. The first type, the TCAs, have been in use for more than 25 years and include such drugs as amitriptyline (Elavil), desipramine (Norpramin), and imipramine (Tofranil). Several exhaustive reviews have established the efficacy of the TCAs for approximately 60% to 70% of patients who receive a standard 4- to 6-week trial (Klein et al., 1980; Morris & Beck, 1974). These rates can be contrasted with the response to placebos, which range from 0% to 50% under controlled conditions.

Research has identified certain features of the depressive syndrome that predict a favorable response to the TCAs. Some of these symptoms include psychomotor disturbance, loss of interest in pleasurable activity, early-morning awakening, weight loss, and lack of responsivity to environmental changes (Bielski & Friedel, 1976; Nelson & Charney, 1981). A poor response to the TCAs is associated with the presence of delusion, generalized anxiety, chronicity, or "neurotic" features. Furthermore, there may be a U-shaped relationship between these TCAs and a favorable clinical response with the best outcome associated with moderate levels of severity (Thase et al., 1985). The new generation of antidepressant medications (e.g., Maptrotiline, Mianserin, and Trazodone) are similar in effect to the TCAs. However, it is expected that some of these compounds will be able to demonstrate increased antidepressant potency with fewer adverse side effects. In addition, it is anticipated that they may act more quickly than TCAs and be less toxic if taken in overdose (Barnes & Bridges, 1982; Berwish & Amsterdam, 1989).

Another family of antidepressant drugs is the MAOIs. Although they are not used as frequently today because of concerns over their high toxicity, the MAOIs have been found to exert a therapeutic effect when used in sufficiently high dosages in the context of proper clinical management (Klein et al., 1980). They may be particularly effective for individuals with "atypical" features of depression, such as hypersomnia, weight gain, or panic attacks (Davidson, 1983; Liebowitz et al., 1984; Nies & Robinson, 1982). Unfortunately, the MAOIs' adverse side effects, which include hypertension, insomnia, and dry mouth, plus their interaction with other drugs and foods rich in tyramine, limit their usefulness (Thase, 1987).

The most widely accepted mechanism of action for the antidepressants is their ability to increase the concentration of monoaminergic transmitters in the synaptic cleft. The TCAs are thought to do this by inhibiting the energy-dependent uptake of monoamines into cytoplasmic stores within the presynaptic membrane (Ashton, 1987) (see Figure 5.3). The MAOIs act to potentiate the effects of the monoamines, particularly serotonin, by controlling the amount held in synaptic storage vesicles.

Although this model of antidepressant action is appealing for its simplicity, it does not explain why the antidepressants' therapeutic onset is delayed despite the immediacy of their effect in the synaptic cleft. It also does not explain why other drugs that increase synaptic levels of these monoamines (e.g., cocaine and amphetamine) are not effective as antidepressants. In addition, since there are other effective antidepressants that are neither reuptake blockers nor monoamine oxidase inhibitors, an increase in the synaptic concentration of monoamines must not be a prerequisite for an antidepressant effect. Although the picture is still unclear, it is probable that these medications exert their therapeutic effectiveness through the stabilization of synaptic transmission, as discussed earlier.

Lithium. Lithium is a metallic element used primarily for its antimanic effects. A number of controlled clinical trials have found that lithium salts are superior to placebo and as effective if not more effective than neuroleptics for the treatment of mania (Klein et al., 1980; Stokes, Stoll, Shamoian, & Patton, 1971). There are differences, however, in the clinical response to neuroleptics and lithium. While neuroleptics may control symptoms more rapidly, lithium provides a more specific effect

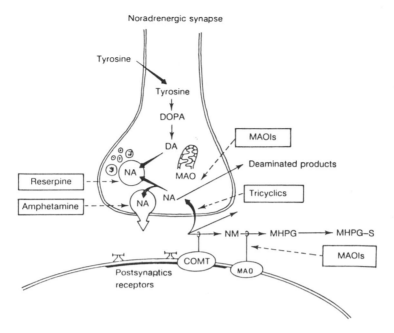

Figure 5.3. Diagram of central noradrenergic synapse illustrating sites of action of anti-depressant drugs. (From H. Ashton [1987], *Brain Systems Disorders and Psychotropic Drugs*, p. 303. Oxford: Oxford University Press. Copyright © 1987 by Heather Ashton. Reprinted by permission.)

on mood by returning affect to normal without the sedation or CNS depression that accompanies the neuroleptics (Gerbino, Oleshansky, & Gershon, 1978; Johnson, Gershon, Burdock, Floyd, & Hekimian, 1971; Prien, Caffey, & Klett, 1972). It is also believed that the long-term use of lithium exerts a prophylactic effect in preventing both depressive and manic relapses (Coppen, Metcalfe, & Wood, 1982).

The mode of action of lithium is unclear (Murray, 1985). It is thought that lithium competes with the four most abundant, positively-charged ions in biological tissue—sodium, potassium, magnesium, and calcium. Alteration of the function of any or all of these cations in the CNS should result in widespread neuronal effects. Consequently, Schildkraut (1973) has suggested that lithium may compete with calcium and magnesium in various monoaminergic transport and release systems, thus decreasing the amount of norepinephrine available to the receptors. Wood (1985) also hypothesized that lithium affected calcium channel transport, but he linked this effect to a reduction in the sensitivity of serotonergic receptors, which are thought to be responsible for the maintenance of euthymic states in bipolar disorder. Bunney and his associates (Bunney, Pert, Rosenblatt, Pert, & Gallaper, 1979) proposed that lithium's antimanic effect is due to its ability to "prevent the development of supersensitivity of dopamine receptors in the CNS" (p. 901). Perhaps all that can be said with some certainty at this point is that lithium probably affects some aspect of neuronal membrane transport, perhaps stabilizing the sensitivity of receptor sites (Bunney et al., 1979; Tosteson, 1981). Whether this reduces responsiveness of serotonergic receptors, blunts excessive discharge of dopaminergic neurons, or exerts a therapeutic effect in some other manner is unknown.

Electroconvulsive Therapy. In terms of endogenous depression, electroconvulsive therapy (ECT) has become established as an effective treatment for patients in whom a rapid response is required because of the severity of the depression and the risk of suicide (Crow & Johnstone, 1979; Fink 1979, 1981). Generally, this sort of patient has failed to respond adequately to a course of antidepressant medications and tends to present with such symptoms as psychomotor retardation, weight loss, and early morning awakening (Kiloh, 1982). Although ECT is probably more effective than drugs for quickly reversing a depressive state, antidepressant medications are thought to be more effective in preventing recurrences of the disorder.

The mode of action for ECT is also unclear. It has been hypothesized that a course of ECT increases post-synaptic responsiveness to norepinephrine, serotonin, and particularly dopamine (Costain, Cowen, Gelder, & Grahame-Smith, 1982; Grahame-Smith, Green, & Costain, 1978), possibly by increasing receptor sensitivity (Green, 1978). This would explain its effectiveness with patients exhibiting psychomotor retardation and weight loss since feeding and locomotion are thought to be regulated to a large extent by dopaminergic systems (Ungerstedt, 1979). Another explanation is based on the observation that repeated convulsions in animals result in the decreased synthesis and concentration of GABA in certain regions of the brain. Consequently, ECT may act to "switch-off" the inhibitory effects of GABA function (Green, 1978).

Because of ethical issues surrounding ECT, certain standards and legal guidelines have been established to control its use (see Winsdale, Liston, Ross, & Weber, 1984). Explicit informed-consent procedures have been adopted in most areas of the United States, and for those patients who are unwilling to receive ECT, certain legal safeguards (e.g., competency proceedings, guardianship, and a second independent opinion) must be insured. Given ECT's potential for misuse, psychologists have generally tended to dispute its therapeutic effectiveness. Nevertheless, the evidence indicating its efficacy for certain types of depressed patients, particulary when alternative treatments have failed, is such that the indiscriminate rejection of ECT as a treatment option is unwarranted.

Adjustment of Circadian Rhythms. Although relatively little is known about the relationship between circadian rhythms and depression, the area merits further study. Evidence is accumulating to suggest that some forms of depression involve the disruption of circadian rhythms (Healy & Williams, 1988). This is seen most clearly in seasonal affective disorder, which is an uncommon but well-documented problem of severe depression that occurs in conjunction with the onset of winter (Wehr et al., 1986). Interestingly, the treatment for this disorder, which involves extending daylight by exposing the person to bright artificial lights, appears to relieve depression but has essentially no other mood effects (Czeisler et al., 1986; N. E. Rosenthal et al., 1985). Likewise, sleep or REM deprivation, which may lessen depressive symptoms, worsens rather than improves the mood of persons who are normal or who suffer from psychological disorders other than depression (Roy-Byrne, Uhde, & Post, 1986).

Attempts to readjust the depressed person's sleep-wake cycle thus represent another type of somatic intervention. One approach involves shifting the sleep period to establish "a more nearly normal temporal relationship between the sleep-wake cycle and circadian rhythms" (Sack, Nurnberger, Rosenthal, Ashburn, & Wehr, 1985, p. 606). It is thought that this type of intervention may potentiate the therapeutic effect of antidepressant medication. A variation of this approach involves keeping a depressed person awake all night (van den Hoofdakker & Elsenga, 1981). This treatment, however, appears to alleviate the symptoms of depression for only a brief period. REM deprivation has also been tried, but again with only a temporary benefit.

Psychosocial Interventions

In addition to somatic treatment, there is often the need for interventions that attend to the patient's maladaptive interpersonal behavior and/or ineffectual way of coping with stress (Klerman & Schechter, 1982; Nezu & Ronan, 1988; Thase, 1983). For example, it has been established that psychosocial interventions that assist in the adaptation process, either by modifying the stressfulness of the situation or by providing effective means for coping with these events, play an important role in the overall treatment effort (cf. Miller, Norman, Keitner, Bishop, &

Dow, 1989). This type of intervention may be of particular importance in the treatment of endogenous depression (Klerman & Schechter, 1982; Thase, 1983).

Interpersonal relationships may be a significant factor as well (Zeiss, Lewinsohn, & Muñoz, 1979). It is thought that reactive depression results, at least in part, from an absence of social reinforcement. In the short run, this may be remedied by the care and attention of persons in the immediate environment. However, if the patient returns to a living arrangement that does not provide satisfying social relationships over the long run, he or she is likely to relapse (Belsher & Costello, 1988). Although antidepressant medication and lithium, both of which enhance serotonergic function, can serve a prophylactic as well as curative role (Klerman, 1978), procedures designed to improve the quality of the patient's social environment are often necessary and may also remove the need for long-term drug maintenance.

In this regard, studies that have focused on the depressed person's social skills have found this intervention to be as effective as or superior to tricyclic antidepressants in alleviating depressive symptoms (Bellack, Hersen, & Himmelhoch, 1983; Hersen, Bellack, & Himmelhoch, 1980; McLean & Hakstian, 1979). In fact, social skill training with placebo was found to be superior to an amitriptyline-only group in terms of dropout rates (15% versus 55%, respectively) and better than all groups (amitriptyline-only, social skills with amitriptyline, and psychotherapy with placebo) in terms of proportion of patients who were substantially improved (Bellack, Hersen & Himmelhoch, 1981). Incidentally, the role serotonin plays in alleviating reactive depression may help explain why alcohol and opiate dependence is so common in persons who are depressed. Opiates activate brain serotonin systems and chronic alcohol consumption may also increase serotonin brain activity (Ahtee & Eriksson, 1973), although this evidence is still controversial (Ellingboe, 1978). Nevertheless, it may be that these behaviors represent a form of self-medication, which, like the antidepressant, fills a need that the social environment is failing to provide.

Summary

Although the mood disorders may be mediated by a common mechanism, they are precipitated by a wide range of etiological factors and respond differentially to a variety of treatment interventions. The picture is made more complex by the observation that many of these disorders overlap among themselves and with other psychopathological conditions. Consequently, the clinician often has to help the patient deal not only with the debilitating effects of a serious depression but also with a concurrent state of anxiety that is affecting its course (Thase, 1987). Distinctions within the mood disorders, such as endogenous and reactive depression, that were once thought to provide a rational basis for making differential treatment decisions may offer only partial guidance in this regard. For example, relying entirely on stress-reducing or somatic interventions for endogenous depression may prove insufficient for the individual whose troubled life style alienates people, reduces social support, and thereby increases his or her vulnerability to the disorder (Briscoe & Smith, 1975).

This state of affairs has lead several reviewers of the treatment literature in the area to conclude that the combination of psychological and somatic interventions is preferred (e.g., Conte, Plutchik, Wild, & Karasu, 1986; Weissman, 1979). The different approaches appear to involve separate mechanisms of action and thus may complement each other in achieving an overall therapeutic effect (Hollon, Spoden, & Chastek, 1986). Although some patients may respond maximally to antidepressant medication, the current state of knowledge does not allow us to identify these individuals with sufficient reliability to warrant so narrow an approach. Furthermore, even the individual who responds well to medication must live and function in a social context so that poor relationships or inadequate support systems must be considered as well. This perspective can be expressed adequately only in a systematic treatment program that takes both psychosocial as well as physiological factors into account.

Chapter **6**

Anxiety Disorders

There are many models of anxiety. Some emphasize cognitive processes, while others focus on mechanisms that are thought to operate more or less independently of higher cortical areas (i.e., without extensive perceptual and cognitive encoding).[1] The debate over the cognitive and noncognitive aspects of anxiety was inaugurated by William James and Walter Cannon in the early part of this century. James (1884) proposed that "reflex currents" initiate visceral reactions and overt muscle activity that are interpreted by the cortex as the experience of emotion (Bindra, 1970). Cannon (1920) responded with the observation that physiological activity (e.g., activation of the autonomic nervous system) is too diffuse to allow for the identification of different emotions. In this regard, physiological arousal may lead to feeling "as if" one is anxious but not to an actual state of anxiety as we normally define it. (See Panel 6.1, "Anxiety Disorders: Diagnostic Summary.")

Both approaches have contributed to our understanding of anxiety. The noncognitive perspective has added to our understanding of anxiety's biochemical and neurophysiological components (e.g., Kety, 1970). In addition, this approach highlights the possibility that genetic factors may play a role in the development of many of these disorders. The cognitive perspective, on the other hand, has broadened our understanding of anxiety to include its subjective aspects (e.g., Schachter, 1964).

Lader (1978, 1980) has attempted to bring together a number of these different theories in the form of a general model of anxiety. As can

---

[1]See Beck and Emery (1985); Lazarus (1982, 1984); and Zajonc (1980, 1984) for examples of cognitive and noncognitive models of anxiety.

PANEL 6.1

Anxiety Disorders: Diagnostic Summary[1]

Anxiety disorders are characterized by feelings of subjective distress (e.g., apprehension, fear, etc.) and avoidance behavior. Some of these disorders have distress as the classic feature, while for others avoidance behavior is the primary characteristic. In all, there are eight disorders in this diagnostic category, not including the residual diagnosis of anxiety disorder not otherwise specified.[2] Of these, the phobias (panic disorder with agoraphobia, agoraphobia without history of panic disorder, social phobia, and simple phobia) are characterized by avoidance behavior. The remaining four disorders have subjective distress as their primary component, although avoidance behavior may also be present. Among these are generalized anxiety disorder and obsessive compulsive disorder, in which distress is experienced if the person attempts to resist the obsessions and compulsions. There is also the diagnosis of panic disorder without agoraphobia. The fourth disorder, posttraumatic stress disorder (PTSD), has as its predominant symptom the reexperiencing of a trauma, although distress and avoidance behavior may occur as well. In addition, two disorders usually first evident in childhood or adolescence, separation anxiety disorder and overanxious disorder, are relevant to this chapter.

Panic disorder with agoraphobia is characterized by recurrent panic attacks which usually lead to a generalized fear of being in places or situations from which escape might be difficult or embarrassing (agoraphobia). As a result of this fear, travel is restricted, a companion is needed when away from home, or the agoraphobic situation is endured despite intense distress. Common situations in which agoraphobia is a problem include being alone outside of the home, being in a crowd or standing in a line, being on a bridge, and traveling in a bus, train, or car.

[1]Material for this section is taken directly from the DSM-III-R (*Diagnostic and Statistical Manual of Mental Disorders* [Third Revision, Revised], American Psychiatric Association, 1987).

[2]There is a separate diagnostic category referred to as adjustment disorders. These disorders involve maladaptive reactions to identifiable psychosocial stressors provided the response does not persist longer than six months. One of the adjustment disorders is "with anxious mood." This disorder will not be dealt with separately here or elsewhere since it is assumed to share many of the physiological characteristics of the anxiety disorders. Another adjustment disorder—"with work (or academic) inhibition"—is also related to the disorders discussed in this chapter in that it reflects the disruption of normal functioning that often accompanies anxiety.

In most cases agoraphobia can be traced directly to recurrent panic attacks, which are periods of intense fear or discomfort that occur unexpectedly. Panic attacks may involve numerous symptoms, including shortness of breath, dizziness, palpitations, trembling or shaking, sweating, choking, nausea, depersonalization, flushes or chills, chest pain or discomfort, fear of dying, or fear of going crazy or doing something uncontrolled. These attacks, however, do not occur in response to specific situations (as is the case in simple phobia) or to circumstances involving other people (social phobia). In fact, it is the unpredictability of the attacks that seems to predispose a person to develop the generalized fear characteristic of agoraphobia.

The average age of onset of panic disorder is in the late 20s. Typically, there are recurrent panic attacks several times a week or even daily, followed by the development of agoraphobia. The latter, by definition, involves varying degrees of constriction in lifestyle and often leads to social and/or occupational impairment. In the case of severe agoraphobia, the person may be nearly or completely housebound.

Panic disorder with agoraphobia is almost twice as common in females as in males and is much more common than panic disorder without agoraphobia. Complications of the disorder may include abuse of psychoactive substances, particularly alcohol and anxiolytic agents. In making the diagnosis of panic disorder with agoraphobia it is particularly important to rule out the presence of such physical problems as hypoglycemia, pheochromocytoma, and hyperthyroidism, all of which can present with similar symptoms. In addition, withdrawal from such substances as barbiturates or intoxication from psychoactive substances such as caffeine or amphetamines can mimic a panic attack.

Both social phobia and simple phobia can be differentiated from panic disorder with agoraphobia by the presence of specific situations or events that invariably precipitate an anxiety reaction. In the case of *social phobia*, the situation involves being in the presence of others who may scrutinize, evaluate, or in other ways open the possibility for embarrassment or humiliation. Examples of such situations include speaking in public, eating in front of others, or urinating in a public lavatory. Social phobia usually begins in late childhood or early adolescence and follows a chronic course. Unless severe, it is rarely incapacitating, although it obviously can interfere with activities involving performance in social situations. The disorder is apparently more common in males than females. There is no reliable information regarding predisposing factors or familial patterns.

Simple phobia is the fear of certain circumscribed situations other than the fear of having panic attack (as in panic disorder) or of humilation or embarrassment in certain social situations (as in social phobia). Examples of these situations involve animals, snakes, bodily injury, closed spaces, heights, or air travel. When confronted with a phobic situation, the person experiences marked anticipatory anxiety usually leading to avoidance of the situation.

Invariably, the person recognizes that his or her fear is unreasonable. Nevertheless, avoidance of the phobic situation continues. It is this interference with the persons's normal routine that is necessary for the diagnosis to be made. Simple phobias can develop at any age, with animal phobias being most common in childhood, blood-injury phobias in adolescence, and other phobias in adulthood. Those that make an appearance in childhood generally disappear without treatment. However, those that persist into adulthood rarely remit if left untreated. Although simple phobias are common in the general population, they rarely result in marked impairment and thus are not seen as frequently in the clinic.

There is an additional disorder involving avoidance behavior—*agoraphobia without history of panic disorder*. There is controversy as to whether this category in a variant of panic disorder with agoraphobia, since it invariably involves the fear of having a limited panic attack. In this regard, a number of symptoms of a panic attack may be experienced, such as becoming dizzy, but are not sufficient for the diagnosis of a panic attack per se.

It is possible to have a *panic disorder without agoraphobia*. As noted earlier, this diagnosis is much less common than panic disorder with agoraphobia. However, a person can experience panic attacks without developing a generalized fear that interferes with his or her social or occupational functioning.

Another disorder that involves subjective distress as its prominent feature is *obsessive compulsive disorder*. Obsessions are persistent ideas, thoughts, impulses, or images that are experienced as repugnant. Examples might include a parent's impulse to kill his or her child or a religious person's blasphemous thoughts. Unlike a delusion, the person recognizes that these obsessions are the product of his or her own mind and are not imposed from without. Compulsions are repetitive, purposeful, and intentional behaviors that are performed in response to an obsession. It is thought that these stereotyped responses neutralize or prevent distress arising from an obsession. Examples might include hand-washing, counting, checking, and touching. In each case the behavior may be related to some danger (e.g., fear of infection) but the person realizes that it is excessive or unreasonable and, at least initially, attempts to resist the compulsion. Resistance, however, is usually met with a mounting sense of apprehension and distress that is relieved by yielding to the compulsion. Obsessive compulsive disorder, which is found equally among males and females, can lead to depression or more generalized anxiety if not treated successfully.

A more pervasive form of anxiety is found with *generalized anxiety disorder* (GAD), which is characterized as unrealistic or excessive distress and worry about two or more life circumstances. For example, a person may worry excessively about finances or about misfortune to family members who are not in danger. To be diagnosed as GAD, however, these worries must occur more days than not for at least six months. Signs of GAD involve three groups of symptoms—motor tension (e.g., muscle tension, restlessness), hyperactivity (e.g., shortness of breath, sweating, nausea), and vigilance and scanning (e.g., feeling keyed up or on edge, exaggerated startle response).

Posttraumatic stress disorder (PTSD) is a relatively recent category that gained widespread attention following the Viet Nam War. The key feature to this disorder is severe symptoms of anxiety (e.g., difficulty falling or staying asleep, hypervigilance, and exaggerated startle response) associated with a psychologically distressing event that is outside the range of usual human experience. The event would be perceived as markedly distressing to anyone and usually involves catastrophic destruction of life and limb, serious personal threat or harm, or seeing someone seriously injured or killed as a result of accident or physical violence. The person's reactions to the stressful event are reexperienced, often in dreams and accompanied by intense psychological distress. Consequently, avoidance of stimuli associated with the stressful event often occurs as does a numbing of general responsiveness not present before the trauma. Over time, generalized anxiety and depression are common for this disorder, which can occur at any age. PTSD is not common but appears to occur equally in males and females.

Finally, there are two anxiety disorders usually first evident in infancy, childhood, or adolescence. The first of these, *separation anxiety disorder*, involves excessive subjective distress concerning separation from someone (usually a parent) to whom the child is attached. The distress is evidenced by clinging behaviors, following the parent around, or a persistent reluctance or refusal to go to sleep. Nightmares and/or physical complaints (e.g., headaches, stomachaches, etc.) may also be present. This disorder, which occurs equally in male and female children, is fairly common and may be precipitated by the death or illness of a loved one (including pets). Furthermore, it appears to be more common among children who have first-degree biological relatives with the disorder than in the general population. Separation anxiety disorder may interfere with school attendance or the child's ability to function independently in an age-appropriate manner.

The second anxiety disorder of childhood, *overanxious disorder*, is characterized by excessive or unrealistic worry about future events, the possibility of injury, or being included in peer group activities. As with separation anxiety disorder, this disorder may involve various physical complaints and even may be accompanied by restlessness or the appearance of nervous habits, such as nail-biting or hair-pulling. Overanxious disorder appears to be fairly common, particularly among the eldest children in small families in which personal achievement is stressed.

be seen in Figure 6.1, a number of various factors are included, although no attempt is made to specify in neurophysiological terms how they interact. Cognition (e.g., appraisal) is given a central role but is not presented as being independent of or as being a prerequisite for the model's noncognitive features. This is because anxiety is seen as pro-

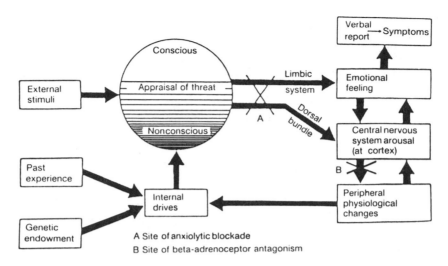

Figure 6.1. Lader's model of anxiety. (From J. M. Lader [1980], The Psychophysiology of Anxiety, in H. M. van Praag [Ed.], *Handbook of biological psychiatry: Part II. Brain mechanisms and abnormal behavior—Psychophysiology*, p. 240. Copyright © 1980 by Marcel Dekker. Reprinted by permission.)

ceeding on both cognitive and noncognitive levels simultaneously (via the limbic system and dorsal bundle). Anxiolytic drugs like the benzodiazepines are thought to affect both pathways at point "A" on the diagram. Lader's model also acknowledges the contributions of genetic factors and past experience, as well as the situational context ("external stimuli"). The box labeled "internal drives" can be interpreted in several ways. As far as physiological factors are concerned, this term might apply to those forms of anxiety, such as panic, that are thought to represent disturbances in metabolic regulation.

On the response side of the model, peripheral physiological changes and subjective experience are included. The latter leads to self-reports of anxiety upon which the diagnosis often depends. The former (peripheral physiological changes) provides yet another avenue for assessment as well as possibly serving to exacerbate anxiety via positive feedback. Medications like the beta-blockers exert their effect at point "B" by interrupting or blocking this feedback. It should be noted, however, that a shortcoming of Lader's model is the failure to indicate how these pathways result in or contribute to avoidance behavior.

Physiological Factors

Secondary Anxiety

The first distinction that needs to be made when considering the physiological aspects of anxiety is whether a particular state is the result of some other psychological or medical condition (Dunn, 1981; Hall, 1980b). More specifically, there are numerous medical conditions that mimic anxiety disorders, more than 25 of which are listed in Table 6.1. One example is mitral valve prolapse syndrome (MVPS) (Kane, Woerner, Zeldis, Kramer, & Saravey, 1981). This relatively common disorder (approximately 5% of the general population have it) is usually asymptomatic. However, more than one-third of patients with MVPS also experience panic attacks (Hartman, Kramer, Brown, & Devereux, 1982).

Another example of secondary anxiety is obsessive-compulsive symptomatology resulting from encephalopathy (especially involving lesions to the globus pallidus) or other neurological dysfunction (e.g., following the allergic reaction to a wasp sting or carbon monoxide poisoning) (Ali-Cherif et al., 1984; Laplane, Baulac, Widlöcher, & Dubois, 1984). Diabetes insipidus (Barton, 1965, 1976) or head injury (Hillbom, 1960) can also result in obsessive or compulsive symptoms. Although most anxiety disorders cannot be traced to medical or neurological causes (Kettl & Marks, 1986), patients with apparent "pathological" anxiety should have physical examinations and clinically appropriate tests (e.g., thyroid function and an electrocardiogram) before a primary diagnosis of anxiety disorder is made (Pi & Simpson, 1987).

Anxiety also may be secondary to or concurrent with other psychological disorders, particularly depression. In some cases, the symptoms of anxiety or panic disorder may precede and thus be symptomatic of a major depressive episode (Sheehan, 1982). One-third of patients with generalized anxiety or panic disorder have been described as having a major affective (i.e., mood) disorder (Dealy, Ishiki, Avery, Wilson, & Dunner, 1981). In most cases, however, separating the two diagnostic groups is difficult, and all that can be said is that both disorders occur together with some frequency. For example, depressive episodes were documented in 44% of patients with anxiety disorders seen in a hospital clinic over a 6-year period (Noyes, Clancy, Hoenk, & Slymen, 1980) and in two-thirds over a 12-year period (Cloninger, Martin, Clayton, & Guze, 1981). Also, a quarter of the obsessional patients followed by Capstick and Seldrup (1973) received a diagnosis of depression that

Table 6.1.   Common Medical Conditions
Mimicking Anxiety Disorders

Cardiovascular system
 Congestive heart failure
 Angina pectoris
 Essential hypertension
 Dysrhythmia, especially paroxysmal atrial tachycardia
 Costal chondritis
 Mitral valve prolapse syndrome (systolic-click-murmur syndrome)
 Myocardial infarction (heart attack)

Respiratory system
 Hypoxic conditions
 Chronic obstructive pulmonary disease

Metabolic and endocrine system
 Hypoglycemia
 Hyper- or hypothyroidism
 Hyper- or hypoadrenalism (Cushing's or Addison's disease)
 Diabetes mellitus

Neurological system
 Brain tumor
 Migraine headache
 Seizure disorders
 Multiple sclerosis
 Other organic brain syndromes (e.g., parkinsonism, encephalopathy)

Hematologic system
 Anemia

Neoplasms
 Pheochromocytoma
 Carcinoid tumor

Drug-related conditions
 Withdrawal reaction of addictive drugs (e.g., alcohol, barbiturates, benzodiazepines)
 Caffeinism
 Tobacco
 Central nervous system stimulants (e.g., amphetamine, cocaine)
 Central nervous system depressants (e.g., neuroleptic-induced side effects [akathisia])

Note. From E. H. Pi and G. M. Simpson (1987), Anxiety Disorders, in R. L. Morrison and A. S. Bellack (Eds.), *Medical Factors and Psychological Disorders: A Handbook for Psychologists*, p. 50. Copyright © 1987 by Plenum Publishing Corporation. Reprinted by permission.

either preceded or followed the obsessional state. And in cases with agoraphobia or panic disorder, it has been estimated that as many as two-thirds of these patients may experience major depressive episodes (Breier, Charney, & Heninger, 1984). Whatever the case, it is clear that persons reporting symptoms of anxiety should also be screened for the presence of other forms of psychopathology. Structured interviews like the Anxiety Disorders Interview Schedule (ADIS) (Di Nardo, O'Brien, Barlow, Waddell, & Blanchard, 1983) and Schedule for Affective Disorders and Schizophrenia (Endicott & Spitzer, 1978) are particularly helpful in this regard.

Physiological Symptoms

The *physiological symptoms* of anxiety (i.e., "peripheral physiological changes" in Lader's model) deserve attention for two reasons. For one, physiological symptoms are central to the assessment process (Hodges, 1976), such as when anxiety is defined as "feelings of tension, apprehension, nervousness and worry, and activation or discharge of the autonomic nervous system" (Spielberger, Pollans, & Worden, 1984, p. 263). The diagnostic criteria for panic disorder, GAD, and PTSD all involve symptoms such as palpitations, sweating, trembling or shaking, or exaggerated startle response. Consequently, measures like heart rate and electrodermal responses are taken as evidence that a person is anxious or experiencing an anxiety disorder. Other physiological measures used in this manner include blood pressure, muscle blood flow, eye pupil size, electromyographic activity, EEGs, and neuroendocrine responses (Lader, 1983; Levitt, 1980; I. Martin, 1961).

A second reason physiological symptoms are important is that these responses can create further problems. This occurs when the body's homeostatic mechanisms become disrupted or exhausted under conditions of prolonged anxiety or stress (Selye, 1976). Chronic anxiety may affect the health of an individual in two ways. For one, the body's organs may become damaged by a period of prolonged overactivation. Second, the immune system may become so weakened that the body is susceptible to infectious diseases. In both cases, the physiological symptoms of anxiety are responsible for initiating a chain of events that causes further physiological damage. This type of problem, however, falls more appropriately under another diagnostic category, psychological factors affecting physical condition.

Individual Differences in Susceptibility to Anxiety

The belief that individuals differ in terms of their susceptibility to anxiety is based, in part, on the observation that persons subjected to the same anxiety-evoking situations do not become incapacitated to the same degree. For example, many thousands of men in Viet Nam experienced the horrors of war but only a small minority developed symptoms of PTSD (Van Putten & Yager, 1984; Yager, Laufer, & Gallops, 1984). Although individual differences in this regard have been explained in psychodynamic, cognitive/perceptual, or learning-based terms, there are also abundant data to suggest that these differences are associated with relatively stable, biological factors, which are largely inherited. (See Panel 6.2, "Heritability of Anxiety.")

An early example of this type of research was "intolerance of ambiguity" (Frenkel-Brunswick, 1949). This trait was characterized by a preference for familiarity or regularity and involved a tendency to make black-or-white generalizations. For example, when a group of subjects were shown a series of drawings in which a cat gradually changed into a dog, persons rated high on this dimension persisted in seeing a cat long after other persons began to notice visual anomalies. Initially, intolerance to ambiguity was linked to anxiety in terms of a person's inability to tolerate personal feelings of ambivalence surrounding sexual or aggressive impulses (Berlyne, 1960). Research during that period on this and a related dimension (simplicity-complexity) revealed a number of psychophysiological differences between persons rated high and low on the constructs. Some of these differences included variations in autonomic responsivity, habituation of electrodermal responses, and lability of EEG waves (Gastaut, 1954; Wenger, 1941).

Another development in the area of individual differences was Hans Eysenck's (1967) biologically-based theory of individual differences. The two basic dimensions of his model are extraversion and neuroticism. The first dimension describes persons who are active, sociable, optimistic, and outgoing in contrast to their opposites, the introverts, who are passive, quiet, and careful. Neither end of the extraversion continuum is problematic in itself. However, pathology enters the picture when we introduce the second dimension, neuroticism, which is concerned with emotional stability. The emotionally stable end of this continuum is epitomized by someone who is calm and even-tempered. He or she can be contrasted to the moody, irritable, and restless highly-neurotic individual.

The introvert who is emotionally stable (i.e., low on neuroticism) behaves in a controlled, thoughtful manner. With increasing instability, however, the introvert becomes more pessimistic, anxious, and moody. In like manner, the unstable extravert may be seen as touchy, restless, and aggressive. This model is similar to that proposed by Jung (1924), who suggested that an extraverted but emotionally unstable person is more likely to develop disorders like hysterical neurosis, whereas the neurotic introvert will display symptoms of "psychasthenia" (i.e., chronic anxiety). The second or "dysthymic" type of disorder is of more

PANEL 6.2

Heritability of the Anxiety Disorders

Over the years there has been a good bit of interest in the question of whether certain people are more genetically predisposed to anxiety than others (e.g., Arkonac & Guze, 1963).

As with other disorders, much of the best work in the area has focused on the diagnosis of anxiety across groups that differ in terms of their biological relatedness. Twin studies, which compare the incidence of anxiety disorders between monozygotic (MZ) and dizygotic (DZ) pairs, are particularly useful in this regard.

An early study using this methodology compared 11 pairs of MZ twins and 11 pairs of DZ twins on several psychophysiological measures thought to be related to anxiety (Lader & Wing, 1966). They found that three variables—rate of electrodermal habituation, number of spontaneous skin conductance fluctuations, and pulse rate—were subject to genetic variation. Torgersen (1983) studied 32 MZ and 53 DZ adult same-sexed twins being treated in Norway for "neurotic and borderline psychotic disorders" (p. 1085). Using the Present State Examination, he found that the frequency of anxiety disorders was twice as high in the MZ as in DZ pairs (60% and 33%, respectively) and three times as high if generalized anxiety disorder (GAD) was excluded (45% and 15%, respectively). Furthermore, panic attacks were five times more likely among the MZ sets. Genetic evidence for GAD was not apparent (i.e., it occurred with the same frequency in MZ and DZ twins).

In terms of the concordance rate among nontwin biologic relatives, Noyes and his associates (Noyes, Clancy, Crowe, Hoenk, & Slymen, 1978) compared the family histories of 112 patients with "anxiety neurosis" to 110 surgical controls. (Anxiety neurosis included such symptoms as "chronic nervousness or apprehension" and "attacks or spells of nervousness" obtained from a structured interview.) The morbidity risk for first-degree relatives of the anxiety patients was 18% as compared to 3% among the control relatives. Relatives of the anxiety patients were also found to be at higher risk for developing alcoholism.

Crowe and his colleagues (Crowe, Noyes, Pauls, & Slymen, 1983) collected data on 278 first-degree relatives of 41 probands with panic disorder and 262 relatives of 41 control probands. The incidence of panic disorder in the first group was 17%, with an additional 7% with probable symptoms. This compared to the incidence rate of 1.8% and 0.4%, respectively, for relatives of the control group. They concluded that panic disorder is a familial disease that affects women twice as often as men and is not associated with an increased familial risk for other psychiatric conditions.

Crowe, Pauls, Slymen, and Noyes (1980) found the incidence of panic among first-degree relatives of persons with the disorder to be 41%, a morbidity rate as high as any in the psychiatric genetics literature. Furthermore, this finding was not related to the presence or absence of mitral valve prolapse syndrome, which also has a genetic component. Although this figure dropped to 31% when based on data from all sources as compared to the interview data only, it still was found to be substantially higher than that for relatives of the controls (4%). Another genetic study of panic disorder pedigrees for 19 kindreds of panic disorder led Pauls, Bucher, Crowe, and Noyes (1980) to conclude that the disorder is transmitted as an autosomal dominant trait, even when the 7 of 19 cases with mitral value prolapse were omitted from the analysis.

Data on obsessive-compulsive disorder is not as extensive. Inouye (1965) found that while all of the pairs of MZ twins he studied in Japan were discordant for conversion reaction and simple phobias, 8 of the 10 pairs exhibiting symptoms of obsessive-compulsive disorder were concordant (i.e., a concordance rate of 80%). This finding is consistent with a case report of two MZ twins who developed symptoms of obsessive-compulsive disorder independently in their early to midtwenties, at which time they led separate lives and had little contact with each other (McGuffin & Mawson, 1980).

In summary, the evidence for a genetic component to panic disorder is fairly definite. Obsessive-compulsive disorder also evidences a fair degree of heritability. On the other hand, while a susceptibility to developing simple phobias may be inherited to a slight degree, GAD has not generated much, if any, evidence for a genetic basis. This variation in heritability across disorders would appear to be consistent with the degree to which environmental factors are thought to play a role in their development.

relevance to this chapter, since hysterical neurosis is now categorized as a somatoform disorder.

It has been proposed that individual differences in extraversion are determined by variability in the reticular formation-neocortical arousal feedback loop (Eysenck, 1983). This variability is thought to involve a "weakened" nervous system. More specifically, the introvert has a diminished capacity for inhibitory (i.e., neocortical) regulation and consequently is characterized by a higher level of excitability. The extravert, on the other hand, displays a greater tendency toward inhibition and thus less arousability. Consequently, introverts should condition more easily than extraverts. (The reader may recall Pavlov's dog, "Brains," from Chapter 2.)

A review by Stelmack (1981) found that, consistent with this hypothesis, introverts show higher levels of EEG activity under conditions of moderate arousal. It has been found that electrodermal activity is generally greater for introverts than extraverts using simple auditory stimuli of moderate intensity and visual stimulation under conditions of nonstress. Also, introverts have shown a slowness to habituate as compared to extraverts (O'Gorman, 1977). In addition, introverts evidence larger tonic pupil size prior to stimulation, suggesting higher levels of cortical arousal (Stelmack & Mandelzys, 1975). This relationship between arousal and introversion, however, is not linear. As predicted by Pavlov, introverts evidence a diminished responsivity at higher levels of stimulation, suggesting the presence of protective inhibition (Eysenck & Levey, 1972). Stelmack concluded that introverts demonstrate an enhanced responsiveness to stimulation over a wide range of psychophysiological measures, the most consistent of which is the electrodermal response.

Individual differences in neuroticism, on the other hand, are thought to be produced by variations in the function of the limbic system. The possibility that the structures mediating extraversion and neuroticism are located in different parts of the brain is consistent with Eysenck's argument that the two dimensions are independent. It also provides a basis for explaining the frequently observed "desynchrony" between response modes (Rachman & Hodgson, 1974; Hodgson & Rachman, 1974; Hugdhal, 1981).

It has been questioned, however, whether extraversion and neuroticism are really independent constructs. Gray (1982, 1983) rotated the two dimensions 45 degrees (see Figure 6.2) and defined anxiety-proneness as a single factor called "trait anxiety." According to Gray, persons high on trait anxiety exhibit a biologically-determined tendency to react more strongly to events in the environment that signal punishment or frustrative nonreward. This disposition represents a reciprocal relationship of excitatory impulses originating from the reticular formation and a downward inhibition from the hippocampal portion of the limbic system. This interaction of physiological arousal in conjunction with behavioral inhibition is responsible for the avoidant, withdrawal, or phobic reactions in everyone, but especially the anxiety-prone individual. The neural structures responsible for this process are referred to as the *behavioral inhibition system*, and activation of this system is said to constitute anxiety.

The Behavioral Inhibition System

Gray's concept of a behavioral inhibition system grew out of his observation of the behavioral effects of antianxiety medications on three

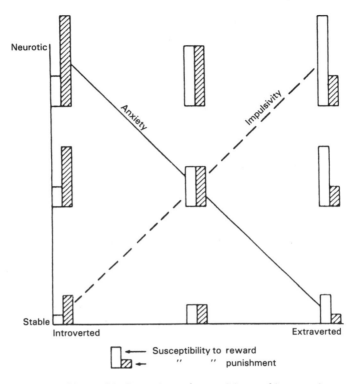

Figure 6.2. Rotation of Eysenck's dimensions of neuroticism and introversion-extraversion proposed by Gray (1970). The dimension of trait anxiety represents the steepest rate of growth in susceptibility to signals of punishment (and other adequate inputs to the behavioral inhibition system); the dimension of Impulsivity represents the steepest rate of growth in susceptibility to signals of reward. Introversion-extraversion now becomes a derived dimension, reflecting the balance of susceptibility to signals of punishment and reward, respectively; and neuroticism similarly reflects the sum of these two types of susceptibility to signals of reinforcement. (From J. A. Gray [1982], *The Neuropsychology of Anxiety*, p. 454. Copyright © 1982 by Jeffrey A. Gray. Reprinted by permission.)

classes of stimuli (Gray, 1977). These are stimuli associated with punishment, stimuli associated with the omission of expected reward (i.e., extinction), and novel stimuli. The behavioral inhibition system is said to act on these stimuli by instigating a tripartite pattern of responses. These include inhibition of ongoing behavior (especially instrumental or reinforced behavior), increased attention to the environment (especially to novel stimuli), and an increased level of autonomic arousal. (The hypothesized relationship between these variables is illustrated in Figure 6.3.)

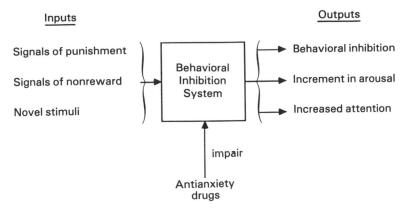

Figure 6.3. The behavioral inhibition system. This system responds to any of its adequate inputs with all of its outputs and comprises the hypothetical substrate on which the antianxiety drugs act to reduce anxiety. (Innate fear stimuli, which represent a fourth type of input in the original figure, are not included here.) (From J. A. Gray [1982], *The Neuropsychology of Anxiety*, p. 12. Copyright © 1982 by Jeffrey A. Gray. Adapted by permission.)

Gray proposed that the central task of the behavioral inhibition system is to compare actual with expected stimuli. The system functions in two modes. If stimuli match an existent neuronal map in the person's brain, it is in the "just checking" mode and behavioral control remains with other (unspecified) brain systems. If there is a mismatch of expected with perceived stimuli, or if the predicted stimulus is aversive, the behavioral inhibition system switches to a "control" mode. This may involve ascending noradrenergic and serotonergic fibers to the hippocampus which appear to open a gate by attaching an "important" tag to the stimulus. When the gate is closed, behavior continues as usual. When it is open, the septo-hippocampal system takes over. This can be seen as analogous to a subroutine in a large computer program. If a certain "if then" condition is met, the program branches to the subroutine and follows its commands. When the subroutine has completed its function, control is returned to the main program for the continuation of normal processing.

When the behavioral inhibition system is in the control mode, its first action is to inhibit any motor program in progress. Second, it increases attentional processes to "check out" the mismatch and, third, it initiates appropriate exploratory and investigative behavior to determine why the mismatch occurred. In short, the system produces behavioral inhibition concomitantly with an increase in physiological arousal, vigilance, and attention. What is striking about this pattern of responses, which Gray recorded in the laboratory with infrahuman subjects, is its direct correspondence to the three symptom clusters of the generalized anxiety disorder (GAD) in the DSM-III-R (e.g., motor tension, autonomic hyperactivity, vigilance and scanning).

Much of Gray's research has taken advantage of the observation that different families of drugs (e.g., benzodiazepines, barbiturates, and alcohol) exert an anxiolytic effect. Consequently, they can be used to "triangulate" the critical behaviors and neural changes that constitute their antianxiety action by allowing the segregation of this effect from their individual side-effects. For example, the benzodiazepines do not affect behavior elicited by other classes of stimuli (e.g., rewards) but they do affect the responses to the three classes of stimuli involved in the behavioral inhibition system.

Histological evidence suggests that the critical site of antianxiety drug action is in the limbic system, specifically the afferent and efferent fibers of the hippocampal system (Gray, 1982). In fact, there is considerable overlap between the profile of behavioral change observed after septal and hippocampal lesions, on the one hand, and the administration of antianxiety drugs on the other. It is known that there are high-affinity receptors for the benzodiazepines located in the septo-hippocampal areas and that there is a relationship between this receptor and the activity of gamma-aminobutyric-acid (GABA) (Braestrup & Nielsen, 1980). However, it does not appear that occupancy of the benzodiazepine receptor is essential for an anxiolytic effect since the barbiturates and alcohol have essentially the same behavioral effects but do not bind there. This suggests that the important element is the facilitation of GABA-ergic transmission, which is produced by the barbiturates as well as the benzodiazepines. (The pharmacodynamics of these drugs are discussed at length in Chapter 7.)

The mechanism of the anxiolytic medications appears to be their ability to reduce the flow of noradrenergic and serotonergic impulses to the septo-hippocampal system. These impulses possibly originate in the locus ceruleus and/or the raphé nuclei, both of which receive GABA-ergic fibers. A reduction of noradrenergic activity in the septo-hippocampal system will result in fewer stimuli being tagged as "important." In addition, it appears that projections of the serotonergic system are responsible for tagging stimuli associated with punishment. When this occurs, the operation of the septo-hippocampal system is even more strongly biased toward inhibition. Ascending cholinergic fibers are thought to facilitate stimulus analysis. Noradrenergic projections *to* the hypothalamus, on the other hand, are thought to prime the autonomic nervous system for action, especially those aspects involved with fight or flight response.

The behavioral inhibition system is related to clinical manifestations of anxiety in several ways. For example, obsessive-compulsive neurosis is thought to represent an excessive checking of potential environmental hazards. Reduction of checking behavior will occur if there is the reduction of the flow of noradrenergic and serotonergic signals reaching the hippocampal system. This can be accomplished either pharmacologically or behaviorally. In the case of the former, anxiolytic medications may serve this purpose.[2] In terms of the latter, interventions involving response prevention are thought to allow for the habituation of the system (Watts, 1979). (Habituation is the waning of a response to a stimulus when the stimulus is repeatedly presented.) In human beings, there are also connections from the septo-hippocampal system and the entorhinal cortex and neocortex so that there is access to verbally coded stores of information. In this way, human anxiety can be triggered by largely verbal stimuli (relatively independently of ascending monoaminergic influences).

Endogenous Anxiety

Gray's model of behavioral inhibition is concerned with how certain types of stimuli instigate a pattern of responses said to be indicative of

[2]Gray's proposal regarding the role of the noradrenergic system in obsessive-compulsive disorder is undercut by the failure of the anxiolytic medications to demonstrate a reliable treatment effect (Ananth, 1985). An alternative theory suggests that obsessive-compulsive disorder is caused by the supersensitive response of another neurotransmitter, dopamine. This theory is based, in part, on the observation that such disorders as tardive dyskinesia, Gilles de la Tourette's syndrome, and amphetamine psychosis, all of which involve increased dopaminergic activity (Creese, Burt, & Snyder, 1977; Ellinwood, 1967), exhibit a pattern of involuntary, repetitive movements that appear similar to the compulsive behaviors characteristic of obsessive-compulsive disorder. Nevertheless, the failure of the neuroleptics, which block dopaminergic activity, to play a significant role in the treatment of obsessive-compulsive disorder raises doubts about this theory as well. A third biochemical theory of obsessive-compulsive disorder suggests that there is a deficiency in serotonin that occurs in conjunction with an increase in dopaminergic activity (Thorén Åsberg, Cronholm, Jörnestedt, & Träskman, 1980). This proposal is based on the finding that clomipramine, which inhibits the re-uptake of serotonin at the presynaptic terminal, is effective in the treatment of the disorder (e.g., Ananth, Peckhold, van den Stern, & Engelsmann, 1981; Karabanow, 1977; Yaryura-Tobias, Neziroglu, & Bergman, 1976). Although the impication of serotonin has some relevance for Gray's model, at present no single physiological explanation of obsessive-compulsive disorder appears to be satisfactory.

anxiety. He does not deal with the possibility that some forms of anxiety can occur spontaneously without reference to external events. This type of disorder is generally referred to as *endogenous anxiety* to distinguish it from anxiety resulting from a person's interaction with his or her external environment (cf. Butler, Gelder, Hibbert, Cullington, & Klimes, 1987). Endogenous anxiety highlights biological factors within an individual operating more or less independently of situational events and is particularly relevant to panic (Sheehan, 1982).

Panic Disorder. Panic disorder is characterized by "sudden, spontaneous, unexplained panic attacks and a feeling of helpless terror or impending disaster, accompanied by a flight response and autonomic manifestations of anxiety" (Sheehan, Ballenger, & Jacobsen, 1980, p. 51). It usually strikes without warning and for no apparent reason (Craske, Grenier, Klosko, & Barlow, 1986; Ley, 1985a). These attacks involve not only autonomic effects but also disrupt normal mental functions and often cause disorientation or feelings of unreality. The sudden, unexpected surge of panic sets this disorder apart from normal response-to-threat anxiety with which we are all familiar. As such, it is not analogous to severe anxiety and requires a different understanding and treatment. Consequently, prescribing rest, relaxation, or minor tranquilizers will most likely be unsuccessful and possibly result in further fear and frustration (Jacob & Rapport, 1984).

If not dealt with properly, panic attacks may lead to a pattern of phobias and eventually agoraphobia (Craske & Barlow, 1988). In the months following the sudden onset of panic, the setting in which the attack occurred will usually determine the nature of the phobia that develops (Brier, Charney, & Heninger, 1986). With time, multiple phobias and avoidance behaviors may develop by way of generalization. This, in turn, can lead to substantial anticipatory anxiety that may precipitate further attacks and result in a vicious cycle (Craske, Rapee, & Barlow, 1988; Margraf, Ehlers, & Roth, 1987). If the process continues to the point of a general avoidance of a wide range of places and situations, agoraphobia has developed. For example, a review of intake information garnered from 60 consecutive clients at an anxiety and stress disorders clinic identified 23 patients who experienced agoraphobia with panic attacks but none who exhibited symptoms of agoraphobia without panic (Di Nardo et al., 1983).

The unusual nature of panic has been recognized for some time. Freud (1935) distinguished between his "neurasthenic" patients and those who were suffering from "anxiety neurosis." Although sexual conflict was seen as the basis for both disorders, the former were somehow different. He wrote, "All that I am asserting is that the symptoms of these patients are not mentally determined or removable by analysis, but that they must be regarded as direct toxic consequences of disturbed sexual chemical processes" (p. 47). This is not incompatible with Sheehan's (1982) argument that panic disorder is a metabolic disorder of the inhibitory neurotransmitters (e.g., GABA, glycine, beta-aline) or of receptor sensitivity to them leading to a failure to dampen excitatory responses.

Physiological Mechanisms of Panic. Although there is general agreement on the clinical features of panic disorder and its relationship to agoraphobia, the picture becomes less clear in regard to how or why it occurs. Several studies have failed to find differences in various metabolic measures, such as blood pH, lactate, pyruvate, ionized calcium, and adrenalin or plasma glucose levels during panic episodes (Gorman, Martinez, Liebowitz, Fyer, & Klein, 1984; Rainey et al., 1984). Nevertheless, two models of panic have been developed, both of which implicate respiration and maintenance of the acid-base balance of the body as the process by which panic is initiated.

The first and more parsimonious of the two models proposes that some individuals tend to overbreathe (i.e., hyperventilate) under conditions that provoke anxiety, thereby increasing their susceptibility for the disorder (Huey & West, 1983; Salkovskis, Jones, & Clark, 1986). An increase in respiration "blows off" carbon dioxide (CO_2) from the lungs, which reduces the partial pressure (i.e., concentration) of carbon dioxide in the blood (pCO_2). As pCO_2 drops, plasma pH rises and results in alkalosis. Some of the effects on the central nervous system of increased alkalosis include dizziness, blurred vision, numbness, tingling in the hands and feet, tachycardia, palpitations, nausea, and breathlessness (Singer, 1958). (See Panel 6.3, "Respiration and Acid-Base Balance.")

Over time, it is thought that low levels of hyperventilation can lead to adjustments in the renal buffering system, which, in turn, lowers the pCO_2 set-point in a manner similar to that observed in persons living at high altitudes (Gledhill, Beirne, & Dempsey, 1975). As a result, the efficiency of the blood buffer systems is reduced so that any sudden increase in pH due to a brief period of acute hyperventilation may trigger the physical sensations of panic (Okel & Hurst, 1961). In some individuals, these symptoms could initiate a cycle of psychological and physiological events to cause a full-blown attack (Clark, 1986, 1988; Clark et al., 1988). (This model is presented in Figure 6.4.)

Steps taken to restore respiratory control may allow for the resetting of the set-point and thus reduce the vulnerability to psychosocial

PANEL 6.3

Respiration and Acid-Base Balance

Maintenance of its acid-base balance is one of the body's most important functions, and a disruption of this balance can have serious, even fatal consequences. The acidity of the body is determined by the concentration of hydrogen ions in the blood and fluid around the cells. If the concentration of hydrogen ions rises too high, which is indicated by a drop in the body's pH, *acidosis* occurs. Extreme acidosis causes a general depression of the nervous system, leading to coma and death if not corrected. A decrease in hydrogen ion concentration (i.e., a rise in pH) results in *alkalosis*. Alkalosis causes nervous system overexcitability so that when a person becomes alkalotic, muscle tetany may occur in addition to the other unpleasant symptoms noted in the text. In extreme cases of alkalosis, a person may die of convulsions.

The acid-base balance of the body can be disrupted in many ways. Physical conditions, such as diarrhea, vomiting, or uremia, can cause metabolic acidosis due to the excessive loss of alkali from the body fluids. Alkalosis may follow the use of certain diuretics that cause an excessive secretion of hydrogen ions in the urine, or the ingestion of alkaline drugs, such as sodium bicarbonate in the treatment of gastritis or peptic ulcer.

There are three defenses the body employs against changes in the concentration of hydrogen ions. These are (1) the buffering compounds in the body's fluids, (2) the respiration system, and (3) the kidneys. Buffering compounds "tie up" hydrogen ions or convert strong bases to water, thus preventing excessive changes in the hydrogen ion concentration. Some of these compounds include bicarbonate, phosphate, and proteins, with proteins being the most plentiful. The kidneys also regulate hydrogen ion concentration by excreting either acid or alkaline urine. Although the renal system is slower to act than the other two defenses, it can work to restore the acid-base balance almost indefinitely, thus providing a powerful negative feedback system (Glednill, Beirne, & Dempsey, 1975).

The respiration system falls between the other two in terms of how quickly it reacts to fluctuations in hydrogen ion concentration and its ability to restore the acid-base balance. The mechanism of action involves regulating the level of carbon dioxide (CO_2) through alterations in the rate of ventilation. CO_2 combines with water (H_2O) in the body fluids to form carbonic acid (H_2CO_3). Carbonic acid, in turn, dissociates into hydrogen and bicarbonate ions, thus lowering the pH level throughout the body. An increase in breathing blows off CO_2, lowering its concentration in the blood (pCO_2) and raising the body's pH. Conversely, an increase in pCO_2, such as occurs when one holds one's breath, lowers pH.

A chemosensitive center on the surface of the medulla regulates the rate of ventilation. Normally, this potent control center responds to increases in pCO_2 with an increase in the frequency of the respiratory rhythm (Guyton, 1981, p. 518). This is because CO_2 passes easily across the blood-brain barrier where it reacts with H_2O to form carbonic acid. The resultant drop in pH in the brain, particularly the cerebrospinal fluid, is known to have a direct stimulatory effect on the chemosensitive area of the medulla. Thus, this system acts to stimulate respiration when CO_2 builds up in the blood.

Like many of the body's systems that are designed to deal with life-threatening situations, the respiratory control system is more easily stimulated than inhibited. In addition, brakes on the system are weak. The vagus nerve inhibits the inspiratory area of the respiratory center, which is also influenced by the pneumotaxic area in the pons. Both of these feedback systems are concerned with turning off the inspiration signal before the lungs become too full of air. Although this has an indirect effect on the rate of respiration, neither appears to play an important role in dampening the respiratory cascade once it has started.

Given the chemoreceptor center's importance in the regulation of the acid-base balance of the body, it can be seen why this system might be implicated in the initiation of panic. Of the three systems designed to defend against changes in hydrogen ion concentration, only the respiratory system is under voluntary control. Consequently, it is more vulnerable to dysregulation when confronted with a metabolic challenge initiated by an anxiety-provoking situation.

stressors (Bonn, Readhead, & Timmons, 1984; Rapee, 1985). Salkovskis, Jones, and Clark (1986) found that patients susceptible to panic attacks did evidence lowered levels of pCO_2 that returned to normal with respiratory control training procedures. Training consisted of three steps. The first step was to induce a panic attack by having the patient hyperventilate. When this occurred, the therapist explained to the patient the reason why overbreathing produced panic. This was followed by training the patient in slow breathing. The procedure was found to reduce both the frequency and severity of panic attacks in a clinical trial of 18 patients with follow-ups at 6 months and 2 years (Clark, Salkovskis, & Chalkley, 1985). The finding was subsequently replicated in a second clinical series with 9 patients and follow-ups at 3 and 6 months (Salkovskis et al., 1986).

The problem with this model is that it is more descriptive than it is explanatory. It fails to explain, for example, why certain individuals have a tendency to overbreathe under conditions of stress. More importantly, the model fails to explain convincingly how the normal negative

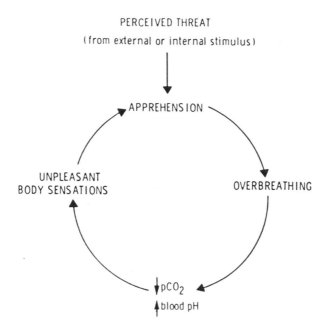

PERCEIVED THREAT
(from external or internal stimulus)

APPREHENSION

OVERBREATHING

UNPLEASANT
BODY SENSATIONS

↓pCO₂
↑blood pH

Figure 6.4. A model of the development of a panic attack. (From D. M. Clark, P. M. Salkovskis, and A. J. Chalkley [1985], Respiratory Control as a Treatment for Panic Attacks, *Journal of Behavior Therapy and Experimental Psychiatry, 16*, p. 24. Copyright © 1985 by Pergamon Press, Ltd. Reprinted by permission.)

feedback mechanisms that control respiration are overridden to the degree that the body's acid-base balance is thrown completely out of balance. Nevertheless, it does provide a rationale for an easily implemented intervention that may be effective, particularly in the early stages of panic, and that may serve a prophylactic purpose for individuals who are susceptible to the disorder.

A possible explanation for instigation of positive feedback in panic is provided by the second model of the disorder (Sheehan, 1982; Carr & Sheehan, 1984). These investigators argue that panic results from a pathological oversensitivity to a drop in pH (i.e., increased acidity) of the respiratory reflex (chemoreceptor) center on the ventral medullary surface in the brain (Dermietzel, 1976). This oversensitivity is thought to trigger a ventilation-arousal cascade, which these central chemoreceptors activate, thus initiating a vicious cycle of increased arousal/anxiety and further increases in the rate of ventilation (see Ley, 1985b, for an extended discussion). They suggest that *local* (i.e., in certain tissues) rather than *systemic* (i.e., pertaining to bodily systems as a whole) changes in pH are responsible for maintaining excessive ventilation in the face of increased alkalosis.

Given the complexity of the body's regulatory functions, it is not unusual for a change in one system to instigate a compensatory response in another that causes the opposite effect. In this case, an increase in ventilation may cause the body's normal autoregulatory mechanism to constrict blood vessels in the face of increased pO_2, which occurs with hyperventilation. The resultant vasoconstriction under these conditions is known to induce ischemia in certain organs of the body, including the liver, heart, and brain (MacMillan & Siesjo, 1973). A reduction in cerebral blood flow allows for a build-up of lactic acid, which is retained or trapped in the brain. This, in turn, causes a drop in cortical pH in spite of the increase in systemic alkalosis. Increased acidity in the medullary region of the brain would stimulate the chemoreceptor zone further, increasing the rate of ventilation, and thus providing a common pathogenic mechanism for panic disorder and hyperventilation syndrome (Carr & Sheehan, 1984; Magarian, 1982). (A schematic interpretation of this hypothesis is provided in Figure 6.5.)

The second model was inspired by M. E. Cohen and White's (1950) observation that patients who had previously experienced panic attacks exhibited an exercise-induced increase in blood lactate that was more pronounced than for normal individuals. Lactic acid is a ubiquitous intermediary metabolite produced by the anaerobic metabolism of carbohydrates.[3] During vigorous exercise, levels of blood lactate increase 10 to 20 times. Confirmation of the early finding by several other investigators (e.g., Holmgren & Ström, 1959; Jones & Mellersh, 1946) prompted Pitts and McClure in 1967 to see if lactate could produce anxiety in susceptible patients. They were able to show that 13 of 14 patients evidenced reliable symptoms of anxiety after the infusion of sodium lactate, as compared to only 2 of 10 normals. This report lead to a series of studies, all of which more or less confirmed that the infusion of sodium lactate (but not of dextrose or saline) was more likely to lead to intense anxiety in panic disorder and/or agoraphobic subjects than in normal controls (e.g., Appleby, Klein, Sachar, & Levitt, 1981; Liebowitz et al., 1984).

An advantage of Sheehan's model is that it highlights those factors that may serve as inappropriate triggers for panic disorder by enhancing the sensitivity of the chemoreceptor zone. For example, caffeine is

[3]Lactic acid is derived solely by the reduction of pyruvate, which requires the oxidation of the cofactor NADH. Although this reaction takes place in the mitochondria of the cells, lactic acid diffuses readily out of the cells into the extracellular fluids and even into the intracellular fluids of less active cells, thus lowering the pH of bodily fluids generally.

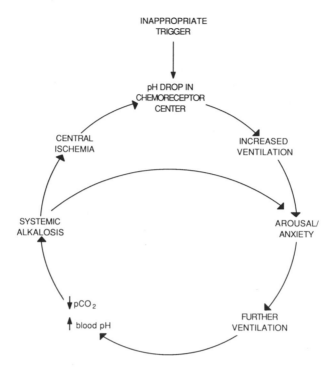

Figure 6.5. A schematic interpretation of Carr and Sheehan's (1984) model of panic. (See text for explanation.)

known to stimulate the central ventilatory drive. Several investigators have demonstrated that patients with agoraphobia and panic attacks exhibit a markedly increased sensitivity to the anxiogenic effects of caffeine as compared to healthy subjects (Boulenger, Uhde, Wolff, & Post, 1984; Charney, Heninger, & Jatlow, 1985). The progestins (e.g., progesterone), which are supplied endogenously during the luteal phase of the menstrual cycle, are also thought to sensitize the susceptible individual to panic (J. B. Martin & Reichlin, 1987). This may explain why females experience panic twice as often as men and why it frequently makes an appearance during early reproductive maturity.

A second advantage of the model is its ability to explain why panic episodes terminate on their own. Psychological theories of panic have difficulty dealing with this aspect of the disorder and usually maintain only that the attacks are "self-terminating" or that they "run their course" (Ley, 1987). Sheehan's model, on the other hand, would predict that, with continued hyperventilation, the pCO_2 of the blood would drop so low that even with central ischemia the level of acidosis in the chemoreceptor trigger zone would not be sufficient to maintain excessive levels of ventilation. In addition, the absence of positive feedback signals from chemoreceptors located outside of the CNS (e.g., the carotid and aortic bodies) would diminish involuntary respiration further and thus move ventilation back toward normal (Guyton, 1981, pp. 518–523).

Despite these advantages, the metabolic evidence upon which the second model is based has been called into question. A review of the lactate infusion research has noted that many of these studies are methodologically unsound, making it hard to separate the anxiety-inducing aspects of the experiment from the substance being studied (Margraf, Ehlers, Roth, Taylor, & Maddock, 1985). For example, one study reported that two of the patients began having the panic attack before the infusion began and that the resultant symptoms did not change in number or intensity during actual infusion (Rainey et al., 1984). Also, while lactate infusions can produce anxiety resembling panic, the experimental state and actual panic are not identical. Furthermore, many of these studies are able to induce panic in only approximately half of the patient subjects while some nonpatients also developed symptoms of panic during the experiment. Finally, a more recent well-controlled lactate study found that both patients with panic disorder and normal controls exhibited similar levels of heart-rate responsivity and self-reported anxiety during infusion (Ehlers et al., 1986). Although the panic patients were more reactive than controls in terms of systolic and diastolic blood pressure, the authors concluded that the response to lactate is not a reliable biological marker of proneness to panic attacks.

Consequently, it can be seen that neither model of panic disorder is without problems. The first fails to explain the mechanism by which positive respiratory feedback occurs, while the second's explanation of this phenomenon is fairly speculative and based on inconsistent data. It is possible that a more adequate theory of endogenous anxiety will need to combine both the behavioral (e.g., respiratory control) and metabolic (e.g., chemoreceptor sensitivity) aspects of the disorder (Ley, 1987).

Whatever the case, there is agreement on panic's distinct clinical picture with its characteristic spontaneity, unpredictability, and pattern of excessive physical symptomatology. Also, it appears that effective interventions for panic differ from those used with other anxiety disorders. Although it is unclear how they work, the success of the antidepressants and the failure of the benzodiazepines for treating panic suggest that panic disorder is somehow different from the other states. The same point can be made by the heritability studies as well. A genetic contribution to panic disorder appears certain, in contrast to the weak and/or inconsistent findings for other anxiety disorders, especially GAD. Consequently, biological models for panic disorder cannot be ignored.

Autonomic Activity in Panic. Both models agree that excessive stimulation of the respiratory reflex center can trigger an outburst of autonomic nervous system (ANS) activity. In this regard, many of the physiological symptoms of panic (e.g., palpitations, hot flashes, chest pain or discomfort, sweating and trembling) are thought to follow rather than precede the onset of panic. Although increased autonomic activity may contribute to or exacerbate an episode once it has started (Ehlers, Margraf, Roth, Taylor, & Birbaumer, 1988), the respiratory model of panic does not see the disorder as resulting from a reaction to or fear generated by excessive autonomic activity (see Ley, 1987, for a discussion of two different approaches to panic disorder). Whatever the case, activity of the ANS is central to our understanding of panic disorder.

One study took six agoraphobic patients who had experienced panic and exposed them to phobic stimuli that had previously elicited their attacks (Ko et al., 1983). Plasma levels of a norepinephrine metabolite, MHPG (3-methoxy-4-hydroxy-phenylglycol), correlated highly with the subjects' ratings of anxiety under all of the experimental conditions (i.e., during baseline, preparation, and panic). The administration of either clonidine (an antihypertensive medication) or imipramine (a tricyclic antidepressant) correlated with a reduction of plasma MHPG levels as well as reports of diminished symptomatology. Another study found that the administration of yohimbine, an alpha$_2$ receptor agonist, provoked significantly greater increases in subject-rated anxiety, nervousness, palpitations, hot and cold flashes, and restlessness among a group of 39 drug-free patients with agoraphobia and panic attacks as compared to 20 healthy controls (Charney, Heninger, & Brier, 1984). MHPG levels were found to be related to subjective ratings of feelings as well as the somatic symptoms.

These findings suggest that the locus ceruleus plays a role in mediating the autonomic component of the panic attack (Redmond, 1977, 1979; Redmond & Huang, 1979; Redmond, Huang, Snyder, & Maas, 1976). Clonidine binds preferentially to alpha$_2$ adrenergic receptors in the locus ceruleus and thus modulates the amount of norepinephrine released (Starke & Altmann, 1973). It is thought to suppress the release of norepinephrine centrally via negative-feedback mechanisms by mimicking the action of the transmitter on alpha-receptor sites. In animals, it also inhibits spontaneous firing of the norepinephrine neurons in the locus ceruleus, which reduces adrenergic turnover in the brain (Svensson, Bunney, & Aghajanian, 1975). (However, tolerance to clonidine develops quickly in the CNS so that it is not of great clinical value.)

The locus ceruleus is normally activated as an emergency response to the triggering of the central chemoreceptor area and is therefore thought to play a central role in mediating the autonomic aspects of a panic attack. It is known to have multiple noradrenergic connections with the cortex, and electrical stimulation of the locus ceruleus, at least in animals, is thought to mimic the effects of anxiety (Redmond & Huang, 1979). Nevertheless, the autonomic discharge in panic is neither a specific nor an exclusive mediator of panic disorder (Ekman, Levenson, & Friesen, 1983). In fact, ANS changes in panic disorder have a profile similar to that found in extreme normal anxiety, although the onset and subjective experience of panic is quite different, as noted earlier.

The tricyclics and benzodiazepines also have been found to decrease central norepinephrine firing in the locus ceruleus (Aghajanian, Cedarbaum, & Wang, 1977; Grant, Huang, & Redmond, 1980). However, it is still difficult to understand how the antidepressants work since they increase adrenergic and serotonergic activity at central synapses and thus might be expected to aggravate rather than alleviate the symptoms of panic (Ashton, 1987; Wilbur & Kulik, 1981). Klein, Zitrin, and Woerner (1978) have suggested that these medications are not working as antidepressants with this population and may be exerting their effect through some other neurotransmission system (also see Tyrer, Candy, & Kelly, 1973). For example, although phenelzine (an MAO inhibitor) increases the synaptic concentration of norepinephrine, it also increases the concentration of several inhibitory neurotransmitters, such as GABA. In like manner, imipramine (a tricyclic) also inhibits re-uptake of GABA thus increasing its activity. This hypothesis also fails to explain why the benzodiazepines, which are thought to enhance GABA transmission as well, have little efficacy in the treatment of agoraphobia (Hafner & Marks, 1976). In this regard, however, Carr and Sheehan (1984) suggest that the GABA-ergic systems affected by the benzodiazepines are not active in the medullary trigger zone. Whatever the case, the mechanism(s) by which the antidepressant medications help control panic is still highly conjectural at this point.

Summary of Physiological Factors

The various physiological theories of anxiety offer distinct but complementary perspectives. All of them view individuals as differing in terms of their vulnerability to developing anxiety states, and, in each case, these differences are thought to be genetically based. However, the individual differences approach is concerned with individual differences in arousal systems (e.g., "nervous types") and thus attempts to describe general predispositions. Gray's behavioral inhibition system focuses on stimulus-response relationships. Consequently, his model allows for greater specificity in the identification of anxiety-provoking stimuli and physiological response patterns said to be characteristic of anxiety. With its emphasis on stimuli that signal novelty or punishment, the behavioral inhibition system is also applicable to such disorders as GAD, overanxious disorder in children, the simple and social phobias, and perhaps PTSD. Stimuli that signal extinction might be seen as particularly relevant to separation anxiety of childhood. Also, as noted earlier, the "just checking" function of the septo-hippocampal system is thought to relate directly to symptoms of obsessive-compulsive disorder. Sheehan's work with endogenous anxiety, on the other hand, has concentrated on anxiety's biochemical basis, particularly as it relates to panic disorder and the subsequent development of agoraphobia. While none of the approaches attempts to deal extensively with the subjective aspects of anxiety, their elaboration of its physiological aspects may serve to flesh out the cognitive or phenomenological models to which they are related (cf. Kenardy, Evans, & Oei, 1988; van den Hout, Boek, van der Molen, Jansen, & Griez, 1988).

Treatment Implications

It is clear that physiological factors play more of a role in some of the anxiety disorders than others. Nevertheless, both cognitive and somatic aspects must be taken into account if the complex interaction between the two sets of factors is to be dealt with successfully (Barlow, 1988; Barlow et al., 1984; Jacob & Rapport, 1984; Turner & Beidel, 1985). An appreciation of this possibility can serve to cut across the paradigmatic boundaries of psychology and medicine so as to make the treatment of anxiety more comprehensive and hopefully more efficacious.

This can occur on the most basic level by recognizing that individuals are very different in terms of their susceptibility to the development of these disorders and that these differences may be fundamental in terms of the person's biological make-up. In addition, it may be important for the psychologist to acknowledge that some aspects of the anxiety disorders may involve biochemical factors that operate more or less independently of life events, interpersonal relationships, or existential dilemmas. It is equally true, on the other hand, that the physician might need to appreciate that the physiology of anxiety always occurs within a psychosocial context and that, while useful in alleviating or controlling some of these conditions, medications have little to offer in terms of modifying the learning that has occurred as a result of these disturbances.

The treatment of panic disorder and agoraphobia with medications is a case in point. In 1962 Klein and Fink suggested that imipramine (a tricyclic antidepressant) was useful for decreasing or eliminating panic attacks. The MAO inhibitors were studied two years later (Klein, 1964), and subsequently the general use of antidepressants for the treatment of agoraphobia and panic became widely accepted (e.g., Kelly, Guirguis, Frommer, Mitchell-Heggs, & Sargant, 1970; Solyom et al., 1973; Sheehan, Ballenger, & Jacobson, 1980; Sheehan et al., 1984). By 1987 there were 21 controlled studies of the treatment of agoraphobia with antidepressants, mostly tricyclics or MAO inhibitors (Marks, 1987). In terms of the tricyclics, the findings varied depending on who was doing the research. Three studies from the Klein group in New York (e.g., Zitrin, Klein, & Woerner, 1980) all found imipramine to be effective in the treatment of agoraphobia. Two studies from the Mavissakalian group in Pittsburgh (Mavissakalian & Michelson, 1986; Michelson & Mavissakalian, 1985) found that imipramine was better than placebo but not superior to therapist-aided exposure. And a study from the Maudsley Hospital (Marks et al., 1983) with follow-ups of 2 (S. D. Cohen, Monteiro, & Marks, 1984) and 5 years (Lelliott, Marks, Monteiro, Tsakiris, & Noshirvani, 1987) found no effect for imipramine, a short-lived effect for therapist-aided exposure, and improvement for all groups (each of which was treated with self-exposure). Data at the 5-year follow-up suggested that the absence of depression accounted for the lack of differences since those subjects with low Hamilton Rating Scale depression scores exhibited more generalized improvement of their phobias than those subjects with moderate pretreatment scores.

The story for MAO inhibitors (7 studies, 6 with phenelzine) is inconsistent as well. Four studies reported favorable outcomes, while a fifth found significant results for social phobia but not agoraphobia. The lack of findings from a sixth study may be explained in terms of a sample that was not significantly depressed (Solyom et al., 1973). A seventh study, which used iproniazid (Lipsedge et al., 1973), found an effect for self-reports of anxiety but not phobic avoidance.

It does appear, however, that antidepressant medications are compatible with exposure treatments of agoraphobia and may enhance treatment effectiveness, especially if the patient's mood is dysphoric to start with (Marks, 1987; Sheehan et al., 1980). Consequently, it may be that behavioral training (i.e., respiratory control) and antidepressants affect panic at different points in the process. Controlled breathing may intervene fairly early in the process by increasing resting levels of pCO_2 in those patients who may be chronically, mildly hyperventilating, thus reducing their susceptibility to panic attack. The antidepressants, on the other hand, may block or dampen autonomic discharge triggered by the hyperventilation-respiratory cascade. Peripheral agents, such as the beta-blockers, may contribute to the disruption of the panic cycle by inhibiting (i.e., blocking) the positive feedback of peripheral physiological changes.

Nevertheless, medications do not provide all of the answers for the treatment of agoraphobia. Among other problems, these medications are slow in terms of onset of therapeutic effect, induce numerous side effects (e.g., drowsiness, dizziness, dry mouth, constipation, etc.), and contribute to treatment dropouts (16% to 36% for imipramine). In addition, relapse rates can be quite high (Marks, 1987; Solyom et al., 1973). In one study, for example, *all* of the phenelzine-treated group relapsed after 2 years in comparison with only 10% of the patients treated with behavior therapy. Furthermore, while the antidepressant medications may be able to dampen the severity of subjective distress or feelings of panic, they have essentially no effect on the avoidance behavior that may develop as a result of these experiences (e.g., Lipsedge et al., 1973). It is therefore not surprising to find that every study that supported the efficacy of antidepressants for agoraphobia also found the need to use conjunctive "psychotherapy" to treat the phobic "symptoms."

A similar picture emerges with drug treatments for other types of phobia. In terms of the simple phobias, Zitrin and her associates (Zitrin, Klein, & Woerner, 1978) found no effect for imipramine over that obtained by a placebo. Socially phobic outpatients were not helped by propranolol (Falloon, Lloyd, & Harpin, 1981). There are two controlled studies of school phobia. In the first (Gittelman-Klein & Klein, 1971), more children receiving imipramine plus caseworker intervention were back in school, had fewer physical complaints, and were less depressed than a placebo group. However, the imipramine group also had more side effects (81% compared to 47%, respectively) and twice as many dropouts (almost one-third of the treatment group). A second double-blind study found no effect of clomipramine on school refusal, although depression improved in the girls (Berney et al., 1981).

Of some 20 controlled drug studies of obsessive-compulsive disorder reviewed by Marks (1987), a majority used clomipramine (a tricyclic antidepressant). The largest and longest of these studies was from the

Maudsley Hospital (Marks, Stern, Mawson, Cobb, & McDonald, 1980; Marks et al., 1983; Mawson, Marks, & Ramm, 1982). Clomipramine improved depression, anxiety, and social adjustment and decreased rituals 2 to 4 months into treatment. However, these gains were reduced by the end of 9 months, no longer significant after 1 year, and had disappeared by the 2-year follow-up. Furthermore, it helped only those patients who were initially depressed. Other studies have yet to find that clomipramine is significantly better than other tricyclics or that its effects are specifically linked to obsessive-compulsive symptoms (Marks, 1987). Relapse is also a problem, as is the problem of dropouts, which range from 11% to 14%.

Consequently, the combination of antidepressant medication with behavioral procedures may provide the best hope for the successful treatment of the obsessive-compulsive (Amin, Ban, Peckhold, & Klingner, 1977; Turner, Hersen, Bellack, Andrasik, & Capparell, 1980), especially for patients who are "very ruminative, doubtful, and highly anxious," (Solyom & Sookman, 1977, p. 49). This is because the two treatment approaches appear to affect different aspects of the disorder. Marks and his associates (1980) found that clomipramine decreased rituals and improved mood, but only for those patients who presented with depressed mood initially. The exposure-based treatment was found to have more lasting effect than the medication on rituals, but it was less likely to improve mood. Consequently, combining of the two forms of treatment had an additive effect. Neverhteless, Marks concluded that exposure remained the treatment of choice. Athough exposure is harder to administer initially and requires "dedication in the face of discomfort," it appears to effect more lasting gains with this population (Marks, 1987, p. 555).

These studies emphasize that pharmacological treatments should not be seen as taking the place of interventions based on psychological, particularly behavioral, principles (Barlow, Craske, Cerny, & Klosko, 1989; Escobar & Landbloom, 1976). This is borne out by a study by Zitrin and her associates (Zitrin et al., 1980), who found that the combination of imipramine and in vivo group exposure was superior to exposure plus a placebo in a randomized, double-blind study of 76 agoraphobic women. However, their results also revealed that approximately two-thirds of the subjects who received the behavioral intervention only also improved. They concluded:

> Although the behavioral techniques of exposure in vivo and desensitization in imagination appear to be more effective when coupled with imipramine therapy, even placebo-treated patients show striking improvement (57% to 78% moderately to markedly improved, depending on the rater) in spite of

the chronicity of the illness (mean duration of 8.6 years). Thus, when a patient is resistant to taking medication or has severe side effects, it certainly seems worthwhile to treat him or her solely with one of these behavioral techniques. (p. 71)

Fortunately, there are several well-controlled studies with adequate follow-up that attest to the efficacy of cognitive-behavioral interventions alone for both agoraphobia and panic disorder (Barlow et al., 1989; Marchione, Michelson, Greenwald, & Dancu, 1987; Michelson, Mavissakalian, & Marchione, 1988).

The importance of nonpharmacological interventions is emphasized further by the observation that in some instances the use of medications for anxiety disorders is contraindicated (Barlow, 1988). For example, the use of benzodiazepines for conditioned anxiety may be harmful to the degree that the drug blocks the habituation process resulting from exposure (Gray, 1982; Marshall & Segal, 1986). In this situation, anxiolytic medications may attenuate or even reverse the benefits of behavioral interventions (Chambless, Foa, Groves, & Goldstein, 1979). Consequently, although medications are useful or even necessary for some anxious clients, they may not be indicated for a group (perhaps a majority) of others (Michelson & Mavissakalian, 1985).

Summary

At the very least, therefore, it can be said that the pharmacological and psychological treatment of the anxiety disorders complement each other (cf. Kandel, 1983). In some cases, drugs may "prime" the patient to face the phobic object or situation and thus allow the therapeutic effects of in vivo exposure to proceed (Hafner & Marks, 1976). In other cases, however, medications may serve as an escape and thus interfere with attempts to confront the situation causing the problem in the first place. The clinician's responsibility, therefore, is to conduct a comprehensive assessment and seek appropriate consultation with colleagues both within and across disciplines. Hopefully, this task is made a bit easier by an appreciation of and respect for the entire range of factors implicated in the development and maintenance of the anxiety disorders.

Chapter 7

Psychoactive Substance Use Disorders

Psychoactive substance use disorders involve physiological symptoms and maladaptive behaviors associated with the regular use of drugs that affect the central nervous system (CNS).[1] Use of psychoactive drugs is said to be maladaptive when it persists despite the presence of social, occupational, psychological, or physical problems. Continued use over time may result in withdrawal symptoms when the drugs are terminated. Substance use disorders are distinguished from substance-induced organic mental disorders in that they deal with problems arising from the use of psychoactive drugs rather than with the acute or chronic effects of these substances on the CNS.

Dependence and Abuse

The essential feature of these disorders is a person's becoming dependent on the substance being used. *Dependence* is characterized by a loss of control that leads to the persistent taking of the drug despite the adverse consequences. (See Panel 7.1, "Psychoactive Substance Use Disorders: Diagnostic Summary.") However, it is also possible that a person may engage in a maladaptive pattern of substance use that falls short of dependence per se. In these cases, an impairment in the ability to function as a consequence of drug use is the key consideration that leads to

[1]Some of these drugs may exert a deleterious effect on the autonomic or peripheral nervous systems as well.

PANEL 7.1

*Psychoactive Substance Use Disorders: Diagnostic Summary**

Psychoactive substance dependence is defined as the continued use of a substance in spite of known aversive consequences. Often dependence includes the physiological symptoms of tolerance and withdrawal, although it is possible for some individuals to have symptoms of both tolerance and withdrawal but not be dependent on the substance. For example, surgical patients may develop a tolerance to prescribed opioids and even experience withdrawal symptoms without demonstrating an inability to control use of these drugs. On the other hand, some people may display impaired control of a substance like cannabis without evidencing either tolerance or withdrawal.

There are nine symptoms of dependence, at least three of which are necessary for the diagnosis to be made. The first of these involves taking the substance in larger and larger amounts over a longer period of time than intended. Second is the desire or unsuccessful attempts to control use of the substance. Third, a great deal of time is spent trying to obtain the substance, taking it, or recovering from its effects. Fourth, frequent symptoms of intoxication or withdrawal interfere with the performance of major role obligations at work, school, or home. The abandonment or reduction of important social, occupational, or recreational activities because of substance use is the fifth symptom. Sixth, use continues despite of knowledge of this persistent disruption of role function. Continued use accompanied by marked tolerance is the seventh symptom, which includes the need for increased amounts of the substance to achieve intoxication or the desired effect. (Tolerance does not apply to all psychoactive substances, such as cannabis, hallucinogens, or phencyclidine.) Eighth, there may be withdrawal symptoms when use is discontinued. Finally, the substance may be used to relieve or avoid withdrawal. The symptoms of dependence are the same across all classes of psychoactive substances, although they may not be as apparent or even apply in a some instances (e.g., withdrawal symptoms do not occur in hallucinogen dependence).

Psychoactive substance abuse is a residual diagnosis indicating a maladaptive pattern of use that does not meet three or more of the criteria for dependence. Abuse is characterized by continued use despite knowledge of persistent or recurrent social, occupational, psychological, or physical problems resulting from or exacerbated by this use. In addition, abuse is said to occur when the substance is used in situations that are physically hazardous (e.g.,

---

*Material for this section is taken directly from the DSM-III-R (*Diagnostic and Statistical Manual of Mental Disorders* [Third Revision, Revised], American Psychiatric Association, 1987).

driving while intoxicated). Often this diagnosis is made with persons who have only recently started taking the psychoactive substances or may involve such substances as cannabis, for which physiological symptoms of withdrawal and the need to use the substance to avoid withdrawal are not problems.

There are nine classes of psychoactive substances associated with dependence and abuse. They are alcohol; amphetamine or similarly acting sympathomimetics; cannabis; cocaine; hallucinogens; inhalants; opioids; phencyclidine (PCP) or similarly acting arylcyclohexylamines; and sedatives, hypnotics, or anxiolytics. A ninth class, nicotine, almost always involves dependence but not abuse (i.e., it is virtually unheard of for someone who is not dependent on nicotine to abuse it). Of these classes, alcohol, sedative-hypnotics and anxiolytics share similar features. There are also similarities between the use of cocaine and amphetamines (or similarly acting sympathomimetics) as well as between the hallucinogens and PCP.

Although a typical diagnosis usually involves a single psychoactive substance, there may be instances in which more than one psychoactive substance is abused, either simultaneously or sequentially. In these cases, either multiple diagnoses are assigned or the diagnosis of polysubstance dependence is made (if at least three different classes of substances not including nicotine are involved).

Although many of the symptoms of dependence or abuse are common to the different classes of drugs, there are also substantial differences between classes. There are several reasons for this. One involves differences in the route of administration. How a drug is used will affect the likelihood of its being abused, the pattern of use, and how quickly the substance reaches the brain. For example, a substance that is injected directly into the blood stream is much more likely to be used in greater amounts and associated with toxic effects than a drug that is absorbed across the intestinal wall. Another difference is based on the drug's duration of action; shorter-acting psychoactive substances, such as amphetamine, cocaine and certain anxiolytics, have a particularly high potential for dependence or abuse. Finally, there are differences between classes in terms of the course of abuse. For drugs like alcohol or cannabis, the course is insidious, occurring over a relatively lengthy period of years. In other instances, such as with amphetamine or cocaine, the course is much more rapid.

Prevalence of abuse and/or dependence of these substances varies as well. From 1981 to 1983 a community study using the DSM-III criteria for psychoactive substance abuse was conducted in the United States. Results indicated that at one time in their lives 13% of the adult population had abused or were dependent on alcohol, 2% on amphetamines, 4% on cannabis, 0.2% on cocaine, 0.3% on hallucinogens, 0.7% on opioids, and 1.1% on sedative-hypnotics. Other data suggest that nicotine dependence is common but that PCP abuse or dependence is rare. Information on the prevalence of inhalant abuse or dependence is lacking. In general, the diagnosis of psychoactive substance use disorder is more common in males than females.

the diagnosis of psychoactive substance *abuse*. The major classes of drugs for which dependence and/or abuse is a problem include alcohol, amphetamine and cocaine, anxiolytics/sedative-hypnotics, cannabis, hallucinogens (including LSD and PCP), inhalants (organic solvents), nicotine, and opioids. Caffeine is also covered in this chapter, although it is unclear whether this substance can actually produce dependence.

The development of dependence begins when the initial effects of the drug are reduced as a result of increasing tolerance or because habituation has occurred (e.g., the substance is perceived as less pleasurable with repeated administrations). This often leads to a craving for the drug and an increase in the amount taken. Dosages may increase until a fairly constant level is maintained. Usage at this level may continue indefinitely unless it is interrupted, which occurs when a person attempts to stop using the drug or, more frequently, when the supply of the substance becomes unavailable (Milby, Jolly, & Beidleman, 1984). If a physical dependence has developed, the cessation of drug administration may result in an abstinence syndrome with its many varied and unpleasant effects.

The natural history of dependence on alcohol and other substances presents a confusing picture. For many years it was assumed that alcoholism represented a chronic disease process, much like cancer or heart disease (Davidson, 1984). This view was an outgrowth of the classic studies on alcoholism by Jellinek in the 1950s (Jellinek, 1952). He suggested that there were four distinguishable states or phases in the development of alcoholism. These include a prealcoholic phase, during which drinking is used for the relief of tension or distress and during which tolerance for increasing amounts of alcohol develops. The second or prodromal phase occurs when the drinker becomes preoccupied with alcohol and is characterized by the appearance of blackouts. This stage leads to the crucial phase during which there is a growing loss of control (i.e., dependence), fear, guilt, and social isolation. Morning drinking, a deterioration of health, and first hospitalizations may occur during this phase. The final or chronic phase involves the complete loss of control and a general deterioration of mental and physical health. Symptoms characteristic of this phase include indefinable fears and persistent tremors. During the final phase there is not only an impairment in thinking and cognitive ability but also, in some cases, the development of episodes of alcoholic psychosis. As many as 40% of alcoholics at this point may offer themselves for treatment since the deterioration of their condition makes denying the severity of the problem difficult to maintain.

It has been argued that the course of alcoholism is more variable than Jellinek's model suggests. For example, blackouts may occur earlier than predicted, later than expected, or not at all (Goodwin, Crane, & Guze, 1969a, 1969b; Trice & Wahl, 1958). Furthermore, several large epidemiological surveys of alcohol consumption in the United States have revealed that people do not report uniform patterns in development of drinking problems (e.g., Cahalan & Room, 1974). Plateaus of severity may develop and remain constant, with many individuals moving in and out of periods of problematic drinking (Clark & Cahalan, 1976). In fact, when individuals are followed over periods as long as 20 years it is found that there may even be a decrease rather than increase in problem drinking among this population (Fillmore, 1975).

An attempt has also been made to identify a consistent pattern of substance abuse for psychoactive drugs other than alcohol. Milby (1981) suggested that use of these substances usually begins with curiosity, excitement, peer pressure, or even medical prescription. The reinforcing effects of the drug and/or peer pressure lead to increasing the size of the dose, the development of tolerance, and eventually dependence. This, in turn, may result in the development of elaborate drug-seeking behavior and the mastery of drug-abuse skills (e.g., the ability to acquire and administer drugs). Nevertheless, it has become apparent that there is also a wide variability in terms of how these substances are used and abused. In fact, it is now generally accepted that the manner in which a substance is abused and the symptoms which occur will vary depending on the pharmacological action of the substance, its legal status, and differences between individuals (Davidson, 1984).

Some of the individual differences that have been associated with differences in drug use are the dimensions of sensation-seeking and introversion-extraversion. Zuckerman has reported that college students who scored high on a measure of sensation-seeking significantly exceeded low-scorers in terms of their use of marihuana, hashish, amphetamine, and LSD (Zuckerman, Neary, & Brustman, 1970). Although occurring infrequently in this 1970 study, cocaine use was reported by the high-sensation-seeking group only. The same was true for glue sniffing. The only drugs used with any frequency among low-sensation groups were marihuana, hashish, and tranquilizers (Zuckerman et al., 1970; Zuckerman, 1972).

A similar pattern has emerged from other studies as well. Eysenck and others (Eysenck & Eysenck, 1975; Golding, Harpur, & Brent-Smith, 1983; Martin, Haertzen, & Hewett, 1978) identified several personality characteristics that tended to identify compulsive drug users. These included risk-taking, impulsivity, sensation- or stimulus-seeking, rebelliousness, aggressiveness, and an intolerance for frustration. As an example, Cherry and Kierman (1976) have linked high scores on Ey-

PANEL 7.2

Heritability of Alcoholism

Alcoholism tends to run in families (Davidson, 1984). This conclusion reflects a consensus that has emerged over the past several decades from two types of studies. One type of study follows the children of alcoholic parents who are adopted at an early age. The second type investigates the degree to which children who share a common genetic makeup (i.e., monozygotic and dizygotic twins) develop the disorder. Both types of studies provide useful information concerning the heritability of alcoholism. The twin studies, however, offer the additional advantage of highlighting mechanisms that may play a role in its development.

There have been a number of well-controlled adoption studies, many of which use the extensive health records maintained in Scandinavian countries over several generations. Goodwin and his colleagues, for example, conducted a series of adoption studies during the 1970s using Danish records (Goodwin, Schulsinger, Hermansen, Guze, & Winokur, 1973; Goodwin, Schulsinger, Knop, Mednick, & Guze, 1977a; Goodwin, Schulsinger, Knop, Mednick, & Guze, 1977b; Goodwin et al., 1974). These investigators followed four groups of subjects—sons of alcoholics raised by either nonalcoholic foster parents or their alcoholic biological parents and daughters raised by either nonalcoholic foster parents or their alcoholic biological parents. The mean age for the groups ranged from 30 to 37 years, and each of the four was paired with a control group matched for age and (for the adoption groups) circumstances of adoption. All of the adoptees were separated from their biological parents in the first few weeks of life and were adopted by nonrelatives. Furthermore, the Danish psychiatrists who conducted the interviews were "blind" to the overall purpose of the study as well as to the identity of the interviewees (e.g., whether they were children of alcoholics or controls).

From these studies, four conclusions emerge (Goodwin, 1979). First, "children of alcoholics are particularly vulnerable to alcoholism, whether raised by their alcoholic parents or by nonalcoholic foster parents" (p. 58). Second, the vulnerability for alcoholism is specific for that disorder only and does not appear to increase the risk for the development of other forms of psychopathology, including the abuse of other psychoactive substances. Third, there are differences between the sons and daughters of alcoholics in terms of drinking patterns and the age at which problems develop. Daughters are less likely to become heavy drinkers, but of those who do, a high percentage are likely to become alcoholic. In addition, alcoholism tends to make its appearance at a later age among women. Finally, it was concluded that alcoholism is not on a continuum with "heavy drinking" or even "problem drinking," a finding that argues against the notion of alcoholism as a progressive disease process.

Other adoption studies have tended to confirm these results. Schuckit and his associates (Schuckit, Goodwin, & Winokur, 1972) found that children whose biological parents were alcoholic but who were raised by nonalcoholic adoptive parents showed a greater probability of becoming alcoholic than children of nonalcoholic biologic parents who were adopted into alcoholic homes. Cadoret and Gath (1978) studied 84 adoptees 18 years of age or older who were separated at birth from their biological parents and who had gone without further contact with them. They found that alcoholism was more frequent in those adoptees whose biological relatives included an individual with alcoholism or for whom heavy drinking had been noted. Furthermore, "age of adoptee, time spent in foster care, age of biological mother at the time of the birth, socio-economic status of adoptive home, psychopathology other than alcoholism in the biological background, and psychiatric or behavioural problems in the adoptive family (parents and sibs) were all unrelated to adult alcoholism in the adoptee" (p. 252).

More recently, Bohman, Sigvardsson, and Cloninger (1981) studied 913 Swedish women adopted by nonrelatives at an early age. They found a three-fold increase in the rate of alcoholism among adopted daughters of alcoholic mothers as compared to daughters whose mothers were nonalcoholic. A companion study followed 862 Swedish men who were also adopted by nonrelatives at an early age (Cloninger, Bohman, & Sigvardsson, 1981). Among those who became alcoholics, two types of alcoholism were identified. The first type occurred in individuals who began drinking in their mid-20s to 30s but who did not develop a problem until midlife. This type involved a high risk of liver disorder and hospitalization but little antisocial behavior and a relatively low risk of social and occupational difficulties. Both biological parents for this type of alcoholism were characterized by mild alcohol abuse, minimal criminality, and a history of no treatment. Postnatal and environmental factors appeared to play an important role in the development of a drinking problem. The first type of alcoholism is therefore thought to reflect a biological susceptibility to the disorder that finds expression only in certain types of social or cultural environments.

The second type of alcoholism was less common (i.e., 24% of the sample) and involved many social but few medical problems. The less common type was more serious in terms of its symptomatology and appeared to be highly heritable over the entire range of social backgrounds observed among the adoptees. The biological parents of this type of alcoholic also evidenced severe problems with drinking that included the need for extensive treatment and a record of criminality. Interestingly, the mothers of these alcoholics were normal in terms of their alcohol use. Thus, this type is referred to as "male-limited" alcoholism because it appears to be transmitted only from father to son. Whether this finding, however, is more a reflection of sociocultural rather than genetic factors has yet to be determined.

Several twin studies have been conducted, all of which support the hypothesis that there is a significant genetic component in the development of alcoholism. Using the files of 109 pairs of Swedish twins, Kaij (cited in Davidson, 1984) found that the rate of alcoholism among monozygotic twins was almost twice that of dizygotic pairs (28% as compared to 54%, respectively). Partanen, Bruun, and Markkanen (1966) conducted a similar study in Finland based on 902 male twins. The consumption of alcohol, whether it was normal drinking, abstinence, or heavy use, did show considerable hereditary variation. No differences between monozygotic and dizygotic twin pairs were observed "for arrests, Social Complications (sic) or presence of addictive symptoms" (p. 19). Consequently, these authors concluded that whether one drinks, how often and how much, is to some degree genetically determined. The disruptive social consequences of this behavior, however, appear to be influenced primarily by factors other than heredity.

Questionnaire data from large numbers of twins have also been used. Loehlin (1977) analyzed the responses of 850 same-sex twins in the United States and concluded that there is a genetic factor in drinking behavior. Jonsson and Nilsson (cited in Goodwin, 1979) reported findings based on the questionnaire data from 7500 twin pairs in Sweden. Monozygotic twins were more concordant in regard to the amount of alcohol consumed than dizygotic pairs. Again, there were no differences between the two groups in terms of the social or occupational consequences of this consumption.

The way in which alcoholism is transmitted genetically is uncertain (Kaij & McNeil, 1979). It does not appear that a single, dominant gene is responsible, since that would predict an incidence rate of approximately 50% in each generation as compared to the usual 30% incidence rate of alcoholism among the offspring of alcoholic parents. It has been suggested that the lower-than-expected rate may reflect a mode of genetic transmission that is sex-linked. This hypothesis gains some support from the observation that males are more likely to develop alcoholism than females. However, a study by Kaij and Dock (1975) found that the sons of daughters of alcoholics had the same probability of alcohol abuse as did the sons of sons.

It is clear, however, that the metabolism of alcohol in the body is genetically determined. This possibility has been suspected for some time given the well-established differences in the response to alcohol across different racial groups (Ewing, Rouse, & Pellizari, 1974; Seto, Tricomi, Goodwin, Kolodney, & Sullivan, 1978; Wolff, 1973). In 1971 Vesell, Page, and Passananti administered a single oral dose of 1 ml per kilogram of body weight of 95% ethanol to 14 sets of nonmedicated, nonhospitalized healthy twins. Half of the twin pairs were monozygotic and half were dizygotic. The rates of elimination were more similar between monozygotic than dizygotic twins, which suggested that individual differences in ethanol elimination were genetically controlled and that "environmental factors played a negligible role" (p. 192). In fact, elimination rates were identical for 5 of the 7 monozygotic twin pairs, whereas only 1 of the 7 dizygotic pairs exhibited exactly the same rate of elimination.

Elimination studies raise the possibility that some individuals have a genetic *intolerance* of alcohol that protects them from developing alcoholism. Thus, the genetic factors in alcoholism may be most important in determining whether an individual is capable of becoming alcoholic. In Goodwin's words, "the potential alcoholic must be able to drink a lot (i.e., lack an intolerance for alcohol)" (1979, p. 60). The development of a *tolerance* to alcohol, on the other hand, appears to be determined more by the frequency and amount of alcohol consumed than by inherited differences in the rate of metabolism. Relapse and resistance to treatment, in turn, is determined to an even greater degree by past learning and environmental factors.

If this is the case, the heritability of alcoholism may be more *permissive* than *deterministic*. In other words, the absence of a genetic intolerance to alcohol may be more important in the development of alcoholism than the presence of an inherited "craving" or need for the drug. This may be particularly true for the first type of alcoholic identified by the Swedish adoption studies. However, the importance of heritability for the second or "male-limited" type is more pronounced than for the first type. Therefore, there may be some forms of alcoholism that are, in fact, strongly determined by one's genetic makeup, although the mechanics by which transmission occurs or how these genetic factors interact with the environment to influence the expression of the disorder are unclear.

senck's neuroticism and extraversion scale to cigarette smoking, while other investigators have found a relationship between high neuroticism and low extraversion and the use of tranquilizing drugs (Ashton, 1984; Golding et al., 1983). Together, these studies suggest that a certain level of emotional instability contributes to a vulnerability for drug abuse. However, stimulants, such as nicotine, may be preferred by individuals who experience high thresholds of arousability (i.e., extraverts), while introverts may prefer substances that take the edge off of their excessive sensitivity.

Differences between individuals in terms of a susceptibility toward substance use as well as a preference for which drug is used would suggest the presence of a genetic component to these disorders (Goodwin, 1971, 1979, 1985). (See Panel 7.2, "Heritability of Alcoholism.") Nevertheless, there does not appear to be any clearly defined trait or constellation of traits that adequately describes all varieties of compulsive drug use or predicts the liability of individuals to relapse (Cloninger & Reich, 1983; Jaffe, 1985; Levison, 1981).

Physiological Factors

Mechanisms of Tolerance and Withdrawal

Drug tolerance is the diminished responsiveness of the body to the actions of a drug that has been administered previously. As a result, a larger dose of the drug is required to elicit a response of the same magnitude or duration as that achieved earlier (Ashton, 1987). The degree of tolerance is not uniform throughout the body. For example, tolerance to the respiratory depressant effects of the barbiturates develops to a lesser degree than to their sedative effects. This is why these drugs lend themselves to overdose, particularly when used in combination with other CNS depressants, such as alcohol.

Tolerance develops in two ways. *Pharmacokinetic tolerance* involves an increase in the rate of metabolism of a drug as a result of increased levels of metabolizing enzymes in the liver. This type of tolerance usually develops over a period of several days before leveling off. The elevated level of enzyme activity declines when administration of the drug is terminated and returns to normal over a period of 6 or 8 weeks (Ashton, 1987). Pharmacokinetic tolerance has little effect on the peak intensity of drug action but does decrease the duration of its activity. It has been estimated that this type of tolerance is capable of decreasing a person's sensitivity to a drug's effects by as much as a third (Jaffe, 1985).

Although pharmacokinetic tolerance occurs for many substances, it is particularly important in the case of the barbiturates and other hypnotics. For example, the usual metabolic pathway for alcohol in the liver requires alcohol dehydrogenase (ADH). However, Lieber and his colleagues (Lieber & DeCarli, 1970, 1972) discovered a non-ADH pathway by which alcohol is metabolized. This pathway, which is termed the microsomal ethanol oxidizing system (MEOS), is activated by heavy drinking and appears to provide a means by which alcoholics can metabolize the excess alcohol they consume.

The second type of tolerance, *pharmacodynamic tolerance*, results from the adaptation of the body's tissues themselves to the drug's effects. This can occur within a matter of minutes or over a period of time. Acute pharmacodynamic tolerance, which often accompanies the sedative/hypnotic effects of alcohol, barbiturates, and benzodiazepines, is most apparent immediately after drug administration when the concentration in the blood is rising (Iversen & Iversen, 1975). The impact of acute tolerance disappears within days if administration of the drug is not repeated (Triggle, 1981).

The mechanism of acute pharmacodynamic tolerance is unclear.

One possibility is the development of *tachyphylaxis* (Bowman, Rand, & West, 1968). Tachyphylaxis is the ability of some drugs to block or antagonize their own action and thus cause a diminution rather than an increase in responding with repeated administrations. In the case of nicotine, this is caused by the drug's persistent occupation of receptor sites. In other cases, such as with the sympathomimetic amines, tachyphylaxis occurs as a result of the depletion of neurotransmitter stores. It is also possible that acute pharmacodynamic tolerance results from short-term changes in receptor affinity for a particular drug due to conformational changes at receptor sites that alter it from an active to an inactive state (Triggle, 1981).

Chronic pharmacodynamic tolerance also occurs over a period of time as the body's regulatory systems respond to the continued administration of a drug with a compensatory increase or decrease in activity. For example, chronic exposure to CNS depressants will result in a compensatory increase in activity of the excitatory systems so as to balance the depressant effects of the drug. Within limits, this allows the person to adapt to the continued presence of a substance in the body. This type of tolerance thus reflects changes in homeostatic regulation that may involve alterations in the output or turnover of excitatory or inhibitory neurotransmitters and/or changes in the sensitivity or density of receptor sites themselves. These changes tend to occur over a period of weeks rather than hours or days and may last for months or even years after the cessation of such drugs as alcohol.

As seen in Figure 7.1, chronic pharmacodynamic tolerance to alcohol may be of two kinds (Littleton, 1983). Decremental tolerance occurs when increasing doses of the drug exert less of a depressant effect on the brain in spite of normal functioning of the CNS when alcohol is not present. In other words, when the individual is not under the influence of alcohol, neuronal activity is normal. However, the person will exhibit less drug effect at higher doses than someone who is nontolerant. Oppositional tolerance, on the other hand, is a general decrease of brain responsiveness to alcohol accompanied by a compensatory increase in CNS activity when the drug is not present. This type of tolerance is more likely to occur under conditions of continuous intoxication. In the case of oppositional tolerance, a person must consume alcohol to feel "normal."

As noted earlier, chronic pharmacodynamic tolerance is thought to occur as the result of changes in the sensitivity of the receptor sites or possibly as a result of modifications in transmitter release. In terms of the first mechanism, it has been demonstrated that increased levels of transmitter substances in the synaptic cleft will result in a decrease in the density of receptor sites, which results in a subsensitivity tolerance. A

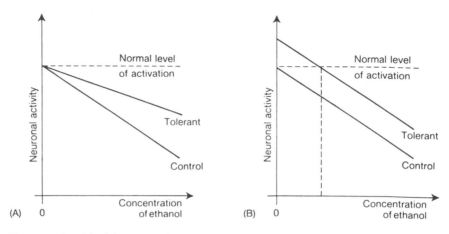

Figure 7.1. Model of decremental and oppositional tolerance to alcohol in the central ner-vous system. In decremental tolerance (A), increasing doses of ethanol have less of a depressant effect on neuronal activity in tolerant as opposed to control subjects. Activity in the absence of ethanol is normal for both groups. In the case of oppositional tolerance (B), neuronal activity is affected less by ethanol in tolerant subjects, but activity in the absence of alcohol is increased above normal levels. Oppositional tolerance is more likely to devel-op following periods of chronic intoxication. (Adapted from J. M. Littleton [1983], Toler-ance and physical dependence on alcohol at the level of synaptic membranes: A review, *Journal of the Royal Society of Medicine, 76,* p. 596. Copyright © 1983 by the Royal Society of Medicine. Reprinted by permission.)

reduction in the levels of a neurotransmitter and/or continued blockage of the nerve terminal will result in a compensatory increase in receptor density and thus induce a supersensitivity tolerance. These changes in receptor sensitivity in response to variations in transmitter availability have been demonstrated in numerous studies (e.g., Barnes, 1981; Ber-ridge, 1981; Perkins, 1982; Sulser, 1981; Triggle, 1981). For example, beta-adrenergic supersensitivity has been demonstrated following the chronic administration of alcohol and opiates. An increased density of muscarinic cholinergic receptors is thought to occur after the ingestion of alcohol and barbiturates, and alcohol appears to the lead to a decrease in the sensitivity of dopamine receptors (Creese & Sibley, 1981).

Modulation of receptor sensitivity postsynaptically is not the only mechanism by which chronic tolerance may occur. As discussed in Chapter 5, the importance of presynaptic positive and negative feedback receptors, called "autoreceptors", has been emphasized (Langer, 1977). Increased levels of a neurotransmitter will have the effect of stimulating negative feedback autoreceptors, thus serving to reduce the release of the transmitter. Under conditions of reduced concentration, positive feedback autoreceptors will stimulate release. The combined mechanisms of changes in post-synaptic sensitivity and presynaptic feedback exert a powerful effect.

The role of transmitter release in the development of tolerance is made complex by the multiplicity of pre- and postsynaptic receptors that exist at serotonergic, dopaminergic, and other synapses and also by the fact that many neurons release more than one neurotransmitter. Because of the elaborate and dynamic interaction of the various transmitters, it is almost impossible for the chronic administration of a drug to exert actions that are limited to only one neurotransmitter or one function of a transmitter system (Ashton, 1987). For example, the barbiturates, opiates, benzodiazepines, and alcohol have all been shown to affect the release and/or turnover of acetylcholine, norepinephrine, dopamine, serotonin, and GABA (Okamoto, 1978). Prolonged administration of the opiates also decreases the synthesis and release of some endogenous opioids (Herz, Höllt, & Przewlocki, 1980; Ho, Brase, Loh, & Way, 1975).

The interaction of the different neurotransmitters under conditions of chronic substance use helps explain the development of *cross-tolerance*. Cross-tolerance, like tolerance, can result from both pharmacokinetic and pharmacodynamic factors. As noted earlier, the former occurs when administration of one drug induces changes in hepatic metabolism that affects the metabolism of other compounds. For example, the chronic ingestion of a barbiturate will not only facilitate the breakdown of other barbiturates but will increase the rate of metabolism of such drugs as warfarin and phenytoin as well (Ashton, 1987).

The pharmacodynamic contribution to cross-tolerance occurs in essentially two ways. First, since different drugs may act similarly on the same receptor sites, changes in receptor sensitivity may affect several related compounds at the same time. Thus, the development of pharmacodynamic tolerance to any of the barbiturates or benzodiazepines is associated with tolerance to all other barbiturates or benzodiazepines. A second mechanism involves the alteration of general homeostatic reactions in the body. For example, increased autonomic activity in response to the chronic administration of alcohol will tend to compensate for the effects of other CNS depressants, including sedative/hypnotics and general anesthetics.

Withdrawal is related to the pharmacodynamic changes that have occurred and is primarily the result of an overswing or rebound of activity in the systems that have become altered as a result of chronic substance use. Largely, symptoms of withdrawal are in the opposite direction of the original drug effects. For example, the abstinence syndrome of CNS depressant drugs is characterized by agitation and hyper-excitability, while withdrawal from stimulant drugs causes fatigue, iner-tia, and general depression. The distribution, duration, and severity of the symptoms depend on which of the body's systems have undergone adaptive modulations and the degree to which these changes have been induced (Ashton, 1987). Withdrawal effects can be reversed if the drug is readministered, which restores the body's equilibrium.

As if the interaction of neurotransmitters, receptor sites, and com-plex feedback mechanisms were not enough, one must also consider the mechanisms of *behavioral tolerance*. Behavioral tolerance refers to com-pensatory adjustments the individual makes under the influence of a particular drug. For example, the deleterious effects of large doses of alcohol on motor performance and speech may be modified by learning how to compensate for the deterioration in performance. The more ex-perience a person has had taking a particular substance, the more likely he or she has been able to learn how to overcome its debilitating effects (Demellweek & Goudie, 1983).

The behavioral effects of repeated administrations of a psychoactive substance may include elements of classical conditioning as well (Beir-ness & Vogel-Sprott, 1984). In these cases, the "learning" that occurs may actually work to delay or lessen the effects of physiological toler-ance. For example, analgesia induced by morphine may become condi-tioned to environmental cues associated with the administration of the drug. Consequently, it is possible to acquire a *hyper*analgesic response under these conditions, even when a placebo is administered (Siegel, 1975). This type of behavioral tolerance would thus tend to counteract the effects of physiological tolerance and provides yet another illustra-tion of how environmental factors play an important role in the develop-ment of substance dependence and abuse.

Substances of Dependence and Abuse

Alcohol. Alcohol is the most widely used and clinically important of drugs that cause dependence (Ashton, 1987). Alcohol is a general CNS depressant that produces a dose-dependent decrease in arousal similar to that obtained from general anesthetics. At small doses there may be the appearance of a slight stimulant effect due to disinhibition. Larger doses, however, are associated with a deterioration of judgment, con-centration, and attention as well as impairment of psychomotor and sexual performance (Crowe & George, 1989).

Alcohol's effects on mood are complex. Small doses may produce a mild euphoria and a pleasant sense of relaxation, similar to that seen with tranquilizing drugs. With increasing dosage, alcohol may precipitate aggressive behavior or a sense of increased poignancy or sentimentality. Higher doses are accompanied by ataxia (uncoordinated motor movements) and slurred speech. Very high doses may induce stupor, deep anesthesia, and even coma. At blood concentrations of 400 ml/m or greater the respiratory response to carbon dioxide becomes depressed, which may result in lethal consequences.

Peripherally, alcohol causes vasodilation in the skin and sweating. Alcohol is also a diuretic, due in part to its ability to suppress the pituitary antidiuretic hormone. As far as the cardiovascular system is concerned, alcohol increases myocardial excitability (Rogers & Spector, 1980) and may induce hypertension in some subjects (Klatsky, Friedman, Siegelaub, & Gérard, 1977). On the other hand, the daily ingestion of alcohol in moderate amounts may increase the concentration of high density lipoproteins and thus provide some protection against coronary heart disease (Ritchie, 1985).

The extended use of alcohol coupled with vitamin deficiencies associated with chronic alcoholism may lead to degenerative changes in brain cells. Wernicke's encephalopathy and Korsakoff's psychosis are two disorders resulting from excessive alcohol consumption over a period of time. Alcohol also increases gastric secretions and thus may contribute to gastritis and peptic ulceration. Other conditions related to chronic alcohol abuse include pancreatitis and hepatic cirrhosis. In pregnancy, fetal alcohol syndrome is found in as many as a third to one-half of babies of mothers who are chronic alcoholics (Jones, Smith, Streissguth, & Myrianthopoulos, 1974).

Alcohol is rapidly absorbed from the gut, primarily in the small intestine. Fats and carbohydrates slow the rate of absorption, and large amounts of alcohol are absorbed relatively slowly. However, the first traces of alcohol may appear in the blood within 5 minutes after ingestion, reaching a peak in 30 minutes to 2 hours, although there is considerable variation between individuals. Alcohol is distributed widely throughout the body and penetrates both the blood-brain and placental barriers easily.

As much as 95% of the alcohol in the body is metabolized in the liver, with the remaining 5% being excreted unchanged in the breath, urine, and sweat. The rate of metabolism, unlike other drugs discussed in this chapter, is linear and occurs at an average rate of 10 ml/hr, although this may be increased modestly in chronic alcoholics. As noted earlier in the chapter, the major pathway for this metabolism involves alcohol dehydrogenase (ADH) with nicotinamide adenine dinucleotide (NAD) as a cofactor (Korsten & Lieber, 1985). This process converts alcohol to acetaldehyde and reduces NAD to NADH (i.e., NAD with the

addition of a hydrogen ion). The generation of high levels of acetaldehyde following the excessive consumption of alcohol and the concomitant shift in the ratio of NADH to NAD is thought to be responsible for a
number of metabolic abnormalities, including the excessive production
of lactic acid, which provides a potential link between excessive alcohol
consumption and panic disorder (see Chapter 6). Some of alcohol's other toxic effects resulting from the accumulation of metabolites include
impaired gluconeogenesis, hypoglycemia, and fatty infiltration of the
liver. Nutritional deficiencies may contribute to this tissue damage.

Chronic alcoholism is associated with reduced concentrations of
ADH in the liver (Jenkins, Cakebread, & Palmer, 1982; Peters, 1983;
Thomas, Halsall, & Peters, 1982). It is unknown whether a preexisting
deficiency in this enzyme predisposes one to alcoholism or whether
heavy drinking causes this deficiency. However, since the enzyme concentration returns to normal during abstinence, it is suspected that excess consumption of alcohol impairs its own metabolism (Agarwal, Harada, Goedde, & Schrappe, 1983; Towell, Cho, Rho, & Wang, 1983).

The areas of the brain that are most sensitive to alcohol are poly-
synaptic structures like the reticular activating system (RAS). Surprisingly, however, little is known about how alcohol affects the CNS
(Myers, 1978). Alcohol's lipid solubility suggests that it operates in a
manner similar to the general anesthetics by decreasing synaptic transmission. This can occur both presynaptically by inhibiting neurotransmitter release or postsynaptically by affecting the sensitivity of the receptors. Presynaptically, it has been suggested that alcohol either binds
to membrane proteins or becomes partitioned into membrane lipids so
as to inhibit the influx of calcium through voltage-dependent channels
in nerve terminals (Franks & Lieb, 1982; Littleton, 1983). This would
prevent a rise in intracellular calcium which normally acts as a trigger for
neurotransmitter release (Harris & Hood, 1980). (A summary of the site
and mechanism of action for alcohol as well as the other substances
covered in this chapter can be found in Table 7.1.)

The release of at least six different neurotransmitters is known to be
inhibited by the presence of alcohol in the brain (Carmichael & Israel,
1975). These include (in order of their sensitivity to alcohol) acetylcholine, serotonin, dopamine, norepinephrine, glutamate, and GABA. The
suppression of acetylcholine has been confirmed in areas of the cerebral
cortex and RAS and may be linked to the behavioral aspects of alcohol
intoxication (Erickson & Graham, 1973). On the other hand, some studies have shown that moderate doses of alcohol may actually increase the
output of norepinephrine and epinephrine (Ritchie, 1985; Myers, 1978).
However, these effects may be related to whether the drug is admin-

Table 7.1. Selected Psychoactive Substances

Substance	Absorbed by	Major site of action	Mechanism of action
Alcohol	gut	CNS (particularly RAS)	Depression of synaptic transmission
Amphetamines	gut	RAS, MRC, lateral hypo-thalamus	Increase release of NE plus direct stimulation of postsynaptic NE recep-tors with some reuptake blockade
Barbiturates	gut	RAS, limbic areas	Hyper-polarization of postsynaptic GABA receptors
Caffeine	gut	RAS, MRC	Increase turnover of monoamines
Cannabis	lungs	Frontal cortex, limbic areas (hyippocampus and amygdala), sensory and motor areas, pons	Unknown, probably multi-ple effects and/or non-specific depressant action on the CNS
Cocaine	skin and mucous membranes	CNS	Blockade of NE re-uptake by presynaptic nerve ter-minals
Heroin	gut	Limbic areas	Stimulation of opioid mu-receptors
Inhalants	lungs	CNS	Possibly similar to alcohol
LSD	gut	Raphe nuclei, limbic areas, visual associational areas, RAS	Decrease in release, turn-over, synthesis, and uti-lization of serotonin
Nicotine	gut and lungs	CNS	Direct stimulation of nic-otinic cholinergic recep-tors
PCP	gut and lungs	CNS and CSF	Unknown, possibly several

Note. CNS = Central Nervous System; CSF = Cerebral-spinal fluid; GABA = Gamma-aminobutyric acid; LSD = Lysergic acid diethylamide; MRC = Medullary respiratory center; NE = Norepinephrine; PCP Phencyclidine; RAS = Reticular Activating System.

istered acutely or chronically. The development of a tolerance to alcohol has been found to be correlated to its effects on dopaminergic activity with reduced sensitivity resulting over time (Mullin & Ferko, 1983). The effects of alcohol on serotonin may also be important, particularly in terms of its sedative effects (Ellingboe, 1978).

The GABA-ergic and endogenous opioid systems have been tied to alcohol. It has been suggested that alcohol, like the benzodiazepines and the barbiturates, produces some of its depressant effects through the enhancement of GABA-ergic activity (Nestoros, 1980). In addition, mod-erate doses of alcohol in mice have been found to increase concentra-tions of enkephalin and beta-endorphin in the brain (Schultz, Wüster,

numerous drugs that belong in both categories, we will focus on the benzodiazepines as the prototypic anxiolytic medication and the barbiturates as representative of the sedative-hypnotic class.

Both drugs exert sedative-hypnotic as well as anticonvulsant effects. In addition, the benzodiazepines are an effective muscle relaxant (Goth, 1978). The benzodiazepines appear to exert a specific anxiolytic effect at low dosages without the sedation that accompanies the barbiturates. The barbiturates, on the other hand, exert more of an anesthetic effect than the benzodiazepines (Richards, 1972).

The benzodiazepines and the barbiturates hasten the onset of sleep and lengthen its duration (Baldessarini, 1985; Evans, Lewis, Gibb, & Cheetham, 1968; Harvey, 1985; Kay, Blackburn, Buckingham, & Karacan, 1976; Wheatley, 1981). However, the pattern of sleep they induce is not normal. More specifically, the duration of slow wave sleep (Stages 3 and 4) is decreased and the onset of REM sleep delayed. Furthermore, "rebound insomnia" is common when either medication is withdrawn after a period of regular use, although the extent of this phenomenon may be related to some hypnotics more than others (Dourdain, Puech, & Simon, 1980; Nicholson, 1980). In addition, there may be a hangover effect that impairs performance and increases irritability following cessation of use. This problem, however, is more marked in the barbiturates than in the benzodiazepines (Bond & Lader, 1981; Clarke & Nicholson, 1978; Dourdain et al., 1980; Johnson & Chernik, 1982). This may be a particular problem in the elderly who may develop depression, confusion, or ataxia following a course of barbiturate medication (MacDonald & MacDonald, 1977).

Both the benzodiazepines and barbiturates are well absorbed when given by mouth and are widely distributed throughout the body with a particularly fast uptake in the vascular areas of the brain (e.g., the gray matter), as well as the limbic system, especially the hypothalamus and amygdala (Tsuchiya & Kitagawa, 1976). This is followed by a slower phase of redistribution into the white matter and adipose tissue. The rate at which this occurs (the beta half-life) is determined by the lipid solubility of the different drugs but usually takes place within a matter of minutes. The elimination half-life shows even greater variability and can range from 2 to 200 hours. Both the benzodiazepines and barbiturates are metabolized in the liver. This process may be slowed in the elderly, in patients with cirrhosis of the liver, or in the presence of other drugs that inhibit the induction of metabolizing enzymes. There appear to be individual or genetic differences in metabolism as well.

The benzodiazepines and barbiturates are thought to exert their effect through the enhancement of GABA-ergic systems in the brain. For the benzodiazepines, this occurs through their occupation of benzodiazepine binding sites, which enhance GABA-ergic activity (Snyder, 1981a). These sites, discovered in 1977 (Möhler & Okada, 1977; Squires & Braestrup, 1977), are concentrated in the cortex, limbic system, and cerebellum. The receptors exhibit a highly stereospecific and selective affinity for benzodiazepines. Consequently, the anxiolytic effect of these medications has lead to the speculation that GABA-ergic receptors mediate anxiety (Gray, 1982; Sepinwall & Cook, 1980).

It is now thought that the benzodiazepine receptor is a membrane protein that makes up part of the postsynaptic GABA receptor complex (see Figure 7.2). This unit appears to consist of at least six components: (1) a GABA recognition site, (2) a chloride channel, (3) a benzodiazepine

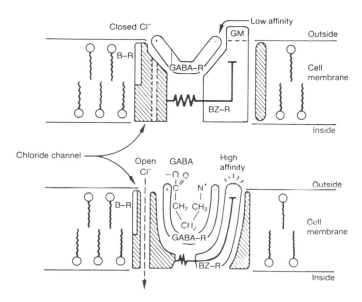

Figure 7.2. Diagram of the postulated postsynaptic GABA receptor complex. BZ-R, benzodiazepine receptor; B-R, barbiturate receptor; GABA-R, GABA recognition site; GM, GABA modulin. Occupation of the GABA recognition site by GABA leads to configurational changes causing opening of chloride channels in the neuronal membrane, with consequent hyperpolarization. The affinity of this site is proposed to be controlled by GABA modulin. Occupation of the benzodiazepine receptor site by benzodiazepines may cause phosphorylation of GABA modulin, favoring the high-affinity state of the GABA receptor and enhancing the inhibitory actions of GABA. Occupation of the barbiturate receptor sites by barbiturates causes prolonged opening of the chloride channel. (Modified from Braestrup and Nielsen, 1980.) (From H. Ashton [1987], *Brain Systems, Disorders, and Psychotropic Drugs*, p. 77. Copyright © 1987 by Heather Ashton. Reprinted by permission.)

binding site, (4) a binding site for barbiturates and some convulsants, (5) one or more enzymes, and (6) a protein that modulates affinity of the complex for GABA. Occupation of the GABA recognition site by GABA causes configurational changes that lead to opening of the chloride channel in the neuronal membrane. Chloride ions enter the cell, hyperpolarizing it and thus making it more resistant to excitation. This is most likely the mechanism by which the GABA-ergic system inhibits postsynaptic activity (Enna, 1981).

The postsynaptic GABA receptor is thought to exist in two states—a high-affinity state that favors reaction with GABA and a low-affinity state which discourages GABA occupation. It has been proposed that the affinity for GABA is controlled by a protein on the membrane surface called a GABA-modulin (Guidotti, Corda, Wise, Vaccarino, & Costa, 1983). The benzodiazepine receptor site is closely linked to GABA-modulin and is thought to affect its ability to alter the affinity of the GABA receptor (Costa, 1981). In other words, the benzodiazepines increase the affinity of the GABA receptors to GABA, which, in turn, enhances the inhibitory activity of GABA throughout the brain.

It is also thought that a receptor site for the barbiturates and for some anticonvulsants is directly tied to the chloride channel and does not immediately involve the GABA-recognition apparatus (Braestrup & Nielsen, 1980). The barbiturates are thought to prolong the opening of the chloride channel with the possible inhibition of calcium uptake (Blaustein & Ector, 1975), which would result in a long-lasting neuronal inhibition due to a continued state of depolarization. This effect may explain, at least in part, the respiratory depression and narcosis that are more profound with the barbiturates than with the benzodiazepines. This may also explain why the barbiturates are effective against repetitive activity in a number of CNS pathways while having little effect on an initial motor impulse (Harvey, 1985).

GABA is a universal inhibitory transmitter present in 30 to 50 % of brain synapses that mediate the activity of cholinergic, adrenergic, dopaminergic, and serotonergic pathways (Haefely, Pieri, Polc, & Schaffner, 1981). Consequently, it has been proposed that the enhancement of GABA activity in various parts of the brain might explain the ability of the benzodiazepines to exert a variety of different effects. For example, their anticonvulsant action may be due to their effect on the hippocampus and cortex, while activity in the reticular formation and cerebellum may be related to their ability to induce muscular relaxation. The limbic system is thought to be the site of their anxiolytic effect, and the arousal areas have been linked to their sedative-hypnotic actions. This model, however, is most likely overly simplified and fails to explain

why tolerance develops much more quickly to the sedative and anticonvulsant effects than the anxiolytic effects (Sepinwall & Cook, 1980). In all
likelihood, there are several types of benzodiazepine receptors that mediate separate actions, just as there are probably several types of GABA
receptors. It is even possible that the various types of GABA-
benzodiazepine receptors are conformational variations of the same
amino acid sequence and that different conformations subserve different
physiological functions (Squires, 1983).

Caffeine. Caffeine and the chemically-related xanthines, theophyl-
line and theobromine, are potent CNS stimulants that have a number of
peripheral effects as well (Sawyer, Julia, & Turin, 1982). Among the CNS
effects are the improvement of cognitive performance and the alleviation
of drowsiness and fatigue. Some of the peripheral effects include increased heart rate, increased vascular resistance, and diuresis (France &
Ditto, 1988).

Caffeine and the xanthines are plant alkaloids that are absorbed
well from the gut and metabolized by the liver. Caffeine has essentially
no therapeutic value, although its use in coffee and soft drinks is well
known. In fact, it has been estimated that caffeine is the most widely
used nonmedical CNS stimulant in the world (Brecher, 1972). The
xanthines in general and theophyllline in particular are used in medicine
for their effect on the respiratory system (e.g., relaxation of bronchial
smooth muscle) and, occasionally, in the treatment of heart failure.

Coffee contains twice as much caffeine as one cup of tea and three
times as much as a standard cola (Schuckit, 1979). Some of the central
effects of caffeine include increased alertness, increased capacity for
sustained intellectual performance, and decreased reaction time (Bruce,
Scott, Lader, & Marks, 1986). Although it enhances motor skills at low
dosages (e.g., less than 200 mg or about two cups of coffee), tasks
requiring fine motor coordination may be adversely affected (Rall, 1985).
At higher dosages persons sensitive to caffeine may experience anxiety,
restlessness, insomnia, tremor, and hyperesthesia (excessive sensitivity
of the senses). Dosages that exceed 500 mg may induce muscle twitches,
rambling thoughts, speech disturbances, and flushing.

Caffeine is not included in the DSM-III-R under the category of
psychoactive substance use disorders because caffeine dependence has
not been established. However, several investigators believe that caffeine dependence exists in the form of *caffeinism* (Goldstein & Kaizer,
1969; Reimann, 1967). This condition is defined as the intake of more
than 500 to 600 mg per day, which is equivalent to six to seven brewed
cups of coffee. In some cases, the variety of symptoms resulting from

doses of caffeine at this level may make it difficult to distinguish between caffeinism and situational anxiety or insomnia (Greden, 1974; Karacan et al., 1977). A lethal dose of caffeine is 10 g or approximately 70 to 100 cups of coffee (Schuckit, 1979). Consequently, it is highly unlikely that a person could run the risk of caffeine overdose, except possibly in graduate school.

The two sites in the brain thought to be most affected by the administration of caffeine are the RAS and the MRC (Rall, 1985). Through its effects on the RAS, caffeine exerts a stimulatory effect on all portions of the cortex as well as increasing the metabolic rate at the cellular level throughout the body (Julien, 1985) and exerting a general stimulatory effect on the sympathetic branch of the autonomic nervous system (Levi, 1967). Stimulation of the MRC increases the respiratory rate, which, in turn, increases oxygen consumption and CO_2 elimination. As noted in Chapter 6, this effect has been linked to the promotion of panic attacks.

It is thought that caffeine's stimulant effect is due to its ability to increase the turnover of monoamines in the brain (Bellet, Roman, DeCastro, Kim, & Keushbaum, 1969). The mechanism for this action, however, is unclear. At one time it was thought that caffeine inhibited phosphodiesterase (the catabolizing agent for cyclic AMP), thus decreasing the breakdown of cyclic AMP and enhancing the central and peripheral action of this nucleotide.[2] Although this seems to be the case with high dosages of caffeine, its clinical effect at lower dosages is questioned. One possible explanation might be the blocking of receptors for adenosine (Snyder, 1981b), a nucleotide thought to be the modulator of central arousal systems (Williams, 1984). It is known, however, that caffeine increases the secretion of epinephrine and norepinephrine by the adrenal medulla, which may account for most of its stimulatory effects (Bellet et al., 1969; Levi, 1967).

There are a number of individual differences that affect a person's response to caffeine. Most importantly, there may be differences in both the metabolism and absorption of the drug (Robertson et al., 1978). Other differences may include age, mental state, and degree of physical fitness. For example, as many persons grow older they become more

---

[2]Cyclic AMP promotes intracellular reactions and the formation and synthesis of many proteins. These effects include activating enzymes, altering cell permeability, initiating the synthesis of specific intracellular proteins, and initiating secretion. The types of effects that will occur are determined by the characteristic of the cell itself. Cyclic AMP is thus an important *second messenger* that plays an important role as an intracellular hormonal mediator throughout the endocrine system. Cyclic AMP also effects the synthesis of the catecholamines.

sensitive to the effects of caffeine, particularly in regard to insomnia (Sawyer et al., 1982). Although the effect of chronic caffeinism is unknown, it is clear that caffeine withdrawal involves both pleasant and unpleasant effects. On the favorable side, blood pressure, heart rate, and gastrointestinal complaints decrease (Edelstein, Keaton-Brasted, & Burg, 1983). On the other hand, headaches may increase dramatically during the withdrawal phase.

Cannabis. *Cannabis sativa*, the hemp plant, is an annual weed that grows freely in most parts of the world. Some sources of cannabis possess great psychoactive potency while other plants produce little or no behavioral changes. This difference has been attributed to the varying concentrations of the naturally occurring substance *delta 9-tetrahydrocannabinol* (delta-9-THC). The concentration of delta-9-THC is influenced by the climate, soil, cultivation, and method of preparation of the plant. Smoking a marihuana cigarette delivers a relatively small quantity of delta-9-THC, the effects of which are variable depending upon the physical health of the individual and various other factors, including diet and the ingestion of such medications as aspirin (Fairbairn & Pickens, 1979, 1980).

Unlike such hallucinogens as LSD, cannabis has a marked sedative effect. Aside from this, the clinical response to the two drugs is similar, although cannabis' effects are less pronounced than those of LSD. These effects, which include changes in perception and mood, usually peak about 30 minutes after initial ingestion and may continue for hours. At higher dosages, psychotic symptoms may occur. All of these effects are influenced by dosage, personality characteristics, the physical and emotional state of the individual just prior to the episode, the surroundings, and the person's expectations (Ashton, Golding, Marsh, Millman, & Thompson, 1981).

Peripherally, cannabis increases heart rate, dries the mouth, decreases sweating, and induces symptoms of gastrointestinal and bronchial irritation, especially in unaccustomed smokers. Perceptual changes affect all sensory modalities. Color perception is heightened; sounds seem more vivid and musical appreciation may be increased. Changes in bodily sensations include feelings of floating, weightlessness, heaviness or swelling, hot and cold sensations, numbness, and tingling. Both spatial perception and the perception of time are distorted. For example, subjective time may seem to be longer than clock time, which contributes to a feeling of timelessness or of time standing still.

Mood alterations may be pleasant or dysphoric. Consequently, the range of emotions expressed under the influence of cannabis can include both laughing or crying with possible alternations between the two. Cognitive changes may include increased speed of thought, rapid and racing thoughts, flight of ideas, or a flooding of thoughts. In some cases, there may be fragmented thinking and mental confusion that impairs performance on complex tasks. Memory, especially short-term memory, is also impaired. Initially, changes in perception, mood, and cognition may contribute to a state of excitement and increased motor activity. However, this is followed by a dose-related CNS depression leading to drowsiness and sleep. At higher doses, cannabis can produce psychotic changes, which may include both visual and auditory hallucinations. Feelings of unreality and out-of-body experiences have also been reported.

Cannabis is highly fat soluble and is therefore quickly and completely absorbed through cell membranes. It is metabolized in the liver and lungs, which results in less bioavailability following oral or respiratory administration than after intravenous injections (Agurell, Lindgren, & Ohlsson, 1979). Once in the blood, delta-9-THC is rapidly distributed throughout the body, concentrating in areas with highest blood flow. It is gradually taken up by the body's fat, from which it is slowly released back into the blood. Consequently, the elimination half-life of delta-9-THC is slow (approximately 56 hours). Repeated use of cannabis may subsequently lead to the accumulation of high levels of delta-9-THC in the body.

The site of action for delta-9-THC's psychoactive effects is probably in the limbic system and the associational sensory areas of the cortex. It has been shown to concentrate in the frontal cortex, sensory areas, and motor areas (including the caudate nucleus, putamen, cerebellum, and pons) (McIsaac, Fritchie, Idänpään-Heikkilä Ho & Englert, 1971). In terms of the limbic system, delta-9-THC appears to have a particular affinity for the hippocampus and amygdala. In animals cannabis has been shown to disrupt the hippocampal theta-rhythm (Miller, 1979) and have both stimulant and depressant effects on hippocampal seizures (Feeney, 1979). Furthermore, lesions of the hippocampus can reproduce many of the functional impairments seen with cannabis (Miller, 1979; Stiglick, Llewellyn, & Kalant, 1984).

In spite of its similarity to LSD in terms of clinical effect, cannabis does not appear to interact with any particular neurotransmitter, such as serotonin (see the discussion of LSD that follows). However, it has been shown that cannabis may alter the uptake of dopamine, norepinephrine, serotonin, and GABA in animal brains. It also may interact with tricyclic antidepressants, amphetamines, beta adrenergic antagonists, and neuroleptics and may block acetylcholine release or affect its re-uptake (Miller, 1979). This is thought to have widespread effects throughout the limbic system leading to impaired memory functioning, lapses in attention, altered speech production, and general problems with complex information processing.

Other investigators have described similarities between cannabis actions and those of the opiates (Kaymakçalan, 1979), which suggests the possibility of an interaction with endogenous opioids or their receptors. Higher dosages of delta-9-THC probably exert a nonspecific central nervous system depressant effect as a result of a generalized uptake into lipid cell membranes similar to the general anesthetics and alcohol (Gill, Jones, & Lawrence, 1972). Nevertheless, cannabis' mechanism of action in the brain remains essentially unknown (Ashton, 1987).

Hallucinogens and Phencyclidine (PCP). There are few drugs more potent than d-lysergic acid diethylamide (LSD). An oral dose of 25 vg (25 millionths of a gram) can produce significant CNS effects in the human being. This is even more remarkable since it is estimated that less than one thousandth of such a dose (i.e, 25 *billionths* of a gram) reaches the brain (Freedman & Boggan, 1982).

Some of the effects produced within minutes of the ingestion of LSD include such somatic symptoms as dizziness, weakness, tremor, nausea, drowsiness, paresthesia (itching), and blurred vision (Hollister, 1982; Jaffe, 1985). Perceptual and mood effects take longer to appear and may last for several hours. Some of these effects include alterations in the perception of shapes and colors, difficulty focusing, heightened perception of hearing and of visual detail, distortion of space with macropsia (objects appear unnaturally large) and micropsia (objects appear unnaturally small), and sometimes the running together of sensory modalities (synaesthesia). After about four hours, major disturbances in cognition are apparent. Initially, thought patterns are altered and thoughts become difficult to express, which is accompanied by a deterioration in performance on tests involving reasoning and memory. This stage is followed by feelings of depersonalization, unreality, and dream-like sensations. Metaphysical preoccupations may dominate, and there may be a feeling of disembodiment and oneness with the world or the cosmos. Hallucinations (visual or auditory) may occur, as well as feelings of omnipotence supervened with irrational beliefs, such as the belief in the ability to fly. The entire syndrome may last from 12 to 24 hours.

In studies in which LSD is administered intravenously, peak concentrations occur in the brain within minutes after injection, and plasma elimination half-life is about 3–4 hours. The onset, severity, and duration of the clinical effects correlate with brain and plasma concentrations, although the symptoms may considerably outlast the half-life of the drug. In the rat and monkey, it has been confirmed that LSD concentrates selectively in the visual and limbic areas of the brain, as well as the pineal gland. Clearance from the brain follows the same time course as from the blood.

It has been established that LSD decreases the release, turnover, synthesis, and utilization of serotonin (Freedman & Boggan, 1982). It has been suggested that LSD binds preferentially to and has a relatively selective stimulant action on serotonin autoreceptors (presynaptic feedback receptors) on the raphé neurons (Aghajanian, 1982). Postsynaptic serotonergic neurons in the limbic and visual areas that receive input from these neurons are thought to be of the inhibitory type. Consequently, a decrease in serotonergic activity in the raphé nuclei, which is induced by LSD's effect on the autoreceptors, results in a disinhibition of activity in the limbic system and secondary visual areas of the brain (see Figure 7.3). This may be responsible for the perceptual distortion and hallucinations produced by LSD.

LSD also has both an agonist and antagonist effect on dopaminergic

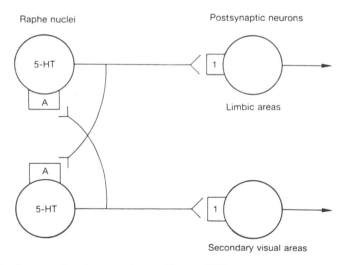

Figure 7.3. Diagram showing postulated effects of LSD at serotonergic receptors in the brain. Autoreceptors (A) inhibit the release of serotonin. Serotonin receptors (1) inhibit the firing of postsynaptic neurons in limbic and sensory areas. LSD is postulated to stimulate the autoreceptors preferentially. This decreases the release of serotonin, which, in turn, disinhibits postsynaptic neurons. (Adapted from Aghajanian, 1982.) (From H. Ashton [1987], *Brain Systems, Disorders, and Psychotropic Drugs*, p. 435. Copyright © 1987 by Heather Ashton. Reprinted by permission.)

and noradrenergic receptors and activates noradrenergic neurons in the locus ceruleus (Aghajanian, 1982; Watson, 1977). In addition, it has been shown that LSD binds to dopamine receptors, alpha- and beta-adrenergic receptors, and histamine-2 receptors (Freedman & Boggan, 1982). Although the importance of these nonserotonergic effects in mediating LSD's pharmacological actions is unclear, it is suspected that they play some role, since mescaline, a related drug with similar effects, does not act on serotonin autoreceptors. On the other hand, lisuride (an analogue of LSD) induces a serotonergic effect similar to LSD and yet does not act as a psychotomimetic agent (Ashton, 1987).

Phencyclidine (PCP) is included with the hallucinogens because it shares clinical features that are similar to LSD and other hallucinogens. At small doses, PCP produces a sense and appearance of drunkenness with staggering gait, slurred speech, nystagmus (involuntary eye movements), and numbness or complete analgesia of the fingers and toes. Subjectively, this stage is experienced as a "high" consisting of euphoria, a sense of intoxication, increased responsiveness to external stimuli, and general excitement. Such somatic symptoms as sweating, catatonic muscular rigidity, disturbances of body image, disorganized thoughts, restlessness, and anxiety may accompany this stage. In addition, bizarre and sometimes aggressive behavior and schizophreniform psychosis may occur. This stage typically lasts 4 to 6 hours and is followed by an extended period of "coming down." At higher dosages, analgesia becomes marked and anarthria (inability to articulate words), drowsiness, stupor, coma, and convulsions may follow. As with LSD, "flashback" psychotic episodes may occur several weeks after cessation of PCP use. The principle causes of death associated with PCP use are homicide and suicide, although respiratory arrest can occur when PCP is taken with barbiturates.

As a lipid-soluble compound, PCP is well-absorbed from any route and consequently is sniffed, smoked, ingested, or injected. It is widely distributed throughout the body and concentrates in the CNS and cerebral-spinal fluid. It is metabolized in the liver with an estimated half-life to elimination of 1 to 2 hours for small doses and up to 3 days after an overdose (Jaffe, 1985).

Although the mechanisms of action of PCP are unclear (Henderson, 1982), changes in the concentration and turnover of dopamine in the brain have been observed (Ary & Komiskey, 1982). This effect may be mediated by enhancement of activity in the inhibitory noradrenergic pathways from the locus ceruleus to the cerebellar Purkinje neurons and is possibly due to the inhibition of norepinephrine re-uptake. It is uncertain, however, whether this mechanism is responsible for psychological effects since other re-uptake blockers, such as the tricyclic antidepressants, do not produce hallucinations.

PCP may also act as an opiate agonist. It has been shown that PCP binds preferentially to the sigma opioid receptors in the rat brain and that it can be displaced by opioids acting on these receptors (Pert & Quirion, 1983). These binding sites are concentrated in the frontal cortex, hippocampus, and subiculum. In addition, Pert and Quirion (1983) have found a good correlation between receptor affinity and behavioral potency for PCP analogues in animal tests. They concluded that the PCP receptor and the sigma opioid receptor are identical and that the psychotomimetic effects of PCP and the opiates may be related. Greenberg and Segal (1986) have extended this hypothesis to include PCP's interaction with mu- as well as sigma-opioid receptors. However, since PCP has many effects that are similar to those of a number of other psychotropic drugs (including general anesthetics, alcohol, narcotics, hallucinogens, cocaine, and amphetamine), it probably has several mechanisms of action.

Inhalants (Organic Solvents). There are more than a dozen substances used in solvent abuse. Some of these include antifreeze, dry-cleaning fluid, glue, ink, oven cleaner, and bronchodilator inhalants for asthma. All of these products contain volatile chemicals that are readily absorbed through the lungs when inhaled (Waldron, 1981). As with most of the other substances covered in this chapter, the organic solvents or inhalants are highly lipid soluble and are thus readily distributed throughout the body, reaching highest concentrations in fat deposits and the CNS.

Like alcohol and the general anesthetics, the inhalants produce a dose-dependent depression of the CNS. Mild intoxication is obtained within minutes of inhalation and lasts up to 30 minutes, although repeated sniffing can maintain this state for up to 12 hours. An initial euphoria, which is most likely due to disinhibition of the CNS, is followed at higher doses by confusion, perceptual distortion, hallucinations, and delusions. This stage may be accompanied by marked aggressive and risk-taking behavior. As depression of the CNS increases, ataxia, nystagmus, and dysarthria (jumbled speech) make an appearance. This may be followed by drowsiness, coma, and sometimes convulsions. Unfortunately, the mechanisms by which the inhalants affect these changes has not been studied systematically (Ashton, 1987). However, it appears that the mode of action for these substances is fundamentally similar to that of alcohol.

Chronic use of inhalants can cause a number of serious and often irreversible changes in the brain. The metabolism of products containing lead, such as gasoline, creates 2,5 hexanedione, which causes peripheral neuropathy due to destruction of axons in the pyramidal system. Atrophy of the optic nerve has also been described (Waldron, 1981). Chronic solvent abusers may complain of a number of psychological and physiological problems, including headache, photophobia, anxiety, irritability, tremor, sleep disturbance, hallucinations, anorexia, nausea, vomiting, abdominal pain, tinnitus, diplopia (double vision), and paresthesia (O'Connor, 1984).

Organic solvents used as inhalants are metabolized by the liver. Some of these, such as chloroform, carbon tetrachloride, and other dry-cleaning products, can cause irreversible damage at high doses. These substances are also nephrotoxic, causing renal failure in some circumstances. Other solvents are capable of inducing cardiac arrhythmias, which may induce sudden death among abusers. As with other highly lipid-soluble compounds, the organic solvents readily cross the placenta during pregnancy, which results in a depression of the neonatal CNS (Ashton, 1985). Although it was thought initially that physical dependence does not occur in solvent abuse, it now appears that dependence may occur among young people who sniff alone (Herzberg & Wolkind, 1983). If continued into adulthood, abuse of inhalants may become part of a wider pattern of drug abuse (Herzberg & Wolkind, 1983).

Nicotine. Nicotine is a volatile, colorless liquid that turns brown upon exposure to air and emits an aroma characteristic of tobacco (Gerald, 1981). This plant alkaloid is structurally related to acetylcholine and acts as a direct agonist on the nicotinic cholinergic receptors throughout the body. Nicotinic receptors are found between the pre- and postganglionic neurons of both the sympathetic and parasympathetic branches of the autonomic nervous system as well as in the membranes of skeletal muscle at the neuromuscular junction. This explains some of nicotine's peripheral effects, which include tachycardia, vasoconstriction, and a rise in blood pressure. It has an antidiuretic effect on the kidneys, with nonsmokers being more susceptible than smokers to this effect. Low dosages of nicotine stimulate the MRC and can induce nausea and/or vomiting via stimulation of the medullary chemoreceptor zone. The usual effect on the gastrointestinal tract is to increase tone and motor activity. This may be related to nicotine's presumed role in the suppression of appetite since it is known that a single cigarette inhibits hunger contractions of the stomach for 15 to 60 minutes (Gerald, 1981). In addition, nicotine appears to elevate fasting levels of blood sugar for a period of a half hour or more.

Nicotine's effect on the cholinergic arousal systems is to increase alertness. This is characterized by increased low voltage EEG activity and increased alpha wave frequency (Knott & Venables, 1977; Murphree, Pfeiffer, & Price, 1967). Also, nicotine may improve learning and memory under certain conditions (Flood, Bennett, Orme, Rosenzweig, & Jarvik, 1978; Mangan & Golding, 1983). However, this effect is complex and reflects a dose-dependent, biphasic mechanism (Morrison & Armitage, 1967).

Nicotine is lipid soluble and thus readily crosses cell membranes and, in the form of cigarette smoke, is absorbed swiftly and efficiently from the lungs. It is also rapidly absorbed from the nasal mucosa when taken as snuff and from the buccal mucosa when delivered in the form of chewing tobacco. It exerts little effect when swallowed because it undergoes a first-pass metabolism in the liver (Ashton, 1987). Nicotine has a half-life of approximately 30 to 60 minutes. Heavy smoking over a period of time will induce variations in the rate of metabolism so that the rate is increased in chronic smokers. Due to hepatic enzyme induction, nicotine also increases the rate of metabolism of several other drugs (Rogers & Spector, 1980).

Once in the blood, nicotine is quickly distributed throughout the body, reaching the brain in 7 to 8 seconds. As a nicotinic acetylcholine receptor agonist, it exerts a biphasic, dose-dependent stimulant/depressant action (Armitage, Hall, & Sellers, 1969). Small to moderate levels of the drug stimulate cholinergic activity. At higher doses or for longer periods of time nicotine may persist in these receptor sites and thus block further responding. This produces the depressant effect of nicotine at high dosages. Lethal dosages block synaptic transmission completely.

Inhaled puffs of smoke produce intermittent, highly concentrated boli of nicotine in the blood (Russell, 1978). This means that the smoker can control the dose rate of nicotine he or she is delivering to the brain. By varying factors such as the size of puff and depth of inhalation, a smoker can obtain predominantly inhibitory or predominantly excitatory effects, or a mixture of both, from one cigarette. This ability to control the psychoactive effects of nicotine is probably the best explanation of why the smoking habit is so popular (Ashton, Millman, Telford, & Thompson, 1974; Ashton & Stepney, 1982; Ashton & Watson, 1970).

Nicotine affects cholinergic pathways throughout the body, although its psychoactive effects are due to its central rather than peripheral effects, particularly in the reward centers of the brain. It is also thought to activate the cerebral cortex generally through stimulation of the RAS and hippocampus, although its mechanism may also involve nicotine-stimulated release of acetylcholine from the cortex. Nicotine's

CNS effects induce pleasurable feelings in 90% of chronic smokers, although it does not produce a "high" comparable to that of many other drugs that induce dependence (Ashton, 1987). In addition, nicotine appears to reduce pain and relieve anxiety in stressful situations (Pomerleau, Turk, & Fertig, 1984). This may be due to nicotine's ability to promote the release of norepinephrine and dopamine from limbic areas and the hypothalamus (Hall & Turner, 1972). It is also possible that nicotine interacts with the opioid reward systems (Karras & Kane, 1980), as well as increasing plasma concentrations of beta-endorphin precursor (beta-endorphin-beta-lipotropin) in man (Pomerleau, Fertig, Seyler, & Jaffe, 1983). At higher dosages, it seems likely that nicotine may reduce activity in the punishment centers of the brain, possibly through a depressant effect at cholinergic synapses in the periventricular system (Ashton, 1987).

Opioids. *Opiates* are products derived from opium and thus refer to its derivatives, such as morphine. *Opioids* are opiates whose actions are specifically antagonized by naloxone. Naloxone (Narcan) is a pure narcotic antagonist that binds to opioid receptors in the brain but does not have morphine-like activity. By definition, effects that are not antagonized by naloxone are not mediated by opioid receptors. *Narcotic analgesics* are agents that act on opioid receptors to produce a naloxone-reversible analgesia (Hughes & Kosterlitz, 1983).

Of this class of drugs, morphine is the main active ingredient of opium and remains the standard against which other agents are measured since other opioids generally have similar actions. Morphine is well absorbed from peripheral sites and is usually administered via subcutaneous, intramuscular, intravenous, or epidural routes. Oral administration is irregular and must overcome first-pass hepatic metabolism and thus requires higher dosages for an equivalent effect. Peak analgesic effects occur approximately one hour after intramuscular injection and two hours after ingestion. Morphine is rapidly distributed through the peripheral areas of the body but crosses the blood-brain barrier rather slowly and reaches the brain in relatively small quantities. The elimination half-life of morphine is 18 to 60 hours.

Heroin (diacetylmorphine), a semisynthetic derivative of morphine, is 1.5 to 3 times more potent than morphine as an analgesic, is more rapidly absorbed by the gastrointestinal tract, and crosses the blood-brain barrier faster than morphine. It is also more quickly metabolized and thus has a shorter duration of action. In the brain, heroin is hydrolyzed to morphine, which is believed to be responsible for its central effects. The potency and quickness of action of heroin is the reason it is usually the drug of choice for opiate abusers. Several synthetic analgesic agents (e.g., meperidine [Demerol], methadone, and propoxyphene [Darvon]) have also been developed. Initially it was hoped that these compounds would exert an analgesic effect that was similar to morphine without offering the same potential for abuse. With the possible exception of pentazocine (Talwin), these opioid agonists appear not to have lived up to this expectation.

The peripheral effects of morphine include arteriolar and venous dilation as well as marked vasodilation of the skin due to the action of peripheral histamine and a suppression of adrenergic tone. This reduction in peripheral resistance may cause postural hypotension. Centrally, morphine produces analgesia, drowsiness, changes in mood, and mental clouding. Morphine affects both the sensation and affective components of pain. At lower doses, pain sensation is selectively depressed while other sensations are unaltered. This is particularly true of continuous dull pain and visceral pain. In cases of sharp intermittent or cutaneous pain, the patient may report that the pain is still present but that it is less distressing.

Morphine and its derivatives are capable of inducing feelings of euphoria, although this varies across individuals. Rapid intravenous injection of heroin in addicts produces an intense "rush" lasting about 45 seconds that is accompanied by warmth and flushing of the skin. This is followed by a period of sustained euphoria or "high." In some case, dysphoria may occur, especially in normal subjects who may complain of an inability to concentrate, difficulty in mentation, and general lethargy (Ashton, 1987).

Other central effects include nausea and vomiting, depression of the cough reflex, and pupillary constriction. Tolerance develops to these effects and to the analgesic and euphoric sensations. At high doses, morphine can cause muscle rigidity, convulsions, and death from respiratory depression. Neuroendocrine effects include increased output of adrenocortical hormone (ACTH), prolactin, and growth hormone. Depression of luteinizing hormone leads to decreased plasma concentration of testosterone and testicular atrophy in men. In women, amenorrhea may occur after prolonged opiate use.

Opioids, by definition, act on the opioid receptors in the brain. Consequently, it was suspected for some time that there must be naturally- occurring compounds in the brain that operate on these receptor sites. The so-called "endogenous opioids" were discovered in 1974 and are categorized into three classes (Hughes, 1983). First, there are the *enkephalins*, which are derived from the precursor pro-enkephalin A. The second class is composed of the *dynorphins*, which are derived from pro-enkephalin B. And finally, there are the *endorphins*, which are deriva-tives of pro-opiomelanocortin. All three classes are closely related struc-turally but differ in the length of their peptide chains. In addition, they have a degree of structural flexibility that allows them to take up differ-ent conformations (Terenius, 1980). This results in an ability to bind to more than one type of opioid receptor and thus to function as either a short-acting neurotransmitter or as a longer-acting neuronal or hormo-nal modulator. In addition to these three classes, several other endoge-nous opioids have been identified (e.g., peptide E, alpha- and beta-neoendorphins), but their function is less clearly understood.

There also appear to be at least three distinct opioid receptor types, each of which has a different pharmacological profile, different tissue distribution, and different binding properties. In addition, it is probable that they mediate different though overlapping actions. *Mu-receptors* are the main sites of action for the narcotic analgesics. The enkephalins and beta-endorphins also act as agonists, but are not specific for mu-receptors. Naloxone and nalorphine are antagonists. The *delta-receptors* are activated by enkephalins, which have a greater affinity for them than for mu-receptors, and by beta-endorphin, which has equal affinity for both delta- and mu-receptors. Naloxone has less antagonist activity at delta- than at mu-receptor sites. It is also thought that delta-receptors play an important role in nociception and probably limbic functions, although it is possible that mu-and delta-receptors represent high- and low-affinity states of a unitary receptor site (Atweh & Kuhar, 1983). *Kappa-receptors* respond to dynorphin, with naloxone exerting some an-tagonist activity at these sites. These receptors also appear to be in-volved in certain types of pain. It has been suggested that mu-, delta-, and kappa-receptors are interchangeable forms of a single opioid recep-tor complex (Barnard & Demoliou-Mason, 1983).

A fourth type, *sigma-receptors*, was originally categorized in *in vivo* pharmacological studies but has not been demonstrated by binding studies. However, PCP may be an agonist for these receptors (Simon, 1981). It has been suggested that activation of sigma-receptors accounts for the hallucinogenic properties of these drugs, although this type may not be a true opioid receptor (Paterson, Robson, & Kosterlitz, 1983). *Eta-receptors* have also been described, but their significance is not known (Ashton, 1987).

The peptides and their receptors are found in particularly high con-centrations in the limbic system, especially the hypothalamus, as well as the pituitary, pons, spinal cord, hippocampus, septum, corpus striatum, and basal ganglia (Atweh & Kuhar, 1983; Cuello, 1983; Khacha-turian, Lewis, Schäfer, & Watson, 1985). This may account for their diverse effects on nociception, metabolism, mood, and behavior. For example, opioid receptors are found in the reward centers of the brain, such as the amygdala and locus ceruleus, where they act in coordination with the monoamines (Koob & Bloom, 1983). Their placement in the hypothalamus and pituitary may explain their widespread hormonal and autonomic effects.

The opioid receptors generally induce cellular inhibition when stimulated. This is thought to be achieved by hyperpolarization of the cell membrane due to the opening of potassium channels and the depression of neurotransmitter release (Henderson, 1983; North & Williams, 1983; Wouters & Bercken, 1980). In this manner, the opioid system operates in the body as a widespread and complex inhibitory signalling mechanism in which selectivity is achieved by the interaction of particular opioid peptides with different receptor types (Thompson, 1984).

It is also apparent that the endogenous opiates interact with a number of other neurotransmitters and neurotransmission systems. This suggests that there may be several overlapping back-up systems that have developed over the course of evolution to deal with this important aspect of sensation and behavior (Sweet, 1980). This includes the presence of multiple neurochemically and anatomically discrete pain suppression systems that respond to different types of stimuli, both physical and psychological. Consequently, the endogenous opiates and the opioid drugs have been implicated in a wide range of psychological disturbances, including depression, anxiety, and schizophrenia. This may also explain the persistence and potency of the opioids in terms of their potential for abuse.

Treatment Implications

The complexity of the interaction of diverse mechanisms in substance dependence and abuse is such as to make simplistic models of treatment for these disorders unrealistic. Not only is there tremendous heterogeneity across different classes of drugs in terms of their action and effect (e.g., some are stimulants, some are depressants), there is also enormous diversity within classes in terms of how and why individuals react to them. When the effects of behavioral adaptation to drug use are added to the picture, the task of successfully treating the individual with a substance use disorder becomes very complex indeed.

Three Challenges

There are three characteristics of the substance use disorders that make their treatment particularly difficult. First, by definition these disorders involve direct, potent biochemical stimulation or depression of the CNS. Consequently, they involve a powerful positive feedback mechanism that makes resistance to treatment and the possibility of relapse highly probable. This situation is not shared by most other disorders in the DSM-III-R. Although some of them (e.g., schizophrenia, see Chapter 4) may involve a strong biological susceptibility, it is not thought that these disorders perpetuate themselves. In other words, schizophrenic symptoms do not in themselves increase one's tendency toward schizophrenia. However, in the case of substance use disorders, the very fact of substance use increases the potential for further abuse.

A second characteristic that makes the treatment of these disorders difficult is that the immediate consequences of their use are rewarding. Although the long-term consequences of use may be aversive, the strength of the reinforcing properties of these substances in the short run will easily outweigh the "morning after" effects. Again, this distinguishes these disorders from the others we have discussed so far. With a few possible exceptions, disorders involving schizophrenia, depression, and anxiety are not inherently reinforcing. In fact, disorders in all three diagnostic categories are usually experienced as aversive and unpleasant, and the person experiencing them is usually highly motivated to seek relief from his or her confused, depressed, or anxious state. This is often not the case with the substance use disorders. To the contrary, it is well known that persons dependent on these drugs will avoid seeking assistance for their problem and often go to great lengths to hide or disguise their abuse.

A final characteristic of these disorders that separates them from others is that, because they involve chemical substances, there may be a tendency to disregard the psychosocial aspects of their treatment. Instead, treatment may be limited to the attempt to balance one biochemical with another. While the value of this type of intervention is without dispute for individuals suffering from an acute abstinence syndrome, it is equally certain that the ultimate solution to these problems is not to substitute one drug for another.

Given the complex interaction of the various neurotransmitter systems discussed above, it should be evident that the use of one substance to counter another will likely continue to disrupt normal homeostatic relationships. This is because our knowledge of these mechanisms and the sophistication with which we can regulate compensatory activity is limited. More importantly, given the mechanisms of cross-tolerance noted earlier, there is also the very present danger of adding breadth to a problem that already exists. The present writer is aware of one case, for example, in which a 50-year-old alcoholic who later committed suicide was treated for his alcoholism with Valium. This seems a bit like throwing stones into a pond to still troubled waters.

The issue is not whether it is important to restore normal biochemical functioning but how to do it. In the case of the severely addicted individual, this might require the assistance of medications over the short run. However, these can not take the place of relearning more adaptive living skills that will allow the individual to proceed adequately through his or her life without developing a dependence on the abused substance again. For some individuals, this may involve exerting better control over such drugs as caffeine that, when used in moderation, do not present a problem. In other cases, however, control is possible only through total and complete abstinence. This is particularly true for those substances (e.g., cocaine, opioids, and perhaps alcohol) whose reinforcing properties are so powerful that it is essentially impossible for the individual to control them once consistent use has begun (Cooper, 1983). Total abstinence may also be appropriate for those individuals with a history of an inability to exert control.

A Multidimensional Approach to Treatment

Solving the problem of control usually requires attention to a number of different aspects of a person's life. Multidimensional treatment programs seeking to meet this need may include pharmacologic, psychotherapeutic, familial, and residential components (e.g., Lowenstein, 1982). Behavioral interventions aimed at reinstating control or maintaining abstinence once it has been obtained have received particular attention in this regard (e.g., Lawson, 1983; Nathan & Niaura, 1985). These programs characteristically involve procedures to develop self-control and problem-solving skills as well as interventions designed to provide a living environment that is supportive of responsible use or abstinence. Self-help programs, such as Alcoholics Anonymous, involve many of the same components, although they are presented in a somewhat different format. What all of these interventions have in common is an emphasis on social reinforcement of control behaviors and the learning of appropriate coping strategies. The latter include not only the instigation of self-control but also the development of social and other life skills. Again, none of these strategies directed at the individual is likely to be successful over the long run unless his or her immediate environment is supportive of these efforts.

The complex nature of successful intervention for the substance use disorders can be illustrated by reference to the treatment of alcoholism, although the "language of recovery" may be universal when it comes to problems of substance use (Ehrlich & McGeehan, 1985; Smith, 1986). A comprehensive review of treatments for alcohol dependence and abuse by W. R. Miller and Hester (1980) concluded that "no treatment method has been shown to be consistently superior to the absence of treatment or to alternative treatments in a sufficient number of well-controlled studies to warrant 'established status'" (p. 108). At best, it can be said that therapists working with substance users must consider a variety of different treatment techniques and adopt a flexible approach in order to tailor the treatment to the individual needs and differences of the patient (P. M. Miller & Foy, 1981). The objectives of such a program might include providing education, modifying the drug-taking behavior itself, reducing the immediate reinforcing consequences of substance use, establishing a natural environment that reinforces controlled use or abstinence, and preparing for the possibility if not probability of relapse.

The education component of treatment involves teaching the patient about the nature of abuse and the effects of the particular substance on his mental and physical health. There are two reasons for including this component. First, it helps deal with the denial that is inherent to these disorders. Second, it may increase the client's motivation to participate in the treatment program (Uecker & Solberg, 1973).

The second component of a comprehensive treatment program focuses on the consummatory behavior itself. In this regard, any of the work on self-control training may be relevant (e.g., W. R. Miller & Muñoz, 1976). An aspect of this training includes stimulus control techniques, which are concerned with identifying the situation, context, times of day, and other cues to consummatory behavior. Self-control training may also include procedures designed to make consumption aversive. Although early work in this area used such painful or discomforting physical stimuli as electrical shocks and emetic drugs, today this approach is more likely to involve covert sensitization (W. R. Miller, 1982). It is important to note, however, that this particular aspect of self-control training will not be successful if used by itself. Aversive techniques are appropriate only as part of a larger, more comprehensive treatment program.

Restructuring the natural environment to maintain treatment goals is a third and crucial component for any comprehensive treatment of substance use. One of the more promising approaches in this regard has been the community-based program developed by Hunt and Azrin (1973). This focuses on the user's work and social settings, marital and familial factors, and leisure activities. The procedure has been found to be even more successful when a "buddy system," a daily-report system, group counseling, and self-administration of disulfiram (Antabuse) were added (Azrin, 1976).

Relapse-prevention training constitutes the final component in a multicomponent program. This component has been influenced by the cognitive-behavioral model of relapse developed by Marlatt (1985). Among other things, this approach focuses on what to do when relapse occurs and how to handle it. An analysis of relapse episodes among 70 alcohol abusers by Marlatt and Gordon (1980) indicated that the vast majority of relapses (74%) occurred in response to negative emotional states, interpersonal conflict, or social pressure to resume substance use. Some of the skills that are thought to help the individual cope with these situations include assertion training (Eisler, Hersen, & Miller, 1974) and problem-solving (Chaney, O'Leary, & Marlatt, 1978). Assertion training is directed toward the goal of substance refusal (i.e., resisting peer pressure to indulge). Problem-solving training is used to provide alternative ways of dealing with frustration, anger, loneliness, depression, or self-experienced urges to consume. In some instances, when abuse is related to marital discord, marital therapy is also indicated at this stage.

Disulfiram (Antabuse)

One of the most powerful ongoing contingencies to insure abstinence in alcohol abuse involves the use of disulfiram (Peachey & Naranjo, 1983). This medication produces an aversive physical reaction characterized by flushing, increased skin temperature, hypotension, and in more severe reactions nausea, vomiting, and physiologic shock (Kwentus & Major, 1979). These reactions are the result of disulfiram's ability to inhibit the action of aldehyde dehydrogenase. This causes a delay in the metabolism of acetaldehyde, which accumulates in the blood. The amount of acetaldehyde that accumulates depends on the dose of disulfiram and the amount of alcohol ingested.

The greatest problem with the use of disulfiram, however, is noncompliance with its administration (Bigelow, Stitzer, & Liebson, 1986). However, when used in conjunction with group counseling designed to assure maintenance, abstinence has been maintained for six months for married (or cohabitating) clients in comparison to a traditional treatment group which suffered an almost complete relapse (Azrin, Sisson, Meyers, & Godley, 1982). (Group counseling, however, was not effective in maintaining medication compliance for clients who lived alone.) When behavior therapy was added to address some of the other concerns noted above, near-total sobriety was observed for both the single and married clients. This provides yet another example of how a physiologically-based intervention must be applied within the larger context of a psychosocial program.

Summary

The end result of this analysis suggests that a piecemeal approach to the treatment of substance use disorders will most likely fail. This would be particularly true for those interventions that focus on only one aspect of this complex problem. It is, of course, possible that in some cases a single factor may be the key to treatment success. This can occur, for example, when all of the other elements of the treatment puzzle (e.g., good social support, nonintrusive environments, lack of genetic disposition, etc.) are in place (cf. Tarter & Edwards, 1986). However, for most patients suffering from this category of disorders, anything less than a comprehensive and multidimensional effort will serve only to sell them short.

Part **III**

Overview

Three conclusions might be drawn from the chapters so far. First, there are no simple explanations for any of the disorders discussed. Second, their expression involves the complex and dynamic interaction of multiple factors, some of which originate within the individual and others of which emanate from the environment. And third, the successful treatment of these disorders inevitably draws on curative powers arising from many different therapeutic strategies. Consequently, it appears that the most reasonable approach to treating these disorders would involve the cooperative intervention of health-care providers representing several disciplines. The reasons for taking an interdisciplinary approach to the treatment of psychological disorders is explored more fully in the final chapter.

Chapter 8

Implications for Practice

The integration of perspectives arising from the complementary yet distinct disciplines of medicine and psychology demands more than a delineation of how physiological factors affect the expression of disorders that are primarily psychological in nature. Such a view requires a fundamentally different way of thinking about these disorders—a model of dysfunction that allows for the peaceful cohabitation of factors that on the surface may appear to be antagonistic if not mutually exclusive.

In Chapter 1 it was suggested that the adoption of a *systemic* approach to understanding these disorders provides a way in which some of the conceptual problems associated with integrating information from disparate literatures can be achieved. This chapter will review the systemic model of dysfunction in light of the information presented in Part II ("Clinical Disorders") and will argue that such an approach provides a compelling rationale for the interdisciplinary treatment of these problems, regardless of political, theoretical, or methodological considerations that tend to interfere with cooperative efforts across disciplines.

Psychological Disorders as Systemic Dysfunctions

In Chapter 1 a distinction was made between a *discrete* and a *systemic* disease. The former represents "a clearly discontinuous change in bodily functioning and traceable to some discrete cause, often external in origin" (Claridge, 1985, p. 9). An example of a discrete disease is an infectious illness like yellow fever.

In comparison, a systemic "disease" occurs as the result of a breakdown of normal functioning. As such, a systemic disease is understood best in terms of the degree to which it deviates from normal. This approach also assumes that there is a continuity between health and illness that underlies the development of this type of problem. Finally, it is thought that a systemic disease results from multiple rather than single causes. In many ways, it might be more appropriate to think of this type of disorder as a systemic *dysfunction* than as a disease.

The three characteristics of a systemic dysfunction highlight several important issues. First, defining a disorder in terms of the degree to which certain thoughts and behaviors deviate from normal introduces such variables as personal opinion and social custom into the diagnostic process. Second, the assumption that there is a continuum between illness and health affects how we conceptualize the mechanisms through which these disorders find expression. Finally, determining what has caused a particular disorder becomes much more complicated when one starts talking about multiple, interacting factors rather than single pathogens or discrete causes.

Diagnosis Revisited

The diagnosis of most psychological disorders is a matter of degree. This means that these disorders are diagnosable primarily in terms of the degree to which they represent a departure from normal functioning. Alcoholism (see Chapter 7) provides an excellent example, for when does "social drinking" become "heavy drinking," when does "heavy drinking" become "problem drinking," and when does "problem drinking" become sufficiently severe to certify that someone is an alcoholic? Not only are there no absolute criteria for making these determinations, there is controversy concerning whether an early pattern of alcohol consumption is predictive of later stages in the progression of the disorder. Furthermore, the diagnosis of alcoholism, whether in terms of the guidelines developed by the American Psychiatric Association, the World Health Organization, or the National Council on Alcoholism, is based primarily on drinking behaviors or the behavioral effects of alcohol consumption rather than a specific biochemical marker or distinctive metabolic process (Mendelson & Mello, 1985).

The same can be said for schizophrenia (see Chapter 4). The thoughts and behaviors that set schizophrenia apart represent a gradual deviation from normal thoughts and behaviors and are thus usually insidious in their onset as well as variable in their course. This is particularly true for the expression of its more "negative" symptomatology. However, even an acute psychotic episode rarely appears out of the blue and is usually preceded by a prodromal phase during which there is a progressive deterioration from the previous level of functioning. Deciding when a person is actively schizophrenic and when he or she is in remission (i.e., normal) is therefore often difficult to determine.

Psychological disorders, as systemic dysfunctions, are thus likely to present with a pattern of cognitive and behavioral deficiencies or excesses that occur gradually over a period of time rather than suddenly. Furthermore, these disorders are not characterized by the presence of a single pathognomonic symptom or specific biochemical marker (Cowdry & Goodwin, 1978). Although the diagnostic criteria developed for the DSM-III and -III-R represent progress in providing guidelines for determining when thoughts and behaviors fall outside normal limits, the diagnosis of psychological disorders is still an inexact science in which social and political considerations as well as questions regarding what constitutes normal variability play an important role (Cantor & Genero, 1986; Rothblum, Solomon, & Albee, 1986). As a result, none of the disorders covered in this book should be thought of or treated independently of the psychosocial context in which they occur.

Individual Differences Revisited

An emphasis on the diagnosis of psychological disorders in terms of the degree to which they deviate from normal functioning suggests that there is a continuum between illness and health. In part, this continuum is thought to reflect an inherited predisposition toward dysfunction. These predispositions are thought to interact with a variety of psychosocial environments so as to make different individuals vulnerable to different types of disorders. A psychological disorder develops "once an individual has passed beyond a certain threshold, determined by a combination of genetic loading and accumulated life experience" (Claridge, 1985, p. 131).

The symptoms of schizophrenia, for example, are thought to represent an aberration in central nervous system (CNS) processes that underlie cognitive and personality characteristics shared by healthy as well as unhealthy persons alike (Claridge, 1987). A schizophrenic break may occur when a "vulnerable" individual is subjected to a series of stressful environmental events that combine to surpass his or her threshold of resistance (Zubin & Spring, 1977). Consequently, it can be argued that there is a continuum between a normal level of functioning and the development of a full-blown psychotic break, with certain conditions (e.g., borderline personality) that are symptomatic of both.

The same basic approach may be applied to other psychological disorders as well. For example, it is thought that individuals differ significantly in terms of their ability to cope with stress, which has been implicated in the development of the mood disorders. Other persons may exhibit evidence of an overly-sensitive nervous system that makes them more susceptible to developing anxiety-based problems. Finally, individual differences in the metabolism of alcohol and responsiveness to it or other psychoactive drugs may play an important role in determining who falls victim to substance dependence or abuse.

Etiology Revisited

It might be said that a person's inherited predispositions provide the *potential* for a particular disorder to occur while his or her life experience supplies the *opportunity*. Sometimes this potential may exert a powerful effect, such as with schizophrenia. At other times, it may serve to increase a person's susceptibility to the disruption of normal physiological functioning, as when hyperventilation precipitates a panic attack. At yet other times, one's physiological potential may only act to facilitate the disruption of the body's normal homeostatic mechanisms, as occurs with the ingestion of psychoactive substances.

Most if not all of the disorders discussed in this book thus manifest a complex etiology that involves multiple factors, some of which reside within the individual (i.e., individual differences) and some of which originate in the environment. Some of the environmental factors include expressed emotion, stressful life situations, fear-evoking stimuli, and social situations that promote or support dysfunctional behaviors. These, in turn, are affected by one's biological make-up, past learning, and current cognitions. Consequently, it is difficult, if not impossible, to determine unequivocally which, if any, play a predominant role.

It is clear, however, that unidimensional explanations of these disorders simply fail to account adequately for the complexity of their expression. An accurate picture of how these disorders originate is more likely to be found by attempting to understand the interaction of environmental, social, personal, and physiological factors together than by focusing on one of them alone.

The Unfulfilled Promise of the Systemic Model

Applying the model of systemic dysfunction to psychological disorders does three things. It asserts that the psychosocial aspects of these disorders can not be ignored; it argues that these disorders are not like discrete diseases; and it highlights the multiplicity of etiological factors inherent to the development of these disorders. Unfortunately, the promise this approach holds for the humane and multidimensional treatment of psychological disorders has, in many ways, gone unfulfilled (cf. Talbott, 1981, 1984).

This is not because the application of the systemic model to psychological problems has been rejected. In fact, this approach was used to justify expanding the DSM-III to include a wide range of disorders that were not included in the DSM-II (Spitzer, Sheehy, & Endicott, 1977). However, in the process the model got turned on its head, for it quickly became the rationale for narrowing (i.e., all disorders are medical in nature) than broadening the scope of treatment (cf. Albee, 1977; Miller, Bergstrom, Cross, & Grube, 1981). (This issue was discussed at length in Chapter 1.)

Therein lies the problem. Rather than being seen as a call for a collaborative effort among different professions, with each contributing in terms of its own area of expertise, the expanded view of what psychological disorders entail has, in some ways, escalated the struggle between professions over access to and control over the treatment of these disorders (cf. Lipowski, 1988).

Among the main combatants are the opposing forces of psychiatry and professional psychology (Buie, 1989). The points of conflict include who controls the purse strings for research support, who determines public policy regarding the provision of health care, and who is reimbursed for the delivery of those services. In Great Britain the locus of this struggle appears to revolve around the allocation of government resources, while in the United States the battle has been joined with particular emphasis on the health-care dollar in the private sector (Kiesler & Morton, 1988b).

The basis of the confrontation is an effort on the part of both psychiatry and professional psychology to expand the scope of their influence and practice. For psychiatrists, this means defining all disorders that involve psychological distress as "a subset of medical disorders" (Spitzer et al., 1977, p.4). Many psychologists, on the other hand, are attempting to extend the scope of their practice to include such activities as hospital admitting privileges and the right to prescribe medications, which traditionally have been within the purview of medicine (Buie, 1988). The question, of course, is whether either profession is capable of encompassing a knowledge base that has sufficient breadth and depth to prepare it to deal with these complex disorders comprehensively.

It is likely that no one profession can or even desires to master both the biomedical and behavioral sciences.[1] In this regard, it may be unrealistic to think that a practitioner can become proficient in the art and

[1]It can be argued that behavioral medicine (i.e., health psychology) does, in fact, represent such an integration of knowledge. There are, however, three points to be made in this

science of both medicine and psychology.[2] This argument may strike some readers as inconsistent, coming as it does in conjunction with a call for the integration of physiological and psychological knowledge. Yet, claiming that one needs to have some understanding and appreciation of both disciplines is not tantamount to maintaining that a practitioner must be competent in both. It would seem that the most reasonable way of dealing with the tremendous range of information that is relevant to the psychological disorders is to take an *interdisciplinary* approach to their treatment. (See Panel 8.1, "Consultation and Referral.")

The Interdisciplinary Treatment of Psychological Disorders

A review of the concepts and information presented in the preceding four chapters (Part II) demonstrates why a single approach to treatment is not enough. At every level the complex interaction of multiple causes requiring the application of a wide range of diverse therapeutic skills is evident. This is seen in terms of CNS structure (i.e., morphology) and function, as well as in terms of the neurochemical systems that mediate both structure and function. Regardless of whether the level of analysis is structural, functional, or neurochemical, the limitations of unidimensional interventions are apparent and the need to deal with the effects of multiple causal factors is obvious.

The Structural Level. The attempt to explain psychological problems

---

regard. First, behavioral medicine, like medicine itself, is a highly specialized endeavor. Researchers and practitioners for the most part focus on specific disorders affecting particular organ systems (e.g., coronary-prone behavior, cardiac rehabilitation, psychoendocrinology). Second, even in such areas as behavioral pediatrics, for which the scope of disorders is broad, the roles of the various professionals who work together are clearly defined and directed toward specific aspects of treatment (Christophersen, 1983). Third, in cases for which a general practice in behavioral medicine is pursued, these efforts often reflect a rather unsophisticated attempt to use a few basic treatment strategies with a broad range of diverse problems. This is perhaps illustrated best when biofeedback is applied indiscriminately to a wide variety of problems for which there is little controlled evidence for its efficacy. (For an extended discussion of the third point, see Hollandsworth, 1986, Chapter 6.)

[2]The reality that health-care needs are not being met in some rural areas means that some practitioners must become proficient with a variety of treatment strategies that may encompass aspects of both medical (i.e., pharmacological) and psychological intervention. It has also been noted that often the experienced professional psychologist knows more about psychotropic medications than many medical practitioners who do not specialize in this area. Nevertheless, the assertion that, in general, individuals should stick to what they know best cannot be denied on the basis of unusual circumstance or variations in individual competence.

PANEL 8.1

Consultation and Referral

Contributed by Patrick Leverett and Rosamond Myers

Outpatient Services

Several salient interdisciplinary treatment issues exist for the professional psychologist in an outpatient treatment setting. Concerns that are particularly important include knowing when to seek the consultation of a physician, which physician to choose, and which of many medical subspecialty areas to refer within.

A realization of the parameters of practice as a professional psychologist is extremely important, particularly from the perspective of the outpatient practitioner who may or may not be accustomed to the treatment team approach in which professional role boundaries are usually clearly delineated. Failure to realize at what point a medical referral is necessary, encouraging a patient* to withdraw from medical treatment, or overstepping the boundaries of psychological practice by offering an opinion as to the existence, nonexistence, or diagnosis of physical disease, is likely to be irresponsible, unethical, and/or illegal. Similarly, misleading a patient, however inadvertently, into thinking that treatment received is being delivered by a physician, constitutes practicing medicine without a license (Knapp & Vandecreek, 1981).

Patients presenting with a clinical picture that includes headache, sweating, chills, tremors, a persistent cough, shortness of breath or other respiratory problems, disturbances in gait or locomotion, ocular problems, dizziness, abdominal distress, chest pain or discomfort, heart palpitations, or any of a host of symptoms of a physiological nature should be referred to a physician to rule out the possibility of biogenic etiology and to evaluate for the appropriateness of the biomedical treatment of such symptoms. Similarly, patients presenting with extreme behavior (e.g., mania, melancholia, or psychosis), patients complaining of or exhibiting symptoms of amnesia or any of the symptoms of organic mental syndromes, substance abuse patients, and patients exhibiting any of the symptoms characteristic of the somatoform disorders should be referred for medical consultation. Patients with sleep disorders as well as patients presenting with sexual dysfunction problems

*To be consistent, the term "patient" is used throughout, although many psychologists prefer "client" instead. This decision, however, should not be interpreted as favoring a medical approach to these problems or as failing to recognize that these "patients" are also "consumers" (i.e., clients) of the services psychologists offer.

should also be referred to a physician for further evaluation (see the DSM-III-R for guidance in all of these areas).

Variability exists between members of any profession in terms of quality of care, preferred patient populations, professional demeanor, and other characteristics of health care. The psychologist seeking medical consultation or considering referring a patient to a physician is well-advised to bear this fact in mind, remembering that the ultimate purpose of consultation/referral is to make the situation for the patient better and not worse. Certainly, the choice of a physician should in most cases be made by the patient himself or herself. For the purpose of offering sound advice, or in the rare instance in which the patient is unable to make a choice either through a lack of knowledge or incapacity, the psychologist should be aware not only of what medical resources are available in his or her community, but should have some knowledge of the professional reputations of local physicians. Such knowledge is traditionally gained through "word-of-mouth" communication with other professionals or through personal experience. More recently, computer data banks containing essential information about physicians have been made available for public use, and may be useful both to the referring psychologist and patient.

In most cases, the decision of what type of physician (i.e., which medical subspecialty) to refer a patient to can best be accomplished by initially referring the patient to a family practice or general practice physician and allowing the physician to either choose to treat the patient or to refer further for specialized treatment. In some cases, however, it is prudent for the psychologist to refer directly to a medical specialist. For example, the patient exhibiting acute symptoms of schizophrenia, mania, or other mental disorders for which adjunctive medical treatment is generally indicated may be referred to a psychiatrist for initial evaluation. Similarly, the patient presenting with symptoms indicative of an organic mental syndrome or disorder may well be referred initially to a physician specializing in neurology. Children are typically referred to a pediatrician. Patients who are pregnant, or for whom pregnancy is suspected, might be best referred initially to a physician specializing in obstetrics and gynecology.

Inpatient Services

When employed in inpatient treatment settings, the professional psychologist will function as a part of a larger interdisciplinary treatment team. Other members of the team are likely to represent such disciplines as medicine, nursing, occupational therapy, psychiatry, recreational therapy, social work, special education, speech therapy, and others. As a member of the treatment team, it will be necessary for the psychologist to understand what each of the other professional's job entails and the type of consultation provided by each.

There are several ways to go about this. The psychologist should talk to different members of the team and find out what they do, how they evaluate patients, and what types of information they can provide. It is also helpful to read the initial and updated evaluations done by various team members in the patient's chart. This allows the psychologist to determine what areas of functioning are measured and assessed by different professionals in the interdisciplinary setting.

Awareness of the functional differences among specialties and what each treats will enable the psychologist to ask informed questions and obtain useful information. It is also important to note that, by taking the time and making the effort to learn something about what other treatment team members do, the psychologist will increase his or her credibility when working within a multidisciplinary treatment setting.

There will be times when questions arise or when consultations regarding medical aspects of treatment are necessary. In order to ask intelligent questions, psychologists must be aware of medication options for the type of disorder they are working with. Clearly it is important to remember that the physician is the expert in this area. However, having a basic knowledge of medication possibilities provides psychologists with an informed basis from which to discuss the case. Likewise, building a thorough knowledge base on physiological reactions allows for the recognition of side effects of medications, which can then be discussed sensibly with the physician.

When discussing cases with other treatment team members, there may be occasions when the psychologist feels less than adequate about his or her knowledge base compared to that of other professionals. At these times it is important to remember that each professional is working toward the same goal (i.e., a successful treatment outcome) and that each discipline comes to the team with different areas of competency and different tools for assessment and treatment. Professionals from different disciplines may have questions about what another area has to offer or what alternative perspectives on the problem are. Other treatment team members will, in all probability, be responsive to discussing their approaches to treatment. At these times basic interpersonal skills often come into play (i.e., presenting questions in a non-threatening, nonchallenging manner, and being open-minded to others' viewpoints when they differ from that of the psychologist).

There will also be times when other professionals will have questions about the role psychology may play in the treatment process. It is important here as well for the psychologist to remember that other disciplines are attempting to work together for the best therapeutic outcome. Thus, the psychologist should not feel uncomfortable or defensive in discussing his or her ideas and conceptualizations with others on the treatment team.

Participating as a member of a multidisciplinary treatment team can be a stimulating and rewarding collaboration. Furthermore, positive experiences in these efforts may play a part in decreasing tensions among disciplines and returning the focus to the successful treatment of the patient.

in terms of differences in bodily structure has a long history. During the last century this interest found expression in the theory and practice of phrenology (e.g., Fowler, 1869; Fowler & Fowler, 1883). However, the simplistic and superficial concepts of phrenology soon fell into disuse and the focus of this approach moved beneath the skull in an attempt to localize different functions in different parts of the brain. However, as more was learned about how the brain operates, the notion that certain functions could be isolated in specific areas of the cortex was also questioned. (For a discussion of these issues, see Luria, 1973, and Hollandsworth, 1986, Chapter 3.) Nevertheless, the morphological study of the CNS is still pursued today for what it might add to an overall understanding of the physiological basis for many of these disorders.

Examples of this approach were provided in Chapter 4, where it was noted that there have been several attempts to determine whether schizophrenic patients are different from normal individuals in terms of the relative weight, thickness, or size of various structures in the brain (e.g., volume of the thalamus, brain weight, average cortical mantle width). One of the more interesting findings to emerge from these studies was the observation that, on average, the corpus callosum of schizophrenic patients may be thicker than that of normals (Bigelow, Nasrallah, & Rauscher, 1983). This was related, in turn, to information-processing models of schizophrenia which suggest that schizophrenics suffer from too much communication between cerebral hemispheres. Other examples of this type of approach include the several theories of schizophrenia which relate structural damage resulting from such diverse causes as brain injury, cerebral atrophy, neurological disease, or viral infection to the development of the disorder (cf. Golden & Sawicki, 1985).

While the structural approach is perhaps the most obvious one, it is also probably the least satisfactory. Part of the problem is that structural differences do not tell us very much about the manner in which the disorder occurs. All of the major structures in the brain serve multiple functions, and injury to or disruption of any one of them can cause a number of diverse dysfunctions.

This point can be illustrated by reviewing what we have learned about the hippocampus. The hippocampus, which lies bilaterally in the temporal lobes of the brain, is well known for its role in the consolidation of memory. It is also generally understood that the hippocampus, in opposition to the amygdala, may serve to dampen affective intensity. However, we have also learned that the functions of the hippocampus are very complex and include, among other things, attaching an "important" tag to incoming stimuli and thus playing a role in the elicitation of anxiety. The hippocampus is also rich in GABA-ergic receptors so that the action of the benzodiazepines here accounts for not only their anxiolytic effect but their anticonvulsant effects as well. Opioid receptors are located in the hippocampus, which implicates this structure in analgesic activity and possibly identifies it as another important reward center of the brain. In addition, nicotine's ability to stimulate hippocampal areas demonstrates that this structure is related to the arousal systems in some manner. Finally, the agonist effects of PCP and delta-9-THC in the hippocampus suggest that this structure is somehow involved in perception and sensation.

The same pattern of multiple function is evident for most of the other major structures in the brain. These structures are usually situated in central locations where numerous neuronal pathways converge. Structures like the hippocampus are, in actuality, communication centers in which messages are processed and passed along to other parts of the brain. Although this means that they play an important role in mediating many disorders, it also means that focusing on any one of these structures by itself will tell us very little about the mechanisms by which this mediation occurs.

This helps explain why surgical interventions (i.e., psychosurgery) have been relatively ineffective in the treatment of psychological disorders. Although at one point there was some hope that lesioning pathways that connect one area of the brain with another might prove to be a viable treatment for certain intractable disorders, psychosurgery has never gained much popularity or acceptance (cf. Miller, 1972). Part of the reason for this is the ethical and social problems inherent to the permanent alteration of a person's functional capacity (Chavkin, 1978).[3] Another aspect of this failure is the lack of clear-cut efficacy for these procedures (Gaylin, 1975). This should not be surprising, however, given the likelihood that psychological disorders, regardless of severity, cannot be localized in any particular part of the brain.

The Functional Level. A more promising approach to understanding the physiology of psychological disorders is to think in terms of the relationships between structures and how this affects their function. This approach has proceeded in two directions. One direction has been to focus on the *vertical* organization of the brain (e.g., the relationship

---

[3]The permanent alteration of anyone's functional capacity is cause for just concern, regardless of how it is accomplished. Although psychosurgery's effects are more dramatic and clearly irreversible, the immutable impairment in function resulting from the chronic administration of psychotropic agents (e.g., tardive dyskinesia) is equally disturbing.

between basic structures in the brain stem and higher areas in the cortex). A second direction has highlighted the interrelatedness of the two halves of the brain and thus has emphasized the brain's *horizontal* arrangement (e.g., across hemispheres).

Perhaps the best example of the vertical approach is found in the work that has investigated the relationship between perception (a higher cortical function) and arousal, which is mediated in the brain stem. This research was discussed in Chapter 4 in terms of the studies of schizophrenics who exhibit a tendency to "augment" or "reduce" the perception of simple stimuli according to variations in stimulus intensity. Other examples of the study of functional relationships between structures may be found in Gray's (1982) work on the behavioral inhibition system. Sheehan (1982) also investigated how certain structures in the brain stem (e.g., the chemoreceptor trigger zone) interact with other structures (e.g., the locus ceruleus) in the mediation of panic attacks.

The horizontal approach, on the other hand, is best exemplified by the study of hemispheric function, much of which has been done with schizophrenic patients. While research on vertical function in this population has focused on perception, hemispheric research has been concerned with how in-coming stimuli are integrated. Initially, this work proceeded under the assumption that the problem with schizophrenia lay in a dysfunction in one of the hemispheres. However, in spite of the relative degree of specialization of the two hemispheres in terms of language and spatial functions, both sides of the brain are involved in the processing of information received from the outside world. Consequently, it has been suggested the problem lies in interhemispheric regulation rather than a dysfunction in either one of the hemispheres. Although there are many theories in this regard, the best that can be said at present is that the two halves of the schizophrenic brain simply do not function in a coordinated manner much of the time.

Although the study of function is useful for understanding why individuals differ in terms of their susceptibility to certain psychological disorders, this approach still does not tell the full story. An individual's functional capacity cannot be thought of independently of the events it is designed to mediate. A schizotypal nervous system, for example, does not by itself insure the development of schizophrenia, just as the behavioral inhibition system will not exert its effect in the absence of appropriate environmental triggers. Consequently, the study of the functional interaction between CNS structures simply highlights the importance of the individual's interaction with his or her environment as well.

The Neurochemical Level. The brain's numerous neurochemical systems provide the communication links between structures that allow the individual to function in his or her environment. These systems involve the synthesis, storage, release, response, and turnover of various neurotransmitters. As such, they exert a pervasive effect throughout the CNS because they are involved with many different structures and affect a wide range of different functions. In addition, these systems are also closely interrelated with one another.

Dopamine provides a good example of just how pervasive these systems are in terms of their effects and the degree to which they interact. As discussed in Chapter 4, an excess of dopaminergic activity is thought to be responsible, at least in part, for schizophrenia. It has been hypothesized that an excess of this activity essentially "turns up the gain" and thus accentuates or exacerbates a process that has been set in motion by some other mechanism, which possibly involves other transmitter substances. Whatever the case, it has been proposed that dopaminergic activity loosens the normal regulatory processes in the CNS and that psychotropic medications block or dampen this excitatory activity.

Although dopamine's role in the etiology of schizophrenia has been established, it is equally clear that this neurotransmitter is involved in a number of other psychological disorders as well. For example, dopamine is thought to play a significant role in the mood disorders. The dopaminergic tuberoinfundibular pathway, which innervates the pituitary, provides a mechanism by which dopamine, perhaps interacting with such other neurotransmitters as serotonin, can affect the function of the endocrine systems of the body in these states. In addition, the nigrostriatal pathway allows for dopamine to play a role in the psychomotor retardation characteristic of major depressive episodes. Dopamine is also known to innervate the reward centers of the brain, although its role here is probably less important than that of norepinephrine. Dopamine may also be involved with the instigation of manic episodes, again possibly in conjunction with serotonin. Lithium may be an effective treatment for mania, in part, because of its ability to prevent the development of a supersensitivity to dopamine and thus blunt the effects of this system.

Dopamine has also been implicated in the development of obsessive-compulsive disorder as well as being a major factor in several of the substance use disorders. In the case of the former, dopaminergic hypersensitivity is thought to explain the compulsive behavior symptomatic of the disorder. On the other hand, CNS depressants, such as alcohol, are known to reduce dopaminergic activity, while CNS stimulants, such as nicotine, amphetamine, and cocaine, serve to enhance its action. Amphetamine, in particular, is known to increase the release of newly-formed dopamine. Tolerance to alcohol involves reduction in the sensitivity to dopamine, while the stereotypic behavior induced by amphetamine or cocaine can be blocked by the administration of a dopamine antagonist or, in animals, lesioning dopaminergic pathways in the corpus striatum. In addition, dopamine is involved with the hallucinogens LSD and PCP.

In addition, it should be noted that dopamine and the other neurotransmitters do not operate in isolation. The regulation of CNS function typically depends on the intricate balance of multiple transmitters operating at multiple sites throughout the brain. The release of dopamine, for example, is apparently mediated by adrenergic activity. Serotonin may also play a role in dopamine's proposed role in schizophrenia by being involved in a three-way interaction with dopamine and norepinephrine. GABA, the inhibitory transmitter, is also thought to influence the activity of many systems throughout the body. This is particularly true in understanding the ability of benzodiazepines, the barbiturates, and alcohol to exert an anxiolytic effect.

The disruption of the balance between neurotransmitters may explain much of the symptomatology in psychological disorders. For example, a relative imbalance in favor of acetylcholine generates symptoms characteristic of the mood disorders, such as the disruption of sleep (acetylcholine and serotonin) and endocrine abnormalities (acetylcholine and norepinephrine). On the other hand, an increase of serotonin in relation to other transmitters has been linked to the increase in aggression and violent behavior, such as violent suicide in the case of depression.

Because of their pervasive effects, the neurochemical systems of the brain are a logical target for therapeutic intervention. Restoring a normal balance between various neurochemical systems is thus the primary goal of medical (i.e., pharmacological) treatment and has allowed for the remediation of many disorders that previously were thought to be unresponsive to any kind of intervention (Klein, Gittelman, Quitkin, & Rifkin, 1980). These pharmacological agents have already revolutionized the treatment of psychological disorders and will become even more sophisticated and effective as we learn more about the actions of the different neurochemical systems.

Nevertheless, the use of medications does not, in itself, provide a total solution to the treatment of psychological disorders. Part of the problem lies in the body's natural capacity to compensate for or even reverse a drug's intended effects. Among the most powerful of these compensatory feedback systems are the presynaptic autoreceptors, which affect the release of many neurotransmitters, especially dopamine, norepinephrine, and serotonin.

A second problem is the fact that all medications have multiple rather than single effects, some of which are desired and others not (i.e., so-called side-effects). This is because receptors activated by a particular drug are located in different parts of the body and initiate a variety of responses depending on the anatomical site on which they are located (Gerald, 1981). In addition, although a drug may preferentially interact with a single receptor, it often interacts with other receptors, albeit less effectively. And finally, given the interrelatedness of neurochemical systems discussed earlier in this section, alteration of one neurotransmitter system will invariably result in modification of other systems as well.

Thus, it can be said that treating psychological disorders with medications alone will offer a partial and inexact cure. Consequently, medications must be combined with other treatment strategies that capitalize on the body's ability to restore itself to healthy functioning.

Conclusion

This review of the three levels of analysis highlights the contribution of physiological factors to psychological disorders and thus stresses the importance of taking these factors into account. It also suggests that the alteration or modification of any single factor by itself will most likely be incapable of exerting a lasting therapeutic effect. Ironically, the single most important conclusion that may be drawn from this book on the physiology of psychological disorders is that physiologically-based treatments are not enough.

This proposal provides the basis for arguing that the contribution of psychologists and other health-care providers is central to the success of the health-care team. Unfortunately, competition between the various health professions may continue to hinder the integration of these converging areas of expertise. However, political, theoretical, and methodological considerations will not alter the reality that one's biological potential and his or her opportunities for growth are inexorably intertwined.

Psychological disorders share characteristics of both physiological and psychological dysfunction. In this regard, they reflect the ability or inability of individuals to handle the difficult task of balancing their biological inheritance with the demands of daily living. Psychological health may thus be likened to a high-wire act in which each of us is a performer. As performers, we bring skills, experience, and natural talent. How well we do will also be influenced by the height of the wire above the floor, how long a balancing pole we hold, whether there is a safety net to catch us if we fall, and whether we have someone standing on our shoulders. All of these factors must be kept in balance if we are to make it successfully across to the other side.

References

Abramowitz, E. S., Baker, A. H., & Fleischer, S. F. (1982). Onset of depressive psychiatric crises and the menstrual cycle. *American Journal of Psychiatry, 139*, 475–478.

Abrams, R. (1988). *Electroconvulsive therapy.* New York: Oxford University Press.

Abrams, R., & Taylor, M. A. (1979). Laboratory studies in the validation of psychiatric diagnoses. In J. Gruzelier & P. Flor-Henry (Eds.), *Hemisphere asymmetries of function in psychopathology* (pp. 363–372). New York: Elsevier/North-Holland.

Achenbach, T. M. (1980). DSM-III in light of empirical evidence on the classification of child psychopathology. *Journal of the American Academy of Child Psychiatry, 19*, 395–412.

Adams, H. B. (1964). "Mental illness" or interpersonal behavior? *American Psychologist, 19*, 191–197.

Adams, H. E., Doster, J. A., & Calhoun, K. S. (1977). A psychologically based system of response classification. In A. R. Ciminero, K. S. Calhoun, & H. E. Adams (Eds.), *Handbook of behavioral assessment* (pp. 47–78). New York: Wiley

Agarwal, D. P., Harada, S., Goedde, H. W., & Schrappe, O. (1983). Cytosolic aldehyde dehydrogenase and alcoholism. *Lancet, 1* 68.

Aghajanian, G. K. (1982). Neurophysiologic properties of psychotomimetics. In F. Hoffmeister & G. Stille (Eds.), *Psychotropic agents. Part III: Alcohol and psychotomimetics, psychotropic effects of central acting drugs* (pp. 89–109). New York: Springer-Verlag.

Aghajanian, G. K., Cedarbaum, J. M., & Wang, R. Y. (1977). Evidence for norepinephrine-mediated colateral inhibition of the locus coeruleus neurons. *Brain Research, 136*, 570–577.

Agras, W. S. (1982). Behavioral medicine in the 1980s: Nonrandom connections. *Journal of Consulting and Clinical Psychology, 50*, 797–803.

Agras, W. S. (Chair). (1985, November). *Behavioral and pharmacological treatment combinations: Depression, anxiety, and eating disorders.* Symposium presented at the convention of the Association for Advancement of Behavior Therapy, Houston.

Agras, W. S. (1987). So where do we go from here? *Behavior Therapy, 18,*, 203–217.

Agurell, S., Lindgren, J.-E., & Ohlsson, A. (1979). Introduction to quantification of cannabinoids and their metabolites in biological fluids. In G. G. Nahas & W. D. M. Paton (Eds.), *Marihuana: Biological effects* (pp. 3–13). Oxford: Pergamon Press.

Ahtee, L., & Eriksson, K. (1973). Regional distribution of brain 5-hydroxytryptamine in rat strains selected for their alcohol intake. *Annals of the New York Academy of Science, 215*, 126–134.

Akiskal, H. S. (1979). A biobehavioral approach to depression. In R. A. Depue (Ed.), *The psychobiology of the depressive disorders: Implications for the effects of stress* (pp. 409–437). New York: Academic Press.

Akiskal, H. S. (1983). Dysthymic disorder: Psychopathology of proposed chronic depressive subtypes. *American Journal of Psychiatry, 140,* 11–20.

Akiskal, H. S., Bitar, A. H., Puzantian, V. R., Rosenthal, T. L., & Walker, P. W. (1978). The nosological status of neurotic depression: A prospective three- to four-year follow-up examination in the light of the primary-secondary and the unipolar-bipolar dichotomies. *Archives of General Psychiatry, 35,* 756–766.

Akiskal, H. S., & McKinney, W. T. (1973). Depressive disorders: Towards a unified hypothesis. *Science, 182,* 20–29.

Akiskal, H. S., & McKinney, W. T. (1975). Overview of recent research in depression: Integration of ten conceptual models into a comprehensive frame. *Archives of General Psychiatry, 32,* 285–305.

Akiskal, H. S., Hirschfeld, R. M. A., & Yerevanian, B. I. (1983). The relationship of personality to affective disorders: A critical review. *Archives of General Psychiatry, 40,* 801–810.

Akiskal, H. S., & Tashjian, R. (1983). Affective disorders: II. Recent advances in laboratory and pathogenetic approaches. *Hospital and Community Psychiatry, 34,* 822–830.

Albee, G. W. (1977). In reply . . . *APA Monitor, 8*(2), 2–3, 10.

Albrecht, P., Torrey, E. F., Boone, E., Hicks, J. T., & Daniel, N. (1980). Raised cytomegalovirus-antibody level in cerebrospinal fluid of schizophrenic patients. *Lancet, 2,* 769–772.

Alford, G. S., & Williams, J. G. (1980). The role and uses of psychopharmacological agents in behavior therapy. In M. Hersen, R. M. Eisler, & P. M. Miller (Eds.), *Progress in behavior modification* (Vol. 10, pp. 207–240). New York: Academic Press.

Ali-Cherif, A., Royere, M. L., Gosset, A., Poncet, M., Salomon, G., & Khalil R. (1984). Troubles du comportement et de l'activité mentale après intoxication oxycarbonée. *Revue Neurologique, 140,* 401–405.

Allen, M. G. (1976). Twin studies of affective illness. *Archives of General Psychiatry, 33,* 1476–1478.

Alpert, M., & Friedhoff, A. J. (1980). An un-dopamine hypothesis of schizophrenia. *Schizophrenia Bulletin, 6,* 387–390.

Altrocchi, J. (1980). *Abnormal psychology.* New York: Harcourt Brace Jovanovich.

American College Dictionary. (1958). New York: Random House.

American Heritage Dictionary of the English Language. (1978). Boston: Houghton Mifflin.

American Psychiatric Association. (1980). *Diagnostic and statistical manual of mental disorders* (3rd ed.). Washington, DC: Author.

American Psychiatric Association. (1987). *Diagnostic and statistical manual of mental disorders* (3rd ed., Revised).. Washington, DC: Author.

Amin, M. M., Ban, T. A., Peckhold, J. C., & Klingner, A. (1977). Clomipramine (Anafranil) and behaviour therapy in obsessive-compulsive and phobic disorders. *Journal of International Medical Research, 5,* (Suppl. 5), 33–37.

Amsterdam, J. D., Winokur, A., Dyson, W., Herzog, S., Gonzalez, F., Rott, R., & Koprowski, H. (1985). Borna disease virus: A possible etiological factor in human affective disorders? *Archives of General Psychiatry, 42,* 1093–1096.

Ananth, J. (1982). Current psychopathological theories of tardive dyskinesia and their implications for future research. *Neuropsychobiology, 8,* 210–222.

Ananth, J. (1985). Pharmacotherapy of obsessive-compulsive disorder. In M. Mavissakalian, S. M. Turner, & L. Michelson (Eds.), *Obsessive-compulsive disorder: Psychological and pharmacological treatment* (pp. 167–211). New York: Plenum.

Ananth, J., Peckhold, J. C., van den Stern, N., & Engelsmann, F. (1981). Double-blind comparative study of clomipramine and amitriptyline in obsessive neurosis. *Progress in Neuro-Psychopharmacology, 5*, 257–262.

Andreasen, N. C. (1982). Concepts, diagnosis and classification. In E. S. Paykel (Ed.), *Handbook of affective disorders* (pp. 24–44). New York: Guilford.

Aneshensel, C. S., & Stone, J. D. (1982). Stress and depression: A test of the buffering model of social support. *Archives of General Psychiatry, 39*, 1392–1396.

Angoff, W. H. (1988). The nature-nurture debate, aptitudes, and group differences. *American Psychologist, 43*, 713–720.

Angrist, B., Rotrosen, J., & Gershon, S. (1980). Differential effects of amphetamine and neuroleptics on negative vs. positive symptoms in schizophrenia. *Psychopharmacology, 72*, 17–19.

Anisman, H., & Zacharko, R. M. (1982). Depression: The predisposing influence of stress. *Behavioral Brain Science, 5*, 89–137.

Annest, J. L., Sing, C. F., Biron, P., & Mongeau, J. G. (1983). Familial aggregation of blood pressure and weight in adoptive families. III. Analysis of the role of shared genes and shared household environment in explaining family resemblance for height, weight and selected weight/height indices. *American Journal of Epidemiology, 117*, 492–506.

Antelman, S. M., & Chiodo, L. A. (1984). Stress-induced sensitization: A framework for viewing the effects of ECS and other antidepressants. In B. Lerer, R. D. Weiner, & R. H. Belmaker (Eds.), *ECT: Basic mechanisms* (pp. 28–32). London: John Libbey.

Appleby, I. L., Klein, D. F., Sachar, E. J., & Levitt, M. (1981). Biochemical indices of lactate-induced panic: A preliminary report. In D. F. Klein & J. G. Rabkin (Eds.), *Anxiety: New research and changing concepts* (pp. 411–423). New York: Raven.

Åsberg, M., Träskman, L. & Thorén, P. (1976). 5–HIAA in the cerebrospinal fluid: A biochemical suicide predictor? *Archives of General Psychiatry, 33*, 1193–1197.

Arkonac, O., & Guze, S. B. (1963). A family study of hysteria. *New England Journal of Medicine, 268*, 239–242.

Armitage, A. K., Hall, G. H., & Sellers, C. M. (1969). Effects of nicotine on electrocortical activity and acetylcholine release from the cat cerebral cortex. *British Journal of Pharmacology, 35*, 152–160.

Ary, T. E., & Komiskey, H. L. (1982). Phencyclidine-induced release of [^{3}H] dopamine from chopped striatal tissue. *Neuropharmacology, 21*, 639–645.

Ashton, H. (1984). Benzodiazepine withdrawal: An unfinished story. *British Medical Journal, 288*, 1135–1140.

Ashton, H. (1985). Disorders of the foetus and infant. In D. M. Davies (Ed.), *Textbook of Adverse Drug Reactions* (3rd ed., pp. 77–127). Oxford: Oxford University Press.

Ashton, H. (1987). *Brain systems, disorders, and psychotropic drugs.* Oxford: Oxford University Press.

Ashton, H., Golding, J., Marsh, V. R., Millman, J. E., & Thompson, J. W. (1981). The seed and the soil: Effects of dosage, personality and starting state on the response to ...^{9}tetrahydrocannabinol in man. *British Journal of Clinical Pharmacology, 12*, 705–720.

Ashton, H., Millman, J. E., Telford, R., & Thompson, J. W. (1974). The effect of caffeine, nitrazepam and cigarette smoking on the contingent negative variation in man. *Electroencephalography and Clinical Neurophysiology, 37*, 59–71.

Ashton, H., & Stepney, R. (1982). *Smoking: Psychology and pharmacology.* London: Tavistock Publications.

Ashton, H., & Watson, D. W. (1970). Puffing frequency and nicotine intake in cigarette smokers. *British Medical Journal, 3,* 679–681.

Atweh, S. F., & Kuhar, M. J. (1983). Distribution and physiological significance of opioid receptors in the brain. *British Medical Bulletin, 39,* 47–52.

Azrin, N. H. (1976). Improvements in the community-reinforcement approach to alcoholism. *Behaviour Research and Therapy, 14,* 339–348.

Azrin, N. H., Sisson, R. W., Meyers, R., & Godley, M. (1982). Alcoholism treatment by disulfiram and community reinforcement therapy. *Journal of Behavior Therapy and Experimental Psychiatry, 13,* 105–112.

Baker, M., Dorzab, J., Winokur, G., & Cadoret, R. (1972). Depressive disease: Evidence favoring polygenic inheritance based on an analysis of ancestral cases. *Archives of General Psychiatry, 27,* 320–327.

Baldessarini, R. J. (1985). Drugs and the treatment of psychiatric disorders. In A. G. Gilman, L. S. Goodman, T. W. Rall, & F. Murad (Eds.), *The pharmacological basis of therapeutics* (7th ed., pp. 387–445). New York: Macmillan.

Barbaccia, M. L., Chuang, D-M., Gandolfi, O., and Costa, E. (1983). Trans-synaptic mechanisms in the actions of impramine. In E. Usdin, M. Goldstein, A. J. Friedoff, and A. Georgatas (Eds.), *Frontiers in Neuropsychiatric Research* (pp. 19–31). London: Macmillan.

Barchas, J. D., Elliott, G. R., & Berger, P. A. (1977). Biogenic amine hypotheses of schizophrenia. In J. D. Barchas, P. A. Berger, R. D. Ciaranello, & G. R. Elliott (Eds.), *Psychopharmacology: From theory to practice* (pp. 100–120). New York: Oxford University Press.

Barchas, J., & Usdin, E. (Eds.). (1973). *Serotonin and behavior.* New York: Academic Press.

Barlow, D. H. (1988). *Anxiety and its disorders: The nature and treatment of anxiety and panic.* New York: Guilford.

Barlow, D. H., Cohen, A. S., Waddell, M. T., Vermilyea, B. B., Klosko, J. S., Blanchard, E. B., & Di Nardo, P. A. (1984). Panic and generalized anxiety disorders: Nature and treatment. *Behavior Therapy, 15,* 431–449.

Barlow, D. H., Craske, M. G., Cerny, J. A., & Klosko, J. S. (1989). Behavioral treatment of panic disorder. *Behavior Therapy, 20,* 261–282.

Barnard, E. A., & Demoliou-Mason, C. (1983). Molecular properties of opioid receptors. *British Medical Bulletin, 39,* 37–45.

Barnes, P. J. (1981). Radioligand binding studies of adrenergic receptors and their clinical relevance. *British Medical Journal, 282,* 1207–1210.

Barnes, T. R., & Bridges, P. K. (1982). New generation of antidepressants. In P. J. Tyrer (Ed.), *Drugs in psychiatric practice* (pp. 219–248). London: Butterworths.

Barnett, P. A., & Gotlib, I. H. (1988). Psychosocial functioning and depression: Distinguishing among antecedents, concomitants, and consequences. *Psychological Bulletin, 104,* 97–126.

Barton, R. (1965). Diabetes insipidus and obsessional neurosis: A syndrome. *Lancet, 1,* 133–135.

Barton, R. (1976). Diabetes insipidus and obsessional neurosis. *American Journal of Psychiatry, 133,* 235–236.

Baum, A., & Nesselhof, S. E. A. (1988). Psychological research and the prevention, etiology, and treatment of AIDS. *American Psychologist, 43,* 900–906.

Baumrind, D. (1971). Current patterns of parental authority. *Developmental Psychology, 4*(1, Pt. 2).

Bayer, R., & Spitzer, R. L. (1985). Neurosis, psychodynamics, and DSM-III. *Archives of General Psychiatry, 42,* 187–196.

Bazhin, E. F., Wasserman, L. I., & Tonkonogii, I. M. (1975). Auditory hallucinations and left temporal lobe pathology. *Neuropsychologia, 13,* 481–487.

Beart, P. M. (1982). Multiple dopamine receptors: New vistas. In J. W. Lamble (Ed.), *More about receptors: Current reviews in biomedicine 2* (pp. 87–92). Amsterdam: Elsevier Biomedical.

Beaumont, J. G., & Dimond, S. J. (1973). Brain disconnection and schizophrenia. *British Journal of Psychiatry, 123,* 661–662.

Beck, A. T. (1983). Cognitive therapy of depression: New perspectives. In P. J. Clayton & J. E. Berrett (Eds.), *Treatment of depression: Old controversies and new approaches* (pp. 265–284). New York: Raven.

Beck, A. T., & Emery, G. (1985). *Anxiety disorders and phobias: A cognitive perspective.* New York: Basic Books.

Beck, J. G. (Chair). (1985, November). *The physiological–cognitive interface in emotional disorders.* Symposium presented at the convention of the Association for Advancement of Behavior Therapy, Houston.

Becker, J., & Schuckit, M. A. (1978). The comparative efficacy of cognitive therapy and pharmacotherapy in the treatment of depressions. *Cognitive Therapy and Research, 2,* 193–197.

Begelman, D. A. (1976). Behavioral classification. In M. Hersen & A. S. Bellack (Eds.), *Behavioral assessment: A practical handbook* (pp. 23–48). New York: Pergamon.

Behrman, R., & Vaughan, V. C. (1983). *Nelson textbook of pediatrics* (12th ed.). Philadelphia: W. B. Saunders.

Beirness, D., & Vogel-Sprott, M. (1984). Alcohol tolerance in social drinkers: Operant and classical conditioning effects. *Psychopharmacology, 84,* 393–397.

Bell, R. Q. (1968). A reinterpretation of the direction of effects in studies of socialization. *Psychological Review, 75,* 81–95.

Bell, R. Q. (1971). Stimulus control of parent or caretaker behavior by offspring. *Developmental Psychology, 4,* 63–72.

Bell, R. Q. (1979). Parent, child, and reciprocal influences. *American Psychologist, 34,* 821–826.

Bellack, A. S. (1986). Schizophrenia: Behavior therapy's forgotten child. *Behavior Therapy, 17,* 199–214.

Bellack, A. S., Hersen, M., & Himmelhoch, J. M. (1981). Social skills training compared with pharmacotherapy and psychotherapy in the treatment of unipolar depression. *American Journal of Psychiatry, 138,* 1562–1567.

Bellack, A. S., Hersen, M., & Himmelhoch, J. M. (1983). A comparison of social skills training, pharmacotherapy and psychotherapy for depression. *Behaviour Research and Therapy, 21,* 101–107.

Bellet, S., Roman, L., DeCastro, O., Kim, K. E., & Keushbaum, A. (1969). Effect of coffee ingestion on catecholamine release. *Metabolism Clinical and Experimental, 18,* 288–291.

Belsher, G., & Costello, C. G. (1988). Relapse after recovery from unipolar depression: A critical review. *Psychological Bulletin, 104,* 84–96.

Benes, F. M., Davidson, J., & Bird, E. D. (1986). Quantitative cytoarchitectural studies of the cerebral cortex of schizophrenics. *Archives of General Psychiatry, 43,* 31–35.

Berger, P. A. (1977). Antidepressant medications and the treatment of depression. In J. D. Barchas, P. A. Berger, R. D. Ciaranello, & G. R. Elliott (Eds.), *Psychopharmacology: From theory to practice* (pp. 174–207). New York: Oxford University Press.

Berger, P. A., & Barchas, J. D. (1977). Biochemical hypotheses of affective disorders. In J. D. Barchas, P. A. Berger, R. D. Ciaranello, & G. R. Elliott (Eds.), *Psychopharmacology: From theory to practice* (pp. 151–173). New York: Oxford University Press.

Bergmann, G. (1956). The contribution of John B. Watson. *Psychological Review, 63,* 265–276.

Berlyne, D. E. (1960). *Conflict, arousal, and curiosity.* New York: McGraw-Hill.

Berney, T., Kolvin, I., Bhate, S. R., Jeans, J., Kay, B., & Scarth, L. (1981). School phobia: A therapeutic trial with clomipramine and short-term outcome. *British Journal of Psychiatry, 138,* 110–118.

Bernstein, A. S. (1964). The galvanic skin response orienting reflex among chronic schizophrenics. *Psychonomic Science, 1,* 391–392.

Bernstein, A. S. (1970). Phasic electrodermal orienting response in chronic schizophrenics: II. Response to auditory signals of varying intensity. *Journal of Abnormal Psychology, 75,* 146–156.

Berridge, M. J. (1981). Receptors and calcium signalling. In J. W. Lamble (Ed.), *Towards understanding receptors* (pp. 122–131). Amsterdam: Elsevier/North-Holland.

Berwish, N. J., & Amsterdam, J. D. (1989). An overview of investigational antidepressants. *Psychosomatics, 30,* 1–18.

Bielski, R. J., & Friedel, R. O. (1976). Prediction of tricyclic antidepressant response: A critical review. *Archives of General Psychiatry, 33,* 1479–1489.

Bigelow, G. E., Stitzer, M. L., & Liebson, I. A. (1986). Substance abuse. In M. Hersen (Ed.), Pharmacological and behavioral treatment: An integrative approach (pp. 289–311). New York: Wiley.

Bigelow, L. B., Nasrallah, H. A., & Rauscher, F. P. (1983). Corpus callosum thickness in chronic schizophrenia. *British Journal of Psychiatry, 142,* 284–287.

Bindra, D. (1970). Emotion and behavior theory: Current research in historical perspective. In P. Black (Ed.), *Physiological correlates of emotion* (pp. 3–20). New York: Academic Press.

Bindra, D. A. (1978). How adaptive behaviour is produced: A perceptual–motivational alternative to response-reinforcement. *Behavioral and Brain Sciences, 1,* 41–91.

Binner, P. R. (1986). DRGs and the administration of mental health services. *American Psychologist, 41,* 64–69.

Blanchard, E. B., McCoy, G. C., Musso, A., Gerardi, M. A., Pallmeyer, T. P., Gerardi, R. J., Cotch, P. A., Siracusa, K., & Andrasik, F. (1986). A controlled comparison of thermal biofeedback and relaxation training in the treatment of essential hypertension: I. Short-term and long-term outcome. *Behavior Therapy, 17,* 563–579.

Blaustein, M. P., & Ector, A. C. (1975). Barbiturate inhibition of calcium uptake by depolarized nerve terminals *in vitro. Molecular Pharmacology, 11,* 369–378.

Blazer, D. (1983). The epidemiology of psychiatric disorder in the elderly population. In L. Grinspoon (Ed.), *Psychiatry update* (Vol. 2, pp. 87–95). Washington, DC: American Psychiatric Press.

Bleuler, E. (1950). *Dementia praecox or the group of schizophrenias,* (J. Zinkin, Trans.). New York: International Universities. (Original work published 1911)

Bleuler, M. (1978). *The schizophrenic disorders: Long-term patient and family studies.* (S. M. Clemens, Trans.). New Haven: Yale.

Bleuler, M. (1979). My sixty years with schizophrenics. In L. Bellak (Ed.), *Disorders of the schizophrenic syndrome* (pp. vii–ix). New York: Basic Books.

Block, J. (1981). Some enduring and consequential structures of personality. In A. I. Rabin (Ed.), *Further explorations in personality* (pp. 27–43). New York: Wiley.

Bloom, B. S. (Ed.). (1985). *Developing talent in young people.* New York: Ballantine.

Blum, K., Hamilton, M. G., Hirst, M., & Wallace, J. E. (1978). Putative role of isoquinoline alkaloids in alcoholism: A link to opiates. *Alcoholism: Clinical and Experimental research, 2,* 113–120.

Bogen, J. E. (1985). The dual brain: Some historical and methodological aspects. In D. F. Benson & E. Zaidel (Eds.), *The dual brain* (pp. 27–43). New York: Guilford.

Bogerts, B., Meertz, E., & Schönfeldt-Bausch, R. (1985). Basal ganglia and limbic system pathology in schizophrenia: A morphometric study of brain volume and shrinkage. *Archives of General Psychiatry, 42,* 784–791.

Bohman, M., Sigvardsson, S., & Cloninger, C. R. (1981). Maternal inheritance of alcohol abuse: Cross-fostering analysis of adopted women. *Archives of General Psychiatry, 38,* 965–969.

Bond, A., & Lader, M. (1981). After-effects of sleeping drugs. In D. Wheatley (Ed.), *Psychopharmacology of sleep* (pp 177–197). New York: Raven.

Bonn, J. A., Readhead, C. P. A., & Timmons, B. H. (1984). Enhanced adaptive behavioural response in agoraphobic patients pretreated with breathing retraining. *Lancet, 2,* 665–669.

Boorstin, D. J. (1983). *The discoverers.* New York: Random.

Börjeson, M. (1976). The aetiology of obesity in children: A study of 101 twin pairs. *Acta Paediatrica Scandinavica, 65,* 279–287.

Boulenger, J.-P., Uhde, T. W., Wolff, E. A., & Post, R. M. (1984). Increased sensitivity to caffeine in patients with panic disorders: Preliminary evidence. *Archives of General Psychiatry, 41,* 1067–1071.

Bowman, W. C., Rand, M. J., & West, G. B. (1968). *Textbook of pharmacology.* Oxford: Blackwell Scientific Publications.

Bradbury, T. N., & Miller, G. A. (1985). Season of birth in schizophrenia: A review of evidence, methodology, and etiology. *Psychological Bulletin, 98,* 569–594.

Bradley, P. B., & Key, B. J. (1958). The effect of drugs on arousal responses produced by electrical stimulation of the reticular formation of the brain. *Electroencephalography and Clinical Neurophysiology, 10,* 97–110.

Braestrup, C., & Nielsen, M. (1980). Benzodiazepine receptors. *Arzneimittel-Forschung/ Drug Research, 30,* 852–857.

Brecher, E. M. (1972). *Licit and illicit drugs.* Boston: Little, Brown.

Breier, A., Charney, D. S., & Heninger, G. R. (1984). Major depression in patients with agoraphobia and panic disorder. *Archives of General Psychiatry, 41,* 1129–1135.

Brier, A., Charney, D. S., & Heninger, G. R. (1986). Agoraphobia with panic attacks: Development, diagnostic stability, and course of illness. *Archives of General Psychiatry, 43,* 1029–1036.

Briscoe, C. W., & Smith, J. B. (1975). Depression in bereavement and divorce: Relationship to primary depressive illness. *Archives of General Psychiatry, 32,* 439–443.

Broadbent, D. E. (1958). *Perception and communication.* Oxford: Pergamon.

Broadbent, D. E. (1971). *Decision and stress.* New York: Academic Press.

Broadbent, D. E. (1977). The hidden preattentive processes. *American Psychologist, 32,* 109–118.

Brook, C. G. D., Huntley, R. M. C., & Slack, J. (1975). Influence of heredity and environment in determination of skinfold thickness in children. *British Medical Journal, 2,* 719–721.

Brown, G. W., Birley, J. L. T., & Wing, J. K. (1972). Influence of family life on the course of schizophrenic disorders: A replication. *British Journal of Psychiatry, 121,* 241–258.

Brown, G. W., Carstairs, G. M., & Topping, G. (1958). Post-hospital adjustment of chronic mental patients. *Lancet, 2* 685–689.

Brown, G. W., Monck, E. M., Carstairs, G. M., & Wing, J. K. (1962). Influence of family life on schizophrenic illness. *British Journal of Preventive and Social Medicine, 16,* 55–68.

Brown, G. W., & Harris, T. (1978). *Social origins of depression: A study of psychiatric disorder in women*. New York: Free Press.

Brown, G. W., & Rutter, M. (1966). The measurement of family activities and relationships: A methodological study. *Human Relations, 19*, 241–263.

Brown, R., Colter, N., Corsellis, J. A. N., Crow, T. J., Frith, C. D., Jagoe, R., Johnstone, E. C., & Marsh, L. (1986). Postmortem evidence of structural brain changes in schizophrenia: Differences in brain weight, temporal horn area, and parahippocampal gyrus compared with affective disorder. *Archives of General Psychiatry, 43*, 36–42.

Bruce, M., Scott, N., Lader, M., & Marks, V. (1986). The psychopharmacological and electrophysiological effects of single doses of caffeine in healthy human subjects. *British Journal of Clinical Pharmacology, 22*, 81–87.

Bryden, M. P., & Ley, R. G. (1983). Right-hemispheric involvement in the perception and expression of emotion in normal humans. In K. M. Heilman & P. Satz, P. *Neuropsychology of human emotion* (pp. 6–44). New York: Guilford.

Buchsbaum, M. S. (1979). Neurophysiological reactivity, stimulus intensity modulation and the depressive disorders. In R.A. Depue (Ed.), *The psychobiology of the depressive disorders: Implications for the effects of stress* (pp. 221–242). New York: Academic Press.

Buchsbaum, M. S., Goodwin, F., Murphy, D., & Borge, G. (1971). AER in affective disorders. *American Journal of Psychiatry, 128*, 19–25.

Buchsbaum, M. S., Haier, R. J., & Johnson, J. (1983). Augmenting and reducing: Individual differences in evoked potentials. In A. Gale & J. A. Edwards (Eds.), *Physiological correlates of human behaviour: Individual differences and psychopathology* (Vol. 3, pp. 107–138). New York: Academic Press.

Buchsbaum, M. S., & Rieder, R. O. (1979). Biological heterogeneity and psychiatric research. *Archives of General Psychiatry, 36*, 1163–1169.

Buie, J. (1988). Practice priorities: Medicare amendments, hospital privileges, HMO reforms, prescription privileges? *APA Monitor, 19*(6), 1, 14–15.

Buie, J. (1989). Psychology confronts efforts to limit practice. *APA Monitor, 20,*(2), 1, 21.

Bunney, B. S. (1984). Antipsychotic drug effects on the electrical activity of dopaminergic neurones. *Trends in Neuroscience, 7*, 212–215.

Bunney, W. E., & Davis, J. M. (1965). Norepinephrine in depressive reactions: A review. *Archives of General Psychiatry, 13*, 483–494.

Bunney, W. E., Pert, A., Rosenblatt, J., Pert, C. B., & Gallaper, D. (1979). Mode of action of lithium: Some biological considerations. *Archives of General Psychiatry, 36*, 898–901.

Burt, C. G., Gordon, W. F., Holt, N. F., & Hordern, A. (1962). Amitriptyline in depressive states: A controlled trial. *Journal of Mental Science, 108*, 711–730.

Buss, A. H. (1966). *Psychopathology*. New York: Wiley.

Buss, A. H., & Plomin, R. (1975). *A temperament theory of personality development*. New York: Wiley.

Buss, A. H., & Plomin, R. (1984). *Temperament: Early developing personality traits*. Hillsdale, NJ: Lawrence Erlbaum.

Butler, G., Gelder, M., Hibbert, G., Cullington, A., Klimes, I. (1987). Anxiety management: Developing effective strategies. *Behaviour Research and Therapy, 25*, 517–522.

Cadoret, R., & Gath, A. (1978). Inheritance of alcoholism in adoptees. *British Journal of Psychiatry, 132*, 252–258.

Cadoret, R. J., & Winokur, G. (1975a). Genetic studies of affective disorders. In F. F. Flach & S.C. Draghi (Eds.), *The nature and treatment of depression* (pp. 335–346). New York: Wiley.

Cadoret, R. J., & Winokur, G. (1975b). X-linkage in manic-depressive illness. *Annual Review of Medicine, 26*, 21–25.

Cahalan, D., & Room, R. (1974). *Problem drinking among American men* (Monograph No. 7). New Brunswick, NJ: Rutgers Center of Alcohol Studies.

Cain, L. F., Levine, S., & Elzey, F. F. (1963). *Cain–Levine Social-Competency Scale*. Palo Alto, CA: Consulting Psychologists Press.

Canaday, J. (1968). Goya and horror. *Horizon, 10*(3), 90–105.

Cannon, W. B. (1920). *Bodily changes in pain, fear, and rage*. New York: Appleton.

Cantor, N., & Genero, N. (1986). Psychiatric diagnosis and natural categorization: A close analogy. In T. Millon & G. L. Klerman (Eds.), *Contemporary directions in psychopathology* (pp. 233–256). New York: Guilford.

Capstick, N., & Seldrup, J. (1973). Phenomenological aspects of obsessional patients treated with clomipramine. *British Journal of Psychiatry, 122*, 719–720.

Carlson, G. A., & Goodwin, F. K. (1973). The stages of mania: A longitudinal analysis of the manic episode. *Archives of General Psychiatry, 28*, 221–228.

Carlsson, A. (1974). Antipsychotic drugs and catecholamine synapses. *Journal of Psychiatric Research, 11*, 57–64.

Carmichael, F. J., & Israel, Y. (1975). Effects of ethanol on neurotransmitter release by rat brain cortical sites. *Journal of Pharmacology and Experimental Therapeutics, 193*, 824–834.

Carney, M. W. P., Roth, M., & Garside, R. F. (1965). The diagnosis of depressive syndromes and the prediction of E.C.T. response. *British Journal of Psychiatry, 111*, 659–674.

Carney, M. W. P., & Sheffield, B. F. (1972). Depression and the Newcastle scales: Their relationship to Hamilton's scale. *British Journal of Psychiatry, 121*, 35–40.

Carney, M. W. P., & Sheffield, B. F. (1974). The effects of pulse ECT in neurotic and endogenous depression. *British Journal of Psychiatry, 125*, 91–94.

Carpenter, W. T., Murphy, D. L., & Wyatt, R. J. (1975). Platelet monoamine oxidase activity in acute schizophrenia. *American Journal of Psychiatry, 132*, 438–441.

Carpenter, W. T., Strauss, J. S., & Bartko, J. J. (1973). Flexible system for the diagnosis of schizophrenia: Report from the WHO International Pilot Study of Schizophrenia. *Science, 182*, 1275–1278.

Carpenter, W. T., & Strauss, J. S. (1974). Cross-cultural evaluation of Schneider's first rank symptoms of schizophrenia: A report from the International Pilot Study of Schizophrenia. *American Journal of Psychiatry, 131*, 682–687.

Carr, D. B., & Sheehan, D. V. (1984). Panic anxiety: A new biological model. *Journal of Clinical Psychiatry, 45*, 323–330.

Carroll, B. J. (1982). The dexamethasone suppression test for melancholia. *British Journal of Psychiatry, 140*, 292–304.

Carson, R. C. (1969). *Interaction concepts of personality*. Chicago: Aldine.

Chambless, D. L., Foa, E. B., Groves, G. A., & Goldstein, A. J. (1979). Flooding with Brevital in the treatment of agoraphobia: Counter-effective? *Behaviour Research and Therapy, 17*, 243–251.

Charney, D. S., Heninger, G. R., & Brier, A. (1984). Noradrenergic function in panic anxiety: Effects of yohimbine in healthy subjects and patients with agoraphobia and panic disorder. *Archives of General Psychiatry, 41*, 751–763.

Charney, D. S., Heninger, G. R., & Jatlow, P. I. (1985). Increased anxiogenic effects of caffeine in panic disorders. *Archives of General Psychiatry, 42*, 233–243.

Charney, D. S., Heninger, G. R., Sternberg, D. E., Redmond, D. E., Leckman, J. F., Maas, J. W., & Roth, R. H. (1981a). Presynaptic adrenergic receptors sensitivity in depression: The effect of long-term desipramine treatment. *Archives of General Psychiatry, 38*, 1334–1340.

Chaney, E. F., O'Leary, M. R., & Marlatt, G. A. (1978). Skill training with alcoholics. *Journal of Consulting and Clinical Psychology, 46,* 1092–1104.

Charney, D. S., Menkes, D. B., & Heninger, G. R. (1981b). Receptor sensitivity and the mechanism of action of antidepressant treatment: Implications for the etiology and therapy of depression. *Archives of General Psychiatry, 38,* 1160–1180.

Chavkin, S. (1978). *The mind stealers: Psychosurgery and mind control.* Boston: Houghton Mifflin.

Cheifetz, D. I., & Salloway, J. C. (1984). Patterns of mental health services provided by HMOs. *American Psychologist, 39,* 495–502.

Cherry, N., & Kierman, K. (1976). Personality scores and smoking behaviour: A longitudinal study. *British Journal of Preventive and Social Medicine, 30,* 123–131.

Chouinard, G., & Jones, B. D. (1978). Schizophrenia as a dopamine-deficiency disease. *Lancet, 2,* 99–100.

Christophersen, E. R. (1983). Behavioral pediatrics: An overview. In P. J. McGrath & P. Firestone (Eds.), *Pediatric and adolescent behavioral medicine: Issues in treatment* (pp. 1–12). New York: Springer.

Ciaranello, R. D., & Patrick, R. L. (1977). Catecholamine neuroregulators. In J. D. Barchas, P. A. Berger, R. D. Ciaranello, & G. R. Elliott (Eds.), *Psychopharmacology: From theory to practice* (pp. 16–32). New York: Oxford University Press.

Ciompi, L. (1980). The natural history of schizophrenia in the long term. *British Journal of Psychiatry, 136,* 413–420.

Claridge, G. S. (1972). The schizophrenias as nervous types. *British Journal of Psychiatry, 121,* 1–17.

Claridge, G. S. (1978). Animal models of schizophrenia: The case for LSD-25. *Schizophrenia Bulletin, 4,* 186–209.

Claridge, G. S. (1985). *Origins of mental illness: Temperament, deviance, and disorder.* New York: Basil Blackwell.

Claridge, G. S. (1987). "The schizophrenias as nervous types" revisited. *British Journal of Psychiatry, 151,* 735–743.

Claridge, G. S., & Broks, P. (1984). Schizotypy and hemisphere function–I: Theoretical considerations and the measurement of schizotypy. *Personality and Individual Differences, 5,* 633–648.

Clark, D. M. (1986). A cognitive approach to panic. *Behaviour Research and Therapy, 24,* 461–470.

Clark, D. M. (1988). A cognitive model of panic attacks. In S. Rachman & J. D. Maser (Eds.), *Panic: Psychological perspectives* (pp. 71–89).

Clark, D. M., Salkovskis, P. M., & Chalkley, A. J. (1985). Respiratory control as a treatment for panic attacks. *Journal of Behavior Therapy and Experimental Psychiatry, 16,* 23–30.

Clark, D. M., Salkovskis, P. M., Gelder, C., Koehler, C., Martin, M., Anastasiades, P., Hackmann, A., Middleton, H., & Jeavons, A. (1988). In I, Hand & H. U. Wittchen (Eds.), *Panic and phobias 2* (pp. 149–158). Berlin: Springer-Verlag.

Clark, W. B., & Cahalan, D. (1976). Changes in problem drinking over a four-year span. *Addictive Behaviors, 1,* 251–259.

Clarke, C. H., & Nicholson, A. N. (1978). Immediate and residual effects in man of the metabolites of diazepam. *British Journal of Clinical Pharmacology, 6,* 325–331.

Clayton, P. J. (1979). The sequelae and nonsequelae of conjugal bereavement. *American Journal of Psychiatry, 136,* 1530–1534.

Cloninger, C. R., Bohman, M., & Sigvardsson, S. (1981). Inheritance of alcohol abuse: Cross-fostering analysis of adopted men. *Archives of General Psychiatry, 38,* 861–868.

Cloninger, C. R., Martin, R. L., Clayton, P., & Guze, S. B. (1981). A blind follow-up and family study of anxiety neurosis. Preliminary analysis of the St. Louis 500. In D. F. Klein & J. G. Rabkin (Eds.), *Anxiety: New research and changing concepts* (pp. 137–154). New York: Raven.

Cloninger, C. R., & Reich, T. (1983). Genetic heterogeneity in alcoholism and sociopathy. In S. S. Kety, L. P. Rowland, R. L. Sidman, & S. W. Matthysse (Eds.), *Genetics of neurological and psychiatric disorders* (pp. 145–166). New York: Raven.

Coble, P., Foster, F., & Kupfer, D. J. (1976). Electroencephalographic sleep diagnosis of primary depression. *Archives of General Psychiatry, 33,* 1124–1127.

Cohen, M. E., & White, P. D. (1950). Life situations, emotions and neurocirculatory asthenia (anxiety neurosis, neurasthenia, effort syndrome). *Research Publications: Association for Research on Nervous and Mental Diseases, 29,* 832–869.

Cohen, R. M., Campbell, I. C., Dauphin, M., Tallman, J. F., & Murphy, D. L. (1982). Changes in α- and β-receptor densities in rat brain as a result of treatment with monoamine oxidase inhibiting antidepressants. *Neuropharmacology, 21,* 293–298.

Cohen, S. D., Monteiro, W., & Marks, I. M. (1984). Two-year follow-up of agoraphobics after exposure and imipramine.*British Journal of Psychiatry, 144,* 276–281.

Colbourn, C. J. (1982). Divided visual field studies of psychiatric patients. In J. G. Beaumont (Ed.), *Divided visual field studies of cerebral organization* (pp. 233–252). New York: Academic Press.

Cole, J. O., Goldberg, S. C., & Davis, J. M. (1966). Drugs in the treatment of psychosis: Controlled studies. In P. Solomon (Ed.), *Psychiatric drugs* (pp. 153–180). New York: Grune & Stratton.

Cole, J. O., Klerman, G. L., & Goldberg, S. C. (1964). Phenothiazine treatment in acute schizophrenia. *Archives of General Psychiatry, 10,* 246–261.

Collins, M. A. (1982). A possible neurochemical mechanism for brain and nerve damage associated with chronic alcoholism. *Trends in Pharmacological Science, 3,* 373–375.

Connolly, J. F., Gruzelier, J. H., Manchanda, R., & Hirsch, S. R. (1983). Visual evoked potentials in schizophrenia: Intensity effects and hemispheric asymmetry. *British Journal of Psychiatry, 142,* 152–155.

Conte, H. R., Plutchik, R., Wild, K. V., & Karasu, T. B. (1986). Combined psychotherapy and pharmacotherapy for depression: A systematic analysis of the evidence. *Archives of General Psychiatry, 43,* 471–479.

Cools, A. R. (1975). An integrated theory of the aetiology of schizophrenia: Impairment of the balance between certain, in series connected dopaminergic, serotonergic, and noradrenergic pathways in the brain. In H. M. van Praag (Ed.), *On the origin of schizophrenic psychoses* (pp. 58–80). Amsterdam: De Erven Bohn.

Cools, A. R. (1982). The puzzling "cascade" of multiple receptors for dopamine: An appraisal of the current situation. In J. W. Lamble (Ed.), *More about receptors: Current reviews in biomedicine 2* (pp. 76–86). Amsterdam: Elsevier Biomedical.

Cooper, J. E., Kendell, R. E., Gurland, B. J., Sharp, L., Copeland, J. R. M., & Simon, R. (1972). *Psychiatric diagnosis in New York and London: A comprehensive study of mental hospital admissions.* London: Oxford University Press.

Cooper, J. R., Bloom, F. E., & Roth, R. H. (1986). *The biochemical basis of neuropharmacology* (5th ed.). New York: Oxford University Press.

Cooper, S. J. (1983). Neural substrates for opiate-produced reward: Solving the dependency puzzle. *Trends in Pharmacological Science, 5,* 49–50.

Coppen, A., Metcalfe, M., & Wood, K. (1982). Lithium. In E. S. Paykel (Ed.), *Handbook of affective disorders* (pp. 276–285). New York: Guilford.

Costa,. E. (1981). The role of gamma-aminobutyric acid in the action of 1,4–benzodiazepines. In J. W. Lamble (Ed.), *Towards understanding receptors* (pp. 176–183). Amsterdam: Elsevier/North-Holland.

Costa, P. T., & McCrae, R. R. (1988). From catalog to classification: Murray's needs and the five-factor model. *Journal of Personality and Social Psychology, 55,* 258–265.

Costain, D. W., Cowen, P. J., Gelder, M. G., & Grahame-Smith, D. G. (1982). Electroconvulsive therapy and the brain: Evidence for increased dopamine-mediated responses. *Lancet, 2,* 400–404.

Cowdry, R. W., & Goodwin, F. K. (1978). Amine neurotransmitter studies and psychiatric illness: Toward more meaningful diagnostic concepts. In R. L. Spitzer & D. F. Klein (Eds.), *Critical issues in psychiatric diagnosis* (pp. 281–303).

Cox, S. M., & Ludwig, A. M. (1979). Neurological soft signs and psychopathology: I. Findings in schizophrenia. *Journal of Nervous and Mental Disease, 167,* 161–165.

Craighead, W. E., Kennedy, R. E., Raczynski, J. M., & Dow, M. G. (1984). Affective disorders–Unipolar. In S. M. Turner & M. Hersen (Eds.), *Adult psychopathology and diagnosis* (pp. 184–244). New York: Wiley.

Craske, M. G., & Barlow, D. H. (1988). A review of the relationship between panic and avoidance. *Clinical Psychology Review, 8,* 667–685.

Craske, M. G., Grenier, V., Klosko, J., & Barlow, D. H. (1986, November). *Night panic.* Paper presented at the convention of the Association for Advancement of Behavior Therapy, Chicago.

Craske, M. G., Rapee, R. M., & Barlow, D. H. (1988). The significance of panic-expectancy for individual patterns of avoidance. *Behavior Therapy, 19,* 577–592.

Cravens, H. (1978). *The triumph of evolution.* Philadelphia: Pennsylvania.

Creese, I. (1982). Dopamine receptors explained. *Trends in Neuroscience, 5,* 40–43.

Creese, I. (1983). Classical and atypical antipsychotic drugs: New insights. *Trends in Neuroscience, 6,* 479–481.

Creese, I., Burt, D. R., & Snyder, S. H. (1977). Dopamine receptor binding enhancement accompanies lesion-induced behavioral supersensitivity. *Science, 197,* 596–598.

Creese, I., & Sibley, D. R. (1981). Receptor adaptations to centrally acting drugs. *Annual Review of Pharmacology and Toxicology, 21,* 357–391.

Creese, I., & Snyder, S. H. (1980). Chronic neuroleptic treatment and dopamine receptor regulation. In F. Cattabeni, G. Racagni, P. F. Spano, & E. Costa (Eds.), *Long-term effects of neuroleptics* (pp. 89–94). New York: Raven.

Cromwell, R. L. (1978). Concluding comments. In L. C. Wynne, R. L. Cromwell, & S. Matthysse (Eds.), *The nature of schizophrenia: New approaches to research and treatment* (pp. 76–83). New York: Wiley.

Cronbach, L. (1967). The two disciplines of scientific psychology. In D. N. Jackson & S. Messick (Eds.), *Problems in human assessment* (pp. 22–39). New York: McGraw-Hill.

Cronbach, L. J. (1975). Beyond the two disciplines of scientific psychology. *American Psychologist, 30,* 116–127.

Cross, A. J., Crow, T. J., & Owen, F. (1981). ^{3}H-flupenthixol binding in post-mortem brains of schizophrenics: Evidence for a selective increase in dopamine D2 receptors. *Psychopharmacology, 74,* 122–124.

Crow, T. J. (1985). Integrated viral genes as the cause of schizophrenia: A hypothesis. In S. D. Iversen (Ed.), *Psychopharmacology: Recent advances and future prospects* (pp. 228–242). Oxford: Oxford University Press.

Crow, T. J. (1980). Molecular pathology of schizophrenia: More than one disease process? *British Medical Journal, 280,* 66–68.

Crow, T. J. (1982). Positive and negative symptoms and the role of dopamine in schizophrenia. In G. Hemmings (Ed.), *Biological aspects of schizophrenia and addiction* (pp. 49–54). New York: Wiley.

Crow, T. J. (1983). Is schizophrenia an infectious disease? *Lancet, 1,* 173–175.

Crow, T. J. (1986). The continuum of psychosis and its implication for the structure of the gene. *British Journal of Psychiatry, 149,* 419–429.

Crow, T. J., Ferrier, I. N., Johnstone, E. C., Macmillan, J. F., Owens, D. G. C., Parry, R. P., & Tyrrell, D. A. J. (1979). Characteristics of patients with schizophrenia or neurological disorder and virus-like agent in cerebrospinal fluid. *Lancet, 1,* 842–844.

Crow, T. J., & Johnstone, E. C. (1979). Electroconvulsive therapy: Efficacy, mechanism of action, and adverse effects. In E. S. Paykel & A. Coppen (Eds.), *Psychopharmacology of affective disorders* (pp. 108–122). Oxford: Oxford University Press.

Crow, T. J., Johnstone, E. C., Longden, A. J., & Owen, F. (1978). Dopaminergic mechanisms in schizophrenia: The antipsychotic effect and the disease process. *Life Sciences, 23,* 562–567.

Crowe, L. C., & George, W. H. (1989). Alcohol and human sexuality: Review and integration. *Psychological Bulletin, 105,* 374–386.

Crowe, R. R, Noyes, R., Pauls, D. L., & Slymen, D. (1983). A family study of panic disorder. *Archives of General Psychiatry, 40,* 1065–1069.

Crowe, R. R., Pauls, D. L., Slymen, D. J., & Noyes, R. (1980). A family study of anxiety neurosis: Morbidity risk in families of patients with and without mitral valve prolapse. *Archives of General Psychiatry, 37,* 77–79.

Cuello, A. C. (1983). Central distribution of opioid peptides. *British Medical Bulletin, 39,* 11–16.

Czeisler, C. A., Allan, J. S., Strogatz, S. H., Ronda, J. M., Sánchez, R., Rios, C. D., Freitag, W. O., Richardson, G. S., & Kronauer, R. E. (1986). Bright light resets the human circadian pacemaker independent of the timing of the sleep-wake cycle. *Science, 233,* 667–671.

Dalton, K. (1984). *The premenstrual syndrome and progesterone therapy* (2nd ed.). Chicago: Year Book Medical.

Davidson, J. (1983). MAO Inhibitors: A clinical perspective. In F. J. Ayd, I. J. Taylor, & B. T. Taylor (Eds.), *Affective disorders reassessed: 1983* (pp. 41–55). Baltimore: Ayd Medical Communications.

Davidson, R. S. (1984). Substance abuse: Alcoholism. In S. M. Turner & M. Hersen (Eds.), *Adult psychopathology and diagnosis* (pp. 73–104). New York: Wiley.

Davis, G. C., Buchsbaum, M. S., van Kammen, D. P., & Bunney, W. E. (1979). Analgesia to pain stimuli in schizophrenics and its reversal by naltrexone. *Psychiatry Research, 1,* 61–69.

Davis, H. P., Rosenzweig, M. R., Becker, L. A., & Sather, K. J. (1988). Biological psychology's relationships to psychology and neuroscience. *American Psychologist, 43,* 359–371.

Davis, J. M. (1974). A two factor theory of schizophrenia. *Journal of Psychiatric Research, 11,* 25–29.

Davis, J. M., Janowsky, D., & Casper, R. C. (1977). Acetylcholine and mental disease. In E. Usdin, D. A. Hamburg, & J. D. Barchas (Eds.), *Neuroregulators and psychiatric disorders* (pp. 434–441). New York: Oxford University Press.

Davis, J. M., Schaffer, C. B., Killian, G. A., Kinard, C., & Chan, C. (1980). Important issues in the drug treatment of schizophrenia. *Schizophrenia Bulletin, 6,* 70–87.

Davis, K. L., Hollister, L. E., Berger, P. A., & Barchas, J. D. (1975). Cholinergic imbalance hypotheses of psychoses and movement disorders: Strategies for evaluation. *Psychopharmacology Communications, 1,* 533–543.

Davison, G. C., & Neale, J. M. (1982). *Abnormal psychology: An experimental clinical approach* (3rd ed.). New York: Wiley.

Dawson, M. E., Schell, A. M., & Catania, J. J. (1977). Autonomic correlates of depression and clinical improvement following electroconvulsive shock therapy. *Psychophysiology*, *14*, 569–578.

Dealy, R. S., Ishiki, D. M., Avery, D. H., Wilson, L. G., & Dunner, D. L. (1981). Secondary depression in anxiety disorders. *Comprehensive Psychiatry*, *22*, 612–618.

DeFeudis, F. V. (1974). *Central cholinergic systems and behavior*. New York: Academic Press.

Deleon-Jones, F., Maas, J. W., Dekirmenjian, H., & Sanchez, J. (1975). Diagnostic subgroups of affective disorders and their urinary excretion of catecholamine metabolites. *American Journal of Psychiatry*, *132*, 1141–1148.

DeLisi, L. E., Goldin, L. R., Hamovit, J. R., Maxwell, E., Kurtz, D., & Gershon, E. S. (1986). A family study of the association of increased ventricular size with schizophrenia. *Archives of General Psychiatry*, *43*, 148–153.

Delworth, U. (1986). APA and DSM. *APA Monitor*, *17*(7), 3.

Demellweek, C., & Goudie, A. J. (1983). Behavioural tolerance to amphetamine and other psychostimulants: The case for considering behavioural mechanisms. *Psychopharmacology*, *80*, 287–307.

Depue, R. A., Kleinman, R. M., Davis, P., Hutchinson, M., & Krauss, S. P. (1985). The behavioral high-risk paradigm and bipolar affective disorder, VIII: Serum free cortisol in nonpatient cyclothymic subjects selected by the General Behavior Inventory. *American Journal of Psychiatry*, *142*, 175–181.

Depue, R. A., & Monroe, S. M. (1978). The unipolar bipolar distinction in the depressive disorders. *Psychological Bulletin*, *85*, 1001–1029.

Depue, R. A., & Monroe, S. M. (1979). The unipolar–bipolar distinction in the depressive disorders: Implication for stress–onset interaction. In R. A. Depue (Ed.), *The psychobiology of the depressive disorders: Implications for the effects of stress* (pp. 23–53). New York: Academic Press.

Depue, R. A., & Monroe, S. M. (1986). Conceptualization and measurement of human disorder in life stress research: The problem of chronic disturbance. *Psychological Bulletin*, *99*, 36–51.

Depue. R. A., Slater, J.F., Wolfstetter-Kausch, H., Klein, D., Goplerud, E., & Farr, D. (1981). A behavioral paradigm for identifying persons at risk for bipolar depressive disorder: A conceptual framework and five validation studies. *Journal of Abnormal Psychology*, *90*, 381–437.

Dermietzel, R. (1976). Central chemosensitivity, morphological studies. In H. H. Loeschcke (Ed.), *Acid base homeostasis of the brain extracellular fluid and the respiratory control system* (pp. 52–65). Littleton, MA: Thieme.

Detera-Wadleigh, S. D., Berrettini, W. H., Goldin, L. R., Boorman, D., Anderson, S., & Greshon, E. S. (1987). Close linkage of c-Harvey-ras-1 and the insulin gene to affective disorder is ruled out in three North American pedigrees. *Nature*, *325*, 806–808.

DeVaul, R. A., & Hall, R. C. W. (1980). Hallucinations. In R. C. W. Hall (Ed.), *Psychiatric presentations of medical illness: Somatopsychic disorders* (pp. 91–103). New York: SP Medical & Scientific Books.

Diamond, S. (1957). *Personality and temperament*. New York: Harper & Brothers.

Dickens, C. (1953). *Great expectations*. London: Oxford University press.

Di Nardo, P. A., O'Brien, G. T., Barlow, D. H., Waddell, M. T., & Blanchard, E. B. (1983). Reliability of DSM-III anxiety disorder categories using a new structured interview. *Archives of General Psychiatry*, *40*, 1070–1074.

Dourdain, G., Puech, A. J., & Simon, P. (1980). Triazolam compared with nitrazepam and with oxazepam in insomnia: Two double-blind, crossover studies analyzed sequentially. *British Journal of Clinical Pharmacology*, *11*,(Suppl. 1), 43S–49S.

Dourish, C. T., & Cooper, S. J. (1985). Behavioural evidence for the existence of dopamine autoreceptors. *Trends in Pharmacological Sciences*, *6*, 17–18.

Dunn, C. G. (1981). The diagnosis and classification of anxiety states. *Psychiatric Annals, 11*(1), 11–16.

Dunner, D. L., Fleiss, J. L., Addonizio, G., & Fieve, R. R. (1976). Assortive mating in primary affective disorder. *Biological Psychiatry, 11,* 31–42.

Dunner, D. L., Greshon, E. S., & Goodwin, F. K. (1976). Heritable factors in the severity of affective illness. *Biological Psychiatry, 11,* 31–42.

Edelstein, B. A., Keaton-Brasted, C., & Burg, M. M. (1983). The effects of caffeine withdrawal on cardiovascular and gastrointestinal responses. *Health Psychology, 2,* 343–352.

Egeland, J. A., Gerhard, D. S., Pauls, D. L., Sussex, J. N., Kidd, K. K., Allen, C. R., Hostetter, A. M., & Housman, D. E. (1987). Bipolar affective disorders linked to DNA markers on chromosome 11. *Nature, 325,* 783–787.

Ehlers, A., Margraf, J., Roth, W. T., Taylor, C. B., & Birbaumer, N. (1988). Anxiety induced by false heart rate feedback in patients with panic disorder. *Behaviour research and Therapy, 26,* 1–11.

Ehlers, A., Margraf, J., Roth, W. T., Taylor, C. B., Maddock, R. J., Sheikh, J., Kopell, M. L., McClenahan, K. L., Gossard, D., Blowers, G. H., Agras, W. S., & Kopell, B. S. (1986). Lactate infusions and panic attacks: Do patients and controls respond differently? *Psychiatry Research, 17,* 295–308.

Ehrlich, P., & McGeehan, M. (1985). Cocaine recovery support groups and the language of recovery. *Journal of Psychoactive Drugs, 17,* 11–17.

Eisler, R. M., Hersen, M., & Miller, P. M. (1974). Shaping components of assertive behavior with instructions and feedback. *American Journal of Psychiatry, 30,* 1344–1347.

Ekman, P., Levenson, R. W., & Friesen, W. V. (1983). Autonomic nervous system activity distinguishes among emotions. *Science, 221,* 1208–1210.

Ellingboe, J. (1978). Effects of alcohol on neurochemical processes. In M. A. Lipton, A. DiMascio, & K. F. Killam (Eds.), *Psychopharmacology: A generation of progress* (pp. 1653–1664). New York: Raven.

Ellinwood, E. H. (1967). Amphetamine psychosis: I. Description of the individuals and the process. *Journal of Nervous and Mental Disease, 144,* 273–283.

Elliott, G. R., Edelman, A. M., Renson, J. F., & Berger, P. A. (1977). Indoleamines and other neuroregulators. In J. D. Barchas, P. A. Berger, R. D. Ciaranello, & G. R. Elliott (Eds.), *Psychopharmacology: From theory to practice* (pp. 33–50). New York: Oxford University Press.

Elliott, G. R., Holman, R. B., & Barchas, J. D. (1977). Neuroregulators and behavior. In J. D. Barchas, P. A. Berger, R. D. Ciaranello, & G. R. Elliott (Eds.), *Psychopharmacology: From theory to practice* (pp. 5–15). New York: Oxford University Press.

Elston, R. C. (1986). Comments on behavioral genetic methodology. *Behavior Therapy, 17,* 362–365.

Emmelkamp, P. M. G. (1982). Anxiety and fear. In A. S. Bellack, M. Hersen, & A. E. Kazdin (Eds.), *International handbook of behavior modification and therapy* (pp. 349–395). New York: Plenum.

Endicott, J., & Spitzer, R. L. (1978). A diagnostic interview: The Schedule for Affective Disorders and Schizophrenia. *Archives of General Psychiatry, 35,* 837–844.

Engel, G. L. (1977). The need for a new medical model: A challenge for biomedicine. *Science, 196,* 129–136.

Enna, S. J. (1981). GABA receptors. In J. W. Lamble (Ed.), *Towards understanding receptors* (pp. 171–175). Amsterdam: Elsevier/North-Holland.

Epstein, L. H., & Cluss, P. A. (1986). Behavioral genetics of childhood obesity. *Behavior Therapy, 17,* 324–334.

Epstein, S. (1979). The stability of behavior: I. On predicting most of the people much of the time. *Journal of Personality and Social Psychology, 37,* 1097–1126.

Erickson, C. K., & Graham, D. T. (1973). Alteration of cortical and reticular acetylcholine release by ethanol *in vivo. Journal of Pharmacology and Experimental Therapeutics, 185,* 583–593.

Escobar, J. I., & Landbloom, R. P. (1976). Treatment of phobic neurosis with clomipramine: A controlled clinical trial. *Current Therapeutic Research, 20,* 680–685.

Evans, J. I., Lewis, S. A., Gibb, I. A. M., & Cheetham, M. (1968). Sleep and barbiturates: Some experiments and observations. *British Medical Journal, 4,* 291–293.

Ewing, J. A., Rouse, B. A., & Pellizzari, E. D. (1974). Alcohol sensitivity and ethnic background. *American Journal of Psychiatry, 131,* 206–210.

Extein, I., Potter, W. Z., Wehr, T. A., & Goodwin, F. K. (1979). Rapid mood cycles after a noradrenergic but not a serotonergic antidepressant. *American Journal of Psychiatry, 136,* 1602–1603.

Eysenck, H. J. (1967). *The biological basis of personality.* Springfield, IL: Charles C. Thomas.

Eysenck, H. J. (1970). The classification of depressive illness. *British Journal of Psychiatry, 117,* 241–250.

Eysenck, H. J. (1982). Neobehavioristic (S-R) theory. In G. T. Wilson & C. M. Franks (Eds.), *Contemporary behavior therapy: Conceptual and empirical foundations* (pp. 205–276). New York: Guilford.

Eysenck, H. J. (1983). Psychophysiology and personality: Extraversion, neuroticism and psychoticism. In A. Gale & J. A. Edwards (Eds.), *Physiological correlates of human behaviour: Individual differences and psychopathology* (Vol. 3, pp. 13–30). New York: Academic Press.

Eysenck, H. J., & Eysenck, S. B. G. (1975). *Eysenck Personality Questionnaire.* San Diego, CA: Educational and Industrial Testing Service.

Eysenck, H. J. & Levey, A. (1972). Conditioning, introversion–extraversion and the strength of the nervous system. In V. D. Nebylitsyn & J. A. Gray (Eds.), *Biological bases of individual behavior* (pp. 206–220). New York: Academic Press.

Fabsitz, R., Feinleib, M., & Hrubec, Z. (1980). Weight changes in adult twins. *Acta Geneticae Medicae et Gemellologiae, 29,* 273–279.

Fabrega, H. (1975). The position of psychiatry in the understanding of human disease. *Archives of General Psychiatry, 32,* 1500–1512.

Fairbairn, J. W., & Pickens, J. T. (1979). The oral activity of δ'-tetrahydrocannabinol and its dependence on prostaglandin E_2. *British Journal of Pharmacology, 67,* 379–385.

Fairbairn, J. W., & Pickens, J. T. (1980). The effect of conditions influencing endogenous prostaglandins on the activity of δ'-tetrahydrocannabinol in mice. *British Journal of Pharmacology, 69,* 491–493.

Falloon, I. R. H. (1985). Behavioral family therapy: A problem-solving approach. In J. Leff & C. Vaughn (Eds.), *Expressed emotion in families: Its significance for mental illness* (pp. 150–171). New York: Guilford.

Falloon, I. R. H., Boyd, J. L., & McGill, C. W. (1984). *Family care of schizophrenia: A problem-solving approach to the treatment of mental illness.* New York: Guilford.

Falloon, I. R. H., Boyd, J. L., McGill, C. W., Razani, J., Moss, H. B., & Gilderman, A. (1982). Family management in the prevention of exacerbations of schizophrenia: A controlled study. *New England Journal of Medicine, 306,* 1437–1440.

Falloon, I. R. H., Lloyd, G. G., & Harpin, R. E. (1981). Treatment of social phobia: Real-life rehearsal and nonprofessional therapist. *Journal of Nervous and Mental Disease, 169,* 180–184.

Fava, G. A., Munari, F., Pavan, L., & Kellner, R. (1981). Life events and depression: A replication. *Journal of Affective Disorders, 3,* 159–165.

Feeney, D. M. (1979). Marihuana and epilepsy: Paradoxical anticonvulsant and convulsant effects. In F. Hoffmeister & G. Stille (Eds.), *Psychotropic agents. Part III: Alcohol and psychotomimetics, psychotropic effects of central acting drugs* (pp. 643–659). New York: Springer-Verlag.

Feighner, J. P., Robins, E., Guze, S. B., Woodruff, R. A., Winokur, G., & Munoz, R. (1972). Diagnostic criteria for use in psychiatric research. *Archives of General Psychiatry, 26*, 57–63.

Feinleib, M., Garrison, R. J., Fabsitz, R., Christian, J. C., Hrubec, Z., Borhani, N. D., Kannel, W. B., Rosenman, R., Schwartz, J. T., & Wagner, J. D. (1977). The NHLBI twin study of cardiovascular disease risk factors: Methodology and summary of results. *American Journal of Epidemiology, 106*, 284–295.

Fenichel, O. (1945). *The psychoanalytic theory of neurosis.* New York: W. W. Norton.

Fillmore, K. M. (1975). Relationships between specific drinking problems in early adulthood and middle age: An exploratory 20-year follow-up study. *Journal of Studies on Alcohol, 36*, 882–907.

Fink, M. (1979). *Convulsive therapy: Theory and practice.* New York: Raven.

Fink, M. (1981). Convulsive and drug therapies of depression. *Annual Review of Medicine, 32*, 405–412.

Fisher, K. (1986a). DSM-III-R: Amendment process frustrates non-MDs. *APA Monitor, 17*(2), 17–18, 24.

Fisher, K. (1986b). DSM-III-R protest: Critics say psychiatry has been stonewalling. *APA Monitor, 17*(7), 4–5.

Fleming, J., & Nichols, K. D. (1986). Victims. *APA Monitor, 17*(7), 3.

Flood, J. F., Bennett, E. L., Orme, A. E., Rosenzweig, M. R., & Jarvik, M. E. (1978). Memory: Modification of anisomycin-induced amnesia by stimulants and depressants. *Science, 199*, 324–326.

Flor-Henry, P. (1976). Lateralized temporal-limbic dysfunction and psychopathology. *Annals of the New York Academy of Sciences, 280*, 777–795.

Flor-Henry, P. (1983). *Cerebral basis of psychopathology.* Boston: John Wright.

Flor-Henry, P., Koles, Z. J., Howarth, B. G., & Burton, L.(1979). Neurophysiology studies of schizophrenia, mania and depression. In J. Gruzelier & P. Flor-Henry (Eds.), *Hemisphere asymmetries of function in psychopathology* (pp. 183–222). New York: Elsevier/North-Holland.

Foa, E. B., Steketee, G. S., & Ozarow, B. J. (1985). Behavior therapy with obsessive-compulsives: From theory to treatment. In M. Mavissakalian, S. M. Turner, & L. Michelson (Eds.), *Obsessive-compulsive disorder: Psychological and pharmacological treatment* (pp. 49–129). New York: Plenum.

Foltz, D. (1980). Judgment withheld on DSM-III: New child classification pushed. *APA Monitor, 11*(1), 1, 33.

Fowler, O. S. (1869). *The practical phrenologist.* Sharon Station, NY: Mrs. O. S. Fowler.

Fowler, O. S., & Fowler, L. N. (1883). *The illustrated self-instructor in phrenology and physiology.* New York: Fowler & Wells.

Fowles, D. C., & Gersh, F. S. (1979). Neurotic depression: The endogenous–neurotic distinction. In R. A. Depue (Ed.), *The psychobiology of the depressive disorders: Implications for the effects of stress* (pp. 55–80). New York: Academic Press.

France, C., & Ditto, B. (1988). Caffeine effects on several indices of cardiovascular activity at rest and during stress. *Journal of Behavioral Medicine, 11*, 473–482).

Franks, N. P., & Lieb, W. R. (1982). Molecular mechanisms of general anaesthesia. *Nature, 300*, 487–493.

Freedman, D. X., & Boggan, W. O. (1982). Biochemical pharmacology of psychotomimetics. In F. Hoffmeister & G. Stille (Eds.), *Psychotropic agents. Part III: Alcohol and psycho-*

tomimetics, psychotropic effects of central acting drugs (pp. 57–88). New York: Springer-Verlag.

Freeman, A. M. (1980). Delusion, depersonalization, and unusual psychopathological systems. In R. C. W. Hall (Ed.), *Psychiatric presentations of medical illness: Somatopsychic disorders* (pp. 75–89). New York: SP Medical & Scientific Books.

Frenkel-Brunswick, E. (1949). Intolerance to ambiguity as an emotional and perceptual personality variable. *Journal of Personality, 18,* 108–143.

Freud, S. (1954). Project for a scientific psychology. In M. Bonaparte, A. Freud, & E. Kris (Eds.), *The origins of psycho-analysis: Letters to Wilhelm Fliess, drafts and notes, 1887–1902* (pp. 347–445; E. Mosbacher & J. Strachey, Trans.). New York: Basic Books.

Freud, S. (1935). *Autobiography* (J. Strachey, Trans.). New York: W. W. Norton.

Freudenberg, R. P., Driscoll, J. W., & Stern, G. S. (1978). Reactions of adult humans to cries of normal and abnormal infants. *Infant Behavior and Development, 1,* 224–227.

Friedman, H. S., & Booth-Kewley, S. (1987). The "disease-prone personality": A meta-analytic view of the construct. *American Psychologist, 42,* 539–555.

Friedman, M. J., & Bennet, P. L. (1977). Depression and hypertension. *Psychosomatic Medicine, 39,* 134–142.

Frith, C. D. (1979). Consciousness, information processing and schizophrenia. *British Journal of Psychiatry, 134,* 225–235.

Frith, C. D., Stevens, M., Johnstone, E. C., & Crow, T. J. (1979). Skin conductance responsivity during acute episodes of schizophrenia as a predictor of symptomatic improvement. *Psychological Medicine, 9,* 101–106.

Frodi, A. (1985). When empathy fails: Aversive infant crying and child abuse. In B. M. Lester & C. F. Z. Boukydis, *Infant crying: Theoretical and research perspectives* (pp. 263–277). New York: Plenum.

Frodi, A. M., Lamb, M. E., Leavitt, L. A., Donovan, W. L., Neff, C., & Sherry, D. (1978). Fathers' and mothers' responses to the faces and cries of normal and premature infants. *Developmental Psychology, 14,* 490–498.

Fulker, D. W. (1979). Some implications of biometrical genetical analysis for psychological research. In J. R. Royce & L. P. Mos (Eds.), *Theoretical advances in behavior genetics* (pp. 337–387). Alphen aan den Rijn, Netherlands: Sijthoff Noordhoff International.

Fulker, D. W. (1981). The genetic and environmental architecture of psychoticism, extraversion and neuroticism. In H. J. Eysenck (Ed.), *A model for personality* (pp. 88–122). New York: Springer-Verlag.

Fuxe, K., Ögren, S. O., Agnati, L. F., Benfenati, F., Cavicchioli, L., Fredholm, B., Andersson, K., Farabegoli, C., & Eneroth, P. (1983). Regional variations in 5-HT receptor populations and ^{3}H-imipramine binding sites in their responses to chronic antidepressant treatment. In E. Usdin, M. Goldstein, A. J. Friedhoff, & A. Georgotas (Eds.), *Frontiers in neuropsychiatric research* (pp. 33–54). London: Macmillian.

Gale, A., & Edwards, J. A. (1983). Introduction. In A. Gale & J. A. Edwards (Eds.), *Physiological correlates of human behaviour: Individual differences and psychopathology* (Vol. 3, pp. 1–11). New York: Academic Press.

Galin, D. (1974). Implications for psychiatry of left and right cerebral specialization. *Archives of General Psychiatry, 31,* 572–583.

Garcia, J. (1981). Tilting at the paper mills of academe. *American Psychologist, 36,* 149–158.

Garcia-Coll, C., Kagan, J., & Reznick, J. S. (1984). Behavioral inhibition in young children. *Child Development, 55,* 1005–1019.

Garcia-Sevilla, J. A., Guimón, J., Garcia-Vallejo, P., & Fuster, M. J. (1986). Biochemical and functional evidence of supersensitive platelet α_2-adrenoceptors in major affective disorder. *Archives of General Psychiatry, 43,* 51–57.

Garfield, S. L. (1986). Problems in diagnostic classification. In T. Millon & G. L. Klerman (Eds.), *Contemporary directions in psychopathology: Toward the DSM-IV* (pp. 99–114). New York: Guilford.

Garmezy, N. (1978). Observations on high-risk research and premorbid development in schizophrenia. In L. C. Wynne, R. L. Cromwell, & S. Matthysse (Eds.). *The nature of schizophrenia: New approaches to research and treatment* (pp. 460–472). New York: Wiley.

Garn, S. M., Cole, P. E., & Bailey, S. M. (1977). Effect of parental fatness levels on the fatness of biological and adoptive children. *Ecology of Food and Nutrition, 7,* 91–93.

Gastaut, H. (1954). The brain stem and cerebral electrogenesis in relation to consciousness. In J. F. Delafresnaye (Ed.), *Brain mechanisms and consciousness: A symposium* (pp. 249–283). Springfield, IL: Charles C. Thomas.

Gaylin, W. D. (1975). The problem of psychosurgery. In W. M. Gaylin, J. S. Meister, & R. C. Neville (Eds.), *Operating on the mind: The psychosurgery conflict* (pp. 3–23). New York: Basic Books.

Gerald, M. C. (1981). *Pharmacology: An introduction to drugs* (2nd ed.). Englewood Cliffs, NJ: Prentice-Hall.

Gerbino, L., Oleshansky, M., & Gershon, S. (1978). Clinical use and mode of action of lithium. In M. A. Lipton, A. DiMascio, & K. F. Killam (Eds.), *Psychopharmacology: A generation of progress* (pp. 1261–1275). New York: Raven.

Gershon, E. S. (1982). Genetic studies of affective disorders and schizophrenia. In B. Bonné-Tamir, T. Cohen, & R. M. Goodman (Eds.), *Human genetics, Part A: The unfolding genome* (pp. 417–432). New York: Alan R. Liss.

Gershon, E. S. (1983). Genetics of the major psychoses. In S. S. Kety, L. P. Rowland, R. L. Sidman, & S. W. Matthysse (Eds.), *Genetics of neurological and psychiatric disorders* (pp. 121–144). New York: Raven.

Gershon, E. S., Baron, M., & Leckman, J. F. (1975). Genetic models of the transmission of affective disorders. *Journal of Psychiatry Research, 12,* 301–317.

Gershon, E. S., Bunney, W. E., Leckman, J. F., Van Eerdewegh, M., & DeBauche, B. A. (1976). The inheritance of affective disorders: A review of data and of hypotheses. *Behavior Genetics, 6,* 227–261.

Gershon, E. S., Dunner, D. L., Sturt, L., & Goodwin, F. K. (1973). Assortative mating in the affective disorders. *Biological Psychiatry, 7,* 63–74.

Gil, D. G. (1970). *Violence against children: Physical child abuse in the United States.* Cambridge, MA: Harvard University Press.

Gill, E. W., Jones, G., & Lawrence, D. K. (1972). Chemical mechanisms of action of THC. In W. D. M. Paton & J. Crow (Eds.), *Cannabis and its derivatives: Pharmacology and experimental psychology* (pp. 76–87). London: Oxford University Press.

Gillin, J. C., Duncan, W., Pettigrew, K. D., Frankel, B. L., & Snyder, F. (1979). Successful separation of depressed, normal, and insomniac subjects by EEG sleep data. *Archives of General Psychiatry, 36,* 85–90.

Gittelman-Klein, R., & Klein, D. F. (1971). Controlled imipramine treatment of school phobia. *Archives of General Psychiatry, 25,* 204–207.

Glassman, A. (1969). Indoleamines and affective disorders. *Psychosomatic Medicine, 31,* 107–114.

Glednill, N., Beirne, G. L., & Dempsey, J. A. (1975). Renal response to short-term hypocapnia in man. *Kidney International, 8,* 376–386.

Gold, M. D., & Pottash, A. L. C. (1983). Thyroid dysfunction or depression? In F. J. Ayd, I. J. Taylor, & B. T. Taylor (Eds.), *Affective disorders reassessed: 1983* (pp. 179–191). Baltimore: Ayd Medical Communications.

Golden, C. J., & Sawicki, R. F. (1985). Neuropsychological bases of psychopathological disorders. In L. C. Hartlage & C. F. Telzrow (Eds.), *The neuropsychology of individual differences: A developmental perspective* (pp. 203–236). New York: Plenum.

Golding, J. F., Harpur, T., & Brent-Smith, H. (1983). Personality, drinking, and drug-taking correlates of cigarette smoking. *Personality and Individual Differences, 4,* 703–706.

Goldman, M. S. (1988, November). *Alcoholism etiology: A biobehavioral perspective.* Clinical round table presented at the convention of the Association for Advancement of Behavior Therapy, New York.

Goldstein, A., Aronow, L., & Kalman, S. M. (1974). *Principles of drug action: The basis of pharmacology* (2nd ed.). New York: Wiley.

Goldstein, A., & Kaizer, S. (1969). Psychotropic effects of caffeine in man. III. A questionnaire survey of coffee drinking and its effects on a group of housewives. *Clinical Pharmacology and Therapeutics, 10,* 477–488.

Goldstein, I. B. (1965). The relationship of muscle tension and autonomic activity to psychiatric disorders. *Psychosomatic Medicine, 27,* 39–52.

Goodwin, D. W. (1971). Is alcoholism hereditary? A review and critique. *Archives of General Psychiatry, 25,* 545–549.

Goodwin, D. W. (1979). Alcoholism and heredity: A review and hypothesis. *Archives of General Psychiatry, 36,* 57–61.

Goodwin, D. W. (1985). Genetic determinants of alcoholism. In J. H. Mendelson & N. K. Mello (Eds.), *The diagnosis and treatment of alcoholism* (2nd ed., pp. 65–87). New York: McGraw-Hill.

Goodwin, D. W., Crane, J. B., & Guze, S. B. (1969a). Phenomenological aspects of the alcoholics "blackout." *British Journal of Psychiatry, 115,* 1033–1038.

Goodwin, D. W., Crane, J. B., & Guze, S. B. (1969b). Alcoholic "blackouts": A review and clinical study of 100 alcoholics. *American Journal of Psychiatry, 126,* 191–198.

Goodwin, D. W., & Guze, S. B. (1984). *Psychiatric diagnosis* (3rd ed.). New York: Oxford University Press.

Goodwin, D. W., Schulsinger, F., Hermansen, L., Guze, S. B., & Winokur, G. (1973). Alcohol problems in adoptees raised apart from alcoholic biological parents. *Archives of General Psychiatry, 28,* 238–243.

Goodwin, D. W., Schulsinger, F., Knop, J., Mednick, S., & Guze, S. B. (1977a). Alcoholism and depression in adopted-out daughters of alcoholics. *Archives of General Psychiatry, 34,* 751–755.

Goodwin, D. W., Schulsinger, F., Knop, J., Mednick, S., & Guze, S. B. (1977b). Psychopathology in adopted and nonadopted daughters of alcoholics. *Archives of General Psychiatry, 34,* 1005–1009.

Goodwin, D. W., Schulsinger, F., Moller, N., Hermansen, L., Winokur, G., & Guze, S. B. (1974). Drinking problems in adopted and nonadopted sons of alcoholics. *Archives of General Psychiatry, 31,* 164–169.

Goodwin, F. K., & Murphy, D. L. (1974). Biological factors in the affective disorders and schizophrenia. In M. Gordon (Ed.), *Psychopharmacological agents* (Vol. 3, 9–37). New York: Academic Press.

Gorman, J. M., Martinez, J. M., Liebowitz, M. R., Fyer, A. J., & Klein, D. F. (1984). Hypoglycemia and panic attacks. *American Journal of Psychiatry, 141,* 101–102.

Goth, A. (1978). *Medical pharmacology: Principles and concepts.* Saint Louis: C. V. Mosby.

Gottesman, I. I. (1978). Schizophrenia and genetics: Where are we? Are you sure? In L. C. Wynne, R. L. Cromwell, & S. Matthysse (Eds.), *The nature of schizophrenia: New approaches to research and treatment* (pp. 59–69). New York: Wiley.

Gottesman, I. I., & Shields, J. (1982). *Schizophrenia: The epigenetic puzzle.* New York: Cambridge University Press.

Grahame-Smith, D. G., Green, A. R., & Costain, D. W. (1978). Mechanism of the antidepressant action of electroconvulsive therapy. *Lancet, 1*, 254–256.

Grant, I., Patterson, T., Olshen, R., & Yager, J. (1987). Life events do not predict symptoms: Symptoms predict symptoms. *Journal of Behavioral Medicine, 10*, 231–240.

Grant, S. J., Huang, Y. H., & Redmond, D. E. (1980). Benzodiazepines attenuate single unit activity in the locus coeruleus. *Life Sciences, 27*, 2231–2236.

Gray, J. A. (1964). *Pavlov's typology*. Oxford: Pergamon.

Gray, J. A. (1970). The psychophysiological basis of introversion-extraversion. *Behaviour Research and Therapy, 8*, 249–266.

Gray, J. A. (1977). Drug effects on fear and frustration: Possible limbic site of action of minor tranquilizers. In L. L. Iversen, S. D. Iversen, & S. H. Snyder (Eds.), *Handbook of psychopharmacology* (Vol. 8, pp. 433–529). New York: Plenum.

Gray, J. A. (1982). *The neuropsychology of anxiety: An enquiry into the functions of the septo-hippocampal system*. New York: Oxford University Press.

Gray, J. A. (1983). Anxiety, personality and the brain. In A. Gale & J. A. Edwards (Eds.), *Physiological correlates of human behaviour: Individual differences and psychopathology* (Vol. 3, pp. 31–43). New York: Academic Press.

Greden, J. F. (1974). Anxiety or caffeinism: A diagnostic dilemma. *American Journal of Psychiatry, 131*, 1089–1092.

Green, A. R. (1978). ECT–How does it work? *Trends in Neuroscience, 1*, 53–54.

Green, P., Glass, A., & O'Callaghan, M. A. J. (1979). Some implications of abnormal hemisphere interaction in schizophrenia. In J. Gruzelier & P. Flor-Henry (Eds.), *Laterality and psychopathology* (pp. 431–448). New York: Elsevier/North-Holland.

Green, P. & Kotenko, V. (1980). Superior speech comprehension in schizophrenics under monaural versus binaural listening conditions. *Journal of Abnormal Psychology, 89*, 399–408.

Greenberg, B. D., & Segal, D. S. (1986). Evidence for multiple opiate receptor involvement in different phencyclidine-induced unconditioned behaviours in rats. *Psychopharmacology, 88*, 44–53.

Greenblatt, M., Grosser, G. H., & Wechsler, H. (1964). Differential response of hospitalized depressed patients to somatic therapy. *American Journal of Psychiatry, 120*, 935–943.

Grunhaus, L., & Birmaher, B. (1985). The clinical spectrum of panic attacks. *Journal of Clinical Psychopharmacology, 5*, 93–99.

Gruzelier, J. H. (1976). Clinical attributes of schizophrenic skin conductance responders and non-responders. *Psychological Medicine, 6*, 245–249.

Gruzelier, J. H. & Flor-Henry, P. (Eds.). (1979). *Hemisphere asymmetries of function in psychopathology*. New York: Elsevier/North-Holland.

Gruzelier, J. H. & Hammond, N. (1976). Schizophrenia: A dominant hemisphere temporal-limbic disorder? *Research Communications in Psychology, Psychiatry, and Behavior, 1*, 33–72.

Gruzelier, J. H., & Hammond, N. V. (1979). Lateralised auditory processing in medicated and unmedicated schizophrenic patients. In J. Gruzelier & P. Flor-Henry (Eds.), *Hemisphere asymmetries of function in psychopathology* (pp. 603–636). New York: Elsevier/North-Holland.

Gruzelier, J. H., & Manchanda, R. (1982). The syndrome of schizophrenia: Relations between electrodermal response, lateral asymmetries and clinical ratings. *British Journal of Psychiatry, 141*, 488–495.

Gruzelier, J. H. & Venables, P. H. (1972). Skin conductance orienting activity in a heterogeneous sample of schizophrenics. *Journal of Nervous and Mental Disorders, 155*, 277–287.

Gudiol, J. (1971). *Goya: 1746–1828*. New York: Tudor.

Guidotti, A., Corda, M. G., Wise, B. C., Vaccarino, F., & Costa, E. (1983). GABAergic synapses. Supramolecular organisation and biochemical regulation. *Neuropharmacology, 22*, 1471–1479.

Gur, R. E. (1977). Motoric laterality imbalance in schizophrenia: A possible concomitant of left hemisphere dysfunction. *Archives of General Psychiatry, 34*, 33–37.

Gur, R. E. (1978). Left hemisphere dysfunction and left hemisphere overactivation in schizophrenia. *Journal of Abnormal Psychology, 87*, 226–238.

Gusella, J. F., Wexler, N. S., Conneally, P. M., Naylor, S. L., Anderson, M. A., Tanzi, R. E., Watkins, P. C., Ottina, K., Wallace, M. R., Sakaguchi, A. Y., Young, A. B., Shoulson, I., Bonilla, E., & Martin, J. B. (1983). A polymorphic DNA marker genetically linked to Huntington's disease. *Nature, 306*, 234–238.

Guyton, A. C. (1981). *Textbook of medical physiology* (6th ed.). Philadelphia: W. B. Saunders.

Haefely, W., Pieri, L., Polc, P., & Schaffner, R. (1981). General pharmacology and neuropharmacology of benzodiazepine derivatives. In F. Hoffmeister & G. Stille (Eds.), *Handbook of experimental pharmacology: Psychotropic agents* (Vol. 55/II, pp. 13–262). Berlin: Springer-Verlag.

Hafner, J., & Marks, I. (1976). Exposure *in vivo* of agoraphobics: Contributions of diazepam, group exposure, and anxiety evocation. *Psychological Medicine, 6*, 71–88.

Haggerty, J. J., Golden, R. N., Evans, D. L., & Janowsky, D. S. (1988). Differential diagnosis of pseudodementia in the elderly. *Geriatrics, 43*(3), 61–69.

Hall, G. H., & Turner, D. M. (1972). Effects of nicotine on the release of ^{3}H-noradrenaline from the hypothalamus. *Biochemical Pharmacology, 21*, 1829–1838.

Hall, R. C. W. (1980a). Anxiety. In R. C. W. Hall (Ed.), *Psychiatric presentations of medical illness: Somatopsychic disorders* (pp. 13–35). New York: SP Medical & Scientific Books.

Hall, R. C. W. (1980b). Depression. In R. C. W. Hall (Ed.), *Psychiatric presentations of medical illness: Somatopsychic disorders* (pp. 37–63). New York: SP Medical & Scientific Books.

Haracz, J. L. (1982). The dopamine hypothesis: An overview of studies with schizophrenic patients. *Schizophrenia Bulletin, 8*, 438–469.

Harris, E. (1971). Goya y Lucientes, Francisco José de. In W. E. Preece (Ed.), *Encyclopaedia Britannica* (Vol. 10, pp. 645–647). Chicago: Encyclopaedia Britannica.

Harris, R. A., & Hood, W. F. (1980). Inhibition of synaptosomal calcium uptake by ethanol. *Journal of Pharmacology and Experimental Therapeutics, 213*, 562–568.

Harrison-Read, P. E. (1981). Synaptic and behavioural actions of antidepressant drugs. *Trends in Neuroscience, 4*, 32–34.

Hartlage, L. C., & Telzrow, C. F. (Eds.). *The neuropsychology of individual differences: A developmental perspective*. New York: Plenum.

Hartman, N., Kramer, R., Brown, W. T., & Devereux, R. B. (1982). Panic disorder in patients with mitral valve prolapse. *American Journal of Psychiatry, 139*, 669–670.

Hartz, A., Giefer, E., & Rimm, A. A. (1977). Relative importance of the effect of family environment and heredity on obesity. *Annals of Human Genetics, 41*, 185–193.

Harvey, S. C. (1985). Hypnotics and sedatives. In A. G. Gilman, L. S. Goodman, T. W. Rall, & F. Murad (Eds.), *The pharmacological basis of therapeutics* (7th ed., pp. 339–371). New York: Macmillan.

Hay, D. A. (1985). *Essentials of behaviour genetics*. Boston: Blackwell Scientific.

Hays, P. (1976). Etiological factors in manic-depressive psychoses. *Archives of General Psychiatry, 33*, 1187–1188.

Healy, D., & Williams, J. M. G. (1988). Dysrhythmia, dysphoria, and depression: The interaction of learned helplessness and circadian dysrhythmia in the pathogenesis of depression. *Psychological Bulletin, 103*, 163–178.

Heilman, K. M., & van den Abell, T. (1979). Right hemisphere dominance for attention. *Neurology, 29,* 586. (Abstract)

Helzer, J. E., & Winokur, G. (1974). A family interview study of male manic depressives. *Archives of General Psychiatry, 31,* 73–77.

Hemsley, D. R. (1975). A two-stage model of attention in schizophrenia research. *British Journal of Social and Clinical Psychology, 14,* 81–89.

Henderson, G. (1982). Phencyclidine: A widely abused but little understood psychotomimetic agent. *Trends in Pharmacological Science, 3,* 248–250.

Henderson, G. (1983). Electrophysiological analysis of opioid action in the central nervous system. *British Medical Bulletin, 39,* 59–64.

Henn, F. A., & Kety, S. (1982). Introduction. In F. A. Henn & H. A. Nasrallah (Eds.), *Schizophrenia as a brain disease* (pp. 3–13). New York: Oxford University Press.

Henn, F. A., & Nasrallah, H. A. (Eds.). (1982). *Schizophrenia as a brain disease.* New York: Oxford University Press.

Hersen, M. (1979). Limitations and problems in the clinical application of behavioral techniques in psychiatric settings. *Behavior Therapy, 10,* 65–80.

Hersen, M. (Ed.). (1983). *Outpatient behavior therapy: A clinical guide.* New York: Grune & Stratton.

Hersen, M. (Ed.). (1985). *Inpatient behavior therapy: A clinical guide.* New York: Grune & Stratton.

Hersen, M. (1986). Introduction. In M. Hersen (Ed.), *Pharmacological and behavioral treatment: An integrative approach* (pp. 5–14). New York: Wiley.

Hersen, M., Bellack, A. S., & Himmelhoch, J. M. (1980). Treatment of unipolar depression with social skills training. *Behavior Modification, 4,* 547–556.

Herz, A., Höllt, V., & Przewlocki, R. (1980). Endogenous opioids and addiction. In W. Wuttke, A. Weindl, K. H. Voigt, & R.-R. Dries (Eds.), *Brain and pituitary peptides* (pp. 183–189). Basel: Karger.

Herzberg, J. L., & Wolkind, S. N. (1983). Solvent sniffing in perspective. *British Journal of Hospital Medicine, 29,* 72–73, 76.

Heston, L. L. (1966). Psychiatric disorders in foster home reared children of schizophrenic mothers. *British Journal of Psychiatry, 112,* 819–825.

Hillbom, E. (1960). After-effects of brain-injuries. *Acta Psychiatrica et Neurologica Scandinavica, 35*(Suppl. 142), 1–195.

Ho, I. K., Brase, D. A., Loh, H. H., & Way, E. L. (1975). Influence of L-tryptophan on morphine analgesia, tolerance and physical dependence. *Journal of Pharmacology and Experimental Therapeutics, 193,* 35–43.

Hobson, J. A., McCarley, R. W., & Wyzinski, P. W. (1975). Sleep cycle oscillation: Reciprocal discharge by two brainstem neuronal groups. *Science, 189,* 55–58.

Hodges, W. F. (1976). The psychophysiology of anxiety. In M. Zuckerman & C. D. Spielberger (Eds.), *Emotions and anxiety: New concepts, methods, and applications* (pp. 175–194). Hillsdale, NJ: Lawrence Erlbaum.

Hodgkinson, S., Sherrington, R., Gurling, H., Marchbanks, R., Reeders, S., Mallet, J., McInnis, M., Peturrson, H., & Brynjolfsson, J. (1987). Molecular genetic evidence for heterogeneity in manic depression. *Nature, 325,* 805–806.

Hodgson, R., & Rachman, S. (1974). II. Desynchrony in measures of fear. *Behaviour Research and Therapy, 12,* 319–326.

Hogarty, G. E., Schooler, N. R., Ulrich, R., Mussare, F., Ferro, P., & Herron, E. (1979). Fluphenazine and social therapy in the aftercare of schizophrenic patients: Relapse analyses of a two-year controlled study of Fluphenazine Deconate and Fluphenazine Hydrochloride. *Archives of General Psychiatry, 36,* 1283–1294.

Hollandsworth, J. G. (1986). *Physiology and behavior therapy: Conceptual guidelines for the clinician.* New York: Plenum.

Hollandsworth, J. G. (1988). Evaluating the impact of medical treatment on the quality of life: A 5-year update. *Social Science and Medicine, 26,* 425–434.

Hollister, L. E. (1977). Antipsychotic medications and the treatment of schizophrenia. In J. D. Barchas, P. A. Berger, R. D. Ciaranello, & G. R. Elliott (Eds.), *Psychopharmacology: From theory to practice* (pp. 121–150). New York: Oxford University Press.

Hollister, L. E. (1982). Pharmacology and toxicology of psychotomimetics. In F. Hoffmeister & G. Stille (Eds.), *Psychotropic agents. Part III: Alcohol and psychotomimetics, psychotropic effects of central acting drugs* (pp. 31–44). New York: Springer-Verlag.

Hollon, S. D., Spoden, F., & Chastek, J. (1986). Unipolar depression. In M. Hersen (Ed.), *Pharmacological and behavioral treatment: An integrative approach* (pp. 199–239). New York: Wiley.

Holman, H. R. (1976). The "excellence" deception in medicine. *Hospital Practice, 11*(4), 11, 18, 21.

Holmgren, A., & Ström, G. (1959). Blood lactate concentration in relation to absolute and relative work load in normal men, and in mitral stenosis, atrial septal defect and vasoregulatory asthenia. *Acta Medica Scandinavica, 163,* 185–193.

Holroyd, K. A. (Chair). (1987, November). *Towards the integration of psychological and pharmacological treatments: Emerging findings with four disorders.* Symposium presented at the convention of the Association for Advancement of Behavior Therapy, Boston.

Hopkins, J., Marcus, M., & Campbell, S. B. (1984). Postpartum depression: A critical review. *Psychological Bulletin, 95,* 498–515.

Hordern, A., Burt, C. G., & Holt, N. F. (1965). *Depressive states: A pharmacological study.* Springfield, IL: Charles C. Thomas.

Hornykiewicz, O. (1973). Dopamine in the basal ganglia: Its role and therapeutic implications (including the clinical use of L-DOPA). *British Medical Bulletin, 29,* 172–178.

Huey, S. R., & West, S. G. (1983). Hyperventilation: Its relation to symptom experience and to anxiety. *Journal of Abnormal Psychology, 92,* 422–432.

Hugdhal, K. (1981). The three-systems-model of fear and emotion–A critical examination. *Behaviour Research and Therapy, 19,* 75–85.

Hughes, J. (1983). Biogenesis, release and inactivation of enkephalins and dynorphins. *British Medical Bulletin, 39,* 17–24.

Hughes, J., & Kosterlitz, H. W. (1983). Introduction. *British Medical Bulletin, 39,* 1–3.

Hunt, G. M., & Azrin, N. H. (1973). A community-reinforcement approach to alcoholism. *Behaviour Research and Therapy, 11,* 91–104.

Inouye, E. (1965). Similar and dissimilar manifestations of obsessive-compulsive neurosis in monozygotic twins. *American Journal of Psychiatry, 121,* 1171–1175.

Iversen, S. D., & Iversen, L. L. (1975). *Behavioral pharmacology.* New York: Oxford University Press.

Jacob, R. G., & Rapport, M. D. (1984). Panic disorder: Medical and psychological parameters. In S. M. Turner (Ed.), *Behavioral theories and treatment of anxiety* (pp. 187–237). New York: Plenum.

Jaffe, J. H. (1985). Drug addiction and drug abuse. In A. G. Gilman, L. S. Goodman, T. W. Rall, & F. Murad (Eds.), *The pharmacological basis of therapeutics* (7th ed., pp. 532–581). New York: Macmillan.

Jahoda, M. (1979). The impact of unemployment in the 1930s and the 1970s. *Bulletin of the British Psychological Society, 32,* 309–314.

James, N. M., & Chapman, C. J. (1975). A genetic study of bipolar affective disorder. *British Journal of Psychiatry, 126,* 449–456.

James, W. (1884). What is emotion? *Mind, 9*(Series I), 188–204.

Janowsky, D. S., El-Yousef, M. K., Davis, J. M., & Sekerke, H. J. (1972). A cholinergic–adrenergic hypothesis of mania and depression. *Lancet, 2,* 632–635.

Janowsky, D. S., Risch, S. C., & Gillin, J. C. (1983). Adrenergic–cholinergic balance and the treatment of affective disorders. *Progress in Neuro-psychopharmacology & Biological Psychiatry, 7,* 297–307.

Janowsky, D. S., Risch, C., Parker, D., Huey, L., & Judd, L. (1980). Increased vulnerability to cholinergic stimulation in affective disorder patients. *Psychopharmacology Bulletin, 16,*(4) 29–31.

Jeffreys, D. B., Flanagan, R. J., Volans, G. N. (1980). Reversal of ethanol-induced coma with naloxone. *Lancet, 1,* 308–309.

Jellinek, E. M. (1952). Phases of alcohol addiction. *Quarterly Journal of Studies in Alcohol, 13,* 673–684.

Jenkins, W. J., Cakebread, K., & Palmer, K. R. (1982). Hepatic aldehyde dehydrogenase and alcoholism. *Lancet, 2,* 1275.

Johnson, G., Gershon, S., Burdock, E. I., Floyd, A., & Hekimian, L. (1971). Comparative effects of lithium and chlorpromazine in the treatment of acute manic states. *British Journal of Psychiatry, 119,* 267–276.

Johnson, L. C., & Chernik, D. A. (1982). Sedative-hypnotics and human performance. *Psychopharmacology, 76,* 101–113.

Johnstone, E. C., Crow, T. J., Frith, C. D., Carney, M. W. P., & Price, J. S. (1978). Mechanism of the antipsychotic effect in the treatment of acute schizophrenia. *Lancet, 1,* 848–851.

Johnstone, E. C., Crow, T. J., Frith, C. D., Husband, J., & Kreel, L. (1976). Cerebral ventricular size and cognitive impairment in chronic schizophrenia. *Lancet, 2,* 924–926.

Johnstone, E. C., Crow, T. J., Frith, C. D., Stevens, M., Kreel, L., & Husband, J. (1978). The dementia of dementia praecox. *Acta Psychiatrica Scandinavica, 57,* 305–324.

Jones, K. L., Smith, D. W., Streissguth, A. P., & Myrianthopoulos, N. C. (1974). Outcome of offspring of chronic alcoholic women. *Lancet, 1,* 1076–1078.

Jones, M., & Melleish, V. (1946). A comparison of the exercise response in anxiety states and normal controls. *Psychosomatic Medicine, 8,* 180–187.

Julien, R. M. (1985). *A primer of drug action* (4th ed.). New York: W. H. Freeman.

Jung, C. G. (1924). *Psychological types: The psychology of individuation.* New York: Harcourt, Brace.

Kagan, J. (1989). Temperamental contributions to social behavior. *American Psychologist, 44,* 668–674.

Kagan, J., Reznick, J. S., Clarke, C., Snidman, N., & Garcia-Coll, C. (1984). Behavioral inhibition to the unfamiliar. *Child Development, 55,* 2212–2225.

Kagan, J., Reznick, J. S., & Snidman, N. (1987). The physiology and psychology of behavioral inhibition in children. *Child Development, 58,* 1459–1473.

Kagan, J., Reznick, J. S., & Snidman, N. (1988). Biological bases of childhood shyness. *Science, 240,* 167–171.

Kagan, J., Reznick, J. S., & Snidman, N., Gibbons, J., & Johnson, M. O. (1988). Childhood derivatives of inhibition and lack of inhibition to the unfamiliar. *Child Development, 59,* 1580–1589.

Kaij, L., & Dock, J. (1975). Grandsons of alcoholics. *Archives of General Psychiatry, 32,* 1379–1381.

Kaij, L., & McNeil, T. F. (1979). Genetic aspects of alcoholism. *Advances in Biological Psychiatry, 3,* 54–65.

Kandel, E. R. (1983). From metapsychology to molecular biology: Exploration into the nature of anxiety. *American Journal of Psychiatry, 140,* 1277–1293.

Kane, J. M., Woerner, M., Zeldis, S., Kramer, R., & Saravay, S. (1981). Panic and phobic disorders in patients with mitral valve prolapse. In D. F. Klein & J. Rabkin (Eds.), *Anxiety: New research and changing concepts* (pp. 327–340). New York: Raven.

Kanfer, F. H., & Saslow, G. (1965). Behavioral analysis: An alternative to diagnostic classification. *Archives of General Psychiatry, 12,* 529–538.

Kaplan, A. R., Sank, D., Allon, R., Lynch, H. T., Hinko, E. N., Powell, W. E., & Moorhouse, A. E. (1976). Genetics, cytogenetics, dermatoglyphics, clinical histories, and schizophrenia etiology. In A. R. Kaplan (Ed.), *Human behavior genetics* (pp. 330–346). Springfield, IL: Charles C. Thomas.

Kaplan, M. (1983a). A woman's view of DSM-III. *American Psychologist, 38,* 786–792.

Kaplan, M. (1983b). The issue of sex bias in DSM-III: Comments on the articles by Spitzer, Williams, and Kass. *American Psychologist, 38,* 802–803.

Karabanow, O. (1977). Double-blind controlled study in phobias and obsessions. *Journal of International Medical Research, 5* (Suppl. 5), 42–48.

Karacan, I., Thornby, J. I., Anch, A. M., Booth, G. H., Williams, R. L., & Salis, P. J. (1977). Dose-related sleep disturbances induced by coffee and caffeine. *Clinical Pharmacology and Therapeutics, 20,* 682–689.

Karlen, A. (1984). *Napoleon's glands and other ventures in biohistory.* Boston: Little, Brown.

Karras, A., & Kane, J. M. (1980). Naloxone reduces cigarette smoking. *Life Sciences, 27,* 1541–1545.

Karson, C. N., Kleinman, J. E., & Wyatt, R. J. (1986). Biochemical concepts of schizophrenia. In T. Millon & G. L. Klerman (Eds.), *Contemporary directions in psychopathology: Toward the DSM-IV* (pp. 495–518). New York: Guilford.

Kass, F., Spitzer, R. L., & Williams, J. B. W. (1983). An empirical study of the issue of sex bias in the diagnostic criteria of DSM-III Axis II Personality Disorders. *American Psychologist, 38,* 799–801.

Kaufmann, C. A., Weinberger, D. R., Yolken, R. H., Torrey, E. F., & Potkin, S. G. (1983). Viruses and schizophrenia. *Lancet, 2,* 1136–1337.

Kay, D. C., Blackburn, A. B., Buckingham, J. A., & Karacan, J. (1976). Human pharmacology of sleep. In R. L. Williams & I. Karacan (Eds.), *Pharmacology of sleep* (pp. 83–210). New York: Wiley.

Kaymakçalan, S. (1979). Pharmacological similarities and interactions between cannabis and opioids. In G. G. Nahas & W. D. M. Paton (Eds.), *Marihuana: Biological effects* (pp. 591–604). Oxford: Pergamon Press.

Kazdin, A. E. (Ed.). (1986). Psychotherapy research [Special issue]. *Journal of Consulting and Clinical Psychology, 54*(1).

Kebabian, J. W., Petzold, G. L., & Greengard, P. (1972). Dopamine-sensitive adenylate cyclase in caudate nucleus of rat brain, and its similarity to the "dopamine receptor." *Proceedings of the National Academy of Sciences (U.S.A.), 69,* 2145–2149.

Kelly, D., Guirguis, W., Frommer, E., Mitchell-Heggs, N., & Sargant, W. (1970). Treatment of phobic states with antidepressants: A retrospective study of 246 patients. *British Journal of Psychiatry, 116,* 387–398.

Kelwala, S., Jones, D., & Sitaram, N. (1983). Monoamine metabolites as predictors of antidepressant response: A critique. *Progress in Neuro-Psychopharmacology and Biological Psychiatry, 7,* 229–240.

Kempton, M. (1989). The fate of Paul Robeson. *New York Review of Books, 36*(7), 2–4, 6–7.

Kenardy, J., Evans, L., & Oei, T. P. S. (1988). The importance of cognitions in panic attacks. *Behavior Therapy, 19*, 471–483.

Kendell, R. E. (1976). The classification of depressions: A review of contemporary confusion. *British Journal of Psychiatry, 129*, 15–28.

Kennedy, J. L., Giuffra, L. A., Moises, H. W., Cavalli-Sforza, L. L., Pakstis, A. J., Kidd, J. R., Castiglione, C. M., Sjogren, B., Wetterberg, L., & Kidd, K. K. (1988). Evidence against linkage of schizophrenia to markers on chromosome 5 in a northern Swedish pedigree. *Nature, 336*, 167–170.

Kettl, P. A., & Marks, I. M. (1986). Neurologic factors in obsessive compulsive disorder: Two case reports and a review of the literature. *British Journal of Psychiatry, 149*, 315–319.

Kety, S. S. (1967). Summary. The hypothetical relationships between amines and mental illness; A critical synthesis. In H. E. Himwich, S. S. Kety, & J. R. Smythies (Eds.), Amines and schizophrenia (pp. 271–277). Oxford: Oxford University Press.

Kety, S. S. (1970). Neurochemical aspects of emotional behavior. In P. Black (Ed.), *Physiological correlates of emotion* (pp. 61–71). New York: Academic Press.

Kety, S. S. (1974). From rationalization to reason. *American Journal of Psychiatry, 131*, 957–963.

Kety, S., (1979). Disorders of the human brain. *Scientific American, 241*(3), 202–214.

Kety, S. S., Rosenthal, D., Wender, P. H., & Schulsinger, F. (1968) The types and prevalence of mental illness in the biological and adoptive families of adopted schizophrenics. In D. Rosenthal & S. S. Kety (Eds.), *The transmission of schizophrenia* (pp. 345–362). New York: Pergamon.

Kety, S. S., Rowland, L. P., Sidman, R. L., & Matthysse, S. W. (Eds.) (1983). Genetics of neurological and psychiatric disorders. New York: Raven.

Khachaturian, H., Lewis, M. E., Schäfer, M. K.-H., & Watson, S. J. (1985). Anatomy of the CNS opioid systems. *Trends in Neuroscience, 8*, 111–119.

Kiesler, C. A., & Morton, T. L. (1988a). Prospective payment system for impatient psychiatry: The advantages of controversy. *American Psychologist, 43*, 141–150.

Kiesler, C. A., & Morton, T. L. (1988b). Psychology and public policy in the "health care revolution." *American Psychologist, 43*, 993–1003.

Kiloh, L. G. (1982). Electroconvulsive therapy. In E. S. Paykel (Ed.), *Handbook of affective disorders* (pp. 262–275). New York: Guilford.

Kiloh, L. G., & Garside, R. F. (1963). The independence of neurotic depression and endogenous depression. *British Journal of Psychiatry, 109*, 451–463.

Kingsbury, S. J. (1987). Cognitive differences between clinical psychologists and psychiatrists. *American Psychologist, 42*, 152–156.

Kinney, D. K., & Jacobsen, B. (1978). Environmental factors in schizophrenia: New adoption study evidence. In L. C. Wynne, R. L. Cromwell, & S. Matthysse (Ed.s). *The nature of schizophrenia: New approaches to research and treatment* (pp. 38–51). New York: Wiley.

Kinsbourne, M. (1974). Mechanisms of hemispheric interaction in man. In M. Kinsbourne & W. L. Smith (Eds.), *Hemispheric disconnection and cerebral function* (pp. 260–285). Springfield, IL: Charles C. Thomas.

Kirkegaard, C. (1981). The thyrotropin response to thyrotropin-releasing hormone in endogenous depression. *Psychoneuroendocrinology, 6*, 189–212.

Klatsky, A. L., Friedman, G. D., Siegelaub, A. B., & Gérard, M. (1977). Alcohol consumption and blood pressure. Kaiser-Permanente multiphasic health examination data. *New England Journal of Medicine, 296*, 1194–1200.

Klawans, H. L. (1973). The pharmacology of tardive dyskinesia. *American Journal of Psychiatry, 130,* 82–86.

Klein, D. F. (1964). Delineation of two drug-responsive anxiety syndromes. *Psychopharmacologia, 5,* 397–408.

Klein, D. F. (1967). Importance of psychiatric diagnosis in prediction of clinical drug effects. *Archives of General Psychiatry, 16,* 118–126.

Klein, D. F. (1974). Endogenomorphic depression: A conceptual and terminological revision. *Archives of General Psychiatry, 31,* 447–454.

Klein, D. F., & Davis, J. M. (1969). *Diagnosis and drug treatment of psychiatric disorders.* Baltimore: Williams & Wilkins.

Klein, D. F., & Fink, M. (1962). Psychiatric reaction patterns to imipramine. *American Journal of Psychiatry, 119,* 432–438.

Klein, D. F., Gittelman, R., Quitkin, F., & Rifkin, A. (1980). *Diagnosis and drug treatment of psychiatric disorders: Adults and children* (2nd ed.). Baltimore: Williams & Wilkins.

Klein, D. F., & Rosen, B. (1973). Premorbid asocial adjustment and response to phenothiazine treatment among schizophrenic inpatients. *Archives of General Psychiatry, 29,* 480–485.

Klein, D. F., Zitrin, C. M., & Woerner, M. C. (1978). Antidepressants, anxiety, panic, and phobia. In M. A. Lipton, A. DiMascio, & K. F. Killam (Eds.), *Psychopharmacology: A generation of progress* (pp. 1401–1410). New York: Raven.

Klerman, G. L. (1975). Overview of depression. In A. M. Freedman, H. I. Kaplan, & B. J. Sadock (Eds.), *Comprehensive textbook of psychiatry-II* (2nd ed., vol. 1, pp. 1003–1012). Baltimore: Williams & Wilkins.

Klerman, G. L. (1978). Long-term treatment of affective disorders. In M. A. Lipton, A. DiMascio, & K. F. Killam (Eds.), *Psychopharmacology: A generation of progress* (pp. 1303–1311). New York: Raven.

Klerman, G. L., & Schechter, G. (1982). Drugs and psychotherapy. In E. S. Paykel (Ed.), *Handbook of affective disorders* (pp. 329–337). New York: Guilford.

Knapp, S., & Vandecreek, L. (1981). Behavioral medicine: Its malpractice risks for psychologists. *Professional Psychology, 12,* 677–683.

Knott, V. J., & Venables, P. H. (1977). EEG alpha correlates of non-smokers, smokers, smoking, and smoking deprivation. *Psychophysiology, 14,* 150–156.

Ko, G. N., Elsworth, J. D., Roth, R. H., Rifkin, B. G., Leigh, H., & Redmond, D. E. (1983). Panic-induced elevation of plasma MHPG levels in phobic-anxious patients: Effects of clonidine and imipramine. *Archives of General Psychiatry, 40,* 425–430.

Kocsis, J. (1981). Somatic treatment for depression. In J. F. Clarkin & H. I. Glazer (Eds.), *Depression: Behavioral and directive intervention strategies* (pp. 295–307). New York: Garland STPM Press.

Kohen, W., & Paul, G. L. (1976). Current trends and recommended changes in extended-care placement of mental patients: The Illinois system as a case in point. *Schizophrenia Bulletin, 2,* 575–594.

Koob, G. F., & Bloom, F. E. (1983). Behavioural effects of opioid peptides. *British Medical Bulletin, 39,* 89–94.

Korsten, M. A., & Lieber, C. S. (1985). Medical complications of alcoholism. In J. H. Mendelson & N. K. Mello (Eds.), *The diagnosis and treatment of alcoholism* (2nd ed., pp. 21–64). New York: McGraw-Hill.

Koslow, S. H. (1977). Biosignificance of *N*- and *O*-methylated indoles to psychiatric disorders. In E. Usdin, D. A. Hamburg, & J. D. Barchas (Eds.), *Neuroregulators and psychiatric disorders* (pp. 210–219). New York: Oxford University Press.

Koslow, S. H., Maas, J. W., Bowden, C. L., Davis, J. M., Hanin, I., & Javaid, J. (1983). CSF and urinary biogenic amines and metabolites in depression and mania: A controlled, univariate analysis. *Archives of General Psychiatry, 40,* 999–1010.

Kraepelin, E. (1902). *Clinical psychiatry: A textbook for students and physicians* (6th ed., A. R. Defendorf, Trans.). New York: Macmillan. (Original work published 1899)

Kraepelin, E. (1921). *Manic-depressive insanity and paranoia* (R. M. Barclay, Trans.). Edinburgh: E. & S. Livingstone.

Kraepelin, E. (1971). *Dementia praecox and paraphrenia* (R. M. Barclay, Trans.). Huntington, NY: Robert E. Krieger Publishing. (Original work published 1919)

Kuhn, R. (1958). The treatment of depressive states with G 22355 (imipramine hydrochloride). *American Journal of Psychiatry, 115,* 459–464.

Kupfer, D. J., & Foster, F. G. (1972). Interval between onset of sleep and rapid-eye-movement sleep as an indicator of depression. *Lancet, 2,* 684–686.

Kuriansky, J. B., Deming, W. E., & Gurland, B. J. (1974). On trends in the diagnosis of schizophrenia. *Archives of General Psychiatry, 131,* 402–408.

Kwentus, J., & Major, L. F. (1979). Disulfiram in the treatment of alcoholism: A review. *Journal of Studies on Alcohol, 40,* 428–446.

Lader, M. H. (1978). Current psychophysiological theories of anxiety. In M. A. Lipton, A. DiMascio, & K. F. Killam (Eds.), *Psychopharmacology: A generation of progress* (pp. 1375–1380). New York: Raven.

Lader, M. H. (1980). The psychophysiology of anxiety. In H. M. van Praag (Ed.), *Handbook of biological psychiatry: Part II. Brain mechanisms and abnormal behavior–Psychophysiology* (pp. 225–247). New York: Marcel Dekker.

Lader, M. H. (1983). Anxiety and depression. In A. Gale & J. A. Edwards (Eds.), *Physiological correlates of human behaviour: Individual differences and psychopathology* (Vol. 3, pp. 155–167). New York: Academic Press.

Lader, M. H., & Wing, L. (1966). *Physiological measures, sedative drugs, and morbid anxiety.* London: Oxford University Press.

Lader, M. H., & Wing, L. (1969). Physiological measures in agitated and retarded depressed patients. *Journal of Psychiatric Research, 7,* 89–100.

Laing, R. D. (1969). *The divided self.* New York: Pantheon Books.

Landau, S. G., Buchsbaum, M. S., Carpenter, W., Strauss, J., & Sacks, M. (1975). Schizophrenia and stimulus intensity control. *Archives of General Psychiatry, 32,* 1239–1245.

Landers, S. (1986). DSM by APA? *APA Monitor, 17*(11), 7.

Langer, S. Z. (1977). Presynaptic receptors and their role in the regulation of transmitter release. *British Journal of Pharmacology, 60,* 481–497.

Langer, S. Z. (1980). Presynaptic receptors and modulation of neurotransmission: Pharmacological implications of therapeutic relevance. *Trends in Neuroscience, 3,* 110–112.

Langer, S. Z., & Arbilla, S. (1984). The amphetamine paradox in dopaminergic neurotransmission. *Trends in Pharmacological Science, 5,* 387–390.

Laplane, D., Baulac, M., Widlöcher, D., & Dubois, B. (1984). Pure psychic akinesia with bilateral lesions of basal ganglia. *Journal of Neurology, Neurosurgery, and Psychiatry, 47,* 377–385.

Lawson, D. M. (1983). Alcoholism. In M. Hersen (Ed.), *Outpatient behavior therapy: A clinical guide* (pp. 143–172). New York: Grune & Stratton.

Lazarus, R. S. (1982). Thoughts on the relations between emotion and cognition. *American Psychologist, 37,* 1019–1024.

Lazarus, R. S. (1984). On the primacy of cognition. *American Psychologist, 39,* 124–129.

Lee, T., & Seeman, P. (1980). Elevation of brain neuroleptic/dopamine receptors in schizophrenia. *American Journal of Psychiatry, 137,* 191–197.

Leff, J., & Vaughn, C. (1985). *Expressed emotion in families: Its significance for mental illness.* New York: Guilford.

Lelliott, P. T., Marks, I. M., Monteiro, W. O., Tsakiris, F., & Noshirvani, H. (1987). Agoraphobics 5 years after imipramine and exposure: Outcome and predictors. *Journal of Nervous and Mental Disease, 175,* 599–605.

Leonhard, K., Kroff, I., & Schultz, H. (1982). Temperaments in the families of monopolar and bipolar phasic psychoses. *Psychiatria et Neurologia, 143,* 416–434.

Lester, B. M. (1985). Introduction: There's more to crying than meets the ear. In B. M. Lester & C. F. Z. Boukydis, *Infant crying: Theoretical and research perspectives* (pp. 1–27). New York: Plenum.

Lester, B. M., & Zeskind, P. S. (1978). Brazelton scale and physical size correlates of neonatal cry features. *Infant Behavior and Development, 1,* 393–402.

Lester, B. M., & Zeskind, P. S. (1979). The organization and assessment of crying in the infant at risk. In T. M. Field, A. M. Sostek, S. Goldberg, & H. H. Shuman (Eds.), *Infants born at risk: Behavior and development* (pp. 121–144). New York: Spectrum.

Levi, L. (1967). Effect of coffee on the function of the sympatho-adrenomedullary system in man. *Acta Medica Scandinavica, 181,* 431–438.

Levison, P. K. (1981). Discussion: An analysis of commonalities in substance abuse and habitual behavior. In T. Thompson & C. E. Johanson (Eds.), *Behavioral Pharmacology of human drug dependence* (Research Monograph No. 37) (pp. 27–41). Rockville, MD: National Institute on Drug Abuse.

Levitt, E. E. (1980). *The psychology of anxiety* (2nd ed.). Hillsdale, NJ: Lawrence Erlbaum.

Lewontin, R. C., Rose, S., & Kamin, L. J. (1984). *Not in our genes; Biology, ideology, and human nature.* New York: Pantheon.

Ley, R. (1985a). Agoraphobia, the panic attack, and the hyperventilation syndrome. *Behaviour Research and Therapy, 23,* 79–81.

Ley, R. (1985b). Blood, breath, and fears: A hyperventilation theory of panic attacks and agoraphobia. *Clinical Psychology Review, 5,* 271–285.

Ley, R. (1987). Panic disorder and agoraphobia: Fear of fear or fear of the symptoms produced by hyperventilation? *Journal of Behavior Therapy and Experimental Psychiatry, 18,* 305–316.

Licht, F. (1979). *Goya: The origins of the modern temper in art.* New York: Universe Books.

Lieber, C. S., & DeCarli, L. M. (1970). Hepatic microsomal ethanol-oxidizing system: In vitro characteristics and adaptive properties in vivo. *Journal of Biological Chemistry, 245,* 2505–2512.

Lieber, C. S., & DeCarli, L. M. (1972). The role of hepatic microsomal ethanol oxidizing system (MEOS) for ethanol metabolism in vivo. *Journal of Pharmacology and Experimental Therapeutics, 181,* 279–287.

Lieberman, R. P., & Davis, J. (1975). Drugs and behavior analysis. In M. Hersen, R. M. Eisler, & P. M. Miller (Eds.), *Progress in behavior modification* (Vol. 1, pp. 307–330). New York: Academic Press.

Lieberman, S. (1986). Books reconsidered [Review of *Psychotherapy by reciprocal inhibition*]. *British Journal of Psychiatry, 149,* 518–519.

Liebowitz, M. R., Fyer, A. J., Gorman, J. M., Dillon, D., Appelby, I. L., Levy, G., Anderson, S., Levitt, M., Palij, M., Davies, S. O., & Klein, D. F. (1984). Lactate provocation of panic attacks: I. Clinical and behavioral findings. *Archives of General Psychiatry, 41,* 764–770.

Liebowitz, M. R., Quitkin, F. M., Stewart, J. W., McGrath, P. J., Harrison, W., Rabkin, J., Tricamo, E., Markowitz, J. S., & Klein, D. F. (1984). Phenelzine *v* imipramine in atypical depression: A preliminary report. *Archives of General Psychiatry, 41,* 669–677.

Lindvall, O., & Björklund, A. (1974). The organization of the ascending catecholamine neuron systems in the rat brain as revealed by glyoxylic acid fluorescence method. *Acta Physiologica Scandinavica Supplementum, 412,* 1–48.

Linehan, M. M. (1987, November). *Suicidal behaviors: Problematic solutions in need of better answers.* Invited address at the convention of the Association for Advancement of Behavior Therapy, Boston.

Link, B., & Dohrenwend, B. P. (1980). Formulation of hypotheses about the true prevalence of demoralization in the United States. In B. P. Dohrenwend, B. S. Dohrenwend, M. S. Gould, B. Link, R. Neugebauer, & R. Wunsch-Hitzig (Eds.), *Mental illness in the United States: Epidemiological estimates* (pp. 114–132). New York: Praeger.

Lipowski, Z. J. (1975). Psychiatry of somatic diseases: Epidemiology, pathogenesis, classification. *Comprehensive Psychiatry, 16,* 105–124.

Lipowski, Z. J. (1988). Linking mental and medical health care: An unfinished task. *Psychosomatics, 29,* 249–253.

Lipsedge, M. S., Hajioff, J., Huggins, P., Napier, L., Pearce, J., Pike, D. J., & Rich, M. (1973). The management of severe agoraphobia: A comparison of iproniazid and systematic desensitization. *Psychopharmacologia, 32,* 67–80.

Lipton, M. A., Breese, G. R., Prange, A. J., Wilson, I. C., & Cooper, B. R. (1976). Behavioral effects of hypothalamic polypeptide hormones in animals and man. In E. J. Sachar (Ed.), *Hormones, behavior, and psychopathology* (pp. 15–29). New York: Raven.

List, S. J., & Seeman, P. (1979). Dopamine agonists reverse the elevated ^{H}-neuroleptic binding in neuroleptic-pretreated rats. *Life Sciences, 24,* 1447–1452.

Littleton, J. M. (1983). Tolerance and physical dependence on alcohol at the level of synaptic membranes: A review. *Journal of the Royal Society of Medicine, 76,* 593–601.

Lloyd, C. (1980). Life events and depressive disorders reviewed. II. Events as precipitating factors. *Archives of General Psychiatry, 37,* 541–548.

Loehlin, J. C. (1977). An analysis of alcohol-related questionnaire items from the National Merit Twin Study. *Annals of the New York Academy of Science, 197,* 117–120.

Loranger, A. W. (1975). X-linkage and manic-depressive illness. *British Journal of Psychiatry, 127,* 482–488.

Lowenstein, I. F. (1982). Glue sniffing: Background features and treatment by aversion methods and group therapy. *Practitioner, 226,* 1113–1116.

Ludwig, A. M. (1975). The psychiatrist as physician. *Journal of the American Medical Association, 234,* 603–604.

Lukas, J. H., & Siegel, J. (1977). Cortical mechanisms that augment or reduce evoked potentials in cats. *Science, 198,* 73–75.

Luria, A. R. (1973). *The working brain: An introduction to neuropsychology.* (B. Haigh, Trans.). New York: Basic Books.

Lyon, L. J., & Antony, J. (1982). Reversal of alcoholic coma by naloxone. *Annals of Internal Medicine, 96,* 464–465.

Maas, J. W. (1975). Biogenic amines and depression: Biochemical and pharmacological separation of two types of depression. *Archives of General Psychiatry, 32,* 1357–1361.

Maas, J. W. (1979). Neurotransmitters in depression: Too much, too little or too unstable? *Trends in Neuroscience, 2,* 306–308.

MacDonald, J. B., & MacDonald, E. T. (1977). Nocturnal femoral fracture and continuing widespread use of barbiturate hypnotics. *British Medical Journal, 2,* 483–485.

MacDonald, N. (1960). Living with schizophrenia. *Canadian Medical Association Journal, 82,* 218–221.

Mackay, A. V. P. (1980). Positive and negative schizophrenic symptoms and the role of dopamine. *British Journal of Psychiatry, 137,* 379–386.

Mackay, A. V. P., Iversen, L. L., Rossor, M., Spokes, E., Bird, E., Arregui, A., Creese, I., & Snyder, S. H. (1982). Increased brain dopamine and dopamine receptors in schizophrenia. *Archives of General Psychiatry, 39*, 991–997.

Mackenzie, A. I. (1979). Naloxone in alcohol intoxication. *Lancet, 1*, 733–734.

MacMillan, V., & Siesjo, B. K. (1973). The influence of hypocapnia upon intracellular pH and upon some carbohydrate substrates, amino acids, and organic phosphates in the brain. *Journal of Neurochemistry, 21*, 1283–1299.

Magarian, G. J. (1982). Hyperventilation syndromes: Infrequently recognized common expressions of anxiety and stress. *Medicine, 61*, 219–236.

Magaro, P. A. (1980). *Cognition in schizophrenia and paranoia: The integration of cognitive processes. Hillsdale, NJ: Lawrence Erlbaum.*

Magaro, P. A. (1984). Schizophrenia. In S. M. Turner & M. Hersen (Eds.), Adult psychopathology and diagnosis (pp. 140–183). New York: Wiley.*

Mahoney, M. J. (1976). *Scientist as subject: The psychological imperative.* Cambridge, MA: Ballinger.

Mangan, G. L., & Golding, J. F. (1983). The effects of smoking on memory consolidation. *Journal of Psychology, 115*, 65–77.

Marchione, K. E., Michelson, L., Greenwald, M., & Dancu, C. (1987). Cognitive behavioral treatment of agoraphobia. *Behaviour Research and Therapy, 25*, 319–328.

Margraf, J., Ehlers, A., & Roth, W. T. (1987). Panic attack associated with perceived heart rate acceleration: A case report. *Behavior Therapy, 18*, 84–89.

Margraf, J., Ehlers, A., Roth, W. T., Taylor, C. B., & Maddock, R. J. (1985). Lactate panic provocation in panic patients and controls: Reactivity vs. baseline differences? *Psychosomatic Medicine, 47*, 88–89. (Abstract)

Marks, I. M. (1987). *Fears, phobias, and rituals: Panic, anxiety, and their disorders.* New York: Oxford University Press.

Marks, I. M., Gray, S., Cohen, D., Hill, R., Mawson, D., Ramm, E., & Stern, R. S. (1983). Imipramine and brief therapist-aided exposure in agoraphobics having self-exposure homework. *Archives of General Psychiatry, 40*, 153–162.

Marks, I. M., Stern, R. S., Mawson, D., Cobb, J., & McDonald, R. (1980). Clomipramine and exposure for obsessive-compulsive rituals. *British Journal of Psychiatry, 136*, 1–25.

Marlatt, G. A. (1985). Relapse prevention: Theoretical rationale and overview of the model. In G. A. Marlatt & J. R. Gordon (Eds.), *Relapse prevention: Maintenance strategies in the treatment of addictive behaviors* (pp. 3–70). New York: Guilford.

Marlatt, G. A., & Gordon, J. R. (1980). Determinants of relapse: Implications for the maintenance of behavior change. In P. O. Davidson & S. M. Davidson (Eds.), *Behavioral medicine: Changing health lifestyles* (pp. 410–452). New York: Brunner/Mazel.

Marshall, W. L., & Segal, Z. (1986). Phobia and anxiety. In M. Hersen (Ed.), Pharmacological and behavioral treatment: An integrative approach (pp. 260–288). New York: Wiley.

Martin, I. (1961). Somatic reactivity: Methodology. In H. J. Eysenck (Ed.), *Handbook of abnormal psychology* (2nd ed., pp. 417–456). San Diego: R. R. Knapp.

Martin, J. B., & Reichlin, S. (1987). *Clinical neuroendocrinology.* Philadelphia: F. A. Davis.

Martin, J. L., & Vance, C. S. (1984). Behavioral and psychosocial factors in AIDS: Methodological and substantive issues. *American Psychologist, 39*, 1303–1308.

Martin, W. R., Haertzen, C. A., & Hewett, B. B. (1978). Psychopathology and pathophysiology of narcotic addicts, alcoholics and drug abusers. In M. A. Lipton, A. DiMascio, & K. F. Killam (Eds.), *Psychopharmacology: A generation of progress* (pp. 1591–1602). New York: Raven.

Mason, J. W. (1975a). A historical view of the stress field: Part I. *Journal of Human Stress,* 1(1), 6–12.

Mason, J. W. (1975b). A historical view of the stress field: Part II. *Journal of Human Stress,* 1(2), 22–36.

Mathew, R. J., Largen, J., & Claghorn, J. L. (1979). Biological symptoms of depression. *Psychosomatic Medicine, 41,* 439–443.

Mathew, R. J., Meyer, J. S., Semchuk, K. M., Francis, D. M., Mortel, K., & Claghorn, J. L. (1980). Cerebral blood flow in depression. *Lancet, 1,* 1308.

Mavissakalian, M., & Michelson, L. (1983). Self-directed in vivo exposure practice in behavioral and pharmacological treatments of agoraphobia. *Behavior Therapy, 14,* 506–519.

Mavissakalian, M., & Michelson, L. (1986). Agoraphobia: Relative and combined effectiveness of therapist-assisted *in vivo* exposure and imipramine. *Journal of Clinical Psychiatry, 47,* 117–122.

Mavissakalian, M., Turner, S. M., & Michelson, L. (1985). Future directions in the assessment and treatment of obsessive-compulsive disorder. In M. Mavissakalian, S. M. Turner, & L. Michelson (Eds.), *Obsessive-compulsive disorder: Psychological and pharmacological treatment* (pp. 213–248). New York: Plenum.

Mawson, D., Marks, I. M., & Ramm, L. (1982). Clomipramine and exposure for chronic obsessive-compulsive rituals: III. Two year follow-up and further readings. *British Journal of Psychiatry, 140,* 11–18.

Maxmen, J. S. (1986). *Essential psychopathology.* New York: W. W. Norton.

McCaffrey, R. J., & Blanchard, E. B. (1985). Stress management approaches to the treatment of essential hypertension. *Annals of Behavioral Medicine, 7,* 5–12.

McCall, R. B. (1981). Nature-nurture and the two realms of development: A proposed integration with respect to mental development. *Child Development, 52,* 1–12.

McCarley, R. W. (1982). REM sleep and depression: Common neurobiological control mechanisms. *American Journal of Psychiatry, 139,* 565–570.

McCarley, R. W., & Hobson, J. A. (1975). Neuronal excitability modulation over the sleep cycle: A structural and mathematical model. *Science, 189,* 58–60.

McClelland, H. A. (1986). Psychiatric reactions to psychotropic drugs. *Adverse Drug Reaction Bulletin, 119,* 444–447.

McCrae, R. R., & Costa, P. T. (1986). Clinical assessment can benefit from recent advances in personality psychology. *American Psychologist, 11,* 1001–1003.

McFarlane, A. H., Norman, G. R., Streiner, D. L., & Roy, R. G. (1983). The process of social stress: Stable, reciprocal, and mediating relationships. *Journal of Health and Social Behavior, 24,* 160–173.

McGhie, A. & Chapman, J. S. (1961). Disorders of attention and perception in early schizophrenia. *British Journal of Medical Psychology, 34,* 103–116.

McGuffin, P., Farmer, A., & Gottesman, I. I. (1987). Is there really a split in schizophrenia? The genetic evidence. *British Journal of Psychiatry, 150,* 581–592.

McGuffin, P., & Mawson, D. (1980). Obsessive-compulsive neurosis: Two identical twin pairs. *British Journal of Psychiatry, 137,* 285–287.

McGuinness, D., & Pribram, K. (1980). The neuropsychology of attention: Emotional and motivational controls. In M. C. Wittrock (Ed.), *The brain and psychology* (pp. 95–139). New York: Academic Press.

McIsaac, W. M., Fritchie, G. E., Idänpään-Heikkilä, J. E., Ho, B. T., & Englert, L. F. (1971). Distribution of marihuana in monkey brain and concomitant behavioural effects. *Nature, 230,* 593–594.

McKusick, V. A. (1969). On lumpers and splitters, or the nosology of genetic disease. Perspectives in Biology and Medicine, 12, 298–312.

McLean, P. D. (1981). Matching treatment to patient characteristics in an outpatient setting. In L. P. Rehm (Ed.), Behavior therapy for depression: Present status and future directions (pp. 197–207). New York: Academic Press.

McLean, P. D., & Hakstian, A. R. (1979). Clinical depression: Comparative efficacy of outpatient treatments. Journal of Consulting and Clinical Psychology, 47, 818–836.

McLemore, C. W., & Benjamin, L. S. (1979). Whatever happened to interpersonal diagnosis?: A psychosocial alternative to DSM-III. American Psychologist, 34, 17–34.

McReynolds, W. T. (1979). DSM-III and the future of applied social science. Professional Psychology, 10, 123–132.

Meakins, J. L., & Christou, N. V. (1979). Defects in host-defense mechanisms. In G. Dick (Ed.), Immunological aspects of infectious diseases (pp. 117–149). Baltimore: University Park.

Meddis, R. (1977). The sleep instinct. London: Routledge & Kegan Paul.

Mednick, S. A., & Schulsinger, F. (1968). Some premorbid characteristics related to breakdown in children with schizophrenic mothers. In D. Rosenthal & S. S. Kety (Eds.), The transmission of schizophrenia (pp. 267–291). New York: Pergamon.

Mednick, S. A., & Schulsinger, F. (1973). A learning theory of schizophrenia: Thirteen years later. In M. Hammer, K. Salzinger, & S. Sutton (Eds.), Psychopathology: Contributions from the social, behavioral, and biological sciences (pp. 343–360). New York: Wiley.

Meehl, P. E. (1962). Schizotaxia, schizotypy, schizophrenia. American Psychologist, 17, 827–838.

Mehr, J. (1983). Abnormal psychology. New York: Holt, Rinehart and Winston.

Meichenbaum , D. (1977). Cognitive-behavior modification: An integrative approach. New York: Plenum.

Meltzer, H. Y. (1979). Biochemical studies in schizophrenia. In L. Bellak (Ed.), Disorders of the schizophrenic syndrome (pp. 45–135). New York: Basic Books.

Meltzer, H. Y. (1980). Relevance of dopamine autoreceptors for psychiatry: Preclinical and clinical studies. Schizophrenia Bulletin, 6, 456–475.

Meltzer, H. Y., & Arora, R. C. (1980). Skeletal muscle MAO activity in the major psychoses: Relationship with platelet and plasma MAO activities. Archives of General Psychiatry, 37, 333–339.

Meltzer, H. Y., Cho, H. W., Carroll, B. J., & Russo, P. (1976). Serum dopamine-β-hydroxylase activity in the affective psychoses and schizophrenia. Archives of General Psychiatry, 33, 585–591.

Meltzer, H. Y., Fang, V. S., Tricou, B. J., Roberston, A., & Piyaka, S. K. (1982). Effect of dexamethasone on plasma prolactin and cortisol levels in psychiatric patients. American Journal of Psychiatry, 139, 763–768.

Meltzer, H. Y., & Stahl, S. M. (1976). The dopamine hypothesis of schizophrenia: A review. Schizophrenia Bulletin, 2, 19–76.

Mendels, J. (1965). Electroconvulsive therapy and depression: II. Significance of endogenous and reactive syndromes. British Journal of Psychiatry, 111, 682–686.

Mendelson, J. H., & Mello, N. K. (1985). Diagnostic criteria for alcoholism and alcohol abuse. In J. H. Mendelson & N. K. Mello (Eds.), The diagnosis and treatment of alcoholism (2nd ed., pp. 1–20). New York: McGraw-Hill.

Mendelson, M. (1974). Psychoanalytic concepts of depression (2nd ed.). Flushing, NY: Spectrum.

Mendlewicz, J., & Fleiss, J. L. (1974). Linkage studies with X-chromosome markers in bipolar (manic-depressive) and unipolar (depressive) illnesses. *Biological Psychiatry, 9,* 261–294.

Mendlewicz, J., Fleiss, J. L., & Fieve, R. R. (1972). Evidence for X-linkage in the transmission of manic-depressive illness. *Journal of the American Medical Association, 222,* 1624–1627.

Mendlewicz, J., & Rainer, J. D. (1977). Adoption study supporting genetic transmission in manic-depressive illness. *Nature, 268,* 327–329. Menninger, K. A. (1926). Influenza and schizophrenia: An analysis of post-influenzal "dementia praecox" as of 1918 and five years later. *American Journal of Psychiatry, 5,* 469–529.

Mered, B., Albrecht, P., Torrey, E. F., Weinberger, D. R., Potkin, S. G., & Winfrey, C. J. (1983). Failure to isolate virus from CSF of schizophrenics. *Lancet, 2,* 919.

Mesulam, M. M. & Geschwind, N. (1978). On the possible role of neocortex and its limbic connections in attention and schizophrenia. In L. C. Wynne, R. L. Cromwell, & S. Matthysse (Eds.), *The nature of schizophrenia* (pp. 161–166). New York: Wiley.

Michelson, L., & Mavissakalian, M. (1985). Psychophysiological outcome of behavioral and pharmacological treatments of agoraphobia. *Journal of Consulting and Clinical Psychology, 53,* 229–236.

Michelson, L., Mavissakalian, M., & Marchione, K. (1988). Cognitive, behavioral, and psychophysiological treatments of agoraphobia: A comparative outcome investigation. *Behavior Therapy, 19,* 97–120.

Milby, J. B. (1981). *Addictive behavior and its treatment.* New York: Springer.

Milby, J. B., Jolly, P. A., & Beidleman, W. B. (1984). Substance abuse: Drugs. In S. M. Turner & M. Hersen (Eds.), *Adult psychopathology and diagnosis* (pp. 105–139). New York: Wiley.

Miller, H. (1972). Psychosurgery and Dr. Breggin. *New Scientist, 55,* 188–190.

Miller, I. W., Norman, W. H., Keitner, G. I., Bishop, S. B., & Dow, M. G. (1989). Cognitive-behavioral treatment of depressed inpatients. *Behavior Therapy, 20,* 25–47.

Miller, L. L. (1979). Cannabis and the brain with special reference to the limbic system. In G. G. Nahas & W. D. M. Paton (Eds.), *Marihuana: Biological effects* (pp. 539–566). Oxford: Pergamon Press.

Miller, L. S., Bergstrom, D. A., Cross, H. J., & Grube, J. W. (1981). Opinions and use of the DSM system by practicing psychologists. *Professional Psychology, 12,* 385–390.

Miller, P. M., & Foy, D. W. (1981). Substance abuse. In S. M. Turner, K. S. Calhoun, & H. E. Adams (Eds.), *Handbook of clinical behavior therapy* (pp. 191–213). New York: Wiley.

Miller, W. R. (1982). Treating problem drinkers: What works? *The Behavior Therapist, 5,* 15–18.

Miller, W. R., & Hester, R. K. (1980). Treating the problem drinker: Modern approaches. In W. R. Miller (Ed.), *The addictive behaviors: Treatment of alcoholism, drug abuse, smoking, & obesity* (pp. 11–141). New York: Pergamon.

Miller, W. R., & Muñoz, R. F. (1976). *How to control your drinking.* Englewood Cliffs, NJ: Prentice-Hall.

Millon, T. (1983). The DSM-III: An insider's perspective. *American Psychologist, 38,* 804–814.

Minke, K. A. (1986, August). Methodological issues in the unification of psychology. In A. W. Staats (Chair), *Unomic psychology: Areas of development in creating a unified science.* Symposium presented at the Convention of the American Psychological Association, Washington, DC.

Mischel, W. (1968). *Personality and assessment.* New York: Wiley.

Mischel, W. (1973). Toward a cognitive social learning reconceptualization of personality. *Psychological Review, 80,* 252–283.

Mischel, W. (1979). On the interface of cognition and personality: Beyond the person–situation debate. *American Psychologist, 34,* 740–754.

Mishra, R., Gillespie, D. P., Youdim, M. B. H., & Sulser, F. (1983). Effect of selective monoamine oxidase inhibition by clorgyline and deprenyl on the norepinephrine receptor-coupled adenylate cyclase system in the rat cortex. *Psychopharmacology, 81,* 220–223.

Möhler, H., & Okada, T. (1977). Benzodiazepine receptor: Demonstration in the central nervous system. *Science, 198,* 849–851.

Monroe, S. M. (1982). Assessment of life events: Retrospective versus concurrent strategies. *Archives of General Psychiatry, 39,* 606–610.

Monroe, S. M., Imhoff, D. F., Wise, B. D., & Harris, J. E. (1983). Prediction of psychological symptoms under high-risk psychosocial circumstances: Life events, social support, and syndrome specificity. *Journal of Abnormal Psychology, 92,* 338–350.

Morris, J. B., & Beck, A. T. (1974). The efficacy of antidepressant drugs: A review of research (1958 to 1972). *Archives of General Psychiatry, 30,* 667–674.

Morrison, C. F., & Armitage, A. K. (1967). Effects of nicotine upon the free operant behavior of rats and spontaneous motor activity of mice. *Annals of the New York Academy of Sciences, 142,* 268–276.

Morrison, R. L., & Bellack, A. S. (Eds.). (1987). *Medical factors and psychological disorders: A handbook for psychologists.* New York: Plenum.

Mullin, M. J., & Ferko, A. P. (1983). Alterations in dopaminergic function after subacute ethanol administration. *Journal of Pharmacology and Experimental Therapeutics, 225,* 694–698.

Murphree, H. B., Pfeiffer, C. C., & Price, L. M. (1967). Electroencephalographic changes in man following smoking. *Annals of the New York Academy of Sciences, 142,* 245–260.

Murphy, D. L., & Buchsbaum, M. S. (1978). Neurotransmitter-related enzymes and psychiatric diagnostic entities. In R. L. Spitzer & D. F. Klein (Eds.), *Critical issues in psychiatric diagnosis* (pp. 305–321). New York: Raven.

Murray, J. B. (1985). Lithium therapy for mania and depression. *Journal of General Psychology, 112,* 5–33.

Murray, R. M., Lewis, S. W., & Reveley, A. M. (1985). Towards an aetiological classification of schizophrenia. *Lancet, 1,* 1023–1026.

Myers, R. D. (1978). Psychopharmacology of alcohol. *Annual Review of Pharmacology and Toxicology, 18,* 125–144.

Nathan, P. E. (1986). Some implications of recent biological findings for the behavioral treatment of alcoholism. *The Behavior Therapist, 9,* 159–161.

Nathan, P. E., & Niaura, R. S. (1985). Behavioral assessment and treatment of alcoholism. In J. H. Mendelson & N. K. Mello (Eds.), *The diagnosis and treatment of alcoholism* (2nd ed., pp. 391–455). New York: McGraw-Hill.

Neale, J. M. & Oltmanns, T. F. (1980). *Schizophrenia.* New York: Wiley.

Nebylitsyn, V. D., & Gray, J. A. (1972). *Biological bases of individual behavior.* New York: Academic Press.

Nelson, J. C., & Charney, D. S. (1981). The symptoms of major depressive illness. *American Journal of Psychiatry, 138,* 1–13.

Nestoros, J. N. (1980). Ethanol selectively potentiates GABA-mediated inhibition of single feline cortical neurons. *Life Sciences, 26,* 519–523.

Newman, G. (1980). Intermittent recurring psychoses. In R. C. W. Hall (Ed.), *Psychiatric presentations of medical illness: Somatopsychic disorders* (pp. 65–73). New York: SP Medical & Scientific Books.

Nezu, A. M., & Ronan, G. (1988). Social problem-solving as a moderator of stress-related depressive symptoms: A prospective analysis. *Journal of Counseling Psychology, 35,* 134–138.

Nicholson, A. N. (1980). Hypnotics: Rebound insomnia and residual sequelae. *British Journal of Clinical Pharmacology, 9,* 223–225.

Niederland, W. G. (1972). Goya's illness: A case of lead encephalopathy? *New York State Journal of Medicine, 72,* 413–418.

Nies, A., & Robinson, D. S. (1982). Monoamine oxidase inhibitors. In E. S. Paykel (Ed.), *Handbook of affective disorders* (pp. 246–261). New York: Guilford.

Nightingale, E. J. (1986). Experience with prospective payment in the Veterans Administration: Its impact on the delivery of mental health services. *American Psychologist, 41,* 70–72.

Noble, P., & Lader, M. (1971a). Salivary secretion and depressive illness: A physiological and psychometric study. *Psychological Medicine, 1,* 372–376.

Noble, P., & Lader, M. (1971b). The symptomatic correlates of the skin conductance changes in depression. *Journal of Psychiatric Research, 9,* 61–69.

North, R. A., & Williams, J. T. (1983). How do opiates inhibit neurotransmitter release? *Trends in Neuroscience, 6,* 337–339.

Noyes, R., Clancy, J., Crowe, R., Hoenk, P. R., & Slymen, D. J. (1978). The familial prevalence of anxiety neurosis. *Archives of General Psychiatry, 35,* 1057–1059.

Noyes, R., Clancy, J., Hoenk, P. R., & Slymen, D. J. (1980). Prognosis of anxiety neurosis. *Archives of General Psychiatry, 37,* 173–178.

O'Connor, D. (1984). *Glue sniffing and volatile substance abuse: Case studies of children and young adults.* Aldershot, Hampshire, England: Gower Publishing.

Oepen, G., Fünfgeld, M., Höll, Zimmermann, P., Landis, T., & Regard, M. (1987). Schizophrenia: An emotional hypersensitivity of the right cerebral hemisphere. *International Journal of Psychophysiology, 5,* 261–264.

O'Gorman, J. G. (1977). Individual differences in habituation of human physiological responses: A review of theory, method, and findings in the study of personality correlates in non-clinical populations. *Biological Psychology, 5,* 257–318.

Ögren, S. O., Fuxe, K., Berge, O. G., & Agnati, L. F. (1983). Effects of chronic administration of antidepressant drugs on central serotonergic receptor mechanisms. In F. Usdin, M. Goldstein, A. J. Friedhoff, & A. Georgotuo (Eds.), *Frontiers in neuropsychiatric research* (pp. 93–108). London: Macmillan.

Okamoto, M. (1978). Barbiturates and alcohol: Comparative overviews on neurophysiology and neurochemistry. In M. A. Lipton, A. DiMascio, & K. F. Killam (Eds.), *Psychopharmacology: A generation of progress* (pp. 1575–1590). New York: Raven.

Okel, B. B., & Hurst, J. W. (1961). Prolonged hyperventilation in man: Associated electrolyte changes and subjective symptoms. *Archives of Internal Medicine, 108,* 757–762.

Oliveau, D., & Willmuth, R. (1979). Facial muscle electromyography in depressed and nondepressed hospitalized subjects: A partial replication. *American Journal of Psychiatry, 136,,* 548–550.

Osmond, H., & Smythies, J. (1952). Schizophrenia: A new approach. *Journal of Mental Science, 98,* 309–315.

Ostwald, P. F., & Murry, T. (1985). The communicative and diagnostic significance of infant sounds. In B. M. Lester & C. F. Z. Boukydis (Eds.), *Infant crying: Theoretical and research perspectives* (pp. 139–158). New York: Plenum.

Owen, F., Crow, T. J., Poulter, M., Cross, A. J., Longden, A., & Riley, G. L. (1978). Increased dopamine-receptor sensitivity in schizophrenia. *Lancet, 2,* 223–226.

Page, I. H. (1954). Serotonin (5-hydroxytryptamine). *Physiological Reviews, 34,* 563–588.

Palmai, G., Blackwell, B., Maxwell, A. E., & Morganstern, F. (1967). Pattern of salivary flow in depressive illness and during treatment. *British Journal of Psychiatry, 113,* 1297–1308.

Parisi, T. (1987). Why Freud failed: Some implications for neurophysiology and sociobiology. *American Psychologist, 42,* 235–245.

Parke, R. D., & Collmer, C. W. (1975). Child abuse: An interdisciplinary analysis. In E. M. Hetherington (Ed.), *Review of child development research* (Vol. 5, pp. 509–590). Chicago: University of Chicago Press.

Parkes, C. M. (1972). *Bereavement: Studies of grief in adult life.* New York: International Universities Press.

Partanen, J., Bruun, K., & Markkanen, T. (1966). *Inheritance of drinking behavior: A study on intelligence, personality, and use of alcohol of adult twins.* Helsinki: Finnish Foundation for Alcohol Studies.

Paterson, S. J., Robson, L. E., & Kosterlitz, H. W. (1983). Classification of opioid receptors. *British Medical Bulletin, 39,* 31–36.

Patterson, T. (1976). Skin conductance responding/nonresponding and pupillometrics in chronic schizophrenia: A confirmation of Gruzelier and Venables. *Journal of Nervous and Mental Disorders, 163,* 200–209.

Pauls, D. L., Bucher, K. D., Crowe, R. R., & Noyes, R. (1980). A genetic study of panic disorder pedigrees. *American Journal of Human Genetics, 32,* 639–644.

Pavlov, I. P. (1928). *Lectures on conditioned reflexes: Twenty-five years of objective study of the higher nervous ability (behaviour) of animals.* (W. H. Gantt, Ed. and Trans.). York, England: Liveright.

Pavlov, I. P. (1960). *Conditioned reflexes: An investigation of the physiological activity of the cerebral cortex* (G. V. Anrep, Ed. and Trans.). New York: Dover. (Original work published 1927)

Paykel, E. S. (1972). Depressive typologies and response to amitriptyline. *British Journal of Psychiatry, 120,* 147–156.

Paykel, E. S., Klerman, G. L., & Prusoff, B. A. (1970). Treatment setting and clinical depression. *Archives of General Psychiatry, 22,* 11–21.

Paykel, E. S., Myers, J. K., Dienelt, M. D., Klerman, G. L., Lindenthal, J. J., & Pepper, M. P. (1969). Life events and depression: A controlled study. *Archives of General Psychiatry, 21,* 753–760.

Paykel, E. S., Prusoff, B., Klerman, G. L. (1971). The endogenous-neurotic continuum in depression: Rater independence and factor distribution. *Journal of Psychiatric Research, 8,* 73–90.

Payne, R. W., Mattussek, P., & George, E. I. (1959). An experimental study of schizophrenic thought disorder. *Journal of Mental Science, 105,* 627–652.

Peachey, J. E., & Naranjo, C. A. (1983). The use of disulfiram and other alcohol-sensitizing drugs in the treatment of alcoholism. *Research Advances in Alcohol and Drug Problems, 7,* 397–431.

Perkins, J. P. (1982). Catecholamine-induced modification of the functional state of β-adrenergic receptors. In J. W. Lamble (Ed.), *More about receptors* (pp. 48–53). New York: Elsevier Biomedical Press.

Perris, C. (1966). A study of bipolar (manic-depressive) and unipolar recurrent depressive psychoses. *Acta Psychiatrica Scandinavica, 42,* (Suppl. 194), 1–189.

Perris, C. (1969). The separation of bipolar (manic-depressive) from unipolar recurrent depressive psychoses. *Behavioral Neuropsychiatry, 1*(8), 17–24.

Perris, C. (1980). Central measures of depression. In H. M. van Praag (Ed.), *Handbook of biological psychiatry. Part II: Brain mechanisms and abnormal behavior—Psychophysiology* (pp. 183–223). New York: Marcel Dekker.

Perris, C. (1982). The distinction between bipolar and unipolar affective disorders. In E. S. Paykel (Ed.), *Handbook of affective disorders* (pp. 45–58). New York: Guilford.

Pert, C. B., & Quirion, R. (1983). The phencyclidine receptor. *Trends in Pharmacological Science, 4,* 12–13.

Peters, T. J. (1983). Aldehyde dehydrogenase and alcoholism. *Lancet, 1,* 364.

Petrie, A. (1960). Some psychological aspects of pain and the relief of suffering. *Annals of the New York Academy of Sciences, 86,* 13–27.

Pétursson, E. (1962). Electromyographic studies of muscular tension in psychiatric patients. *Comprehensive Psychiatry, 3,* 29–36.

Phillips, L. (1953). Case history data and prognosis in schizophrenia. *Journal of Nervous and Mental Disease, 117,* 515–525.

Pi, E. H., & Simpson, G. M. (1987). Anxiety disorders. In R. L. Morrison & A. S. Bellack (Eds.), *Medical factors and psychological disorders: A handbook for psychologists* (pp. 41–60). New York: Plenum.

Pitt, B. (1973). 'Maternity blues.' *British Journal of Psychiatry, 122,* 431–433.

Pitts, F. M., & McClure, J. N. (1967). Lactate metabolism in anxiety neurosis. *New England Journal of Medicine, 277,* 1329–1336.

Plaut, S. M., & Friedman, S. B. (1981). Psychosocial factors in infectious disease. In R. Ader (Ed.), *Psychoneuroimmunology* (pp. 3–30). New York: Academic Press.

Plomin, R. (1989). Environment and genes; Determinants of behavior. *American Psychologist, 44,* 105–111.

Plomin, R., DeFries, J. C., & Loehlin, J. C. (1977). Genotype–environment interaction and correlation in the analysis of human behavior. *Psychological Bulletin, 84,* 309–322.

Plomin, R., DeFries, J. C., & McClearn, G. E. (1980). *Behavioral genetics: A primer.* San Francisco: W. H. Freeman.

Pomerleau, O. F., Fertig, J. B., Seyler, L. E., & Jaffe, J. (1983). Neuroendocrine reactivity to nicotine in smokers. *Psychopharmacology, 81,* 61–67.

Pomerleau, O. F., Turk, D. C., & Fertig, J. B. (1984). The effects of smoking on pain and anxiety. *Addictive Behaviors, 9,* 265–271.

Post, R. M., Fink, E., Carpenter, W. T., & Goodwin, F. K. (1975). Cerebrospinal fluid amine metabolites in acute schizophrenia. *Archives of General Psychiatry, 32,* 1063–1069.

Potkin, S. G., Cannon, E., Murphy, D. L., & Wyatt, R. J. (1978). Are paranoid schizophrenics biologically different from other schizophrenics? *New England Journal of Medicine, 298,* 61–66.

Prechtl, H., & Beintema, D. (1964). *The neurological examination of the full-term newborn infant* (Little Club Clinics in Developmental Medicine No. 12). London: William Heineman.

Prien, R. F., Caffey, E. M., & Klett, C. J. (1972). Comparison of lithium carbonate and chlorpromazine in the treatment of mania. *Archives of General Psychiatry, 26,* 146–153.

Quay, H. C. (1986). A critical analysis of DSM-III as a taxonomy of psychopathology in childhood and adolescence. In T. Millon & G. L. Klerman (Eds.), *Contemporary directions in psychopathology: Toward the DSM-IV* (pp. 151–165). New York: Guilford.

Rabkin, J. G., & Struening, E. L. (1976). Life events, stress, and illness. *Science, 194,* 1013–1020.

Racagini, G., and Brunello, N. (1984). Transynaptic mechanisms in the action of antidepressant drugs. *Trends in Pharmacological Science, 5,* 527–531.

Rachman, S. J., & Hodgson, R. (1974). I. Synchrony and desynchrony in fear and avoidance. *Behaviour Research and Therapy, 12,* 311–318.

Rachman, S. J., & Wilson, G. T. (1980). *The effects of psychological therapy.* New York: Pergamon.

Rado, S. (1956). *Psychoanalysis of behavior.* New York: Grune & Stratton.

Rado, S., & Daniels, G. E. (1956). *Changing concepts of psychoanalytic medicine.* New York: Grune & Stratton.

Rainey, J. M., Pohl, R. B., Williams, M., Knitter, E., Freedman, R. R., & Ettedgui, E. (1984). A comparison of lactate and isoproterenol anxiety states. *Psychopathology, 17*(Suppl. 1), 74–82.

Rall, T. W. (1985). Central nervous system stimulants: The methylxanthines. In A. G. Gilman, L. S. Goodman, T. W. Rall, & F. Murad (Eds.), *The pharmacological basis of therapeutics* (7th ed., pp. 589–603). New York: Macmillan.

Ramey, C. T., Hieger, L., & Klisz, D. (1972). Synchronous reinforcement of vocal responses in failure-to-thrive infants. *Child Development, 43,* 1449–1455.

Randall, P. L. (1980). A neuroanatomical theory on the aetiology of schizophrenia. *Medical Hypotheses, 6,* 645–658.

Rapee, R. M. (1985). A case of panic disorder treated with breathing retraining. *Journal of Behavior Therapy and Experimental Psychiatry, 16,* 63–65.

Rapee, R. M. (1986). Differential response to hyperventilation in panic disorder and generalized anxiety disorder. *Journal of Abnormal Psychology, 95,* 24–28.

Raskin, A., & Crook, T. H. (1976). The endogenous–neurotic distinction as a predictor of response to antidepressant drugs. *Psychological Medicine, 6,* 59–70.

Redmond, D. E. (1977). Alterations in the function of the nucleus locus coeruleus: A possible model for studies of anxiety. In E. Usdin & I. Hanin (Eds.), *Animal models in psychiatry and neurology* (pp. 293–306). New York: Pergamon.

Redmond, D. E. (1979). New and old evidence for the involvement of a brain norepinephrine system in anxiety. In W. E. Fann, I. Karacan, A. Pokorny, et al., (Eds.), *Phenomenology and the treatment of anxiety* (pp. 152–203). New York: SP Medical and Scientific Books.

Redmond, D. E., & Huang, Y. H. (1979). New evidence for a locus coeruleus–norepinephrine connection with anxiety. *Life Sciences, 25,* 2149–2162.

Redmond, D. E., Huang, Y. H., Snyder, D. R., & Maas, J. W. (1976). Behavioral effects of stimulation of the nucleus locus coeruleus in the stump-tailed monkey *Macaca arctoides). Brain Research, 116,* 502–510.

Rehm, L. P. (1981). (Ed.). *Behavior therapy for depression: Present status and future directions.* New York: Academic Press.

Reider, R. O., & Gershon, E. S. (1978). Genetic strategies in biological psychiatry. *Archives of General Psychiatry, 35,* 866–873.

Reich, T., Clayton, P. J., & Winokur, G. (1969). Family history studies: V. The genetics of mania. *American Journal of Psychiatry, 125,* 1358–1369.

Reimann, H. A. (1967). Caffeinism: A case of long-continued, low-grade fever. *Journal of the American Medical Association, 202,* 1105–1106.

Reis, D. J., Fink, J. S., & Baker, H. (1983). Genetic control of the number of dopamine neurons in the brain: Relationship to behavior and responses to psychoactive drugs. In S. S. Kety, L. P. Rowland, R. L. Sidman, & S. W. Matthysse (Eds.), Genetics of neurological and psychiatric disorders (pp. 55–75). New York: Raven.

Reveley, M. A., Glover, V., Sandler, M., & Spokes, E. G. (1981). Brain monoamine oxidase activity in schizophrenics and controls. *Archives of General Psychiatry, 38,* 663–665.

Reznick, J. S., Kagan, J., Snidman, N., Gersten, M., Baak, K., & Rosenberg, A. (1986). Inhibited and uninhibited children: A follow-up study. *Child Development, 57,* 660–680.

Richards, C. D. (1972). On the mechanism of barbiturate anaesthesia. *Journal of Physiology, 227,* 749–767.

Rimón, R., Roos, B. E., Räkköläinen, V., & Alanen, Y. (1971). The content of 5–

hydroxyindoleacetic acid and homovanillic acid in the cerebrospinal fluid of patients with acute schizophrenia. *Journal of Psychosomatic Research, 15,* 375–378.

Rimón, R., Sternbäck, A., & Huhmar, E. (1966). Electromyographic findings in depressed patients. *Journal of Psychosomatic Research, 10,* 159–170.

Risch, S. C., Cohen, R. M., Janowsky, D. S., Kalin, N. H., & Murphy, D. L. (1980). Mood and behavioral effects of physostigmine on humans are accompanied by elevations in plasma β-endorphin and cortisol. *Science, 209,* 1545–1546.

Ritchie, J. M. (1985). The aliphatic alcohols. In A. G. Gilman, L. S. Goodman, T. W. Rall, & F. Murad (Eds.), *The pharmacological basis of therapeutics* (7th ed., pp. 372–386). New York: Macmillan.

Ritchie, J. M., & Greene, N. M. (1985). Local anaesthetics. In A. G. Gilman, L. S. Goodman, T. W. Rall, & F. Murad (Eds.), *The pharmacological basis of therapeutics* (7th ed., pp. 302–321). New York: Macmillan.

Robbins, E., & Guze, S. B. (1972). Classification of affective disorders: The primary–secondary, the endogenous–reactive, and the neurotic–psychotic concepts. In T. A. Williams, M. M. Katz, & J. A. Shield (Eds.), *Recent advances in the psychobiology of the depressive illnesses* (DHEW Publication No. HSM 70–9053, pp. 283–293). Washington, DC: U.S. Government Printing Office.

Roberts, E. (1975). GABA in nervous system function–an overview. In R. O. Brady (Ed.), *The nervous system. Vol. I: The basic neurosciences* (pp. 541–552). New York: Raven.

Roberts, E. (1977). The γ-aminobutyric acid system and schizophrenia. In E. Usdin, D. A. Hamburg, & J. D. Barchas (Eds.), *Neuroregulators and psychiatric disorders* (pp. 347–357). New York: Oxford University Press.

Robertson, D., Frölich, J. C., Carr, R. K., Watson, J. T., Hollifield, J. W., Shand, D. G., & Oates, J. A. (1978). Effects of caffeine on plasma renin activity, catecholamines and blood pressure. *New England Journal of Medicine, 298,* 181–186.

Roebuck, J. B., & Kessler, R. G. (1972). *The etiology of alcoholism: Constitutional, psychological, and sociological approaches.* Springfield, IL: Charles C. Thomas.

Rogers, C. R. (1951). *Client-centered therapy: It's current practice, implications, and theory.* New York: Houghton Mifflin.

Rogers, H., & Spector, R. (1980). *Aids to pharmacology.* New York: Churchill Livingstone.

Rosenthal, D. (1970). *Genetic theory and abnormal behavior.* New York: McGraw-Hill.

Rosenthal, D., Wender, P.H., Kety, S. S., Schulsinger, F., Welner, J., & Østergaard, L. (1968). Schizophrenics' offspring reared in adoptive homes. *Journal of Psychiatric Research, 6*(Suppl. 1), 377–391.

Rosenthal, D., Wender, P. H., Kety, S. S., Welner, J., & Schulsinger, F. (1971). The adopted-away offspring of schizophrenics. *American Journal of Psychiatry, 128,* 307–311.

Rosenthal, N. E., Sack, D. A., Carpenter, C. J., Parry, B. L., Mendelson, W. B., & Wehr, T. A. (1985). Antidepressant effects of light in seasonal affective disorder. *American Journal of Psychiatry, 142,* 163–170.

Rosenthal, R., & Bigelow, L. B. (1972). Quantitative brain measurements in chronic schizophrenia. *British Journal of Psychiatry, 121,* 259–264.

Rosenthal, S. H., & Klerman, G. L. (1966). Content and consistency in the endogenous depressive pattern. *British Journal of Psychiatry, 112,* 471–484.

Ross, A. O. (1980). *Psychological disorders of children: A behavioral approach to theory, research, and therapy* (2nd ed.). New York: McGraw-Hill.

Rothblum, E. D., Solomon, L. J., & Albee, G. W. (1986). A sociopolitical perspective of DSM-III. In T. Millon & G. L. Klerman (Eds.), *Contemporary directions in psychopathology* (pp. 167–189). New York: Guilford.

Rowe, D. C. (1987). Resolving the person–situation debate: Invitation to an interdisciplinary dialogue. *American Psychologist, 42,* 218–227.

Roy-Byrne, P. P., Uhde, T. W., & Post, R. M. (1986). Effects of one night's sleep deprivation on mood and behavior in panic disorder. *Archives of General Psychiatry, 43,* 895–899.

Rubens, R. L., & Lapidus, L. B. (1978). Schizophrenic patterns of arousal and stimulus barrier functioning. *Journal of Abnormal Psychology, 78,* 199–211.

Rush, A. J., Hollon, S. D., Beck, A. T., & Kovacs, M. (1978). Depression: Must pharmacotherapy fail for cognitive therapy to succeed? *Cognitive Therapy and Research, 2,* 199–206.

Rush, A. J., Schlesser, M. A., Roffwarg, H. P., Giles, D. E., Orsulak, P. J., & Fairchild, C. (1983). Relationships among the TRH, REM latency, and dexamethasone suppression tests: Preliminary findings. *Journal of Clinical Psychiatry, 44* (Sec. 2), 23–29.

Russell, M. A. H. (1978). Cigarette smoking: A dependence on high-nicotine boli. *Drug Metabolism Reviews, 8,* 29–57.

Russo, D. C. (1988, November). *A requiem for the passing of the three-term contingency.* Presidential address at the convention of the Association for Advancement of Behavior Therapy, New York.

Sachar, E. J. (1982). Endocrine abnormalities in depression. In E. S. Paykel (Ed.), *Handbook of affective disorders* (pp. 191–201). New York: Guilford.

Sack, D. A., Nurnberger, J., Rosenthal, N. E., Ashburn, E., & Wehr, T. A. (1985). Potentiation of antidepressant medications by phase advance of the sleep-wake cycle. *American Journal of Psychiatry, 142,* 606–608.

Salkovskis, P. M., Jones, D. R. O., & Clark, D. M. (1986). Respiratory control in the treatment of panic attacks: Replication and extension with concurrent measurement of behaviour and pCO_2. *British Journal of Psychiatry, 148,* 526–532.

Sarason, I. G., de Monchaux, C., & Hunt, T. (1975). Methodological issues in the assessment of life stress. In L. Levi (Ed.), *Emotions–Their parameters and measurement* (pp. 499–509). New York: Raven.

Sarason, I. G., & Sarason, B. R. (1984). *Abnormal psychology: The problem of maladaptive behavior* (4th ed.). Englewood Cliffs, NJ: Prentice-Hall.

Sarason, S. B. (1981). An asocial psychology and a misdirected clinical psychology. *American Psychologist, 36,* 827–836.

Sartwell, P. E., & Last, J. M. (1980). Epidemiology. In J. M. Last (Ed.), *Public health and preventive medicine* (11th ed., pp. 9–85). New York: Appleton-Century-Crofts.

Sawyer, D. A., Julia, H. L., & Turin, A. C. (1982). Caffeine and human behavior: Arousal, anxiety, and performance effects. *Journal of Behavioral Medicine, 5,* 415–439.

Scarr, S. (1985). Constructing psychology: Making facts and fables for our times. *American Psychologist, 40,* 499–512.

Scarr, S., & McCartney, K. (1983). How people make their own environments: A theory of genotype → environment effects. *Child Development, 54,* 424–435.

Scarr, S., & Weinberg, R. A. (1977). Intellectual similarities within families of both adopted and biological children. *Intelligence, 1,* 170–191.

Scarr, S., & Weinberg, R. A. (1978). The influence of "family background" on intellectual attainment. *American Sociological Review, 43,* 674–692.

Scarr, S., & Weinberg, R. A. (1983). The Minnesota adoption studies: Genetic differences and malleability. *Child Development, 54,* 260–267.

Schacht, T. E. (1985). DSM-III and the politics of truth. *American Psychologist, 40,* 513–521.

Schacht, T. E., & Nathan, P. E. (1977). But is it good for the psychologist?: Appraisal and status of DSM-III. *American Psychologist, 32,* 1017–1025.

Schachter, S. (1964). The interaction of cognitive and physiological determinants of emotional state. In L. Berkowitz (Ed.), *Advances in experimental social psychology* (Vol. 1, pp. 49–80). New York: Academic Press.

Schildkraut, J. J. (1965). The catecholamine hypothesis of affective disorder: A review of supporting evidence. *American Journal of Psychiatry, 122,* 509–522.

Schildkraut, J. J. (1973). Pharmacology: The effects of lithium on biogenic amines. In S. Gershon & B. Shopsin (Eds.), *Lithium: Its role in psychiatric research and medical treatment* (pp. 51–73). New York: Plenum.

Schildkraut, J. J. (1982). The biochemical discrimination of subtypes of depressive disorders: An outline of our studies on norepinephrine metabolism and psychoactive drugs in the endogenous depressions since 1967. *Pharmacopsychiatry, 15,* 121–127.

Schildkraut, J. J., Herzog, J. M., Orsulak, P. J., Edelman, S. E., Shein, H. M., & Frazier, S. H. (1976). Reduced platelet monoamine oxidase activity in a subgroup of schizophrenic patients. *American Journal of Psychiatry, 133,* 438–440.

Schildkraut, J. J., & Kety, S. S. (1967). Biogenic amines and emotion. *Science, 156,* 21–30.

Schimel, J. (1976). The retreat from a psychiatry of people. *Journal of the American Academy of Psychoanalysis, 4,* 131–135.

Schneider, K. (1959). *Clinical psychopathology.* New York: Grune & Stratton.

Schoenewolf, G. (1986). 'Holy cows.' *APA Monitor, 17*(4), 2.

Schooler, N. R. (1986). The efficacy of antipsychotic drugs and family therapies in the maintenance treatment of schizophrenia. *Journal of Clinical Psychopharmacology, 6*(Suppl.), 11S–19S.

Schuckit, M. A. (1979). *Drug and alcohol treatment.* New York: Plenum.

Schuckit, M. A., Goodwin, D. A., & Winokur, G. (1972). A study of alcoholism in half siblings. *American Journal of Psychiatry, 128,* 1132–1136.

Schulsinger, F., Kety, S. S., Rosenthal, D., & Wender, P. H. (1979). A family study of suicide. In M. Schou & E. Strömgren (Eds.), *Origin, prevention and treatment of affective disorders* (pp. 277–287). New York: Academic Press.

Schultz, R., Wüster, M., Duka, T., & Herz, A. (1980). Acute and chronic ethanol treatment changes endorphin levels in brain and pituitary. *Psychopharmacology, 68,* 221–227.

Schwartz, G. E., Fair, P. L., Mandel, M. R., Salt, P., Mieske, M., & Klerman, G. L. (1978). Facial electromyography in the assessment of improvement in depression. *Psychosomatic Medicine, 40,* 355–360.

Schwartz, G. E., Fair, P. L., Salt, P., Mandel, M. R., & Klerman, G. L. (1976a). Facial expression and imagery in depression: An electromyographic study. *Psychosomatic Medicine, 38,* 337–347.

Schwartz, G. E., Fair, P. L., Salt, P., Mandel, M. R., & Klerman, G. L. (1976b). Facial muscle patterning to affective imagery in depressed and nondepressed subjects. *Science, 192,* 489–491.

Schwartz, G. E., & Weiss, S. M. (1977). What is behavioral medicine? *Psychosomatic Medicine, 39,* 377–381.

Seeman, P., Lee, T., Chau-Wong, M., & Wong, K. (1976). Antipsychotic drug doses and neuroleptic/dopamine receptors. *Nature, 261,* 717–718.

Seidman, L. J. (1983). Schizophrenia and brain dysfunction: An integration of recent neurodiagnostic findings. *Psychological Bulletin, 94,* 195–238.

Seligman, M. E. P., & Hager, J. L. (1972). *Biological boundaries of learning.* New York: Appleton-Century-Crofts.

Selye, H. (1976). *The stress of life* (rev. ed.). New York: McGraw-Hill.

Sepinwall, J., & Cook, L. (1980). Mechanism of action of the benzodiazepines: Behavioral aspect. *Federation Proceedings, 39,* 3024–3031.

Seto, A., Tricomi, S., Goodwin, D. W. Kolodney, R., & Sullivan, T. (1978). Biochemical correlates of ethanol-induced flushing in Orientals. *Journal of Studies in Alcohol, 39,* 1–18.

Shagass, C. (1977). Early evoked potentials. *Schizophrenia Bulletin, 3,* 80–92.

Shagass, C., Ornitz, E. M., Sutton, S., & Tueting, P. (1978). Event related potentials and psychopathology. In E. Callaway, P. Tueting, & S. H. Koslow (Eds.), *Event-related brain potentials in man* (pp. 443–496). New York: Academic Press.

Sheehan, D. V. (1982). Panic attacks and phobias. *New England Journal of Medicine, 307,* 156–158.

Sheehan, D. V., Ballenger, J., & Jacobsen, G. (1980). Treatment of endogenous anxiety with phobic, hysterical and hypochondriacal symptoms. *Archives of General Psychiatry, 37,* 51–59.

Sheehan, D. V., Coleman, J. H., Greenblatt, D. J., Jones, K. J., Levine, P. H., Orsulak, P. J., Peterson, M., Schildkraut, J. J., Uzogara, E., & Watkins, D. (1984). Some biochemical correlates of panic attacks with agoraphobia and their response to a new treatment. *Journal of Clinical Psychopharmacology, 4,* 66–75.

Sherrington, R., Brynjolfsson, J., Petursson, H., Potter, M., Dudleston, K., Barraclough, B., Wasmuth, J., Dobbs, M., & Gurling, H. (1988). Localization of a susceptibility locus for schizophrenia on chromosome 5. *Nature, 336,* 164–167.

Shipman, W. G., Oken, D., Goldstein, I. B., Grinker, R. R., & Heath, H. A. (1964). Study in psychophysiology of muscle tension. II. Personality factors. *Archives of General Psychiatry, 11,* 330–345.

Shuttlesworth, D., Neill, D., & Ellen, P. (1984). The place of physiological psychology in neuroscience. *Physiological Psychology, 12,* 3–7.

Siegel, S. (1975). Evidence from rats that morphine tolerance is a learned response. *Journal of Comparative Physiological Psychology, 89,* 498–506.

Siever, L. J. (1985). Biological markers in schizotypal personality disorder. *Schizophrenia Bulletin, 11,* 564–574.

Silverman, J. (1967). Variations in cognitive control and psychophysiological defense in the schizophrenias. *Psychosomatic Medicine, 29,* 225–251.

Simon, E. J. (1981). Opiate receptors: Some recent developments. In J. W. Lamble (Ed.), *Towards understanding receptors* (pp. 159–165). Amsterdam: Elsevier/North-Holland.

Singer, E. P. (1958). The hyperventilation syndrome in clinical medicine. *New York State Journal of Medicine, 58,* 1494–1500.

Sitaram, N., Nurnberger, J. I., Gershon, E. S., & Gillin, J. C. (1982). Cholinergic regulation of mood and REM sleep: Potential model and marker of vulnerability to affective disorders. *American Journal of Psychiatry, 139,* 571–576.

Skinner, B. F. (1950). Are theories of learning necessary? *Psychological Review, 57,* 193–216.

Skinner, B. F. (1987). Whatever happened to psychology as the science of behavior? *American Psychologist, 42,* 780–786.

Skutsch, G. M. (1985). Manic depression: A multiple hormone disorder? *Biological Psychiatry, 20,* 662–668.

Slater, E. (1966). Expectation of abnormality on paternal and maternal sides: A computational model. *Journal of Medical Genetics, 3,* 159–161.

Slater, E., & Cowie, V. (1971). The genetics of mental disorders. New York: Oxford University Press.

Small, S. A., Zeldin, R. S., & Savin-Williams, R. C. (1983). In search of personality traits: A multimethod analysis of naturally occurring prosocial and dominance behavior. *Journal of Personality, 51,* 1–16.

Smith, D., & Kraft, W. A. (1983). DSM-III: Do psychologists really want an alternative? *American Psychologist, 38*, 777–785.

Smith, D. E. (1986). Cocaine-alcohol abuse: Epidemiological, diagnostic and treatment considerations. *Journal of Psychoactive Drugs, 18*, 117–129.

Snyder, S. H. (1976). The dopamine hypothesis of schizophrenia: Focus on the dopamine receptor. *American Journal of Psychiatry, 133*, 197–202.

Snyder, S. H. (1981a). Opiate and benzodiazepine receptors. *Psychosomatics, 22*, 986–989.

Snyder, S. H. (1981b). Dopamine receptors, neuroleptics and schizophrenia. *American Journal of Psychiatry, 138*, 460–464.

Sokolov, E. N. (1963). *Perception and the conditioned reflex* (S. W. Waydenfeld, Trans.). New York: Pergamon.

Solyom, L., Heseltine, G. F. D., McClure, D. J., Solyom, C., Ledwidge, B., & Steinberg, G. (1973). Behavior therapy versus drug therapy in the treatment of phobic neurosis. *Canadian Psychiatric Association Journal, 18*, 25–32.

Solyom, L., & Sookman, D. (1977). A comparison of clomipramine hydrochloride (Anafranil) and behaviour therapy in the treatment of obsessive neurosis. *Journal of International Medical Research, 5* (Suppl. 5), 49–61.

Spielberger, C. D., Pollans, C. H., & Worden, T. J. (1983). Anxiety disorders. In S. M. Turner & M. Hersen (Eds.), *Adult psychopathology and diagnosis* (pp. 263–303). New York: Wiley.

Spitzer, R. L. (1985). DSM-III and the politics–science dichotomy syndrome. *American Psychologist, 40*, 522–526.

Spitzer, R. L., Sheehy, M., & Endicott, J. (1977). DSM-III: Guiding principles. In V. M. Rakoff, H. C. Stancer, & H. B. Kedward (Eds.), *Psychiatric diagnosis* (pp. 1–24). New York: Brunner/Mazel.

Spohn, H. E., & Patterson, T. (1979). Recent studies of psychophysiology in schizophrenia. *Schizophrenia Bulletin, 5*, 581–611.

Squires, R. F. (1983). Benzodiazepine receptor multiplicity. *Neuropharmacology, 22*, 1443–1450.

Squires, R. F., & Braestrup, C. (1977). Benzodiazepine receptors in rat brain. *Nature, 266*, 732–734.

Staats, A. W. (1983) *Psychology's crisis of disunity: Philosophy and method for a unified science.* New York: Praeger.

Starke, K., & Altmann, K. P. (1973). Inhibition of adrenergic neurotransmission by clonidine: An action on prejunctional alpha-receptors. *Neuropharmacology, 12*, 339–347.

Stelmack, R. M. (1981). The psychophysiology of extraversion and neuroticism. In H. J. Eysenck (Ed.), *A model for personality* (pp. 38–64). New York: Springer-Verlag.

Stelmack, R. M. & Mandelzys, N. (1975). Extraversion and pupillary response to affective and taboo words. *Psychophysiology, 12*, 536–540.

Stenstedt, A. (1952). A study in manic-depressive psychosis: Clinical, social and genetic investigations. *Acta Psychiatrica et Neurologica Scandinavica,*(Suppl. 79), 1–111.

Stephens, J. H. (1978). Long-term prognosis and follow-up in schizophrenia. *Schizophrenia Bulletin, 4*, 25–47.

Stephens, J. H., Astrup, C., & Mangrum, J. C. (1967). Prognosis in schizophrenia: Prognostic scales cross-validated in American and Norwegian patients. *Archives of General Psychiatry, 16*, 693–698.

Stern, R. S. (1978). Behavior therapy and psychotropic medication. In M. Hersen & A. S. Bellack (Eds.), *Behavior therapy in a psychiatric setting* (pp. 40–57). Baltimore: Williams & Wilkins.

Stevens, J. R. (1982). Neuropathology of schizophrenia. *Archives of General Psychiatry, 39,* 1131–1139.

Stevens, J. R., Bigelow, L., Denney, D., Lipkins, J., Livermore, A. H., Rauscher, F., & Wyatt, R. J. (1979). Telemetered EEG-EOG during psychotic behaviors of schizophrenia. *Archives of General Psychiatry, 36,* 251–262.

Stiglick, A., Llewellyn, M. E., & Kalant, H. (1984). Residual effects of prolonged cannabis treatment on shuttle-box avoidance in the rat. *Psychopharmacology, 84,* 476–479.

Stiles, W. B., Shapiro, D. A., & Elliot, R. (1986). "Are all psychotherapies equivalent?". *American Psychologist, 41,* 165–180.

Stokes, P. E., Stoll, P. M., Koslow, S. H., Maas, J. W., Davis, J. M., Swann, A. C., & Robins, E. (1984). Pretreatment DST and hypothalamic-pituitary-adrenocortical function in depressed patients and comparison groups: A multicenter study. *Archives of General Psychiatry, 41,* 257–267.

Stokes, P. E., Stoll, P. M., Shamoian, C. A., & Patton, M. J. (1971). Efficacy of lithium as acute treatment for manic-depressive illness. *Lancet, 1,* 1319–1325.

Stone, E. A. (1979). Subsensitivity to norepinephrine as a link between adaptation to stress and antidepressant therapy: An hypothesis. *Research Communications in Psychology, Psychiatry and Behavior, 4,* 241–255.

Stone, M. H. (1980). *The borderline syndromes: Constitution, personality, and adaptation* New York: McGraw-Hill.

Straube, E. R. (1979). On the meaning of electrodermal non-responding in schizophrenia. *Journal of Nervous and Mental Disorders, 167,* 601–611.

Strauss, J. S., & Carpenter, W. T. (1977). Prediction of outcome in schizophrenia: III. Five-year outcome and its predictors. *Archives of General Psychiatry, 34,* 159–163.

Strickland, B. R. (1985, November). *Bridging biology and behavior therapy or don't mistake asthma for passion.* Paper presented at the convention of the Association for Advancement of Behavior Therapy, Houston.

Stunkard, A. J., Sorensen, T. I. A., Hanis, C., Teasdale, T. W., Chakraborty, R., Schull, W. J., & Schulsinger, F. (1986). An adoption study of human obesity. *New England Journal of Medicine, 314,* 193–198.

Sturgeon, D., Kuipers, L., Berkowitz, R., Turpin, G., & Leff, J. (1981). Psychophysiological responses of schizophrenic patients to high and low expressed emotion relatives. *British Journal of Psychiatry, 138,* 40–45.

Sturgeon, D., Turpin, G., Kuipers, L., Berkowitz, R., & Leff, J. (1984). Psychophysiological responses of schizophrenic patients to high and low expressed emotion relatives: A follow-up study. *British Journal of Psychiatry, 145,* 62–69.

Sullivan, J. L., Cavenar, J. O., Stanfield, C. N., & Hammett, E. B. (1978). Reduced MAO activity in platelets and lymphocytes of chronic schizophrenics. *American Journal of Psychiatry, 135,* 597–598.

Sulser, F. (1981). New perspectives on the mode of action of antidepressant drugs. In J. W. Lamble (Ed.), *Towards understanding receptors* (pp. 99–104). Amsterdam: Elsevier/North-Holland.

Susser, M. (1973). *Causal thinking in the health sciences: Concepts and strategies of epidemiology.* New York: Oxford University Press.

Svensson, T. H., Bunney, B. S., & Aghajanian, G. K. (1975). Inhibition of both noradrenergic and serotonergic neurons in brain by the α-adrenergic agonist clonidine. *Brain Research, 92,* 291–306.

Svensson ,T. H., & Usdin, T. (1978). Feedback inhibition of brain noradrenaline neurones by tricyclic antidepressants: α-receptor mediation. *Science, 202,* 1089–1091.

Sweet, W. H. (1980). Neuropeptides and monoaminergic neurotransmitters: Their relation to pain. *Journal of the Royal Society of Medicine, 73,* 482–491.

Szasz, T. S. (1971). *The manufacture of madness: A comparative study of the Inquisition and the mental health movement.* London: Routledge & Kegan Paul.

Szasz, T. S. (1974). *The myth of mental illness: Foundations of a theory of personal conduct* (rev. ed.). New York: Harper & Row.

Szasz, T. S. (1979). *The myth of psychotherapy: Mental healing as religion, rhetoric, and repression.* Oxford: Oxford University Press.

Szasz, T. S. (1987). *Insanity: The idea and its consequences.* New York: Wiley.

Talbott, J. A. (Ed.). (1981). *The chronic mentally ill: Treatment, programs, systems.* New York: Human Sciences Press.

Talbott, J. A. (Ed.). (1984). *The chronic mental patient: Five years later.* New York: Grune & Stratton.

Targum, S. D. (1983). Neuroendocrine challenge studies in clinical psychiatry. *Psychiatric Annals, 13,* 385–395.

Tarrier, N., Cooke, E. C., & Lader, M. H. (1978a). Electrodermal and heart-rate measurements in chronic and partially remitted schizophrenic patients. *Acta Psychiatrica Scandinavica, 57,* 369–376.

Tarrier, N., Cooke, E. C., & Lader, M. H. (1978b). The EEG's of chronic schizophrenic patients in hospital and in the community. *Electroencephalography and Clinical Neurophysiology, 44,* 669–673.

Tarrier, N., Vaughn, C., Lader, M. H., & Leff, J. P. (1979). Bodily reactions to people and events in schizophrenics. *Archives of General Psychiatry, 36,* 311–315.

Tarter, R., & Edwards, K. (1986). Antecedents to alcoholism: Implications for prevention and treatment. *Behavior Therapy, 17,* 346–361.

Taylor, M. A. (1972). Schneiderian first-rank symptoms and clinical prognostic features in schizophrenia. *Archives of General Psychiatry, 26,* 64–67.

Telch, M. J., Agras, W. S., Taylor, C. B., Roth, W. T., & Gallen, C. C. (1985). Combined pharmacological and behavioral treatment for agoraphobia. *Behaviour Research and Therapy, 23,* 325–335.

Tepper, J. M., Groves, P. M., & Young, S. J. (1985). The neuropharmacology of the autoinhibition of monoamine release. *Trends in Pharmacological Sciences, 6,* 251–256.

Terenius, L. (1980). Opiates and their receptors. In W. Wuttke, A. Weindl, K. H. Voigt, & R.-R. Dries (Eds.), *Brain and pituitary peptides* (pp. 27–34). Basel: Karger.

Thase, M. E. (1983). Cognitive and behavioral treatments for depression: A review of recent developments. In F. J. Ayd, I. J. Taylor, & B. T. Taylor (Eds.), *Affective disorders reassessed: 1983* (pp. 234–243). Baltimore: Ayd Medical Communications.

Thase, M. E. (1987). Affective disorders. In R. L. Morrison & A. S. Bellack (Eds.), *Medical factors and psychological disorders: A handbook for psychologists* (pp. 61–91). New York: Plenum.

Thase, M. E., Frank, E., & Kupfer, D. J. (1985). Biological processes in major depression. In E. E. Beckham & W. R. Leber (Eds.), *Handbook of depression: Treatment, assessment, and research* (pp. 816–913). Homewood, IL: Dorsey.

Thoenen, H., Otten, U., & Oesch, F. (1973). Trans-synaptic regulation of tyrosine hydroxylase. In E. Usdin & S. Snyder (Eds.), *Frontiers in catecholamine research* (pp. 179–186). New York: Pergamon.

Thomas, A., & Chess, S. (1977). *Temperament and development.* New York: Brunner/Mazel.

Thomas, A., Chess, S., & Birch, H. G. (1968). *Temperament and behavior disorders in children.* New York: New York University Press.

Thomas, A., Chess, S., Birch, H. G., Hertzig, M. E., & Korn, S. (1963). *Behavioral individuality in early childhood.* New York: New York University Press.

Thomas, M., Halsall, S., & Peters, T. J. (1982). Role of hepatic acetyldehyde dehydrogenase in alcoholism: Demonstration of persistent reduction in cytosolic activity in abstaining patients. *Lancet, 2,* 1057–1059.

Thompson, J. W. (1984). Opioid peptides. *British Medical Journal, 288,* 259–261.

Thorén, P., Åsberg, M., Cronholm, B., Jörnestedt, L., & Träskman, L. (1980). Clomipramine treatment of obsessive-compulsive disorder: I. Controlled clinical trial. *Archives of General Psychiatry, 37,* 1281–1285.

Torgersen, S. (1983). Genetic factors in anxiety disorders. *Archives of General Psychiatry, 40,* 1085–1089.

Tosteson, D. C. (1981). Lithium and mania. *Scientific American, 244*(4), 164–166, 168, 171–172, 174.

Towell, J. F., Cho, J-K., Rho, B. L., & Wang, R. I. H. (1983). Aldehyde dehydrogenase and alcoholism. *Lancet, 1,* 364–365.

Träskman, L., Åsberg, M., Bertilsson, L., & Sjöstrand, L. (1981). Monoamine metabolites in CSF and suicidal behavior. *Archives of General Psychiatry, 38,* 631–636.

Trice, H. M., & Wahl, J. R. (1958). A rank order analysis of the symptoms of alcoholism. *Quarterly Studies on Alcohol, 19,* 636–648.

Triggle, D. J. (1981). Desensitization. In J. W. Lamble (Ed.), *Towards understanding receptors* (pp. 28–33). Amsterdam: Elsevier/North-Holland.

Tronick, E. Z. (1989). Emotions and emotional communication in infants. *American Psychologist, 44,* 112–119.

Tsuang, M. T., & Vandermey, R. (1980). *Genes and the mind: Inheritance of mental illness.* New York: Oxford University Press.

Tsuchiya, T., & Kitagawa, S. (1976). Effects of benzodiazepines and pentobarbital on the evoked potentials in the cat brain. *Japanese Journal of Pharmacology, 26,* 411–418.

Turner, F. J. (1984). *Adult psychopathology: A social work perspective.* New York: Free Press.

Turner, S. M., & Beidel, D. C. (1985). Empirically derived subtypes of social anxiety. *Behavior Therapy, 16,* 384–392.

Turner, S. M., & Hersen, M. (Eds.). (1984). *Adult psychopathology and diagnosis.* New York: Wiley.

Turner, S. M., Hersen, M., Bellack, A. S., Andrasik, F., & Capparell, H. V. (1980). Behavioral and pharmacological treatment of obsessive-compulsive disorders. *Journal of Nervous and Mental Disease, 168,* 651–657.

Turpin, G. (1983). Psychophysiology, psychopathology and the social environment. In A. Gale & J. A. Edwards (Eds.), *Physiological correlates of human behaviour: Individual differences and psychopathology* (Vol. 3, pp. 265–280). New York: Academic Press.

Tyrer, P. J. (1981). Drug-induced depression. *Prescribers Journal, 21,* 237–242.

Tyrer, P., Candy, J., & Kelly, D. (1973). A study of the clinical effects of phenelzine and placebo in the treatment of phobic anxiety. *Psychopharmacologia, 32,* 237–254.

Tyrrell, D. A. J., Parry, R. P., Crow, T. J., Johnstone, E., & Ferrier, I. N. (1979). Possible virus in schizophrenia and some neurological disorders. *Lancet, 1,* 839–841.

Uchalik, D. C. (Chair). (1978, November). *Neurology, physiology, pharmacology and behavior therapy: Completing the gestalt.* Symposium presented at the convention of the Association for Advancement of Behavior Therapy, Chicago.

Uecker, A. E., & Solberg, K. B. (1973). Alcoholics' knowledge about alcohol problems: Its relationship to significant attitudes. *Quarterly Journal of Studies on Alcohol, 34,* 509–513.

Ungerstedt, U. (1971). Stereotaxic mapping of the monoamine pathways in the rat brain. *Acta Physiologica Scandinavia,* (Suppl. 367), 1–48.

Ungerstedt, U. (1979). Central dopamine mechanisms and unconditioned behaviour. In A. S. Horn, J. Korf, & B. H. C. Westerink (Eds.), *The neurobiology of dopamine* (pp. 577–596). New York: Academic Press.

Uyeda, M. K., & Moldawsky, S. (1986). Prospective payment and psychological services: What difference does it make? Psychologists aren't in Medicare anyway! *American Psychologist, 41,* 60–63.

van den Hoofdakker, R. H., & Elsenga, S. (1981). Clinical effects of sleep deprivation in endogenous depression. In W. P. Koella (Ed.), *Sleep 1980: Circadian rhythms, dreams, noise and sleep, neurophysiology, therapy* (pp. 2–9). Basel: S. Karger.

van den Hout, M. A., Boek, C., van der Molen, G. M., Jansen, A., & Griez, E. (1988). Rebreathing to cope with hyperventilation: Experimental tests of the paper bag method. *Journal of Behavioral Medicine, 11,* 303–310.

van Praag, H. M. (1980). Central monoamine metabolism in depression: I. Serotonin and related compounds. *Comprehensive Psychiatry, 21,* 30–43.

van Praag, H. M. (1982). Depression, suicide and the metabolism of serotonin in the brain. *Journal of Affective Disorders, 4,* 275–290.

Van Putten, T., & Yager, J. (1984). Posttraumatic stress disorder: Emerging from the rhetoric. *Archives of General Psychiatry, 41,* 411–413.

VandenBos, G. R. (Ed.). (1986). Psychotherapy research [Special issue]. *American Psychologist, 41*(2).

Vaughn, C. E., & Leff, J. P. (1976). The influence of family and social factors on the course of psychiatric illness: A comparison of schizophrenic and depressed neurotic patients. *British Journal of Psychiatry, 129,* 125–137.

Vaughn, C. E., & Leff, J. P. (1977). The measurement of expressed emotion in the families of psychiatric patients. *British Journal of Social and Clinical Psychology, 15,* 157–165.

Venables, P. H. (1964). Input dysfunction in schizophrenia. *Progress in Experimental Personality Research, 1,* 1–47.

Venables, P. H. (1973). Input regulation and psychopathology. In M. Hammer, K. Salzinger, & S. Sutton (Eds.), *Psychopathology: Contributions from the social, behavioral, and biological sciences* (pp. 261–284). New York: Wiley.

Venables, P. H. (1977). The electrodermal psychophysiology of schizophrenics and children at risk for schizophrenia: Controversies and developments. *Schizophrenia Bulletin, 3,* 28–48.

Venables, P. H. (1981). Psychophysiology of abnormal behavior. *British Medical Bulletin, 37,* 199–203.

Venables, P. H. (1983). Some problems and controversies in the psychophysiological investigation of schizophrenia. In A. Gale & J. A. Edwards (Eds.), *Physiological correlates of human behaviour: Individual differences and psychopathology* (Vol. 3, pp. 207–232). New York: Academic Press.

Venables, P. H. (1984). Cerebral mechanisms, autonomic responsiveness, and attention in schizophrenia. In W. D. Spaulding & J. K. Cole (Eds.), *Theories of schizophrenia and psychosis* (pp. 47–91). Lincoln, NE: Nebraska University Press.

Venables, P. H., Fletcher, R. P., Dalais, J. C., Mitchell, D. A., Schulsinger, F., & Mednick, S. A. (1983). Factor structure of the Rutter 'Children's Behaviour Questionnaire' in a primary school population in a developing country. *Journal of Child Psychology and Psychiatry, 24,* 213–222.

Venables, P. H., Mednick, S. A., Schulsinger, F., Raman, A. C., Bell, B., Dalais, J. C., & Fletcher, R. P. (1978). Screening for risk of mental illness. In G. Serban (Ed.), *Cognitive defects in the development of mental illness* (pp. 273–303). New York: Brunner/Mazel.

Venables, P. H., & Wing, J. K. (1962). Level of arousal and the sub-classification of schizophrenia. *Archives of General Psychiatry, 7,,* 114–119.

Vesell, E. S., Page, J. G., & Passananti, G. T. (1971). Genetic and environmental factors affecting ethanol metabolism in man. *Clinical Pharmacology and Therapeutics, 12,* 192–201.

Vessie, P. R. (1932). On the transmission of Huntington's chorea for 300 years–the Bures family group. *Journal of Nervous and Mental Diseases, 76,* 553–573.

Wachs, T. D. (1983). The use and abuse of environment in behavior-genetic research. *Child Development, 54,* 396–407.

Wachtel, P. L. (1977). *Psychoanalysis and behavior therapy: Toward an integration.* New York: Basic Books.

Waldron, H. A. (1981). Effects of organic solvents. *British Journal of Hospital Medicine, 26,* 645–647, 649.

Wallace, C. J., Donahoe, C. P., & Boone, S. E. (1986). Schizophrenia. In M. Hersen (Ed.), *Pharmacological and behavioral treatment: An integrative approach* (pp. 357–381). New York: Wiley.

Waller, N. G., & Ben-Porath, Y. S. (1987). Is it time for clinical psychology to embrace the five-factor model of personality? *American Psychologist, 42,* 887–889.

Walton, J. N. (1977). *Brain's diseases of the nervous system* (8th ed.). Oxford: Oxford University Press.

Watson, S. J. (1977). Hallucinogens and other psychotomimetics: Biological mechanisms. In J. P. Barchas, P. A. Berger, R. D. Ciaranello, & G. R. Elliott (Eds.), *Psychopharmacology: From theory to practice* (pp. 341–354). New York: Oxford University Press.

Watts, F. N. (1979). Habituation model of systematic desensitization. *Psychological Bulletin, 86,* 627–637.

Weckowicz, T. E., Yonge, K. A., Cropley, A. J., & Muir, W. (1971). Objective therapy predictors in depression: A multivariate approach. *Journal of Clinical Psychology, 27,* 4–29.

Wehr, T. A., Jacobsen, F. M., Sack, D. A., Arendt, J., Tamarkin, L., & Rosenthal, N. E. (1986). Phototherapy of seasonal affective disorder. *Archives of General Psychiatry, 43,* 870–875.

Weinberger, D. R., Bigelow, L. B., Kleinman, J. E., Klein, S. T., Rosenblatt, J. E., & Wyatt, R. J. (1980). Cerebral ventricular enlargement in chronic schizophrenia: An association with poor response to treatment. *Archives of General Psychiatry, 37,* 11–13.

Weinberger, D. R., DeLisi, L. E., Neophytides, A. N., & Wyatt, R. J. (1981). Familial aspects of CT abnormalities in chronic schizophrenic patients. *Psychiatry Research, 4,* 65–71.

Weinberger, D. R., & Wyatt, R. J. (1982). Brain morphology in schizophrenia: *In vivo* studies. In F. A. Henn & H. A. Nasrallah (Eds.), *Schizophrenia as a brain disease* (pp. 148–175). New York: Oxford University Press.

Weissman, M. M. (1979). The psychological treatment of depression: Evidence for the efficacy of psychotherapy alone, in comparison with, and in combination with pharmacotherapy. *Archives of General Psychiatry, 36,* 1261–1269.

Wenger, M. A. (1941). The measurement of individual differences in autonomic balance. *Psychosomatic Medicine, 3,* 427–434.

Wells, C. E. (1979). Pseudodementia. *American Journal of Psychiatry, 136,* 895–890.

Wexler, B. E. (1980). Cerebral laterality and psychiatry: A review of the literature. *American Journal of Psychiatry, 137,* 279–291.

Wexler, B. E. & Heninger, G. R. (1979). Alterations in cerebral laterality during acute psychotic illness. *Archives of General Psychiatry, 36,* 278–284.

Whatmore, G. B. (1966). Some neurophysiologic differences between schizophrenia and depression. *American Journal of Psychiatry, 123,* 712–716.

Wheatley, D. (1981). Effects of drugs on sleep. In D. Wheatley (Ed.), *Psychopharmacology of sleep* (pp. 153–176). New York: Raven.

Where next with psychiatric illness? (1988). *Nature, 336,* 95–96.

Whybrow, P. C., & Prange, A. J. (1981). A hypothesis of thyroid-catecholamine-receptor interaction: Its relevance to affective illness. *Archives of General Psychiatry, 38,* 106–113.

Wiggins, J. S. (1973). *Personality and prediction: Principles of personality assessment.* Boston: Addison-Wesley.

Wilbur, R., & Kulik, A. V. (1981). Gray's cybernetic theory of anxiety. *Lancet, 2,* 803.

Williams, A. W., Ware, J. E., & Donald, C. A. (1981). A model of mental health, life events, and social support applicable to general populations. *Journal of Health and Social Behavior, 22,* 324–336.

Williams, J. B. W., & Spitzer, R. L. (1983). The issue of sex bias in DSM-III. *American Psychologist, 38,* 793–798.

Williams, M. (1984). Adenosine–a selective neuromodulator in the mammalian CNS? *Trends in Neuroscience, 7,* 164–168.

Willner, P. (1985). *Depression: A psychobiological synthesis.* New York: Wiley.

Willner, P., & Montgomery, T. (1980). Neurotransmitters and depression: Too much, too little, too unstable–or not unstable enough? *Trends in Neuroscience, 3,* 201.

Wilson, P. H. (1982). Combined pharmacological and behavioural treatment of depression. *Behaviour Research and Therapy, 20,* 173–184.

Wing, J. K., Cooper, J. E., & Sartorius, N. (1974). *The measurement and classification of psychiatric symptoms.* London: Cambridge University Press.

Winokur, G., Clayton, P. J., & Reich, T. (1969). *Manic depressive illness.* St. Louis: C. V. Mosby.

Winsdale, W. J., Liston, E. H., Ross, J. W., & Weber, K. D. (1984). Medical, judicial, and statutory regulation of ECT in the United States. *American Journal of Psychiatry, 141,* 1349–1355.

Wolff, P. H. (1973). Vasomotor sensitivity to ethanol in diverse mongoloid populations. *American Journal of Human Genetics, 25,* 193–199.

Wood, K. (1985). The neurochemistry of mania: The effect of lithium on catecholamines, indoleamines and calcium mobilization. *Journal of Affective Disorders, 8,* 215–223.

Wouters, W., & Bercken, J. van den. (1980). Effects of meta-enkephalin on slow synaptic inhibition in frog sympathetic ganglion. *Neuropharmacology, 19,* 237–243.

Wyatt, R. J., Murphy, D. L., Belmaker, R., Cohen, S., Donnelly, C. H., & Pollin, W. (1973). Reduced monoamine oxidase activity in platelets: A possible genetic marker for vulnerability to schizophrenia. *Science, 179,* 916–918.

Wyatt, R. J., Potkin, S. G., & Murphy, D. L. (1979). Platelet monoamine oxidase activity in schizophrenia: A review of the data. *American Journal of Psychiatry, 136,* 377–385.

Yager, J., Laufer, R., & Gallops, M. (1984). Some problems associated with war experience in men of the Vietnam generation. *Archives of General Psychiatry, 41,* 327–333).

Yaryura-Tobias, J. A., Neziroglu, F., & Bergman, L. (1976). Chlorimipramine, for obsessive-compulsive neurosis: An organic approach. *Current Therapeutic Research, 20,* 541–548.

Young, D., & Scoville, W. B. (1938). Paranoid psychosis in narcolepsy and the possible danger of benzedrine treatment. *Medical Clinics of North America, 22,* 637–646.

Zahn, T. P. (1976). On the bimodality of the distribution of electrodermal orienting responses in schizophrenic patients. *Journal of Nervous and Mental Disease, 162,* 195–199.

Zahn, T. P., Rosenthal, D., & Lawlor, W. G. (1968). Electrodermal and heart rate orienting reactions in chronic schizophrenia. *Journal of Psychiatric Research, 6,* 117–134.

Zajonc, R. B. (1980). Feeling and thinking: Preferences need no inferences. *American Psychologist, 35,* 151–175.

Zajonc, R. B. (1984). On the primacy of affect. *American Psychologist, 39,* 117–123.

Zeiss, A. M., Lewinsohn, P. M., & Muñoz, R. F. (1979). Nonspecific improvement effects in depression using interpersonal skills training, pleasant activity schedules, or cognitive training. *Journal of Consulting and Clinical Psychology, 47,* 427–439.

Zeskind, P. S. (1980). Adult responses to cries of low and high risk infants. *Infant Behavior and Development, 3,* 167–177.

Zeskind, P. S., & Lester, B. M. (1978). Acoustic features and auditory perceptions of the cries of newborns with prenatal and perinatal complications. *Child Development, 49,* 580–589.

Zigler, E., & Glick, M. (1988). Is paranoid schizophrenia really camouflaged depression? *American Psychologist, 43,* 284–290.

Zigler, E., & Phillips, L. (1961). Psychiatric diagnosis: A critique. *Journal of Abnormal and Social Psychology, 63,* 607–618.

Zis, A. P., & Goodwin, F. K. (1982). The amine hypothesis. In E. S. Paykel (Ed.), *Handbook of affective disorders* (pp. 175–190). New York: Guilford.

Zitrin, C. M., Klein, D. F., & Woerner, M. G. (1978). Behavior therapy, supportive psychotherapy, imipramine, and phobias. *Archives of General Psychiatry, 35,* 307–316.

Zitrin, C. M., Klein, D. F., & Woerner, M. G. (1980). Treatment of agoraphobia with group exposure in vivo and imipramine. *Archives of General Psychiatry, 37,* 63–72.

Zubin, J. (1972). Scientific models for psychopathology in the 1970's. *Seminars in Psychiatry, 4,* 283–296.

Zubin, J. (1977–78). But is it good for science? *Clinical Psychologist, 31*(2), 1, 5–7.

Zubin, J. (1986). Implications of the vulnerability model for DSM-IV with special reference to schizophrenia. In T. Millon & G. L. Klerman (Eds.), *Contemporary directions in psychopathology: Toward the DSM-IV* (pp. 473–494). New York: Guilford.

Zubin, J., & Spring, B. (1977). Vulnerability: A new view of schizophrenia. *Journal of Abnormal Psychology, 86,* 103–126.

Zuckerman, M. (1972). Drug usage as one manifestation of a "sensation-seeking" trait. In W. Keup (Ed.), *Drug abuse: Current concepts and research* (pp. 154–163). Springfield, IL: Charles C. Thomas.

Zuckerman, M. (1979). *Sensation seeking: Beyond the optimal level of arousal.* Hillsdale, NJ: Lawrence Erlbaum.

Zuckerman, M. (Ed.). (1983). *Biological bases of sensation seeking, impulsivity, and anxiety.* Hillsdale, NJ: Lawrence Erlbaum.

Zuckerman, M. (1984). Sensation seeking: A comparative approach to a human trait. *Behavioral and Brain Sciences, 7,* 413–471.

Zuckerman, M., Neary, R. S., & Brustman, B. A. (1970). Sensation-Seeking Scale correlates in experience (smoking, drugs, alcohol, "hallucinations," and sex) and preference for complexity (designs). In *Proceedings of the 78th Annual Convention of the American Psychological Association* (pp. 317–318). Washington, DC: American Psychological Association.

Zung, W. W. K. (1973). From art to science: The diagnosis and treatment of depression. *Archives of General Psychiatry, 29,* 328–337.

Author Index

Subject Index